C000070068

Create, Copy, Disrupt

Create, Copy, Disrupt

India's Intellectual Property Dilemmas

Prashant Reddy T.
Sumathi Chandrashekaran

OXFORD
UNIVERSITY PRESS

OXFORD
UNIVERSITY PRESS

Oxford University Press is a department of the University of Oxford.
It furthers the University's objective of excellence in research, scholarship,
and education by publishing worldwide. Oxford is a registered trademark of
Oxford University Press in the UK and in certain other countries

Published in India by
Oxford University Press
YMCA Library Building, 1 Jai Singh Road, New Delhi 110 001, India

© Oxford University Press 2017

The moral rights of the authors have been asserted

First Edition published in 2017

All rights reserved. No part of this publication may be reproduced, stored in
a retrieval system, or transmitted, in any form or by any means, without the
prior permission in writing of Oxford University Press, or as expressly permitted
by law, by licence, or under terms agreed with the appropriate reprographics
rights organization. Enquiries concerning reproduction outside the scope of the
above should be sent to the Rights Department, Oxford University Press, at the
address above

You must not circulate this work in any other form
and you must impose this same condition on any acquirer

ISBN-13: 978-0-19-947066-2
ISBN-10: 0-19-947066-9

Typeset in Trump Mediaeval LT Std 10/14
by The Graphics Solution, New Delhi 110 092
Printed in India by Rakmo Press, New Delhi 110 020

For Amma, Naana, and Vikasanna
(Prashant Reddy T.)

For my parents, Shanti and Chandrashekaran
(Sumathi Chandrashekaran)

CONTENTS

Foreword by Shamnad Basheer   ix
Acknowledgements   xi
List of Abbreviations   xvii
Introduction   xxi

1. Indian Patent Law Declares Independence   1

2. Surrender at Geneva   36

3. Life after Marrakesh   55

4. Novartis Trips Over Section 3(d)   84

5. New Delhi Challenges the Berne Convention   115

6. The Moving Picture   153

7. Akhtar Rescripts Copyright Law   184

8. Digital India Seeks 'Safe Harbour'   216

9. The Traditional Knowledge Trilogy   250

10. The Queen of All Rices   286

11. Of Gods and Gurus   322

Index   359
About the Authors   373

FOREWORD

To say that intellectual property (IP) is a contentious issue in India is a gross understatement. Indeed, our debates have often generated more heat than light. This monumental work by two leading IP thinkers will fill a gaping void in the present debate. It throws much-needed light on a number of IP issues that have plagued India for long and divided our debaters into polemical positions—positions propelled more by emotions and less by logic.

While the life of a law cannot and should not be logic alone (given the limits of rationality and logic in an utterly chaotic and complex world) and emotion ought to find some place in it, emotions cannot be allowed to run amok and must be reined in to make space for a decent amount of logic and dispassionate analysis as well. The authors do decently well here, and attempt a relatively objective analysis of a tricky terrain.

But dispassionate does not mean dry—quite the contrary! With their stellar penmanship and stimulating sweep of a narrative, the authors bring to life the myriad facets of Indian IP law and policy— infusing the various chapters with a rare combination of historical insight, present predicament, rigorous doctrinal analysis, and a take on macro-level policy.

Indeed, this is the key USP of the book. That it is not a dry doctrinal one. Neither is it a pure historical or contemporary narrative. Rather, in combining these various elements into a cogent, cohesive (and perhaps even eclectic) whole, the book promises to appeal to a wide constellation of academics, practitioners, policymakers, judges, and students.

But more importantly, this book is one of the rare few that breaks down the legalese of the law (and an esoteric, arcane one at that) into language more readily accessible to the common man—resuscitating it from the clutches of a privileged priesthood (comprising lawyers and policymakers) who have dominated the debates for way too long.

The book's admirable appeal lies in its legible lingo, which helps democratize the discourse around IP—a theme that is central to the mission of *SpicyIP*, a blog that I founded many years ago. And a blog fortunate enough to have been led, at different points in time, by these two gifted writers. In many ways, I am personally grateful to them for having produced what I had been meaning to produce for many years—a book that decodes IP and permits a wider panoply of the public to engage with it.

Forewords should be short, as they merely introduce the book and its importance (or lack of it!). Long-windedness is a sin common to us lawyers and law professors. So let me not stand in the way of those eager to embark on an exciting expedition into the world of Indian IP—a journey that promises to inform as much as inspire, for chaotic as it sounds, Indian IP has managed to make a distinct mark in a world where the pressures to conform to a largely uniform IP script are intense—a script devised for the most part by Western industrial powers and one that (paradoxically enough) has remained largely static, despite its avowed objective to encourage creativity and innovation; ideals that, at their very heart, call for experimentation and risk taking.

Shamnad Basheer
Honorary Research Chair Professor of IP Law,
Nirma University
Visiting Professor of Law, National Law School, Bengaluru
Founder: IDIA/SpicyIP/P-PIL

ACKNOWLEDGEMENTS

This book has been in the making for several years now, and we can confidently say that it would not have reached anywhere near completion without help from our friends and acquaintances. We brainstormed on the outline and structure of this book many times over (there are perhaps a dozen versions in our inboxes) with Shamnad Basheer, who not only helped identify topics that would be of relevance and interest to the audience we wanted to reach out to, but also reviewed some of the chapters at different stages over the years. We received fabulous research assistance from Aparajita Lath, a keen blogger at *SpicyIP* and an upcoming lawyer, who pulled out the most obscure material from the depths of various libraries, offline and online, and put together extremely useful research notes as background material for the manuscript, besides doubling up as reviewer for some of the chapters. We are grateful also to Goutam Lath, whose translation skills came in handy when we had to wade through documents written in Hindi officialese. Sai Vinod, another friend from *SpicyIP* and an emerging young lawyer, was always available to bounce off ideas, file applications under the Right to Information (RTI) Act, 2005 on behalf of the authors, and also review chapters, when needed.

Research into many of the stories in this book began as anecdotes told to us in conversations we had with R.S. Seshadri of Tilda Rice, Malathi Lakshmikumaran and R. Parthasarathy of Lakshmikumaran and Sridharan, and Latha Nair of K&S Partners. Achille Forler has been an endless source of interesting information on the copyright issues faced by the music industry.

Delving into the archives involved visiting the Department of Industrial Policy and Promotion (DIPP), Ministry of Commerce and Industry, several times for applications filed under the RTI Act, and much of the research would not have been possible without the support of the officers and staff there, particularly Chandni Raina and S.K. Lal. We also met G.R. Raghavender, Registrar of Copyrights, for some of our research.

Libraries across the world were raided for information, too, including those at the Central Secretariat and the National Institute of Public Finance and Policy in New Delhi, the National University of Juridical Sciences in Kolkata, Stanford Law School of California, USA, Harvard University, USA, and the collection of manuscripts available with Sterling Publishers, and we are particularly thankful to the library staff who humoured our queries and our requests for obscure information with great patience. Two digital databases which were most useful in building the historical narrative in this book were the *Economic & Political Weekly* and the *New York Times*.

When libraries were not accessible, we approached offices through the route of applications made under the RTI Act. Though our success rate was mixed, much of the narrative contained in this book, particularly pertaining to Indian legislative history, was built on the foundation of the replies we received to the RTI applications. Many of the offices replied to our applications in considerable detail, notably the Council of Scientific and Industrial Research, the Traditional Knowledge Digital Library, the Parliament Library, the Lok Sabha and Rajya Sabha Secretariats, the Agricultural and Processed Food Products Export Development Authority, and the Copyright Office.

There were also many documents that could not be procured by us in India, but were easily available in libraries abroad. Our friends and colleagues at various institutes and universities across the world were roped in to assist us in this search. Simi George, Akshar Saxena, Subramanian Natarajan, and Shubha Ghosh were generous enough to spare valuable time to try and procure these documents from their home libraries, variously at Harvard University, the University of Chicago's Centre for Research Library, the British Library, and the London School of Economics. Without these, the stories we have told would have been woefully incomplete.

Even as we thought the chapters and the manuscript were near completion, our anonymous Oxford University Press (OUP) reviewers pointed out several issues. Their perceptive comments, as also the comments of Darren Smyth, Chaitanya Ramachandran, and Anushree Rauta, were immensely useful and improved the manuscript considerably.

Several of the stories told here first saw light of day as smaller pieces of analyses and news reports that appeared on the *SpicyIP* blog written by one of the authors. Those pieces invariably were commented upon by various fellow bloggers, blog readers, and commentators, which eventually helped sculpt the larger essays that form part of this book. To all of them, who are too numerous to name without missing someone out, we remain ever grateful.

Finally, this book would most certainly not have been possible without the faith that our editors at OUP had in us. They humoured our skipping deadlines regularly, dealt with our incessant queries and the mistakes we made as novice authors, and kept encouraging us whenever we expressed scepticism about the future of this manuscript.

———

As a law student, when I* was getting more than my share of rejections for articles or papers that I used to submit to publications, I never quite imagined that I would someday get an opportunity to publish a book on intellectual property (IP) law with OUP. This was possible only because of opportunities, encouragement, and experience that were provided to me by many wonderful people in my life. I would like to thank a few of them over here.

First and foremost, I would like to thank my incredible parents, Satya and Sudhakar, for making sure that I had the best of opportunities to reach my potential and enjoy life. I grew up in a city and community obsessed with sending their children to engineering college and at one point of time I appeared destined to end up a failed software engineer

* This section is by Prashant Reddy T.

responsible for writing code that crashed computer networks across the world. The fact that I became the first lawyer from my family was mostly because of opportunities shown to me by my parents. I also absolutely have to thank my elder brother, Vikas, for generally being around in life. I have learnt many things from him, especially the virtues of being irreverent and frank while expressing one's opinion— both of which values have held me in good stead while writing about the law.

Amongst the most important influences in my academic and professional life is Shamnad Basheer. He has given me many opportunities, as a young student and as a lawyer, to observe and learn IP law from the frontlines: as a co-author in academic publications, a research assistant at a university, and a blogger on *SpicyIP*. I have lost track of the number of recommendation letters that he has written for me, each of which has opened new opportunities at universities, scholarship funds, and law firms. Although Shamnad and I are rarely on the same page of any IP debate, he always had my back when I got flak for my less than diplomatic writing on *SpicyIP*. The liberty to write freely and in opposition to a mainstream viewpoint is a surprisingly rare commodity and I am thankful to Shamnad for ensuring that I had an opportunity to do so on *SpicyIP*.

Amongst my many law school professors, I am especially grateful to T. Ramakrishna at the National Law School of India University who introduced me to the subject of IP law while I was studying for my BA, LLB (Honours) degree. At Stanford Law School, where I earned an LLM degree, I had the good fortune of studying IP and related technology laws under leading lights such as Professors Mark Lemley, Paul Goldstein, Robert Merges, Henry Greely, and Barbara van Schewick, amongst others. My education at Stanford was possible, in part, due to a scholarship from the J.N. Tata Endowment which selected me as a J.N. Tata Scholar after an interview with Nawaz Mody and Zia Mody. I am very grateful for the Endowment's generosity. I am also forever indebted to my dear grandfather, N. Varada Reddy whose generosity and encouragement made it possible for me to study at Stanford.

From the many superb lawyers that I have worked with, I would like to especially thank Pravin Anand, the Managing Partner of Anand and Anand, and R. Parthasarathy, who heads the IP practice of Lakshmikumaran & Sridharan. My time at both law firms gave me valuable opportunities to learn from these two leading IP lawyers in India while working on cutting-edge IP cases. A short stint at the San Francisco offices of Schiff Hardin provided a fascinating insight into the practice of IP law in the USA. I am grateful to Sailesh Patel and the late Christopher Ohly for enabling this opportunity and to the wonderful George Yu for being a great mentor during my time at Schiff Hardin. The experience was an eye-opener and showed me the distance required to be travelled by Indian legal practice in general, and IP law in specific, to achieve the intellectual rigour demanded by a justice system actually aimed at uncovering the truth.

Last but not the least, I am grateful to my several friends who have encouraged me to complete this book at times when I lost steam. You know who you are. Thank you!

The first piece I[†] ever wrote on IP was as a high school student, on something vaguely to do with biotechnology and intellectual property rights (IPRs). My mother decided to put up my piece of adolescent writing on the bulletin board outside her laboratory for her colleagues, students, and visitors to read. As embarrassed as I was then, I realize now that she was the first one to 'publish' my IP writing, and will always remain the one person who truly believed I could do crazy things like writing a book. I am sure if she were around today, while being extremely happy and proud to see someone properly publish my work, she would probably have said, 'I told you so!'

This was, of course, before blogs became popular as avenues for self-publishing, and many years before I discovered *SpicyIP*. An open call for bloggers by Shamnad way back in 2007 made me send him an email from Singapore, where I was studying then, and it started a fascinating journey into the world of IP. I (still) have had no formal education in IP, but those few years on the blog taught me more about the subject than a classroom might have, in more ways than one.

---

† This section is by Sumathi Chandrashekaran.

I also got the opportunity to briefly dabble in IP practice, for which I have Obhan and Associates to thank, where I learnt a lot of my basics about the subject. I must also admit that I would never have become a lawyer at all, if it were not for three very special people, Ashima Gadi, Shefali Sewak, and Aparna Wilson, who are responsible for my having adventured into this discipline in the first place.

Somewhere along the way, my friend Ahana Mullick sowed the seed in my head of putting together a book like this on IP, and were it not for her constant prodding, I might never have kept at it. Rajni Raman, Kavitha Ravikumar, Unni K. Narayanan, Pragyan Acharya, my aunts Geeta Narayan and Sudha Sundaram, and my grandmother Radha Balakrishnan religiously tracked every milestone on this book, and ensured that I moved on to the next. There are far too many others, who kept encouraging me to stay with this project, to list here—mentors, classmates, colleagues, friends, family, and well-wishers—all of whom I remain indebted to.

Finally, the book itself would have never come to fruition in any form if it were not for my father, who has taught me to think, ask questions, and write.

ABBREVIATIONS

AGM	Annual General Meeting
AOC	Appellation d'origine contrôlée
AOL	America Online
APEDA	Agricultural and Processed Food Products Export Development Authority (India)
AYUSH	Ayurveda, Yoga and Naturopathy, Unani, Siddha, and Homeopathy (India)
BBS	Bulletin Board Service
BIRPI	Bureaux Internationaux Réunis pour la Protection de la Propriété Intellectuelle
CBI	Central Bureau of Investigation (India)
CCC	Copyright Clearance Center
CD	Compact Disc
CEO	Chief Executive Officer
CERT-IN	Computer Emergency Response Team, India
CISAC	Confédération Internationale des Sociétés d'Auteurs et Compositeurs
CIVC	Comité Interprofessionnel du vin de Champagne
CLB	Company Law Board (India)
CML	Chronic Myeloid Leukaemia
CPAA	Cancer Patients Aid Association
CPI(M)	Communist Party of India (Marxist)
CSIR	Council of Scientific and Industrial Research (India)
CUP	Cambridge University Press

DG-CSIR	Director-General of the Council of Scientific and Industrial Research (India)
DIPP	Department of Industrial Policy and Promotion (India)
DIT	Department of Information Technology (India)
DMCA	Digital Millennium Copyright Act (USA)
DSB	Dispute Settlement Body
DU	University of Delhi
EC	European Communities
ECRRD	European Community Rental Rights Directive
ED	Enforcement Directorate (India)
EIA	Export Inspection Agency (India)
EMRs	Exclusive Marketing Rights
EPA	Environmental Protection Agency (USA)
EPO	European Patent Office
EU	European Union
FSA	Food Standards Agency
FTC	Federal Trade Commission (USA)
GATT	General Agreement on Tariffs and Trade
GIs	Geographical Indications
GIPAP	Glivec International Patient Access Program
GoM	Group of Ministers (India)
HRD	Human Resource Development
IARI	Indian Agricultural Research Institute
ICANN	Internet Corporation for Assigned Names and Numbers
ICAR	Indian Council of Agricultural Research
IFOAM	International Federation of Organic Agricultural Movements
IIPA	International Intellectual Property Alliance
IIS	Institute for Inner Studies
IMF	International Monetary Fund
IMI	Indian Music Industry
INAO	Institut national de l'origine et de la qualité (France)
IP	Intellectual Property
IPAB	Intellectual Property Appellate Board (India)
IPMD	Intellectual Property Management Department (CSIR)
IPOs	International Patent Offices

IPOA	Intellectual Property Owners Association
IPRs	Intellectual Property Rights
IPRS	Indian Performing Right Society
IRRO	Indian Reprographic Rights Organisation
ISP	Internet Service Provider
IT	Information Technology
JPC	Joint Parliamentary Committee (India)
KRRS	Karnataka Rajya Raitha Sangha
MoU	Memorandum of Understanding
MP	Member of Parliament
MSF	Médecins Sans Frontières
NARS	National Agricultural Research System (India)
NASSCOM	National Association of Software and Services Companies
NBT	National Basmati Trials (India)
NCE	New Chemical Entity
NDA	National Democratic Alliance
NGO	Non-governmental Organization
NRI	Natural Resources Institute
NSP	Network Service Provider
NWGPL	National Working Group on Patent Laws
OCILLA	Online Copyright Infringement Liability Limitation Act
OHIM	Office for Harmonisation in the Internal Market
OIF	Osho International Foundation
OSP	Online Service Provider
OSYU	Open Source Yoga Unity
OUP	Oxford University Press
PEN	Poets, Essayists, and Novelists
PhRMA	Pharmaceutical Research and Manufacturers of America
PMI	Permanent Mission of India
PMO	Prime Minister's Office (India)
PPL	Phonographic Performance Limited
PPRADS	Payyannur Pavithra Ring Artisans and Development Society
RFSTE	Research Foundation for Science, Technology and Ecology

RSGB	Research Services of Great Britain
RTI	Right to Information
SAUs	State Agricultural Universities
SCIL	Super Cassettes Industries Ltd.
SIM	Self Instructional Material
SIMCA	South Indian Music Companies Association
SLP	Special Leave Petition
SRC	States Reorganisation Commission
SWA	Scotch Whisky Association
TKDL	Traditional Knowledge Digital Library
TKRC	Traditional Knowledge Resource Classification
TRIPS	Agreement on Trade-Related Aspects of Intellectual Property Rights
TTAB	(United States) Trademark Trial and Appeal Board
TWN	Third World Network
UCC	Universal Copyright Convention
UK	United Kingdom
UN	United Nations
UNESCO	United Nations Educational, Scientific and Cultural Organization
UPA	United Progressive Alliance
URL	Uniform Resource Locator
US	United States
USPTO	United States Patent and Trademark Office
USTR	United States Trade Representative
WIPO	World Intellectual Property Organization
WTO	World Trade Organization

INTRODUCTION

The story of Indian intellectual property (IP) law is a saga in its own right. Despite being an area of law impacting everyone's access to medicine, technology, books, music, and movies, IP in India has historically been regarded as an esoteric subject, one that has no room in public debate. Over the past decade, though, this narrative has altered dramatically: student-led protests after academic publishers sued a photocopy shop in the University of Delhi (DU); judicial websites hacked in disapproval of court-imposed bans on access to file-sharing websites; resellers lobbying for parallel imports; Bollywood producers threatening strikes to oppose mandatory royalty-sharing with composers; and rallies by patient groups during the Glivec case are some of the recent examples where the IP debate has spilled onto the streets. Several of these confrontations would have been unimaginable 60 years ago, when it was mainly the government driving Indian IP policy. The deepening of democracy, an expanding middle class, and a new breed of academics, lawyers, and activists have pushed IP into the spotlight of public debate.

Having been commentators on *SpicyIP* for many years, we have often been asked by students and other readers for recommendations of a book that could explain the story of Indian IP in a simple and jargon-free language. But most of the (meagre) IP scholarship that has been published in India has catered to either lawyers or academics. This book attempts to fill this gap in IP writing by presenting the debate in a form that is accessible to a general, non-specialist reader. Rather than explaining the black letter of the law, this book tries to explain the evolution of Indian IP law and policy through the lens of history and politics, peppered with judicial decisions at occasional intervals.

The debate in India has conventionally been bucketed into those who are in favour of protecting IP (the 'pro' IP lobby) and those who are against such protections (the 'anti' IP lobby). But this book has deliberately avoided this binary distinction, and chosen instead to examine the debate more detachedly. It delves into many complex and multilayered facets of the issue, a lot of which has remained hidden even from academic view. For instance, in the 1950s, India was all set for a radical overhaul of its copyright law, including a possible exit from the Berne Convention. But a strong lobby of politician-authors in Parliament blocked these efforts, despite other parliamentarians contending that an expansive copyright law would affect India's ability to make books (and, by extension, education) accessible to its people. Similarly, in the 1960s, although there was broad political consensus to narrow Indian patent law, the Swatantra Party remained steadfast in its opposition, arguing instead that India would benefit through greater technology transfer by respecting IP even if it belonged to foreigners. These issues remain relevant in India even today, whether it is in the guise of the DU photocopy case or the access to medicines debate. The turn of the century has seen a new churn in India's approach to IP law, which has led to a more distinctive identity emerging. India is now increasingly emboldened in asserting its rights and interests, as demonstrated by the law on geographical indications, the vociferous debates on traditional knowledge surrounding plants such as neem, turmeric, and basmati, and the protections that many believe various communities are entitled to. The money-spinners that religion and spirituality are in India have not been left far behind in the IP debate either, the most well-known being the questions about the IP around yoga.

IP is slowly becoming an inflexion point in public conversations; views remain polarized and India remains in search of conclusions for many aspects of IP protection in this day and age, but exciting times lie ahead.

The content of this book can be categorized as follows.

Chapter 1, 'Indian Patent Law Declares Independence', deals with patents and pharmaceuticals in India after it gained independence from the British. This discussion has four stages. The first stage is a narration of how India abolished pharmaceutical patents in 1970, and the lengthy debate that preceded such a move. This abolition came after 22 years, two expert committees, two parliamentary standing committees, and some rather intense opposition from the Swatantra Party, which was the only political party supporting a patent regime for pharmaceuticals at the time. The second stage is described in Chapter 2, 'Surrender at Geneva', of how India was slowly convinced and nudged into becoming a member of the World Trade Organization (WTO) by the United States Trade Representative. Joining the WTO and becoming a signatory to the Agreement on Trade-Related Intellectual Property Rights (TRIPS) required India to reinstate a pharmaceutical patent regime in exchange for greater trading benefits in other sectors like textiles. The third stage is the amendment of India's patent law to comply with TRIPS, discussed in Chapter 3, 'Life after Marrakesh'. This effort spanned a stormy decade of parliamentary debates and culminated in (the infamous) Section 3(d) of the Patents Act, 1970, a provision that was inserted into the law, literally, at the last minute. This enactment eventually led to the fourth stage, explained in Chapter 4, 'Novartis Trips Over Section 3(d)', where India's new patent law, and especially Section 3(d), was tested by Novartis all the way to the Supreme Court of India.

The next series of chapters deal with Indian copyright law and policy, with each chapter discussing a different creative industry. Chapter 5, 'New Delhi Challenges the Berne Convention', deals with the book publishing industry, in the context of India's attempt to rewrite its own copyright law immediately after Independence and its efforts to renegotiate its international obligations under the Berne Convention. A determined lobbying effort led by the poet laureate Ramdhari Singh 'Dinkar' and his contemporaries forced the Government of India to roll back contentious reforms such as a reduced copyright term and a mandatory registration requirement for copyright enforcement. Chapter 6, 'The Moving Picture', explains how India's movie industry dealt with the evolution of copyright law and vice versa. In particular, we chronicle the rich history of litigation, first within the Indian industry and then the litigation between foreigners and Indian cinema, for example, where an Indian producer in Karnataka accused the

Hollywood producers of *Independence Day* of infringing his copyright. Chapter 7, 'Akhtar Rescripts Copyright Law', details the background to the revolutionary Copyright (Amendment) Act, 2012, which sought to radically alter the equations in the Indian music industry. This chapter is the story of how the lyricist and scriptwriter Javed Akhtar took it upon himself to lead Indian lyricists and poets in a successful lobbying effort that pitted the creative community against the moneybags who controlled the production houses and music labels. Chapter 8, 'Digital India Seeks "Safe Harbour"', narrates the Indian experience in developing a safe harbour exception in copyright law that would shield Internet intermediaries from copyright infringement. The lack of a 'safe harbour' provision led to promising start-ups like Guruji.com being shut down after the Bengaluru police arrested the graduates from the Indian Institute of Technology who founded the company. This chapter reminds us that India still has a long way to go to enforce a balanced regime to protect copyrights on the Internet.

The last set of chapters deal with traditional knowledge, religion, and IP law. Chapter 9, 'The Traditional Knowledge Trilogy', deals with a series of patent controversies in the 1990s, where Indian traditional knowledge associated with neem, turmeric, and basmati was allegedly patented by foreign corporations. Much of the debate surrounding these events was completely misguided and the government response, in the form of the Traditional Knowledge Digital Library (TKDL), is problematic because it does little else than showcasing India's 'glorious past'. Chapter 10, 'The Queen of All Rices', discusses the Indian government's several unsuccessful attempts to protect the uniqueness of basmati rice by registering it as a geographical indication (GI). The taste and success of basmati is a credit to the generations of farmers who have skilfully bred their respective traditional varieties of basmati, only to face stiff competition from government-sanctioned hybrids such as Pusa basmati. More worryingly, the Government of India has virtually 'nationalized' the basmati GI by allowing its own agencies to seek ownership of the GI, rather than empower the community of farmers, millers, and traders who developed basmati over centuries. Chapter 11, 'Of Gods and Gurus', covers the issue of IP in the context of gods, gurus, and traditions. As religions become commercialized, gurus who proclaim themselves to be the messengers of gods leave behind fortunes in the form of IP, either as books or audio and video recordings. Temples are not far behind, with several of them claiming trademark rights in symbols representing various deities. Indian trademark law is rare in having a provision forbidding the registration of symbols that hurt religious feelings.

This book is by no means a comprehensive or exhaustive detailing of the various stories around IP in India. Many stories still remain un-researched and untold. Our objective in putting this book together was singular—to aid the non-specialist reader in understanding complex but fascinating issues in Indian IP, and use this book as a stepping-stone to explore and debate the subject further, with greater nuance and analysis. The theme laid out in the selection of stories is also reflected in the title to this work: Create, Copy, Disrupt. The title is a play on the usual slogan of 'Create, Protect, Innovate' that has been adopted by IP agencies and IP conferences across the world. Arguably, an IP policy need not focus on creation and innovation alone, and a developing country like India can consider following a policy of imitation, which although disruptive can still serve the country's economic interests.

Since this book was never meant to be an academic text, it has been a challenge to break down the language of the law into readable prose for a non-specialist audience. Lawyers have a habit of forgetting that legal jargon is incomprehensible to most, but we have tried our best to keep the legalese to a minimum. We hope we have succeeded towards this in some measure.

1

INDIAN PATENT LAW DECLARES
INDEPENDENCE

On 1 April 2013, the Supreme Court of India delivered a ruling that upheld a 2006 decision of the Indian Patent Office to deny Novartis a patent for Glivec, a breakthrough wonder-drug used to treat patients suffering from chronic myeloid leukaemia (CML). This landmark ruling, which interpreted Section 3(d) of India's patent law, was the latest in a series of setbacks faced by the innovator pharmaceutical industry which had always regarded India as a 'problem child' when it came to pharmaceutical patents. This tension between India and the innovator pharmaceutical industry is decades old. For example, in 1944, Haffkine Institute—a government institute named after scientist Waldemar Mordecai Haffkine who invented vaccines against cholera and plague—under the stewardship of S.S. Sokhey, unsuccessfully fought a compulsory licensing dispute against the pharmaceutical industry.[1] The Haffkine Institute, funded by the erstwhile government of Bombay, sought a compulsory licence for the manufacture of patented sulfathiazole on the grounds that existing supplies did not meet demand and the prices were excessively high. In a letter dated 16 August 1957 to Jawaharlal Nehru, Sokhey wrote that a representative of the British pharmaceutical company May and Baker told him soon after that they would not let their pricing policy be questioned in public; and that since it was the first such case for compulsory licensing, the pharmaceutical industry had collected funds of Rs 600,000 to argue the matter. An offer of a voluntary licence to manufacture the drug in India was also made to Sokhey, provided he withdrew his charges and sold the drug at the same price as the imported price. Sokhey turned down the offer, fought the case, and lost.[2]

After Independence, India made several attempts to reform its patent law in the face of stiff opposition from the pharmaceutical lobby. In 1970, an independent India finally enacted its own patent legislation, repealing the British-era Patents and Designs Act, 1911, thereby doing away with patents for pharmaceutical products, and reducing the terms of all patents in India. Why did a newly independent India take almost 22 years to abolish patents for pharmaceutical products? Why did India retain process patents for the pharmaceutical sector? Who were the main players lobbying against the law? What were the political debates that took place in the Parliament over the reform of patent law? This chapter tries to explain the story of how Indian policymakers took the decision to enact a patent law that transformed the global pharmaceutical industry and made India the pharmacy of the developing world.

The Experts and Their Reports

Between 1947, when India became independent, and 1970, when Parliament enacted a new patent law, two expert committees and two Joint Parliamentary Committees (JPCs) debated the direction of India's new patent policy—a feat not replicated since for any of India's other intellectual property laws. The first committee, the Patent Enquiry Committee, was constituted in 1948 and headed by retired Justice Bakshi Tek Chand, who was also a member of the Constituent Assembly that drafted the Indian constitution.[3] The second committee, the Committee on Revision of Patent Law, was set up in 1957 and was headed by Justice Rajagopala Ayyangar—then a judge of the Madras High Court, who went on to become a Justice of the Supreme Court of India.[4] Both expert committees had a key focus on patents related to chemicals, food, and medicine.

Under the Patents and Designs Act, 1911, imposed on India during British rule, there were no special restrictions on the patenting of chemicals, food, and medicine.[5] The position of law was the same in the UK until 1919, when the British Parliament introduced several restrictions on the patenting of certain inventions related to chemicals, food, and medicine. In the ensuing years, the British amended their patent law multiple times over, notably in 1932 and 1949 as a response to the needs of their evolving industry. However, for many decades, the Patent and Designs Act of 1911 continued to be followed in India.

With the change in its law in 1919, the UK introduced special restrictions for chemical inventions, later extended to food and medicine. Before 1919, the UK's patent law, like the Indian patent law, protected only 'methods of manufacture', and not *substances* resulting from such methods of manufacture.[6] However, this position of law was not entirely clear in its application. Accounts of British patent law from that era suggest that several patent applications claimed protection for even *new* chemical substances, independent of their processes of manufacture, and such claims were often granted.[7] In the UK, these patents for new chemical substances, especially industrial dyes, were hampering the development of the domestic chemical industry. This was because a large number of patents in the UK for new chemical substances, including dyes, were owned by the Germans.[8]

The German chemical industry was at an advantage because Germany itself did not offer protection for new chemical substances under its own patent law. Introduced in 1877, and followed across most of Europe, the German patent law at the time protected only chemical processes (that is, methods of manufacture), along with the chemical substances that resulted from such processes (as a result, a competitor could still manufacture the same substance through a different non-patented process).[9] Chemical substances, in their own right, were not protected under the German patent law in that era. Similar restrictions also applied to products or substances related to food and medicines. Therefore, if a company patented a particular process for the manufacture of a chemical, food, or medicine, a competitor could manufacture the same substance with a new non-infringing process. This feature of the law encouraged German chemical industries to invest significantly in the development of new processes as well as circumvent processes already patented, thereby leading to increased competition and innovation in more efficient methods of manufacturing chemical substances.[10]

Not only did the German patent law ensure that local manufacturing of new chemical substances was quick and easy, but the Germans also had first-mover advantage in filing and obtaining patents for new chemical substances (or products) in the UK and the US since both the countries, unlike Germany, granted product patents in that era. Once the substances were patented, the UK and the US industries could no longer manufacture the same product with new processes or methods of manufacture. The Germans would usually manufacture these patented chemical substances (or products) in their own country and export the patented chemical substances (or products) to the US and the UK.[11] Thus, the product patent system in both the UK and the US for chemical, food, and medicine substances led to their own industries stagnating to a point where changes in the law became necessary to ensure the survival of domestic industries.

In the US, the legal position changed after the First World War, when it enacted a legislation to confiscate all enemy property. At the time, enemy property included all patents owned by the Germans, and it is believed that this confiscation was the turning point in the growth of the US chemical industry.[12]

The UK, on its part, amended its patent law in 1919 to introduce a new Section 38(A)(1), modelled, interestingly, on German law. Under this new provision, only 'special' chemical processes were patentable along with the substances resulting from these special processes. The phrase 'special' was understood to mean a new process of manufacturing that produced a new substance by its own chemical reaction.[13] This amendment barred the earlier practice of claiming patents for chemical substances themselves. Effectively, competitors could now manufacture the same substance through non-infringing processes. This contributed significantly to the growth of the Britain's chemical industry.[14] By 1931, when the Sargant Committee was reviewing the patent protection to be offered to chemical inventions in the UK, British industry apparently complained that Section 38(A)(1) hindered the protection of new substances that were developed through processes not considered to be 'special' by the Patent Office.[15] As the British chemical industry was considered to have advanced by then, Section 38(A)(1) was amended in 1932, and the requirement for having a 'special' process was deleted.[16]

The only requirement under the 1932 amendment, according to experts, was for the patent specification to describe the method or process of manufacture of the product or substance. Effectively, the law recognized patents for products and substances in the UK, because the product or substance no longer had to be manufactured by a 'special' process.[17] Thus, a product could be patented as long as the process was disclosed in the specification. In 1949, the UK amended its law to do away with even this requirement to disclose the manufacturing process, and substances or products related to chemicals, food, or medicine could be claimed by themselves.[18]

This explanation of the UK law is crucial as it served as a template for changes to the Indian patent law. Both the Tek Chand Committee and the Ayyangar Committee referred to the British patent law while debating the level of patent protection to be offered to chemicals, food, and medicine. However, both committees approached the same issue very differently. The first interim report was submitted by the Tek Chand Committee to Syama Prasad Mookerjee, the then Minister for Industry and Supply, on 4 August 1949. The committee explained that the respondents it surveyed agreed that 'patent protection should be granted for inventions in the field of food and medicine, both for new products and new processes' and that it was 'in entire agreement with these views'.[19] Such a consensus was rather unusual since most countries at the time did not protect new products or substances related to food or medicine under their patent laws. Though, few exceptions to this trend existed, such as the US and the UK. However, in its final report in April 1950, the Tek Chand Committee came to a diametrically opposite conclusion. Referring to the insertion of Section 38(A)(1) in the UK law in 1919, the committee cryptically noted that '[t]he absence of these provisions undoubtedly favoured the foreigner and enabled him to abuse his patent rights in India to the detriment of the people of this country.'[20] In an equally cryptic conclusion, the committee noted, '[s]ubstances prepared or produced by chemical processes or intended for food or medicine should not be patentable except when made by the invented processes or their obvious equivalent.'[21] This was similar to the language of Section 38(A)(1) of the UK law after the 1919 amendments except the word 'special' had been replaced with the word 'invented'.

Why did the committee take polar opposite views in its interim and final reports? Its recommendations were likely to have far-reaching implications for the Indian economy, and provoke reactions from foreign investors. Surely, the committee should have provided a more detailed explanation. Instead, it merely outlined the laws of Japan, France, Germany, and the UK, explaining how those countries imposed similar special restrictions on the patenting of inventions related to food and medicine.[22] The mandate of the Patents Enquiry Committee ended with the submission of its final report in April 1950.[23]

Three years later, the Patents Bill, 1953, was introduced in the Lok Sabha by the then Minister of Commerce, T.T. Krishnamachari. This was the second patent legislation introduced in independent India. The first—the Indian Patents and Designs (Amendment) Act, 1950—had amended the British-era Patents and Designs Act, 1911, to provide for more liberal compulsory licensing provisions. The 1953 Bill sought to repeal the existing patent law and replace it with an entirely new law. The 'Statement of Objects and Reasons' accompanying the 1953 Bill, explaining the reasons for the introduction of the Bill, stated:

> The Indian Patents and Designs Act, 1911 was enacted at a time when India had not developed industrially. The experience of the working of this Act coupled with the progress of industrial development in the country indicated clearly the need for a more comprehensive legislation so as to ensure that patent rights are not abused to the detriment of the consumer or to the prejudice of the trade or of the industrial development of the country ... The final report of the Patents Enquiry Committee was submitted in 1950. The object of this Bill is to give effect to such of the recommendations of the final report of the Patents Enquiry Committee as have been accepted by Government.

This 'Statement of Objects and Reasons' does not explain the government's stance on the Patent Enquiry Committee's recommendations regarding pharmaceutical patents. However, from the draft of the Bill it appears that someone inside the government had either decided to reject the committee's recommendation on limiting patents for food, medicine, and chemicals, *or* had made a drafting error. As introduced in Parliament, Clause 3(d) of the Patents Bill, 1953 *prohibited* the patenting of 'a substance prepared or produced by a chemical process or intended for food or medicine other than a substance prepared or produced by any method or process of manufacture particularly described in the complete specification of the invention or by its obvious chemical equivalent'.

This provision was in fact a verbatim copy of Section 38(A)(1) of the UK Patents Act as it existed *after* the amendments in 1932. As explained earlier, in the UK, this provision had led to a *de facto* product patent regime, because patentees tended to claim all possible processes of manufacture, and made it impossible for competitors to enter the market. But the Tek Chand Committee had actually recommended the version of Section 38(A)(1) which existed *after* the 1919 amendment, and *before* the 1932 amendment, because it wanted patent protection for only *invented* processes, and products made specifically by those invented processes.[24] It did not recommend a product patent regime. The deletion of the word 'invented' from the Tek Chand Committee's proposal, in Clause 3(d), therefore, completely changed the meaning of the provision. By importing this into Indian law as Clause 3(d), the government went against a key recommendation of the Tek Chand Committee. The reason for this divergence was not clear. Did special interest groups influence the government or did the drafters of the law simply copy the wrong provision of law? Nevertheless, the Patents Bill, 1953 was not enacted into a law by the Parliament.

Instead, the Indian government constituted a second committee in 1957 under Justice Ayyangar 'to review the Patent Laws in India with a view to ensure that the patent system was more conducive to national interests'.[25] Unlike the Tek Chand Committee's report, which merely skimmed over several contentious issues, Justice Ayyangar's report was exceptionally well-researched, and his report is the source for much of the discussion on the evolution of patent law in Germany and the UK provided earlier in this chapter. Besides a broader historical understanding of restrictions on patenting products in various countries at different stages of development, this report also examined the impact of such restrictions on innovation in the chemical industry. For example, in one footnote, Ayyangar listed the position of patents for chemical products and processes of manufacture in 22 countries.[26] Of these countries, Ayyangar noted that some allowed patents for new processes of manufacture of chemicals, but disallowed patents for either *all* the chemical products, or for chemical products related to food and medicine *per se*. These countries were Austria, Chile, Czechoslovakia, Denmark, Finland, Germany (Federal Republic), Germany (Democratic Republic), Holland, Hungary, France, Japan, Mexico, Norway, Poland, Spain, Sweden, Switzerland, the Union of Soviet Socialist Republics (USSR), and Yugoslavia. Some, like Italy, had abolished product and process patents for pharmaceutical inventions altogether.

This restriction on patenting food and medicine, Ayyangar explained, was because these countries did not want any single producer to monopolize the manufacture of such vital products as it would lead to high prices. At the time, the Indian Patents and Designs Act, 1911 was similar to pre-1919 British law, that is, 'invention' was defined as a 'manner of new manufacture'. However, there was a difference between law and practice. Ayyangar noted that the Controller of Patents of the Indian Patent Office explained to him 'that in effect the Indian Patent practice proceeds on the basis of section 38(A)(1) of the U.K. Act of 1907 as amended in 1932.'[27] This meant that new products or substances, including those related to food and medicine, were being protected under Indian patent law.

For India, which was just beginning to build its industry after independence, it made even less sense to allow product patents, as foreigners held 90 per cent of all Indian patents.[28] Citing contemporary economic literature, Ayyangar concluded that product patents would only send royalties from India out to foreign countries, and also hamper domestic manufacturing. The only reasonable conclusion, according to Ayyangar, was to prohibit product patents for chemicals, food, and medicine altogether, and allow patents for only processes used to manufacture those products. In this manner, industry would have incentives to create newer and cheaper manufacturing processes. To this end, Ayyangar disagreed with the proposed Clause 3(d) of the Patents Bill, 1953, since it would allow patenting of products or new substances provided the process of manufacturing the substance was also disclosed.[29] Instead, Ayyangar drafted an alternate provision:

(2) No patent shall after the commencement of this Act be granted in respect of inventions claiming—(a) substances intended for or are capable of being used as food or beverage or as medicine (for men or animals) including sera, vaccines, antibiotics and biological preparations, insecticide, germicide or fungicide, and (b) substances produced by chemical processes including alloys but excluding glass.

(3) Notwithstanding anything in sub-section (2) inventions of chemical processes for the manufacture or production of the substances mentioned in that subsection shall be patentable.[30]

Ayyangar's draft provision, which was part of his final report submitted to the government in September 1959, offered more clarity than Clause 3(d) of the 1953 Bill, avoiding the convoluted phraseology earlier on offer. This draft was clear that some substances in certain fields of technology would not be patentable even if the processes used to manufacture those substances would still be patentable.

Strangely, Ayyangar remained silent on the possibility of the abuse of a process patent regime. For instance, a patentee could file multiple patent applications for all the different processes used to manufacture the same product, and thus create a *de facto* product patent regime. The problem of multiple process patents was a reality in Indian industry, and was highlighted by several scientists and industrialists during hearings conducted by a JPC examining patent law in 1969.

One such person was K.A. Hamied, entrepreneur and founder of Cipla, and father of Yusuf Hameid, who made Cipla one of the most successful generic pharmaceutical companies in India. Testifying before the JPC, K.A. Hamied said:

... chemical science has advanced in Europe and other places for the manufacture of certain items like Talbutumite. I can manufacture it by a certain process, it can be manufactured by another process. Now, in these foreign countries—highly developed countries—they take a patent of all the conceivable processes so that when I give the problem to my scientist in National Chemical Laboratory, Poona or National Drugs Research Institute, Lucknow he says it is patented. He discovers another process and finds that is also patented; he makes to another process and he is surprised to find that is also patented. So, if a manufacturer or patentee wants to manufacture a substance by a certain process, let him patent only that one process by which he is manufacturing. Now what is happening is that because of his vast scientific knowledge he covers all conceivable processes with the result that others cannot do anything, and their scientific research work is hampered.[31]

He also highlighted the uncertainty regarding the scope of a granted process patent. Hamied asserted, '[w]e evolve a process, but then we do not know whether that process is covered by patent. You know the case of Unichem Laboratory. Dr Ganapathy thought that it was quite a different process, but they filed a suit saying that it was almost the same as theirs. He lost the case after having spent so much money on that'.[32] The reference was most likely to the case of *Farbewerke Hoechst Aktiengesellschaft Vormals Meister Lucius & Bruning Corporation* v. *Unichem Laboratories and Ors*,[33] decided by the Bombay High Court in 1968. In its final judgment, the court restrained Unichem Laboratories from infringing a process patent owned by Hoechst for the manufacture of Tolbutamide, an anti-diabetic compound. Unichem had claimed that it was actually a process patented by the Haffkine Institute of Bombay, for which it (Unichem) had obtained a licence. The All India Manufacturers' Organization (AIMO), Bombay, and the Indian Drug Manufacturers' Association (IDMA) echoed Hamied's complaint, making similar despositions before the JPC.

Why did Ayyangar recommend retaining process patents? Probably, he hoped to tackle patent thickets through a more stringent compulsory licensing policy. The government, though, approached the issue differently, as was obvious from the Patents Bill it later introduced in the Parliament. Before discussing the journey of this new patent law in the 1960s, it is useful to understand the raging debate on patent law reform in the US at the same time because of its impact on Indian policymakers.

Kefauver Instigates the Patent versus Prices Debate in the US

In 1957, as Ayyangar began writing his masterly report on reworking Indian patent law, a US Senator by the name Carey Estes Kefauver embarked on one of the most audacious, ambitious, and searing inquiries into the affairs of the country's pharmaceutical industry. By this time, Senator Kefauver had earned a stellar public reputation by heading a Senate investigation into organized crime, with *Time* magazine, in a cover story in 1951, describing him as Crime Hunter Kefauver.[34] Towards the end of the 1950s, Kefauver, now head of the Senate Sub-Committee on Anti-trust and Monopoly, turned his guns on the increasing monopolies within the American industry by examining their effects on domestic consumers. For this purpose, he investigated the administered pricing regimes in four major industries: steel, automobiles, bread, and pharmaceutical drugs. The highly-publicized investigation into the pharmaceutical industry ended in a 384-page report, backed with empirical evidence and submitted on 8 May 1961.[35] The report presented a picture that the pharmaceutical industry was guilty of making astonishing profits through the sale of medicines of doubtful efficacy, and an expansive patent law that lent itself to abuse. Kefauver's report was criticized for acting as a witch-hunt trying to push an agenda of 'socialist control of healthcare', a serious charge in an America that was still recovering from the worst excesses of McCarthyism.[36]

Regardless of the criticism, Kefauver's research into the profits and business structure of the pharmaceutical industry was headline-grabbing. The report compared the profit margins of the top 15 pharmaceutical companies in the US with those of leading companies in 50 other industries, and found that the pharmaceutical industry had the highest profit margins:

> Not one of these companies has a gross margin above production costs as high as the lowest gross margin shown among the 15 drug companies, i.e., 59 percent. Among the 50 non-drug industries, in only one case, soft drinks, does the margin of the firm shown, Coca-Cola Co., approach this figure. In 6 of the 15 drug companies listed, the gross margin is more than 70 percent of sales, while in 41 of the 50 nondrug companies the margin is below 35 percent. Indeed, two-thirds (33) of the nondrug companies have margins which are less than half of the lowest margin reported for any of the 15 drug companies.[37]

As shocking as these facts were, Kefauver's true genius was in his effective use of the press to publicize the hearings. For instance, the highly-respected daily newspaper, *The New York Times*, ran a story on 8 December 1959 titled 'Senate Panel Cites Mark-ups on Drugs Ranging to 7,079%'.[38] This news report contained details of the clash at a hearing between Kefauver and Francis Brown, the President of Schering Corporation, who strongly defended the industry against allegations of overcharging, pointing, in a refrain that sounds familiar even today, to the cost of failed drugs to justify the profit margins on successful drugs. Nevertheless, the justification did not help. Kefauver's investigators had evidence of highly disparate pricing of the same drug in different countries, with the US prices often being the highest. This finding, too, was widely publicized. *The New York Times* story in January 1960 titled 'Big profits found in tranquilizers—one 6 times costlier than in Paris—Senate Inquiry Challenges Maker' reported how Kefauver grilled Walter A. Munns, President of the Smith, Kline & French Laboratories on the cost of a tranquilizer, chlorpromazine, credited for having 'dramatically depopulated mental hospitals in the last five years'.[39] Rhone-Poulenc of France had originally invented this drug, and then licensed the patents to Smith, Kline & French, which then marketed the drug in the US under the brand name Thorazine. This drug, sold in Paris for 51 cents, was sold in the US at six times the price at USD 3.03. Thorazine was just one among many examples of pharmaceutical companies charging considerably different prices across markets. Clearly, it appeared that these companies were massively overcharging in some markets, even after accounting for differences in manufacturing costs and raw materials.

These investigations had an almost indelible impact on Indian policymakers. It would not be an exaggeration to state that no other lines in history have influenced Indian policy on pharmaceutical patents, as much as the following extract from Kefauver's final report to the US Senate:

> India which does grant patents on drug products, provides an interesting case example. The prices in India for the broad-spectrum antibiotics, Aureomycin, are among the highest in the world. As a matter of fact, in drugs generally, India ranks among the highest priced nations of the world—a case of inverse relationship between per capita income and the level of drug prices.[40]

That this was the conclusion of a US Senator with strong credentials, for taking on monopolistic industries, served as a propaganda coup for those against pharmaceutical patents in India. Widely reported in Indian newspapers, these lines from Kefauver's report were emphasized by numerous opponents of India's pharmaceutical patent regime in the 1960s. They demanded that pharmaceutical patents be scrapped because patents were responsible for the high cost of drugs in India. This excerpt from Kefauver's report also repeatedly figured in the parliamentary debates on the country's pharmaceutical patent regime in 1965, 1967, and 1970.

S.S. Sokhey of Haffkine Institute, a vocal critic of India's pharmaceutical patent regime, wrote a long piece in the February 1962 issue of the venerable *Economic and Political Weekly* (*EPW*), demanding the abolition of pharmaceutical patents in India on the basis of Kefauver's report.[41] Sokhey had lost a compulsory licensing dispute with pharmaceutical companies before the Calcutta High Court in the 1940s. He was initially a member of the Tek Chand Committee, but having simultaneously been appointed the Assistant Director General of the World Health Organization (WHO), he did not sign the final report.[42] He also actively lobbied the Indian government for collaborations with the Soviet Union to develop pharmaceutical plants within India.[43] In his *EPW* article, Sokhey listed examples from Kefauver's report of blatant overcharging by pharmaceutical companies to draw a link between high prices and patents. Attacking Ayyangar for recommending the retention of patents for novel processes, Sokhey demanded nothing short of a complete abolition of pharmaceutical patents, for both process and product. He reminded readers of India's efforts at economic self-sufficiency and said:

> The country is making a great effort to attain self-sufficiency in drugs and a new Patents Bill is in the offing. We should see to it that inventions relating to drugs and foods are made non-patentable both as regards the product and process. If the drugs patents are not abrogated we shall have to pay crores of rupees every year as royalties to foreign firms which own almost 100 per cent drug process patents.[44]

In a reply by A. Gupta published in the *EPW* in May 1962, the cost of drugs cited by Sokhey from Kefauver's report, was neatly rebutted.[45] Gupta insisted that the drugs mentioned by Sokhey were available in India at prices amongst the lowest in the world, and went on to provide the actual cost of the drugs in the Indian market. Gupta said, '[t]his clearly shows that these life-saving drugs are available at quite a cheap rate in the Indian market, even though the patent rights for the manufacture of these drugs are held by some foreign manufacturers'.[46] In a rejoinder published in the *EPW* on 26 May 1962, Sokhey admitted that the high prices mentioned in Kefauver's report were of brands sold by American companies and he did not dispute the figures provided by Gupta[47]. Nevertheless, he maintained that, '[o]n the other hand, the prices quoted by Dr Gupta are those of the non-branded drugs, and even then the prices are several times the cost of production.'

The most strident *criticism* of Kefauver's report in India came from the Organisation of Pharmaceutical Producers of India (OPPI), an organization of innovator pharmaceutical companies, most of who were based out of western countries. In its memorandum to the JPC examining the Patents Bill, 1965, OPPI stated that:

> Senator Kefauver and some of his colleagues on the Committee launched a most vindictive attack on the pharmaceutical industry and the publicity and notoriety gained by the proceedings of the Committee, and its report has led to the belief that the allegations made against the pharmaceutical industry were substantiated. These allegations were refuted by well-documented submissions of many witnesses who appeared in opposition. Senator Roman Hruska, a member of the Kefauver Sub-committee, said, 'It has been my judgment that the hearings so far have been prejudiced and distorted. They have lacked balance. They are unfair to the industry, the Government agencies, the Senate itself, and to the public.'[48]

OPPI further reminded the committee that the US Congress rejected Kefauver's patent reform legislation.[49] Seeking to debunk other findings of the Kefauver Committee, the OPPI memorandum provided evidence to demonstrate that, for several drugs not under patent, the prices of imported drugs were cheaper than the ones manufactured by production units owned by the Government of India.[50] On differential drug pricing in different countries and high markups on production costs, OPPI strongly condemned the practice of picking up one or two drugs from the entire portfolio of a company and comparing the same based on international exchange rates.[51]

Those famous lines from Kefauver's report on patents and pharmaceutical prices in the Indian market, which continue to be cited in India today, may not have provided the entire story.

The Politics of Patents in Parliament

Ayyangar's report recommending revisions to Indian patent law was followed by two attempts to enact a new patent law. The first was the Patents Bill, 1965, which lapsed after the Lok Sabha was dissolved, and the second was the Patents Bill, 1967, which was eventually enacted as the Patents Act, 1970.

Although there were slight differences between the 1965 and 1967 legislation, both proposed a deliberately weakened patent law. Besides restrictions on product patents for pharmaceuticals, chemicals, and certain other technologies, both laws also sought to reduce the term of protection from the existing 16 years to 14 years. The term of process patents for food, medicine, chemicals, and other technologies, would be further restricted to 10 years. Process patents for such technologies would also be subject to a system of licenses of right, where any person could use the patented process three years after the sealing of the patent (a patent would be sealed three months after it was found in order for grant, if there was no opposition from any interested person), by paying the patentee a royalty of up to four per cent of the sales price. In effect, the period of market exclusivity for patentees was reduced to three years. Unlike compulsory licences, where the person demanding such a licence had to convince the Controller of Patents that the patentee was abusing its monopoly, a 'license of right' did not require any such prior adjudication by the Controller of Patents. It was granted as a matter of right. These measures were most likely introduced by the government to deal with complaints by Indian industry that foreign patentees were creating thickets around products by patenting all known processes.

Interestingly, Kefauver had made similar proposals in the US in the early 1960s. In the legislation introduced in the US Congress in 1960, he proposed reducing the exclusivity of a patent from 17 years to a mere three-year period, after which the patent would be available for compulsory licensing on payment of royalty to the patentee.[52]

One controversial provision in the 1965 and 1967 Bills was the absolute right vested in the central government to import patented medicines into India without having to pay compensation to the patentees.[53] All these provisions existed in addition to extensive compulsory licensing provisions which allowed the Controller to issue compulsory licences on the grounds that the patented product was being sold at a high price.[54]

As was the practice at the time, both the 1965 and 1967 Bills were referred to JPCs for examination, who in turn invited views from several stakeholders. The final reports of these JPCs came with lengthy dissent notes from both the ideological right and left.[55]

At the time, Indian politics had three main political parties representing the entire spectrum of views. On the ideological left was an assortment of communist parties, headed by the Communist Party of India (CPI), which demanded complete abolition of all patents. On the ideological right was the conservative Swatantra Party, then the only party supporting free market capitalism and stronger property rights including intellectual property rights for all technologies without discrimination. Minoo Masani, a founding member of the Swatantra Party, had played a pivotal role in opposing the dilution of Indian copyright law in the previous decade. After independence, the ruling Indian National Congress (INC) party, with the most number of Members of Parliament (MPs) had put India on the path of a mixed economy, that is, a primarily socialist economy with limited opportunity for private capitalist industries that were subject to a litany of state controls. But even the INC was divided on the subject of pharmaceutical patents. While some MPs demanded complete abolition of all patents, a few questioned the logic of doing away with product patents. But both bills were supported by most members of the JPCs, suggesting that a majority of MPs broadly supported the government's version, subject to some amendments.

Dissenting notes filed by MPs from the INC, Swatantra Party, and CPI, to the Report of the JPC on the 1965 Bill, provide an interesting reflection of the diversity in political opinions in the Parliament. Four notes are of particular interest, representing not only diversity in opinion, but also an incredibly well-informed set of parliamentarians.

The dissent note filed by Ramachandra Vithal Bade of the INC, along with another MP, opened with the line 'we are strongly of the opinion that all foreign patents should be abrogated'. Citing extensively from Kefauver's and Ayyangar's reports, they argued that patents were the cause of high prices and that a patent system did not benefit India since it primarily imported technology from foreign countries, who would in turn repatriate royalties back home. They also questioned the fundamental utility of patents, quoting Edsel Ford (of the Ford Motor Company) and Eugene Schinder (a managing partner in a French company manufacturing arms). Ford had reportedly answered a question on whether inventions would continue even without patents by saying, 'I feel quite definitely, it will be carried on', and Schinder had similarly said that, 'I am quite of the opinion that there would be very little difference in respect of rapid progress if patents were abolished.'[56]

The dissent note filed by three MPs from the INC and an independent MP, L.M. Singhvi struck a more balanced position. They explained the possible detrimental effects of abolishing certain kinds of pharmaceutical patents, including its effects on technology transfer to India. This group sought to play down, with evidence, concerns regarding the pricing of medicines, and the adverse effect of patents on the growth of the pharmaceutical industry. Seeking a middle path which included compulsory licensing and government use of crucial patents, they pitched for retaining a patent system which created 'a proper investment climate in India for the rapid growth of the pharmaceutical and chemical industries both by Indian entrepreneurs and by import of foreign technology and investment where necessary'.[57]

The dissent note by M.R. Masani and Dahyabhai Patel of the Swatantra Party was emphatically in line with the party's proclaimed ideology in demanding a full-fledged patent system. Pointing to the paradox of abolishing patents while demanding greater industrialization, Masani and Patel said, '[u]nfortunately there is a kind of schizophrenia to be found in regard to the granting of adequate patent protection for inventions. On the one hand, many people want scientific and industrial development; on the other hand, they get obsessed with all kinds of claptrap about monopoly, pricing, social justice and making medicines and drugs available cheaply to everybody all over the country'. On the issue of discrimination against pharmaceutical inventions, Masani and Patel wrote, '[t]here does not appear to us to be any reason for discrimination between inventions in different fields of production or enterprise. Since it is generally agreed that patent protection advances progress, we fail to understand why an important need of the consumer such as drugs and medicines should be denied the advantage of such protection and promotion'.[58]

The fourth dissent note of interest was submitted by MPs from the CPI and the Dravida Munnetra Kazhagam (DMK). This note criticized not only the Bill but also the fundamental notion that patents created incentives for research, especially in India where research was mainly conducted in publicly-funded institutions. The MPs pointed out how countries like Italy, Japan, and USSR had enacted patent laws only after reaching a certain level of development, and that India would be mistaken to adopt a patent system in its present condition. Regarding patents for food and medicines, they quoted Kefauver's report as evidence of drug prices in India being the highest in the world to demand the abolition of pharmaceutical patents in order to ensure the growth of the industry. Condemning the Indian government for being 'influenced more by the views of foreign monopolies and their Indian collaborators than by those of people who are interested in genuine development of our national industry' they termed the Patents Bill a 'tragic situation'.[59]

Ultimately, the 1965 Bill never became a law because the Lok Sabha dissolved shortly after the JPC report was tabled. After the lapse of the Patents Bill, 1965, a new Patents Bill, 1967 was introduced in Parliament, which was, once again, referred to a JPC. Foreign witnesses from 17 organizations located in the US, the UK, Japan, Italy, West Germany, Switzerland, and Yugoslavia were invited to depose.[60] West Germany and Japan were of particular interest to the Indian legislators as both countries had miraculously rebuilt devastated economies after losing the Second World War. Yugoslavia was one of the few socialist economies to have a patent system. Italy had abolished both product and process patents for the pharmaceutical sector. Many Indian witnesses also deposed before the JPC. The verbatim record of the depositions runs into more than 561 pages, representing an impressive consultative exercise. Each foreign expert witness who deposed before the JPC was cross-examined by well-prepared MPs, ready to challenge their testimony.

Foreigners Depose for Patents Before Parliament

The common thread in the testimonies of the foreign witnesses was a complete opposition to the radical reforms proposed by the Patents Bill, 1967.

Harry Seid, representing the Pharmaceutical Manufacturers Association, US and National Association of Manufacturers, US, opposed the proposed reduction of patent terms, the abolition of product patents, the mandatory 'licenses of rights' for all process patents related to the pharmaceutical, chemicals, and food, and the proposed power to allow the government to import medicines or drugs into India without paying compensation to patentees. Extolling the virtues of patents, Seid preached to the JPC that '[a] strong patent law which respects due process, which shuns discrimination, which grants fair compensation, and which joins in a comity of nations, operating in accordance with tested precepts, is bound to make treasured progress—but if followed in reverse is fraught with unfathomed risks'.[61]

Explaining the cost and difficulty in developing a new drug, Seid said, 'It is estimated that the drug industry spends on an average approximately $7 million in research and development costs for each new drug discovery. Research costs continue to mount'.[62] Given the investment made by patentees in developing new inventions, Seid argued that, '[i]t is inconceivable that any person or company in a civilized country such as India should be deprived of property without compensation or be deprived of the right of judicial appeal when property is taken by Government action'.[63] On these grounds of 'due process', Seid wanted the clause that allowed for importation of patented medicines without compensation to the patentee dropped from the Bill. Similarly, Seid objected to the 'license of rights' for all process patents for medicine and food at a fixed royalty of up to four per cent. Seid explained, '[n]ot only is such an arbitrary small percentage inadequate, but I respectfully submit that it is wholly discriminatory. Not even the wisdom of Solomon can set in advance a fixed royalty or fixed compensation which is fair and not discriminatory'.[64]

Some MPs on the JPC were in a combative mood and asked Seid tough questions. In a veiled reference to Kefauver's report, C.C. Desai asked, '[h]ow would you explain the tendency in your own country for having a weak patent law?' Seid defensively replied,

> Let me tell you something about U.S.A. In respect of U.S.A. you will find in some particular report some statements have been made about a number of things. I will tell you right now that no effective action has ever been taken in respect of scrapping of the patent law or to amend the patent law so as to reduce the period of patents.

Another MP, Srinibas Misra, was more pointed and asked Seid, '[y]ou are aware that the Kefauver Committee pronounced that India is the mostly highly priced country, so far as drugs are concerned?' Seid replied by asserting, 'I do not know whether drug prices in India are higher than in the UK or Europe or USA etc. I read the report of the Kefauver Committee in the newspapers. But experience has shown that in Italy they are dumping their drugs abroad to get foreign currency and yet the prices at home are high'.[65] At the time, Italy did not provide for either product or process patents for pharmaceutical inventions, and logically, it should have had the lowest prices because no one company had a monopoly on manufacture of any pharmaceutical. Then why did Seid conclude that Italy had high drug prices?

Other witnesses like O.H. Nowotny, representing the Swiss Society of Chemical Industries, made similar statements about drug prices in Italy. He deposed that:

> Italy where no drug patents exist is a shining example for such a situation. Every time a new drug has been developed and patented outside Italy, the numerous domestic drug manufacturers have rushed to the Italians with their own imitations, often arriving there before the original inventor had time to introduce his own drug. This has led to such an unnatural fragmentation of the market that drug prices in Italy are today just as high, and in some cases even higher, than in countries where drug patents are being granted.[66]

These testimonies on Italian drug prices were not taken at face value by the JPC, which cross-checked these facts with the Italian witness who was also deposed. C.C. Desai asked Franco Niccolai from Farmitalia, a pharmaceutical company in Italy, '[w]hat is the justification for the high prices in spite of the fact that you do not have to pay for patents?'[67] Niccolai responded in the negative telling Desai that this was 'absolutely not' the case as the prices in Italy were strictly controlled by the government. Even though Italy had managed to grow an extensive pharmaceutical industry because of lack of a patent regime for pharmaceuticals, the Italians were planning to introduce patent protection for the pharmaceutical industry. Niccolai explained that Italy was doing so because it was the only way to create incentives for research in the pharmaceutical industry. This may not have been the only reason. As pointed out by Nambiar, an MP on the JPC, Italy was under pressure from the European Common Market to change its patent law to protect pharmaceutical inventions. Niccolai replied by saying that, 'the common market certainly helps in this regard'. This caused Nambiar to say, '[w]e have got much admiration for Italy. We feel that we do not have anything similar to that of European Common Market or an Asian Common Market here. We can follow the footsteps of Italy with regard to the patent law so far as pharmaceuticals are concerned without a protection, which you were doing all these years'.[68]

Besides the link between patents and prices, there was also the question of whether patent protection was necessary for India to attract the latest technology and investment into the country, in response to which German and Japanese witnesses offered useful testimonies.

The German experience, with only process patents, had significantly moulded Ayyangar's final report and by extension, the Patents Bill, 1967. By the time, the Germans deposed before the JPC in January 1969, Germany had enacted a patent law recognizing even product patents. A. Kraft of the Department of Law and Economics, Johannes Gutenberg University at Mainz, deposed, '[f]rom 1911 to 1967, the patent system has remained almost the same. Then, as you know, we also introduced the product patent for chemical substances'.[69] Kraft, like other foreign witnesses, was not in favour of India diluting its patent law, warning that it would affect foreign investment in India. Another German who deposed before the JPC was Hans Harms, the Chairman of Merck AG, who was also representing the Association of Pharmaceutical Manufacturers of Federal Republic of Germany. Conveying the sentiments of the German industry, Harms said, 'It is the official opinion of the entire German industry that it cannot be the intention of the Indian legislation to give, through this Patents Bill, third parties a legal possibility to copy inventions of others practically free of charge. This would not at all correspond to the traditional fairness your country is known for'.[70] Warning that the enactment of the Patents Bill would be fatal to India's economic development, Harms told the Indian lawmakers that,

> if and when this Patents Bill would be accepted the readiness of foreign companies to invest in your country would decline considerably. No private company would decide to build new plants or to invest money in already existing facilities in India for the exploitation of its inventions if there were the danger that third parties easily could copy those inventions or could import imitations with the official approval of Indian authorities as provided for in the Patents Bill.[71]

Harms instead suggested a different approach where India protected even foreign patent rights so as to attract investment, technology, and most importantly, *know-how*, which requires an element of human experience and cannot be learnt from just reading a patent specification. He explained that, '[a]fter the Second World War in Germany the absolute protection of foreign property was an essential supposition for the speedy recovery of our economy and for the steadily increasing influx of foreign investment. We never doubted that we made the right decision despite of the fact that we have still today a negative license balance'. Drawing parallels with Japan, he continued, '[i]n this connection I should like to mention that Japan, who has a strong patent law, has a negative patent license balance, too, which is not an unimportant reason why Japan's industry reached a level which today is admired at by the whole world'.[72]

Shoji Matsui, a spokesperson for the Japan Patent Association and Federation of Economic Organisation, Japan who also deposed before the JPC, broadly corroborated Harms' claim. Matsui explained that Japan continued to import technology, paying around USD 1.2 billion for technology import (versus technology exports worth only USD 56 million), because such imports contributed to building an industrial base that fuelled exports from Japan. Matsui said,

> The foreign exchange paid by Japan for the introduction of technology has produced much greater value and effects than that paid for mere importation of raw material or finished products. One of the key factors having enabled Japan to expand export of goods 'Made in Japan' is the patented technologies and technical know-how introduced in the past ten decades.[73]

Matsui warned against diluting patent law for short term benefits, saying:

> I frankly admit that the Indian Government could save the outflow of foreign exchange, at least temporarily, by taking full advantage of the rights to work any patented invention, almost ignoring patentee's will under the provisions of this Bill. However, it had to be admitted, on the other hand, that technical know-how would not come into India smoothly under the situation because no one would risk his technical investment in a country where his investment might scarcely be protected.[74]

None of the testimony offered by these various American, German, Italian, Japanese, and Swiss witnesses swayed the JPC's opinion. In fact, its final report, tabled before Parliament on 27 February 1970 recommended diluting the Patents Bill, 1967 even further. For example, the term of process patents for food, drug, and medicine was recommended to be further reduced from the originally proposed 10 years to a mere 7 years.

The Attorney General's 'Disquieting' Deposition

An important issue flagged by the JPC was whether Parliament could curtail the term of existing patents granted under the existing Patents and Designs Act, 1911, since this would dilute private patent rights. The JPC had particular reason to worry about this, because the past 19 years had witnessed immense tension between Parliament and the Supreme Court over the issue of land reform legislation that allowed the state to acquire and redistribute land without paying just and adequate compensation to landowners. The Patents Bill, 1967, had two provisions that interfered with the enjoyment of private patent rights without any necessity to pay compensation to the patentees. The first provision was Clause 48 (now Section 47(4)), which gave the central government the right to import patented medicines and drugs into the country without paying compensation to the patentee. The second provision was Clause 53, which curtailed the term of existing patents. Both provisions ran the risk of constitutional challenge, and so the JPC requested for a legal opinion from Attorney General Niran De, who later also deposed before the Committee.[75]

The Attorney General's opinion could not be traced by the authors, but the transcript of his deposition before the JPC reveals the broad conclusions of his opinion along with the incisive questioning that he was subjected to. It appears that the Attorney General had presented the following conclusion to the committee: '[i]t is not now open to Parliament not to have any patent law with regard to invention, in cases where patent rights have already been conferred by the existing law, namely the Patents and Designs Act'.[76] For Masani and his Swatantra Party colleagues, the Attorney General's opinion offered a ray of hope in a battle they were otherwise losing. The other MPs on the JPC, unhappy with the Attorney General's opinion, subjected him to an intense interrogation, especially on whether he had changed his opinion after instructions from the government. C.C. Desai began by asking him why the opinion was not dated, to which the Attorney General replied that he 'cannot answer the question'. When the question was repeated, the Attorney General's answer revealed perhaps more than what was intended '[i]t should have borne a date. I can tell you that is my opinion. Sometimes when I have given an opinion, I have asked for it to be brought back and change it myself without any influence from any quarter.' The last few words, hinted at the possibility of great pressure on the Attorney General. Smelling blood, Desai asked the Attorney General a pointed question: '[i]f there is an earlier opinion, can that be circulated to us?' The Attorney General defensively replied:

> I cannot answer that. I hope you will appreciate my position. My opinions are supposed to be confidential. I can answer questions here on the basis of the final opinion which I gave; whether I have given three or four opinions is not relevant. But I want to say one thing: no power on earth can influence me in my opinion.[77]

Attorney General's evasive responses did not go down well with most people on the JPC. Two MPs in particular, Madhu Limaye and Godey Murahari, questioned the veracity of the Attorney General's opinion in their dissent note stating, '[t]he examination by the Committee of the Attorney General also revealed that the law officer gave two opinions, and, perhaps, the Government had something to do with the modification by the Attorney General of his earlier opinion. This is very disquieting'.[78]

Perhaps, some of these MPs were being unfair to the Attorney General. The transcript of his deposition reveals how he made some intelligent drafting suggestions to insulate the legislation from future constitutional challenges. For example, he recommended making the grant of patents contingent on certain conditions, which included the right of the government to import a patented invention without any payment, rather than the existing format where patent rights could be granted, and then taken away without any compensation. Eventually, the Attorney General's drafting suggestions were accepted.[79]

The Attorney General had also suggested that it would be unconstitutional to reduce the term of patents already granted under previous legislation. This is apparent from the dissent note of Ananda Nambiar who stated:

> Another serious stumbling block which came in our way in limiting the duration of the Patent period is the limitation placed by the legal interpretation of our Constitution. After the Golak Nath's case, it is interpreted that the Parliament has no right to legislate on restricting the existing property rights and therefore the Attorney General opined that since the existing Patents Rights are those already granted by an Act (though of 1911) the same cannot be taken away now and therefore the period granted already should continue. Or else there is the danger of it being struck down by the Supreme Court.[80]

The JPC accepted the Attorney General's advice, for it did not curtail the term of existing patents under the Patents and Design Act, 1911. In the notes to clause 53, the report states that the '[c]ommittee feels that the term of patents granted under the Indian Patents and Designs Act, 1911 should not be curtailed'.[81]

The MPs of the Swatantra Party were unhappy with the final recommendations of the JPC. A dissent note by two MPs from the party, stated that the provisions allowing for 'licenses of right' along with right of the government to import patented pharmaceuticals, without paying compensation to the patentees was in violation of the right to property and at risk of being struck down by the Supreme Court. On the issue of patent terms, the Swatantra Party MPs argued that far from reducing patent terms, the law should have actually provided for patent term extensions. They argued:

> ... in the case of medicines and drugs, the period taken from the first discovery of a new chemical compound which may hold out some hopes of a new drug, through the long processes of evaluation and clinical

testing and finally the emergence of a new drug that is safe for human treatment, is becoming longer and longer, as drugs become more and more powerful and their side effect require more intensive examination. If ever there was a case for increasing the term of patents, rather than decreasing it, it is in respect of this class of patents.[82]

The lack of such provision, they warned, would place Indian inventors at a disadvantage and impede the development of the country.

India Finally Gets a New Patent Law

By 1970, the political landscape of India had changed vastly from the days when Jawaharlal Nehru was the prime minister. His daughter, Indira Gandhi was appointed the prime minister in 1966 after some deft political manoeuvring, and put India on a decidedly socialist path. Her policies included nationalizing all the private banks in the country and even amending the *Preamble* to the Constitution in 1976 to expressly mention that India was a socialist country.

Hence, when the Patents Bill was posted for a final vote in the Lok Sabha in August 1970, more than two decades after the Indian government constituted the Patents Enquiry Committee under Justice Tek Chand in 1948, it was a foregone conclusion that the Bill would sail through the Parliament with the support of the INC. However, this did not stop the opponents from making floundering attempts to delay the Bill. One such protest was by Piloo Mody, a founding member of the Swatantra Party. The reason for his outrage was the fact that the Parliament took up this Bill for debate on a Saturday, which was a holiday under the rules of the Lok Sabha. The Speaker, however, brushed Mody's objection aside.[83] The debate that followed was an impressive display of the intellectual faculties available in the fourth Lok Sabha, with articulate arguments being made for and against the patent system.

Opening the debate for the Indian government was Dinesh Singh, the Minister of Industrial Development and Internal Trade, who explained the rationale of the patent system, the recommendations of the expert committees, and the policy objectives of the government. Concluding with a reference to Indian press coverage of 'depositions made before United States Senate Committee of how developing countries are being swindled by some large companies manufacturing pharmaceuticals', Singh justified the Patents Bill as a legitimate effort by India to protect itself from 'international cartels'.[84]

While most speakers from the INC and the CPI broadly supported the Bill, they were scathing in their criticism on the 20-year delay in bringing the new Patents Bill to vote. Sushila Nayar, an MP from INC, speculated that '[the] new patents law will touch the pockets of the drug concerns, [which is why] they have obstructed all the efforts to amend these laws'.[85] She also commented on how the drug industry had actively lobbied against the Bill, saying that, '[a]ll the Memoranda, all the deputation and the hectic lobbying that was done amongst Members of Parliament were, more than 95 per cent and probably 99.9 per cent of these organized form of the drug interests. The reason is obvious'.[86] This was supported by other MPs like Ananda Nambiar, a communist from Tiruchirapalli, Tamil Nadu, who pointed to the long list of foreigners deposing before the JPCs. Nambiar said:

> All those persons who came from abroad strongly objected to our Patents Bill. They said that in their countries they were having patent protection, therefore their countries flourished, and that in India too we must have patent protection and then only it will beneficial to us. That is the sort of advice that these people gave. But we had also evidence from an Italian that in his country there was no patent protection, that it had been introduced only recently. In Japan also it was not there and has been [introduced] only recently. The industry in both Italy and Japan has fared well.[87]

While a few communists like Nambiar supported the new patent law, other communists like H.N. Mukherjee slammed the government for not trying hard enough to dilute patent rights. After quoting extensively from Indian press coverage on the Kefauver Report, Mukherjee called for junking the entire patent system, angrily saying, 'to hell with patent rights. Did Japan care about patent rights when Japan was going ahead? Did the Soviet Union care for patent rights? ... So, without the botheration of patent [rights] we can go ahead. Far too long we have suffered this long and sordid story of exploitation.'[88]

The most powerful dissent came from N. Dandekar of the Swatantra Party, whose main line of attack was that both the government and the Bill's supporters in the Lok Sabha were confused about the objectives of patent law. He reminded his colleagues that India already had separate laws to prevent monopolies, control prices, and regulate foreign exchange. According to Dandekar, the primary objective of patent law was 'to ensure that people are not discouraged but encouraged to undertake research, to undertake inventions and to devote all their time and all those resources that are required for the purpose of research invention and development'.[89] Dandekar objected to three particular clauses of the Bill. The first was doing away with product patents for food, medicines, and chemicals; the second was the reduction of the patent term for chemical processes to merely seven years; and the third was against a provision (that still exists in Indian law as Section 47(4)) which allows the government to import patented pharmaceuticals into the country without having to pay compensation to patentees. The third clause was a sore point for the innovator industry and the Swatantra Party as it allowed the government to override the rights of patentees. Concluding his speech, Dandekar said, 'Let the man and his invention be both nationalized, and let him become their slave. But let us not talk at the same time about democracy and liberty and individual rights and all that kind of thing on the one hand and on the other, have this kind of business of depriving a person of the results of his labours'.[90] This was a rare instance where a parliamentarian articulated his concerns regarding the Bill in the language of liberty and rights.

A good measure of the impact of Dandekar's speech was the retort it drew from H.N. Mukherjee, who, being a communist, was a natural ideological foe of the Swatantra Party. Mukherjee said:

> When Mr. Dandekar of the Swatantra Party was speaking, I was reminded of what Gandhiji said in regard to those who participated in the sucking of the blood of the Indian people in the process of exploitation. When he was being tried in March 1922, he told the court that the profits and the brokerage are sucked from the masses and the brokerage obtained by the Indian collaborators of foreign imperialist interests. There is no reason at all why life-saving drugs and food for infants and expectant and nursing mothers, sick people and convalescing people should be subject to the law of patents at all.[91]

Regardless of Mukherjee's barbs, one issue raised by Dandekar is particularly important, and that is of price control. Why could the central government not tackle rising drug prices through price control, especially since it had such powers under the Essential Commodities Act, 1955 and the Drug Price Control Order, 1955 (DPCO)? It turns out that the government of the day was unable to effectively administer drug prices under the DPCO. This was the assessment provided by Sushila Nayar, from the ruling INC, who pointed out that the government was:

> ... well-known for bungling as they have done in the recent Drugs (Price Control) Order. The price control which was in force from 1 April 1963 and which had prevented rise in prices till 1967 was hurriedly removed. The prices rose. Then they re-imposed the price control order which was so defective that they have had to change it a number of times within a few days, causing confusion upon confusion. Every time it was confusion worst confounded. As a result, prices have risen sharply and drugs have become scarce.[92]

Regardless of the opposition by Dandekar and his allies like S.K. Somani to the Bill and their attempts to introduce amendments for strengthening patent rights, the majority of the Lok Sabha voted in favour of the Patents Bill, 1970.

However, the Patents Bill still had to be passed by the Rajya Sabha, the upper house of the Parliament, before it could become law. The Rajya Sabha posted the Bill for a debate and vote on 3 September 1970. The debate proceeded on virtually the same lines as in the Lok Sabha. Those who supported the Bill referred to the Kefauver Report and blamed the high prices of pharmaceutical drugs in India on the patent laws of the country. The only two dissenting voices were a lone MP from the INC and one, again, from the Swatantra Party.

Babubhai M. Chinai, MP of INC, argued that India needed a strong patent legislation to attract the best technology. Referring to the central government's failure to control drug prices despite several laws that gave it the power to intervene, Chinai identified the lack of political will in the government as the reason for the high prices. Drawing attention to post-war Japan's miraculous economic growth, Chinai reasoned that Japan's strong patent law had enabled the country to access the latest technology to produce and export, and thereby earn revenues far outstripping the royalties paid for using the patents.[93]

Expressing his discontent with the Bill, Chinai concluded by saying, 'I cannot help pointing out that the overall impression with the new Patents Bill gives is that our Government is completely out of date with the economics of modern technology.'[94] Predictably, a CPI MP, Balachandra Menon, attacked Chinai and his proposals as representing 'a Chamber of Commerce, and the most reactionary Indian monopolist'.[95]

The only other dissenting voice was that of Dahyabhai V. Patel of the Swatantra Party. He was the son of Sardar Vallabhbhai Patel, the 'Ironman', credited with unifying the princely states into India after the British left, and a life-long member of the INC Party. In his speech, Dahyabhai launched a fierce attack on the control economy imposed by INC, arguing that, '[a]ll industry has been stagnated because of this idea of control, control, control. Too much of control has hampered the growth of industry'.[96] He warned the Rajya Sabha that a weak patent law would only add to the brain drain because scientists and engineers would have no incentive to conduct research in India with a weak patent law.[97]

Like other members of his party in Lok Sabha, Dahyabhai Patel also made multiple attempts to push through amendments for a patent extension clause, longer terms for chemical process patents, changes to the compulsory licensing provisions, and so on. However, almost the entire House had spoken out in favour of the Bill, and all these amendments were defeated. Finally after 22 long years of expert committees, parliamentary committees, and debates, the Patents Act, 1970, was passed by both houses of Parliament.

This law would forever change the global pharmaceutical industry. Over the next two decades, the generic drug industry in the Indian private sector would flourish to become one of the largest generic drug industries in the world. By the end of the twentieth century, the generic pharmaceutical industry would earn India the moniker of 'pharmacy of the world'. This law was supported by the socialists and communists, and criticized by the Swatantra Party for trampling on private property rights. Nevertheless, this law gave rise to one of the most prosperous and successful private sector industries in Indian history. However, the fight to reverse this law would begin less than two decades later through a treaty called the Agreement on Trade-Related Aspects of Intellectual Property Rights (TRIPS)—a treaty that would be signed by India after it was out-manoeuvred and out-negotiated by the US.

———

Notes

1. *The Haffkine Institute*, available at http://www.haffkineinstitute.org/instiprofile.htm (Last visited on 30 March 2015).
2. Nasir Tyabji, Aligning with Both the Soviet Union and with the Pharmaceutical Transnationals: Dilemmas Attendant on Initiating Drug Production in India, at 20–1. (ISID Working Paper No. 2010/08, 2010).
3. MINISTRY OF INDUSTRY AND SUPPLY, REPORT OF THE PATENTS ENQUIRY COMMITTEE (1948–50).
4. JUSTICE N. RAJAGOPALA AYYANGAR, REPORT ON THE REVISION OF THE PATENTS LAW (September 1959).
5. AYYANGAR, REPORT, ¶ 47, at 21.
6. AYYANGAR, REPORT, ¶ 68, at 27.
7. AYYANGAR, REPORT, ¶ 68, at 27.
8. AYYANGAR, REPORT, ¶ 82, at 30.
9. AYYANGAR, REPORT, ¶ 58, at 23.
10. AYYANGAR, REPORT, at 23, 24.
11. AYYANGAR, REPORT, ¶ 127, at 49.
12. AYYANGAR, REPORT, *Restrictions on the Patentability of Inventions: Patents for Chemical Substances, Food and Medicine etc*, at 31; Luigi Palombi, The Search for Alternatives to Patents in the 21st century (Paper presented at the International Seminar INCT-PPED: Promoting Strategic Responses to Globalization, November 2009), at 6–8.
13. AYYANGAR, REPORT, ¶ 78, at 30–1.
14. AYYANGAR, REPORT, at 31.
15. AYYANGAR, REPORT, at 31.
16. AYYANGAR, REPORT, at 33.
17. AYYANGAR, REPORT, ¶ 83, at 33.

18. AYYANGAR, REPORT, ¶ 88, at 33.
19. MINISTRY OF INDUSTRY AND SUPPLY, REPORT, *Annexure A: First Interim Report of the Patents Enquiry Committee*, at 171.
20. MINISTRY OF INDUSTRY AND SUPPLY, REPORT, *The Patent System: Its Origin and Development with Particular Reference to Patent Legislation in India*, at 30.
21. MINISTRY OF INDUSTRY AND SUPPLY, REPORT, *Recommendations for Improving the Law of Patents in India*, at 65.
22. MINISTRY OF INDUSTRY AND SUPPLY, REPORT, *Recommendations for Improving the Law of Patents in India*, at 62–3.
23. MINISTRY OF INDUSTRY AND SUPPLY, REPORT, *Forwarding Letter*, at 3.
24. MINISTRY OF INDUSTRY AND SUPPLY, REPORT, *Recommendations for Improving the Law of Patents in India*, at 65.
25. AYYANGAR, REPORT, at 3.
26. AYYANGAR, REPORT, *Restrictions on the Patentability of Inventions: Patents for Chemical Substances, Food and Medicine etc*, at 25.
27. AYYANGAR, REPORT, ¶ 89, at 34.
28. MINISTRY OF INDUSTRY AND SUPPLY, REPORT, *Annexure A: First Interim Report of the Patents Enquiry committee*, at 165.
29. AYYANGAR, REPORT, *Practice of the Indian Patent Office regarding patents for chemical products*, at 34.
30. AYYANGAR, REPORT, *Notes on Clauses*, at 121.
31. INDIA, LOK SABHA, JOINT COMMITTEE ON THE PATENTS BILL, 1967, *Minutes of Evidence* 233 (14 February 1969).
32. LOK SABHA, JOINT COMMITTEE, *Minutes of Evidence*, at 238.
33. AIR 1969 Bombay 255.
34. *Crime Hunter Kefauver*, TIME, 12 March 1951.
35. UNITED STATES SENATE (Subcommittee on Antitrust and Monopoly), STUDY OF ADMINISTERED PRICES IN THE DRUG INDUSTRY, 87th Congress Report No. 448 (8 May 1961).
36. *Drug Industry Hits 3 Year Patent Bill*, THE NEW YORK TIMES, 27 July 1961.
37. UNITED STATES SENATE, STUDY OF ADMINISTERED PRICES, at 28.
38. John W. Finney, *Senate Panel Cites Mark Ups on Drugs Ranging to 70,079%*, THE NEW YORK TIMES, 8 December 1959.
39. Joseph A. Loftus, *Big Profit Found in Tranquilizers: One 6 Times Costlier than in Paris*, THE NEW YORK TIMES, 22 January 1960.
40. UNITED STATES SENATE, STUDY OF ADMINISTERED PRICES, at 112.
41. Saheb Singh Sokhey, *Manufacture of Modern Drugs Forging Ahead But Menaced by Patent Laws*, EPW (1962).

42. MINISTRY OF INDUSTRY AND SUPPLY, REPORT, *Forwarding Letter*, at 3.

43. Nasir Tyabji, *Aligning with Both the Soviet Union and With the Pharmaceutical Transnationals: Dilemmas Attendant on Initiating Drug Production in India*, at 4 (August 2010) (on file with the Institute of Studies in Industrial Development Working Paper No. 2010/08, 2010).

44. Sokhey, *Manufacture of Modern Drugs*, at 235, 241.

45. A. Gupta, *Manufacture of Drugs: A Comment*, EPW 841–2 (1962).

46. Gupta, *Manufacture of Drugs*.

47. Sahib Singh Sokhey, *Rejoinder*, EPW 843 (1962).

48. Organisation of Pharmaceutical Producers of India, *Memorandum on the Patents Bill 1965*, at 21–2 (June 1966).

49. Organisation of Pharmaceutical Producers of India, *Memorandum*, at 22.

50. Organisation of Pharmaceutical Producers of India, *Memorandum*, at 17.

51. Organisation of Pharmaceutical Producers of India, *Memorandum*, at 22–5.

52. Jeremy A. Greene, *Reform, Regulation, and Pharmaceuticals—The Kefauver–Harris Amendments at 50*, N ENGL J MED 1481–3 (2012).

53. The Patents Act, 1970, § 47(4).

54. The Patents Bill, 1967, Chap. XVI.

55. LOK SABHA, REPORT OF THE JOINT COMMITTEE ON THE PATENTS BILL, 1965 (31 October 1966) *Gazette of India Extraordinary*—(Part II–Section 2), at 1016 ('LOK SABHA, REPORT, 1966') and LOK SABHA, REPORT OF THE JOINT COMMITTEE ON THE PATENTS BILL, 1967 (27 February 1970) ('LOK SABHA, REPORT, 1970').

56. LOK SABHA, REPORT, 1966, at 1027–33.

57. LOK SABHA, REPORT, 1966, at 1051–61.

58. LOK SABHA, REPORT, 1966, at 1033–6.

59. LOK SABHA, REPORT, 1966, at 1047–50.

60. LOK SABHA, REPORT, 1970, at Appendix V.

61. LOK SABHA, JOINT COMMITTEE, *Minutes of Evidence*, at 47 (20 January 1969).

62. LOK SABHA, JOINT COMMITTEE, *Minutes of Evidence*, at 44.

63. LOK SABHA, JOINT COMMITTEE, *Minutes of Evidence*, at 44.

64. LOK SABHA, JOINT COMMITTEE, *Minutes of Evidence*, at 46.

65. LOK SABHA, JOINT COMMITTEE, *Minutes of Evidence*, at 56.

66. LOK SABHA, JOINT COMMITTEE, *Minutes of Evidence*, at 94 (22 January 1969).

67. LOK SABHA, JOINT COMMITTEE, *Minutes of Evidence*, at 197 (25 January 1969).

68. LOK SABHA, JOINT COMMITTEE, *Minutes of Evidence*, at 191 (20 January 1969).

69. LOK SABHA, JOINT COMMITTEE, *Minutes of Evidence*, at 129 (22 January 1969).

70. LOK SABHA, JOINT COMMITTEE, *Minutes of Evidence*, at 137 (23 January 1969).

71. LOK SABHA, JOINT COMMITTEE, *Minutes of Evidence*, at 138 (23 January 1969).

72. LOK SABHA, JOINT COMMITTEE, *Minutes of Evidence*, at 138 (22 January 1969).

73. LOK SABHA, JOINT COMMITTEE, *Minutes of Evidence*, at 169 (24 January 1969).

74. LOK SABHA, JOINT COMMITTEE, *Minutes of Evidence*, at 169 (24 January 1969).

75. LOK SABHA, REPORT, 1970, at 134.

76. LOK SABHA, REPORT, JOINT COMMITTEE ON THE PATENTS BILL, 1967, *Minutes of Evidence*—Vol. 2, at 4 (29 January 1970)

77. LOK SABHA, REPORT, JOINT COMMITTEE ON THE PATENTS BILL, 1967, *Minutes of Evidence*—Vol. 2, at 7 (29 January 1970).

78. LOK SABHA, REPORT, at 12

79. LOK SABHA, REPORT, JOINT COMMITTEE ON THE PATENTS BILL, 1967, *Minutes of Evidence*—Vol. 2, at 4–5 (29 January 1970); The Patents Act, 1970, §47 and §48 (clause 47 of the Patents Bill, 1967 is Section 48 of The Patents Act, 1970 and clause 47 of the Patents Bill, 1967 is Section 47 of The Patents Act, 1970).

80. LOK SABHA, REPORT, 1970, at 22.

81. LOK SABHA, REPORT, 1970, at 8.

82. LOK SABHA, REPORT, 1970, at 16.

83. India, LOK SABHA, *Debate on the Patents Bill*, (29 August 1970), at 2.

84. Lok Sabha, *Debate*, at 11.

85. Lok Sabha, *Debate*, at 19.

86. Lok Sabha, *Debate*, at 14.

87. Lok Sabha, *Debate*, at 42.

88. Lok Sabha, *Debate*, at 50.

89. Lok Sabha, *Debate*, at 31.

90. Lok Sabha, *Debate*, at 37.

91. Lok Sabha, *Debate*, at 46.

92. Lok Sabha, *Debate*, at 161.

93. India, Rajya Sabha, *Debate on the Patents Bill 1970*, 3 September 1970, at 50.

94. Rajya Sabha, *Debate*, at 53.
95. Rajya Sabha, *Debate*, at 74–5.
96. Rajya Sabha, *Debate*, at 67.
97. Rajya Sabha, *Debate*, at 68.

2

SURRENDER AT GENEVA

In 1947, a group of 23 countries, including India, entered into a multilateral agreement called the General Agreement on Tariffs and Trade (GATT). The aim of GATT was to progressively reduce tariffs and other trade barriers to facilitate the flow of international trade. With time, the GATT talks covered a wider range of topics and included more members. The sixth round of these talks, which began in 1986 at Punta del Este in Uruguay, was called the Uruguay Round, and involved 123 countries. For the first time, intellectual property rights (IPRs) were a part of the agenda in the form of the Agreement on Trade-Related Aspects of Intellectual Property Rights (TRIPS).[1] Several multilateral intellectual property (IP) treaties already existed, such as the Patent Co-operation Treaty or the Berne Convention for the Protection of Literary and Artistic Works (Berne Convention), but none of these had been linked to trade, and they had always been independent of GATT.

Crowbar Diplomacy

The politics of putting IP on the agenda was straightforward. For developed countries, such as the United States (US), IPRs over movies, music, books, pharmaceuticals, and new technology counted towards an increasing percentage of exports to the developing countries, most of which did not have strong IP laws. Approximately, one-fourth of all the US exports were IPs, and the lack of IP protection in export markets was causing serious losses to the US, and increasing its trade deficit.[2] The idea behind linking IP and trade was to create incentives for developing countries to commit to stronger IP law and enforcement, in return for greater access to the markets of developed countries. A key demand of the developed countries, due to lobbying by their pharmaceutical industry, was that national patent laws be prohibited from discriminating against any technologies. This demand was particularly targeted at countries like India. The Pharmaceutical Research and Manufacturers of America (PhRMA), an association of innovator companies, and one of the most influential lobbies in the US, has candidly said that 'the Indian patent system was the most direct motivation for US efforts in the Uruguay Round negotiations relating to patents'.[3] The reason for India being the most 'direct motivation' was a new patent law enacted by the Indian Parliament in 1970, which virtually abolished patents for several technologies, especially substances intended to be used for food, medicines, and chemicals. The law allowed process patents (that is, patents over processes or methods of manufacture) for these technologies, but after a three-year period of exclusivity, even these process patents were subject to 'licenses of right' which allowed any person in the market to use these technologies for a fixed royalty capped at four per cent. The virtual abolition of patents over medicines came as a boon for the domestic pharmaceutical industry. Freed from the fetters of patents, it was only a matter of time before India's abundant supply of chemical engineers and chemists turned entrepreneurs. Indian companies like Ranbaxy, Dr. Reddy's, Cipla, Sun Pharmaceuticals, and Aurobindo grew rapidly, fulfilling India's domestic pharmaceuticals needs as well as catering to foreign markets. The threat to the foreign pharmaceutical industry from India had doubled. Foreign companies could not patent or compete in the Indian market, and Indian generic exports were competing with them in lucrative markets, such as the US and the European Communities (EC). The only solution for the foreign pharmaceutical industry, especially innovators whose new drugs were imitated without payment of royalty, was to force countries like India to adopt a product patent regime for pharmaceutical inventions. This was in the form of the new TRIPS agreement that proposed setting certain minimum standards of IP protection for all signatories.

International multilateral treaties on the protection of IP date back to the nineteenth century. But TRIPS is considered a landmark in the history of international IP law because the Uruguay Round proposed linking IP protection to trading privileges and market access of non-IP goods. This linking was done to facilitate cross-retaliation in case of any treaty violations. Initially, any violations could be brought before a permanent enforcement mechanism under the aegis of the newly created World Trade Organization (WTO). The Dispute Settlement Body (DSB) of the WTO would adjudicate complaints. After a decision was issued, the offending nation would have to carry out corrective action, failing which the complainant country could cross-retaliate with economic sanctions such as raising tariffs, as authorized by the WTO. For example, if the US complained about weak patent laws in India, and India continued to breach international obligations to strengthen its patent laws, the DSB could authorize the US to cross-retaliate against India by raising its import tariffs in other sectors, such as textiles from India.

When the US first proposed the inclusion of IP at Punta del Este in 1986, developing countries, such as India and Brazil, expressed staunch opposition.[4] India's stance, as explained in its communication to the Negotiating Group on TRIPS, was that IP had no relationship with international trade. The communication said, 'The protection of intellectual property rights has no direct or significant relationship to international trade. It is because substantive issues of intellectual property rights are not germane to international trade that GATT itself has played only a peripheral role in this area and the international community has established other specialized agencies to deal with them'.[5]

India and Brazil had emerged as leaders in the developing world during the Uruguay Round, and any opposition from these countries could lead to the failure of the trade talks. But the US government was under extreme domestic pressure to push forward an aggressive trade agenda,[6] faced as it was with an increasing trade deficit due to competition from Asia and the EC. As a result, domestic constituents in the US, ranging from corporations to workers' unions to politicians, were urging their government to retaliate against countries perceived to be engaging in unfair trade practices against American exports. The more reasonable among them pointed out that the US was already quite protectionist, and that the Americans had to become more competitive. But popular sentiment swung the other way, and the political class had to take action. One such manifestation of domestic politics in America was the Omnibus Trade and Competitiveness Act of 1988, which placed certain responsibilities on the United States Trade Representative (USTR).[7]

The US President had always had powers under Section 301 of the existing Trade Act of 1974 to take retaliatory action against countries for specific complaints made by American companies on specific products. Throughout the 1980s, the US government liberally retaliated on an industry-by-industry basis. In 1982, President Reagan increased tariffs on Japanese leather and leather goods because of a petition by the Footwear Industries of America. Similarly, in 1988, a complaint by the Pharmaceutical Manufacturers Association against the lack of patent protection for their products in Brazil, led to the US President imposing 100 per cent tariffs on Brazilian paper products, pharmaceuticals, and consumer electronics.[8]

Under the new Omnibus Trade and Competitiveness Act, 1988, the USTR had to formally study the trading practices of America's trading partners, submit reports to the US Congress, and take action against offenders. The revised Section 301 now had two components: Super 301, which studied unfair trade practices as a whole and Special 301, which focused exclusively on IP policies of foreign nations that hurt US interests.[9] The reports had a list of 'priority countries' that would be targeted for negotiations. This list came to be known as the USTR 'watch-list', with some, in jest, referring to it as a 'hit-list'. If negotiations regarding the opening up of markets or changing IP policies failed, the USTR could recommend sanctions against that country. Moreover, the USTR was placed under significant oversight by the US Congress, putting each of its actions under the spotlight.[10]

The Section 301 strategy was referred to as 'crowbar diplomacy', since it used American economic power as a lever to force open foreign markets to American exports. It earned one USTR, Carla Hills, the nickname 'Crowbar Carla'. Her more trenchant critics preferred to call her 'Cowboy Carla', issuing 'Rambo-style' threats after walking into trade negotiations with her '301' gun pointed at troublesome trading partners.[11]

The 1988 law was severely criticized not only by foreign governments, who warned that it could end up derailing the Uruguay Round of talks, but also by domestic votaries of free international trade, who were distressed that this legislation could lead to trade wars.[12] There was no denying that in the age of multilateralism, the US had embarked on a blatantly unilateral path.

But crowbar diplomacy had its intended effects. Several countries who ran the risk of being cited by the USTR, like South Korea and Taiwan (both having huge trade surpluses with the US), immediately opened bilateral negotiations and promised to open their markets.[13] Other potential targets like the EC, which had the economic might to retaliate, came out with their own list of protectionist measures adopted by the Americans, in a report running into 41 pages.[14]

The Geneva Surrender

By April 1989, the Government of India also buckled to US pressure by agreeing, during negotiations at Geneva, to put trade-related IP on the table during the Uruguay Round. Some labelled this concession, which was a reversal from its original position, as the 'Geneva Surrender', because it fundamentally changed India's stance on linking IP and trade.[15] The *Economic and Political Weekly* (*EPW*), in an editorial titled 'Volte Face on Patents', called the decision a 'setback to the national interests of the third world countries as a whole', concluding that '[i]t is with a sense of anguish that patriotic and people-oriented scientists are watching the recent developments on the patents front'.[16]

It is still not clear as to why the Government of India reversed its stand in Geneva. Was it the 'stick' of possible Section 301 sanctions, or was it the 'carrot' of greater access to the global market? In a book published in 2015, India's lead negotiator, A.V. Ganesan explained that at the time, the Indian government *was* worried about Section 301 sanctions on Indian garment exports to the US. Further, according to Ganesan, India wanted to integrate with the global economy, and the Indian government felt that it was only a matter of time before other developing countries agreed to American demands.[17]

The 'Geneva Surrender' marked a turning point in the debate at home in India. It sparked the creation of a strong anti-TRIPS alliance, comprising domestic industry, scientists from the public sector, and public health activists. This alliance was called the National Working Group on Patent Laws (NWGPL). The idea of the alliance began in 1988, when a senior staffer at Ranbaxy, noticing the winds of change, invited two self-described 'anti-corporate activists' to his office to discuss the possibility of an alliance between the generic pharmaceutical industry and the activist community to stall changes in the Indian laws in response to TRIPS.[18]

The senior staffer was Bal Krishan Keayla, formerly with the government before becoming a director at Ranbaxy. The other two were left-leaning activists, Amit Sen Gupta and Amitava Guha, who, unusually, chose to team up with industry. In Sen Gupta's own words, while reminiscing about Keayla and his unconventional idea for the alliance, '[w]e had never worked with the industry and saw them as uncompromising enemies.... But Keaylaji persuaded us as only he could.'[19] The first meeting was held in the Ranbaxy boardroom. As Sen Gupta commented later, it 'was the first time some of us had been in any boardroom'.[20] Ranbaxy soon severed ties with the alliance, but the NWGPL, under the leadership of Keayla, grew into one of the most formidable civil society groups of the 1990s.[21] The range of its research and advocacy in the patent law space left an indelible impact on Indian patent policy in the 1990s and beyond.

One of the NWGPL's first events was the December 1989 National Conference of Scientists on Science, Technology, and Patents. The day-long event aimed at educating, or rather, advocating the downside of TRIPS, to an audience consisting largely of scientists. The tone of the conference was decidedly anti-patents, and it ended with a resolution to call upon the Indian government to make 'an unequivocal policy statement that there will not be any change in the law and policy relating to Patents and Intellectual Property and this position would be maintained in GATT and other National, International and Bilateral fora'.[22]

Faced with widely reported criticism and resistance from groups like the NWGPL, the Indian government clarified that it had only agreed to talk about the issue and had not made any commitments.

What was wrong about this? As an opinion piece by Srinivasa Raghavan in the *Economic Times* in 1989 pointed out:

> Plenty, say critics, because readiness to talk implies a readiness to change. The government denies this, but the Americans are convinced that they have scored a major victory in getting India to give up its rigid stance. Not only have they broken up the formidable India–Brazil duo which had caused the US much sorrow in trade talks, they have also managed to initiate a process that must in all reasonableness culminate in India going about half-way to meet US demands. All we have to do, say the Americans, is to wait.[23]

This dire prediction would eventually come true.

The Sanctions Threat

In the last week of May 1989, USTR Carla Hills announced that the US President George Bush, Sr, had cited India, along with Brazil and Japan, under Super 301, for unfair trade practices.[24] The US had also cited India under Special 301, along with 16 other countries, for poor IP laws. The unfair trade practices included trade-related investment measures and insurance market practices, while the IP issues were related to patent protection for all classes of inventions, effective protection of well-known trademarks, and improved enforcement against piracy, among others. Citing India under Section 301 did not automatically result in economic sanctions, but India would now have to negotiate the highlighted issues with the USTR and resolve them within three years, failing which the US could impose nearly 100 per cent tariffs on Indian imports.[25]

The decision to cite India caught several experts by surprise because India was the 27th-largest trading partner of the US and enjoyed a USD 670 million trade surplus with the US through bilateral trade that stood at around USD 5.4 billion in 1988–9.[26] Both figures were tiny in the context of the US economy, which was suffering from a trade deficit of USD 153 billion in 1987.[27] Indian trade practices were hardly likely to have hurt the American economy. So why did the USTR cite India, especially when the Indian economy was already slowly opening up, and when India had already agreed to discuss IP in the Uruguay Round?

Some speculated that the USTR was under immense public pressure to act against foreign countries, and chose India since it was a convenient target that could not retaliate.[28] Others were quite certain that the US was using the Section 301 process as leverage to steamroll Indian opposition against TRIPS. *India Today* quoted Howard Rosen of the Washington-based Institute for International Economics as saying, '[a]t GATT, the US had watched India and Brazil walk away after blocking its efforts to push its trade interests. This is a way of bringing them back. It is no accident that the 18-month deadline for negotiations coincides with the conclusion of GATT's Uruguay round of talks in December 1990.'[29] Rosen was perhaps right, because Carla Hills, in a statement released on 25 May 1989, said 'Super and Special 301, like other Trade Policy Tools at our disposal, will be able to create an ever-expanding Multilateral Trading System based upon clear and enforceable Rules'.[30]

The announcement by the US to place India on the priority list was met with outrage and disappointment at home. Dinesh Singh, the commerce minister, in an interview with the *Economic Times* said, 'I am dismayed that the US Administration should have named India under the provisions of Super 301. When the US itself has built and retained so many barriers against access to its markets, it is hardly in a position to ask others to lift barriers—without itself doing so.'[31]

The announcement was also condemned by US experts. Jim Powell in the *Wall Street Journal* called Super 301 'the economic equivalent of civilian bombing'.[32] The *Business Standard* reported that Jagdish Bhagwati, a Columbia University professor, had petitioned US President George Bush, Sr, warning him that the use of Super 301 would invite retaliation from the strong, while the weak would regard it as 'the way of the bully reviving the image of the ugly American'.[33] This petition was signed by 36 top economists, including some from conservative think-tanks like the American Enterprise Institute. In a moral dimension, the petitioners pointed out that the US had not mentioned the EC because it had prepared its own list of US unfair trade practices. The pundits of free trade were worried that the US action would cause irreversible damage to the multilateral trading system, which had even benefited the Americans themselves.

Some critics blamed the Indian government for bringing the 301 citations upon itself. Chitra Subramaniam of the *Hindu*, better known for having broken the story on the Bofors scandal, wrote from Geneva:[34]

> The battle for TRIPS was lost well in advance at the Trade Negotiations Committee ... when India did a dramatic somersault and agreed to negotiate adequate norms and standards for TRIPS. Ironically India was hoping to appease Ms. Hills and company by appearing flexible... If India had not agreed to negotiate norms and standards in April, it would have had negotiating leverage now.

She further noted:

> It is being suggested unanimously here—by some Third World diplomats and informed observers—that India should retaliate by blocking the negotiations and threaten to wreck the Uruguay round process if the U.S. does not get off its high horse. India can also draw up a list of its imports from the U.S. and impose restrictions on them in a manner that is akin to the American style.

Though compelling, this suggestion discounted the fact that the Uruguay Round offered a substantial opportunity for India to boost exports to lucrative Western markets, especially in textiles. Also, since India was the 27th-largest trading partner of the US, it did not have the economic might to hurt America through a trade war. If anything, such a trade war would only have served to exacerbate the balance of payments crisis being faced by the country in 1989. That crisis eventually blew into a full-fledged economic crisis in 1990–1, without the US even imposing any sanctions on India.

The economic crisis of 1990–1 would change the Indian economy forever. It forced India to open its economy. Foreign investment and access to international markets became supremely important, and every passing day made it clear that India would become a part of the proposed multilateral trading system emerging out of the Uruguay Round. Speaking at the ministerial level trade talks in Brussels in December 1990, Subramanian Swamy, the then minister for commerce, while expressing his government's concerns about the impact of TRIPS on medicines, did not outright reject the possibility of India amending its patent law. However, he made it clear that India was concerned about linking IP protection under TRIPS to trade in services or trade in goods under GATT: 'We are not opposed to the idea of a new organization by whatever name it is called, as long as it is structured to service three distinct agreements. We reject any proposal which tends to link up three distinct agreements with a view to facilitating cross-retaliation.'[35]

The Government of India's position as articulated by Swamy at Brussels gradually diluted as USTR Carla Hills ramped up pressure on India through the threat of trade sanctions. Although the Uruguay Round involved multilateral talks, it was well known that the USTR was also negotiating directly with trading partners to influence the outcome of the talks. Even as late as 1990, India had publicly stated that it would not discuss trade-related IP issues directly with the US Government in bilateral talks. The *New York Times*, in June 1990, quoted an Indian diplomat who said, '[a]s a sovereign independent country, we cannot be subject to another sovereign independent country's laws.'[36] Off the record, however, one Indian minister said, '[s]ince we cannot, and must not, conduct official negotiations, I would favour quiet, informal behind-the-scenes talks'.[37]

But by October 1991, USTR Hills was in India, holding talks with the Indian government. In her statements to the Indian press, she made it absolutely clear that patents for pharmaceuticals was one of the key issues.[38] Strangely, the Indian government steadfastly held on to the public stand that the Uruguay Round and bilateral talks with the US were two separate issues.[39] This schizophrenic public stand on multilateral and bilateral talks was possibly necessary to avoid attacks from domestic opponents.

US Imposes Trade Sanctions

When the strict timelines under Section 301 expired, the US imposed sanctions on India on 30 April 1992 for failing to amend its IP policies. The sanctions involved taking 'the $35-million drugs and pharmaceutical imports off its duty free list, imposing 5 per cent customs duty'.[40] These sanctions were mild and did not cause much panic in India. What New Delhi feared more was the possibility of the sanctions being extended to the USD 700-million textile exports from India to the US.[41] Any action on textile exports would have hurt the Indian economy. Would India finally commit to signing TRIPS as a part of the GATT package, and bring back pharmaceutical patents?

Contemporary media reports suggest that India's political resolve was quickly melting in the face of pressure from the US, now the sole superpower after the dissolution of the USSR. Bureaucrats admitted that '[i]f the US hits back, there's little we can do'.[42]

According to the *EPW* in January 1992, despite public criticism of the draft treaties by commerce minister P. Chidambaram, a secret note had been circulated within the ministry, with the minister's approval, recommending that the government accept the proposal on TRIPS and cross-retaliation, since the benefits of increased trading privileges with the developed world in agriculture and textiles would result in a net gain for India.[43]

One of the many problems with the Indian government's stand during the GATT negotiations was the lack of transparency of its intentions even when it came to the Parliament. Under the Constitution of India, the political executive can enter into international treaties without prior sanction of the Parliament, although Parliamentary approval is required to amend existing domestic laws. This was perhaps one reason why the Indian government and its ministers were not candid about its official stand. Even so, between 1992 and 1994, the Rajya Sabha discussed the Dunkel Draft (eponymously named after Arthur Dunkel, the Director General of the WTO, who was given the task to prepare the final text for negotiations of GATT in the Uruguay Round) on more than 50 occasions, either during the question hour or in general discussions. Most of the times, commerce minister Chidambaram, a reputed lawyer by profession, fielded the questions with grace and skill, without revealing any of the government's actual intentions.

The only clear answer Chidambaram provided was to the following question posed by a group of Parliamentarians from the Bharatiya Janata Party (BJP) and Communist Party of India (Marxist) (CPI(M)) with regard to the Dunkel proposals: 'whether [the] Government propose[s] to issue a white paper on this issue?' Chidambaram replied with a terse 'No, Sir'.[44] Given that it took India two expert committee reports, two joint parliamentary committee reports, and three legislative attempts over a period of 22 years to enact the Patents Act, 1970, it was surprising that the government was negotiating a binding international treaty on India's behalf without so much as a white paper.

Parliament Conducts Hearings on the Dunkel Draft

The saving grace of an otherwise appalling phase of Indian democracy was the intervention of the Department-related Parliamentary Standing Committee on Commerce, a relatively recent institution in Indian democracy. Historically, the Indian Parliament voted to create ad hoc Select or Standing Committees, comprising members of the Lok Sabha and Rajya Sabha, to examine issues or bills of importance. In April 1993, the Parliament constituted a system of Department-related Parliamentary Standing Committees that would oversee different departments of the Government of India and examine legislations introduced by these departments in the Parliament. Given the permanent nature of these committees, the political executive had little control over them. The first Department-related Parliamentary Standing Committee on Commerce was headed by I.K. Gujral, who later became the Prime Minister. The issue of TRIPS fell within this committee's mandate, which studied the Dunkel Draft in detail, inviting a cross-section of Indian society to testify.

Statements made by senior bureaucrats before the committee shed light on the exact happenings during the negotiations on TRIPS and GATT. It was during these hearings that A. Hoda, the Special Secretary, ministry of commerce, revealed the reason for the Government of India agreeing to discuss IP issues in the GATT framework. He claimed that once the other developing countries buckled, India no longer had a choice.[45] Anti-TRIPS activists, who also deposed before the Standing Committee, claimed that this explanation was a cover-up, and that the Government of India had, in fact, caved in before any of the other developing countries.[46]

A.V. Ganesan, India's chief negotiator at the Uruguay Round of multilateral trade talks, also deposed before the committee. Ganesan and his team had a tough job of balancing India's needs with the onerous demands of the Americans. Explaining the contentious Indian position of reinstating pharmaceutical product patents, Ganesan unexpectedly informed the committee that this reinstatement was in India's interests. Ganesan argued that it was not possible to acquire advanced technology from abroad without granting product patents for such inventions.[47] While there may have been other valid reasons to sign TRIPS, such as increased trading benefits in other sectors, Ganesan's reasons were arguably incorrect. The growing pharmaceutical industry was proof that Indian industry had all the skills to reverse-engineer the latest chemical and pharmaceutical products. On the contrary, patents owned by foreigners would have curbed Indian industry. Ganesan, though, also pointed out that any price rise of essential pharmaceuticals could be handled by broad compulsory licensing provisions which India had insisted on retaining in the negotiating text.[48] This balance of reinstating pharmaceutical product patents with the promise of diluting such rights through compulsory licences formed the bedrock of Ganesan's negotiating strategy. As frustrating as this strategy may have been for US and European negotiators, it paid off when India managed to retain broad compulsory licensing provisions in TRIPS.

On two other issues, Ganesan staunchly opposed proposals made by developed countries. The first related to the patenting of naturally occurring microorganisms which had not been genetically modified. The second was whether a patent could be 'worked' in India through importation, or whether a patented invention had to be necessarily manufactured in India. 'Working' a patent was an important requirement in Indian law, and the failure to manufacture locally could result in a compulsory licence being issued. Developed countries like the US opposed local 'working' requirements, since they preferred the flexibility of manufacturing patented inventions in low-cost territories, and shipping the final product to the global market. Ganesan made it clear to the committee that such obligations should be disobeyed even if approved as a part of the final text.[49]

After receiving extensive testimony on all aspects of the Dunkel Draft, the Standing Committee produced a 66-page report, in which it made four recommendations. First, Indian patent law should protect only process patents and not product patents; second, the patent term should not be extended to 20 years since it would discourage research and development; third, India should retain 'licenses of right' which result in automatic compulsory licensing for certain patents; and fourth, patenting of microorganisms and biological processes should be prohibited.[50] In other words, the committee did not want the Indian government to concede the most important provisions that were introduced through the Patents Act, 1970. The government is generally not bound by the recommendations of a Parliamentary Standing Committee, although most recommendations are usually accepted. The final text of TRIPS agreed to by India, in 1994, did not adhere to any of these recommendations of the Standing Committee.

India Prepares to Sign TRIPS

As it became obvious that the Indian government had every intention to sign TRIPS, some sought judicial intervention to restrain the government from signing the treaty. On 7 April 1994, one week before India signed TRIPS at Marrakesh, the High Court of Delhi was petitioned by four persons, 'seeking a writ of mandamus restraining the Union of India from signing/ratifying the existing version of [the] GATT Treaty, or to restrain the Union of India from, agreeing to sign and signing Art. 27.3(b) of the TRIPS Agreement'.[51] Two of these petitioners were Vandana Shiva of Research Foundation for Science, Technology and Ecology (RFSTE) and Nanjundaswamy of the Karnataka Rajya Raitha Sangha (KRRS). Shiva and Nanjundaswamy were also involved in the high-decibel controversy against the neem patents granted to the US company, W.R. Grace.[52] Article 27.3(b) of TRIPS allowed member states to exclude plants from domestic patent law, provided they enacted sui generis, that is, separate legislation to protect new plant varieties. Domestic opposition to TRIPS was severe, on the grounds that pharmaceuticals would become more expensive. But there was very little public debate on Article 27.3(b) of TRIPS. This was surprising because if India did comply with TRIPS and protect plant varieties under a sui generis law, it would most likely drive up the prices of new seed varieties, and impact national agricultural policies. In the case filed before the Delhi High Court, the petitioners sought a direction to exclude 'patents on life-forms including plants, animals, human beings produced through biological or microbiological processes, whether natural or modified on grounds of public morality and public order.' The petitioners basically argued that TRIPS would violate the fundamental rights of Indian citizens, especially the right of farmers to breed their own plants.

Within two weeks of its filing, the Delhi High Court on 22 April 1994 dismissed the petition on the grounds that the mere signing of a treaty would not violate the fundamental rights of the petitioner. The Court also held that on economic policy, as per precedent of the Supreme Court, the judiciary had to defer to the decisions of the elected government.

At the concluding ministerial meeting of the WTO talks in Morocco on 13 April 1994, Pranab Mukherjee, India's then minister for commerce, told his counterparts from other countries that India had 'negotiated in good faith', and that while it had joined the consensus, it 'would have preferred these results to be different'. While welcoming 'the promise of the integration of the textiles and clothing sector into the General Agreement', Mukherjee warned that '[f]ears have also been expressed in many developing countries regarding the possible increases in the prices of patented drugs under the new TRIPS regime', and that India stood 'committed to the prevention of exploitative pricing of life-saving drugs in … [the] … country'.[53]

Mukherjee's speech revealed two things: that the Indian government had made a trade-off, increasing textile exports at the cost of hurting its pharmaceutical industry and patient population by reinstating pharmaceutical product patents; and that India would exploit all safeguards to keep in check the rise of prices in the pharmaceuticals sector.

As the Government of India would soon learn, negotiating and signing the new WTO treaties was the easy part. The true challenge would be to convince the Parliament to enact the laws required to enforce India's obligations under TRIPS. A counter-movement had already begun, with a broad-based coalition of unlikely allies. Over the next decade, India would furiously debate the deal struck with the developed world during the Uruguay Round of talks.

Notes

1. For an excellent history of the TRIPS, see JAYASHREE WATAL, INTELLECTUAL PROPERTY RIGHTS IN THE WTO AND DEVELOPING COUNTRIES (2003).

2. Rita Manchanda, *Super 301 and Special 301: America Gets Tough on Trade*, in BACKGROUND PAPERS SUBMITTED FOR THE NATIONAL CONFERENCE OF SCIENTISTS ON SCIENCE, TECHNOLOGY AND PATENTS (NATIONAL WORKING GROUP ON PATENT LAWS) 3 (4 December 1989).

3. 'Special 301' Report on Intellectual Property Barriers, *Submission of the Pharmaceutical Research and Manufacturers of America* (16 February 1999).

4. Paul Lewis, *Aims on Trade Talks Outlined*, THE NEW YORK TIMES, 19 July 1986, available at http://www.nytimes.com/1986/07/19/business/aims-on-trade-talks-outlined.html (Last visited on 22 March 2015).

5. Group of Negotiations on Goods (GATT), *Standards and Principles Concerning the Availability, Scope and Use of Trade-Related Intellectual Property Rights (Communication from India)*, Multilateral Trade Negotiations (The Uruguay Round), MTN.GNG/NG11/W/37 (10 July 1989), at 19.

6. Paul Lewis, *U.S. Issues Threat in Talks on Trade*, THE NEW YORK TIMES, 7 September 1986, available at http://www.nytimes.com/1986/09/07/world/us-issues-threat-in-talks-on-trade.html (Last visited on 22 March 2015).

7. Manchanda, *Super 301 and Special 301*, at 7.

8. Jim Powell, *Why Trade Retaliation Closes Markets and Impoverishes People*, Cato Institute Policy Analysis No. 143 (20 November 1990), available at http://object.cato.org/sites/cato.org/files/pubs/pdf/pa143.pdf (Last visited on 22 March 2015).

9. See generally Elizabeth K. King, *The Omnibus Trade Bill of 1988: Super 301 and Its Effects on the Multilateral Trade System Under the GATT*, 12 U. PA. J. INT'L BUS. L. 245 (1991).

10. *Congress Lays Out Strict Timetable for 'Special' and 'Super' 301 Actions*, in BACKGROUND PAPERS SUBMITTED FOR THE NATIONAL CONFERENCE OF SCIENTISTS ON SCIENCE, TECHNOLOGY AND PATENTS (NATIONAL WORKING GROUP ON PATENT LAWS) (4 December 1989) (this article appeared in the Economic Times in May 1989).

11. Louis Uchitelle, *A Crowbar for Carla Hills*, THE NEW YORK TIMES, 10 June 1990, available at http://www.nytimes.com/1990/06/10/magazine/a-crowbar-for-carla-hills.html (Last visited on 22 March 2015); Chitra Subramaniam, *U.S. Threat & India's Options*, THE HINDU, 14 June 1989; *Hills' Hard Line on Trade Draws Protests in S. Korea*, LOS ANGELES TIMES, 12 October 1989, available at http://articles.latimes.com/1989-10-12/business/fi-398_1_south-korea-s-population (Last visited on 22 March 2015).

12. Powell, *Trade Retaliation*.

13. U.S. Trade Representative Fact Sheet, *'Super 301' Trade Liberalization Priorities (3920) (GLS401 05/25/89)*, in BACKGROUND PAPERS SUBMITTED FOR THE NATIONAL CONFERENCE OF SCIENTISTS ON SCIENCE, TECHNOLOGY AND PATENTS (NATIONAL WORKING GROUP ON PATENT LAWS) (4 December 1989).

14. Powell, *Trade Retaliation*, at 3.

15. *Intellectual Property Rights: The Geneva Surrender*, XXIV (22) EPW 1201 (3 June 1989).

16. *Volte-Face on Patents*, XXIV (17) EPW 895 (29 April 1989).

17. A.V. Ganesan, *Negotiating for India*, in THE MAKINGS OF THE TRIPS AGREEMENT: PERSONAL INSIGHTS FROM THE URUGUAY ROUND NEGOTIATIONS: 2015 (Jayashree Watal and Antony Taubman, eds, 2015).

18. Amit Sen Gupta, *B K Keayla: A Personal Reminiscence*, XLV (51) EPW 25 (18 December 2010).

19. Sen Gupta, *B K Keayla*, at 25–6.

20. Sen Gupta, *B K Keayla*, at 25–6.

21. Sen Gupta, *B K Keayla*, at 26.

22. B.K. Keayla (Convenor), Resolution Adopted at the National Conference of Scientists on Science, Technology and Patents (4 December 1989).

23. T.C.A. Srinivasa Raghavan, *US Omnibus Act: The Pressure Principle*, in BACKGROUND PAPERS SUBMITTED FOR THE NATIONAL CONFERENCE OF SCIENTISTS ON SCIENCE, TECHNOLOGY AND PATENTS (NATIONAL WORKING GROUP ON PATENT LAWS) (4 December 1989) (this article appeared in the Economic Times on 29 May 1989).

24. Clyde H. Farnsworth, *U.S. Cites Japan, India and Brazil as Unfair Traders*, THE NEW YORK TIMES, 26 May 1989, available at http://www.nytimes.com/1989/05/26/business/us-cites-japan-india-and-brazil-as-unfair-traders.html (Last visited on 29 March 2015).

25. U.S. Trade Representative Fact Sheet, *'Special 301' on Intellectual Property (2780) (GS4040525 05/25/89)*, in BACKGROUND PAPERS SUBMITTED FOR THE NATIONAL CONFERENCE OF SCIENTISTS ON SCIENCE, TECHNOLOGY AND PATENTS (NATIONAL WORKING GROUP ON PATENT LAWS) (4 December 1989); Bruce Odessey, *U.S. Names Japan, Brazil, India Super 301 Priorities (790) (GS4050525 05/25/89)*, in BACKGROUND PAPERS SUBMITTED FOR THE NATIONAL CONFERENCE OF SCIENTISTS ON SCIENCE, TECHNOLOGY AND PATENTS (NATIONAL WORKING GROUP ON PATENT LAWS) (4 December 1989).

26. N.C. Joshi, *Terrorism in Trade*, in BACKGROUND PAPERS SUBMITTED FOR THE NATIONAL CONFERENCE OF SCIENTISTS ON SCIENCE, TECHNOLOGY AND PATENTS (NATIONAL WORKING GROUP ON PATENT LAWS) (4 December 1989) (this article appeared in the Indian Post on 15 July 1989).

27. Daniel Griswold, *America's Maligned and Misunderstood Trade Deficit*, Cato Institute Trade Policy Analysis No. 2 (20 April 1998), available at http://www.cato.org/publications/trade-policy-analysis/americas-maligned-misunderstood-trade-deficit (Last visited on 22 March 2015).

28. Arvind Panagariya, *India as Scapegoat: U.S. Actions Under Super-301*, in Background Papers Submitted for the National Conference of Scientists on Science, Technology and Patents (National Working Group on Patent Laws) (4 December 1989) (this article appeared in the Times of India on 23 June 1989).

29. Paranjoy Guha Thakurta, Rita Manchanda, and Salil Tripathi, *Indo-US Trade: US Accuses India of Using Unfair Means*, India Today, 30 June 1989, available at http://indiatoday.intoday.in/story/us-accuses-india-of-using-unfair-means/1/323590.html (Last visited on 22 March 2015).

30. Statement by USTR Hills, *Hills Says Purpose of 301 Actions is to Expand Trade (GS4020525 05/25/89)*, in Background Papers Submitted for the National Conference of Scientists on Science, Technology and Patents (National Working Group on Patent Laws) (4 December 1989).

31. I.C. Singhal (Interview), *We Have to Decide if We Should Have a Dialogue with the US*, in Background Papers Submitted for the National Conference of Scientists on Science, Technology and Patents (National Working Group on Patent Laws) (4 December 1989) (this interview appeared in the Economic Times on 6 June 1989).

32. *US Expert Flays Trade Action by Bush Regime*, in Background Papers Submitted for the National Conference of Scientists on Science, Technology and Patents (National Working Group on Patent Laws) (4 December 1989) (this article appeared in the Business Standard on 1 June 1989).

33. *Top US Economists Warn against Use of Super 301*, in Background Papers Submitted for the National Conference of Scientists on Science, Technology and Patents (National Working Group on Patent Laws) (4 December 1989) (this article appeared in the Business Standard on 4 June 1989).

34. Subramaniam, *U.S. Threat & India's Options*.

35. Trade Negotiations Committee (GATT), *Statement by Dr. Subramanian Swamy, Union Minister of Commerce, Law and Justice*, Multilateral Trade (The Uruguay Round), MTN/TNC/MIN(90)/ST/46 (4 December 1990), at 4.

36. Clyde H. Farnsworth, *U.S. Likely to Forgo Sanctions against India*, The New York Times, 14 June 1990, available at http://www.nytimes.com/1990/06/14/business/us-likely-to-forgo-sanctions-against-india.html (Last visited on 22 March 2015).

37. Guha Thakurta, Manchanda, and Tripathi, *Indo-US Trade*.

38. Sunil Jain, *Indo-US Trade: Patent Pressure*, INDIA TODAY, 31 October 1991, available at http://indiatoday.intoday.in/story/india-has-not-liberalized-enough-says-us-trade-representative/1/318986.html (Last visited on 22 March 2015).

39. Jain, *Indo-US Trade*.

40. Sunil Jain, *First Blood*, INDIA TODAY, 14 June 2013, available at http://indiatoday.intoday.in/story/special-301-us-imposes-5percent-customs-duty-on-drugs-and-pharmaceutical-imports/1/306918.html (Last visited on 22 March 2015).

41. Jain, *First Blood*.

42. Guha Thakurta, Manchanda, and Tripathi, *Indo-US Trade*.

43. *GATT, the Dunkel Draft and India*, XXVII(4) EPW 140 (25 January 1992).

44. India, Rajya Sabha, *Written Answers to Government's Reaction on Dunkel's Proposals* (25 February 1992), at 90.

45. INDIA, RAJYA SABHA, PARLIAMENTARY STANDING COMMITTEE ON COMMERCE, DRAFT DUNKEL PROPOSALS 29–30 (14 December 1994).

46. RAJYA SABHA, PARLIAMENTARY STANDING COMMITTEE ON COMMERCE, DRAFT DUNKEL PROPOSALS, at 30.

47. RAJYA SABHA, PARLIAMENTARY STANDING COMMITTEE ON COMMERCE, DRAFT DUNKEL PROPOSALS, at 34.

48. RAJYA SABHA, PARLIAMENTARY STANDING COMMITTEE ON COMMERCE, DRAFT DUNKEL PROPOSALS, at 34.

49. RAJYA SABHA, PARLIAMENTARY STANDING COMMITTEE ON COMMERCE, DRAFT DUNKEL PROPOSALS, at 35.

50. RAJYA SABHA, PARLIAMENTARY STANDING COMMITTEE ON COMMERCE, DRAFT DUNKEL PROPOSALS, at 46.

51. Vandana Shiva and Ors. v. Union of India, 1995 (32) DRJ 447, available at http://indiankanoon.org/doc/1110085/ (Last visited on 12 August 2014).

52. See Chapter 9, *The Traditional Knowledge Trilogy*, in this volume.

53. Trade Negotiations Committee (GATT), *Statement by Mr. Pranab Mukherjee, Minister of Commerce*, Multilateral Trade (The Uruguay Round), MTN.TNC/MIN(94)/ST/38 (13 April 1994).

3

LIFE AFTER MARRAKESH

W hen India signed the Marrakesh Agreement in 1994 (which established the World Trade Organization [WTO]), eight years after the Uruguay Round of talks began in Punta del Este, it agreed to be bound by the Agreement on Trade-Related Aspects of Intellectual Property Rights (TRIPS). To comply with TRIPS, India had to amend its Patents Act, 1970, significantly. For example, it had to repeal Section 5 that prohibited the grant of pharmaceutical patents; extend patent terms from 14 to 20 years; and abolish 'licenses of right'. These changes required the Indian Parliament to enact a law amending the Patents Act, 1970. This was not going to be easy because the Indian government had already left the Parliament annoyed over its actions in the run up to 1994: It did nothing to mollify the many Members of Parliament (MPs) who were opposed to TRIPS and the WTO system; and worse, it had become a member of the WTO without seeking parliamentary approval. As a result, when the Amendment Bills were brought to vote, the government had to face an angry Parliament that staged walkouts, sought further debates on the proposed amendments, and delayed the process of complying with TRIPS. Only after the WTO's Dispute Settlement Body (DSB) ruled against India in complaints filed by the United States (US) and the European Communities (EC) did the Parliament begin the process of amending India's patent laws.

These events took place between 1995 and 2005 in three stages: first, there was denial and refusal to comply with international obligations; second, India lost at the DSB and realized that it had no choice but to follow the law if it wanted to be a member of the WTO;

and third, India looked for ways to exploit the flexibilities of TRIPS to outwit developed countries at their own game. This chapter tells the story of India's journey from the failed Patents (Amendment) Ordinance, 1994 to the Patents (Amendment) Act, 2005.

The Failed Amendments

Under TRIPS, like other developing countries, India had until 2005 to amend its patent law to grant product patents for pharmaceutical inventions. As an interim measure, under the transitional provisions of TRIPS, by 1 January 1995, countries like India had to bring into effect a regime of exclusive marketing rights (EMRs) for technologies discriminated against under existing national patent laws. Parliament was not in session at the time, so to meet this deadline, the government issued the Patents (Amendment) Ordinance, 1994, amending the Patents Act, 1970. The Ordinance provided for a mechanism called the 'mailbox', through which patent applications for hitherto unpatentable technologies could be filed, and the priority date of these applications would be 'frozen' until India amended its patent laws to comply with TRIPS. The ordinance also granted EMRs to mailbox applicants, who acquired patent-like monopoly rights until the mailbox applications were examined under India's (future) amended patent law.[1] With the promulgation of this ordinance, India was in compliance with its immediate obligations under TRIPS. But ordinances are valid for only six months from the day Parliament reconvenes after the ordinance is promulgated, or at best, seven-and-a-half months from the date of promulgation.[2] If the ordinance lapsed, India would be in violation of its TRIPS obligations. Therefore, a law was still needed to make the amendments brought by the ordinance permanent, which the government introduced in Parliament as the Patents (Amendment) Bill, 1995.

In the run up to the amendment, while negotiating TRIPS, the government had studiously ignored calls from the Parliament for a more informed debate, and did not even release a 'white paper' on the topic.[3] As payback, a determined opposition was ready to fight the government over the amendment. When the Patents (Amendment)

Bill, 1995 was finally debated in the Lok Sabha, the opposition berated the government for how it had promulgated the ordinance, and for not having taken the Parliament into confidence before agreeing to become part of the WTO. As Rabi Ray, a Lok Sabha MP, said during the debate, '[t]he Parliament was not taken into confidence before signing the Marrakesh agreement. The Government kept Parliament in the dark and did everything and has now brought this ordinance.... Our submission is that the entire Opposition and many [honourable] Members from the Congress oppose the basic principles behind [the] issuance of the Ordinance.'[4] Several MPs expressed similar sentiments, and called for the ordinance to be withdrawn before debating the Amendment Bill.

But the government did not agree, and the opposition was forced to debate the bill. After a brief, acrimonious debate, a section of the opposition walked out of the Parliament in protest. But the Lok Sabha had a quorum, and most of those present voted in favour of the bill, as a result of which the bill was passed. India's bicameral system, though, meant that the bill also had to be passed in the Rajya Sabha before it could become a law. The Rajya Sabha referred the bill to a Select Committee, consisting of MPs from the Rajya Sabha, for a more detailed examination. Select Committees usually invite evidence from all stakeholders and take time to deliberate before submitting a final report. While the Select Committee scrutinized the bill, the Lok Sabha dissolved for elections, and the Patents (Amendment) Bill, 1995 automatically lapsed.[5] Meanwhile, the ordinance also expired on 26 March 1995. In this legislative void, India was at risk of breaching its TRIPS commitments.

Under the Marrakesh treaty, which set up the WTO, any member aggrieved by the failure of a fellow member to comply with TRIPS could seek redressal of its grievances under the dispute resolution mechanism. This dispute resolution mechanism is administered by the DSB of the WTO. The first stage of the dispute resolution process requires the aggrieved member to request consultations with the member which is allegedly in violation of its obligations under the WTO rules. The two members are required to consult with each other and attempt to resolve the issue amicably. If consultations fail, the DSB will be requested to set up a Panel comprising adjudicators who will hear the arguments of both parties and deliver a report to the DSB with a list of recommendations based on the law. Although this report is formally referred to as 'recommendations', it is in reality a final ruling since it can be rejected by the DSB only if there is complete consensus against adopting the report. The Panel report, though, can be appealed before a permanent Appellate Body set up by the DSB. If a particular member is found to be in breach of its obligations, it is given time to comply with the recommendations of the DSB, but if it fails to carry out remedial measures in time, the complainant-member may request the DSB to authorize 'retaliation' by suspending trading privileges or imposing tariffs on imports from the member country that is refusing to comply with the DSB ruling.[6]

WTO Trade Disputes

From February 1996, the US began to invoke the WTO dispute settlement mechanism to ensure that its trading partners under the WTO Agreement started complying with their TRIPS obligations. Its first three complaints were against Japan, Pakistan, and Portugal.[7] The fourth complaint was against India. Filed on 2 July 1996, the complaint alleged that India had violated its TRIPS obligations because it failed to provide for transitional protection pending the deletion of Section 5 of its then Patents Act, which prohibited patents for pharmaceutical and agrochemical inventions.[8]

The US had a strong case before the DSB, since Article 70 of TRIPS was clear that all member states had to provide transitional protection until they amended their national patent laws to allow patents for all technologies without any discrimination against any field of technology. In fact, the preamble to the Patents (Amendment) Ordinance, 1994 had said that it was being enacted 'to meet ... India's obligations under [TRIPS] while safeguarding its interests'.[9] Given this admission, the fact that the Indian Ordinance had lapsed was reason enough for the US to allege that India was in violation of TRIPS.

Surely enough, India suffered a comprehensive defeat before the Panel that heard the dispute. In a report circulated on 5 September 1997, the Panel found that India had failed in its obligations under TRIPS.

Specifically, it had found that India failed to establish an effective mailbox system to preserve priority of patent applications for pharmaceutical and agricultural chemical inventions, besides also failing to provide EMRs for these inventions, pending a transition to a patent system from 1 January 2005.[10] An appeal by India also failed. The Appellate Body, in a report circulated on 19 December 1997, agreed substantially with the Panel report, and the DSB adopted both the Appellate Body report and the Panel report on 16 January 1998.[11] Even before the appellate proceedings could conclude, the EC also initiated proceedings against India on the same grounds as the US. India lost this case as well, with the Panel submitting a report in the EC's favour in August 1998.[12] This report was adopted by the DSB on 22 September 1998.

Failure to comply with the DSB's ruling would give both the US and the EC opportunities to 'retaliate' against India under the WTO Agreement by increasing tariffs on Indian imports. Faced with the possibility of trade sanctions, and after consulting the US, India informed the DSB on 21 April 1998 that both parties had agreed to a reasonable timeline of 15 months to implement the DSB's recommendations.[13] India, therefore, had until 19 April 1999 to amend its patent law.

In June 1998, five months after the DSB adopted the Panel report and the Appellate Body report, the Parliamentary Standing Committee on Commerce decided to study and invite testimony on the subject of 'India and the World Trade Organization'. In its final report, tabled before the Parliament on 4 December 1998, the committee speculated that it remained an open question as to '[w]hether retaliations will actually be applied against India should it fail to meet the April, 1999 deadline'.[14] Pointing to the existing record, the committee astutely observed that even 'where it has won its battles in the Disputes Settlement Panel, the U.S.A. has desisted from taking retaliatory action against the offending countries'.[15] But the committee also noted India's vulnerability if retaliatory action were to take place, especially in the blossoming software industry that exported software and services worth billions of dollars to the US.[16] Soon after, the Government of India introduced the Patents (Amendment) Bill, 1998 to enforce EMRs for pharmaceuticals and agrochemicals.

The First Amendment

By 1998, the political situation, both within India and between India and the rest of the world, had changed dramatically. A coalition led by the right-wing Bharatiya Janata Party (BJP) had won the electoral mandate for the first time since the party's creation in the 1980s. The coalition installed Atal Bihari Vajpayee, a senior BJP politician, as India's new Prime Minister. Interestingly, not only had Vajpayee led the walkout by the BJP from the Lok Sabha in 1995 over the amendment to the patent law, he had also written a dissent note in 1970 as a member of the Joint Parliamentary Committee (JPC) examining the Patents Bill, 1967. Vajpayee had filed this dissent note with two other parliamentarians, Kanwar Lal Gupta and Pitamber Das. At the time, all three were members of the Bharatiya Jana Sangh, the BJP's political predecessor. That dissent note had supported the government's move to do away with product patents for pharmaceutical products. Vajpayee's dissent was that the government should have gone further to ensure that patents were granted to only Indians and not foreigners, and that there would be no international retaliation since very few Indians had foreign patents. The note also pointed out that European countries were trading with the Chinese, despite there being no patent regime in China.[17]

On assuming office in 1998, one of Prime Minister Vajpayee's first decisions was to authorize the testing of nuclear bombs, with an aim to declare India a nuclear power. The fallout of the nuclear bombs reverberated far beyond the testing grounds of Pokhran, Rajasthan. The US, which had pressured India to cancel nuclear tests earlier that decade, was outraged, complicating the already difficult diplomatic relationship between India and the developed world.[18]

As the party in power, the BJP, contrary to its stand in 1995, now had to introduce and pilot the Patents (Amendment) Bill, 1998. To ensure the bill's passage, the BJP-led government would have to negotiate with the Congress party (now sitting in the opposition), which had been in power when India became a member of the WTO. In other words, both the ruling party and the principal opposition party were now on the same page.

Thus, when the Rajya Sabha took up the Patents (Amendment) Bill, 1998 for debate, the Congress and the BJP, with a few exceptions, spoke almost the same language. The opposition to the bill came from left-wing and regional parties, both of whom were unhappy at not having been consulted on such an important issue.

The MPs from the Communist Party of India (Marxist) (CPI(M)) had a simple opposition strategy: They would delay the Bill for as long as possible. They demanded that the bill be referred to a Select Committee, comprising parliamentarians from the Rajya Sabha. Veteran communist MP Gurudas Dasgupta made an impassioned plea to the Speaker: 'I only implore you, Sir, that the Bill may kindly be sent to a Select Committee and the Select Committee may kindly be asked to complete its deliberations in the next session.'[19] This was not an unusual demand because the Rajya Sabha had previously referred the Patents (Amendment) Bill, 1995 to a Select Committee as well. But the circumstances in 1998 were very different. Parliament was now debating this bill under the direct threat of WTO-authorized trade sanctions. Another left-wing MP, Biplab Dasgupta, though, argued, 'even if we fail to meet the deadline, is it that the heaven is going to fall on us? We violated this part of the agreement in 1995, when we allowed the Ordinance to lapse.'[20] A resolution moved by the left-wing MPs for referring the bill to a Select Committee was eventually defeated in the Rajya Sabha.[21]

Other members of the opposition, notably the Congress party, staunchly supported the bill. In fact, the strongest argument favouring the Bill came not from the BJP, but from a Congress MP, Kapil Sibal, also a successful lawyer. In his speech in Parliament, Sibal explained that the Bill was balanced and had enough safeguards to protect India from possible negative repercussions of the EMR system. Sibal explained the procedure that the patent office would have to follow before granting an EMR, that is, each mailbox application would be scrutinized by the patent office for compliance with Section 3 of the Patents Act, which listed unpatentable subject matter, and also Section 2(1)(j), which defined 'invention'. With the many safeguards in TRIPS, and the provisions of Indian patent law that allowed for compulsory licensing of EMRs, Sibal assured, the bill would protect public interest.[22]

Sibal's speech was admired and praised by many in the Parliament, especially by BJP MPs. For instance, Arun Shourie, a former editor-in-chief of the *Indian Express*, a known supporter of free market trade, and by then, a BJP MP, stated, 'it is a great pleasure to follow Mr. Kapil Sibal's educated exposition of this provision. With what he has said, I doubly endorse and warmly endorse this Bill'.[23] Shourie then proceeded to present an eloquent defence of the WTO Agreement. With great clarity, he explained how the WTO Agreement had insulated India from trade sanctions by the US after the Pokhran nuclear tests. Before the WTO Agreement, the US could have hurt India economically by prohibiting or imposing higher tariffs on Indian imports, but now, the US was prohibited from taking unilateral action on issues of trade covered under the agreement. He also informed the Parliament that there were lucrative benefits for India, and that because of the WTO Agreement, Indian textile exports had risen three to four times.[24] In the vote that followed the debate on 22 December 1998, the Rajya Sabha passed the Patents (Amendment) Bill, 1998. Even before the Bill could be voted on by the Lok Sabha, the Government of India surprisingly promulgated the Patents (Amendment) Ordinance, 1999 on 8 January 1999.[25]

A few months later, in March, the Lok Sabha, too, passed the bill, but with relatively more resistance. Several MPs were upset with the government for having adopted the ordinance route again, while others disliked the Indian government's caving into pressure from the US. Congress MP Jaipal Reddy accused the government of not having 'the political will and the moral stamina to discuss a Bill with the Government of the United States' and questioned whether the BJP-led government was really a 'sovereign Government'.[26] To drive home his point of how India should place domestic interests over international obligations, Reddy cited instances of the US having made it clear that its domestic law was superior to WTO law. Pointing out to unilateral actions by the US, he told the House that:

> A big trade war has broken out between the most like-minded allies, between the two biggest trade partners, the European Union and America. And it revolves [a]round only 500 million dollars. It does not entail billions of dollars. The United States has not cared to go to [the] WTO. It has unilaterally decided to impose sanctions against the European Union. The point I am trying to make is that when it comes to [the] United States, [the] WTO is helpless. Just as in political and military matters the United States overtakes the United Nations, in commercial matters the United States, overtakes the WTO.[27]

Other MPs opposed the Bill for reasons ranging from a lack of consultation with state governments, to simple arguments of economic nationalism. Possible increase in drug prices and harm to the domestic pharmaceutical industry due to the bill were also discussed. The most-cited reason for opposition was that India was enacting this law under pressure from developed countries and the WTO system. Members of Parliament from the communist parties staged a walkout in protest before the bill was put to vote, accusing the government of supporting an 'anti-national' legislation.[28] But the majority of the members present in the Lok Sabha passed the bill, and the Patents (Amendment) Act, 1999 came into effect from 26 March 1999. With this law, India now had EMRs, and was, therefore, compliant with its immediate obligations under TRIPS.

The Second Amendment

The Patents (Amendment) Act, 1999 was only the first of three pieces of legislation passed between 1995 and 2005, amending India's patent law to ensure TRIPS compliance. The second was the Patents (Second Amendment) Bill, 1999, introduced in the Rajya Sabha on 20 December 1999. This time, the government itself requested that the bill be referred to a JPC, comprising 10 MPs from the Rajya Sabha and 20 MPs from the Lok Sabha.[29]

The 1999 Bill was perhaps the least controversial of the three amendments to Indian patent law. Its main aim was to amend the law to ensure TRIPS compliance while incorporating all the flexibilities allowed by TRIPS. The bill made several changes: It had a new definition of the term 'invention'; expressly recognized parallel imports of patented products; introduced an exception to patent infringement in the form of what is referred to as a 'Bolar' exception, which is derived from American law, and exempts manufacturers from liability for patent infringement if they manufacture or test patented inventions with the intention to submit test data for regulatory purposes; increased the term of patents from 14 to 20 years; and deleted the 'licenses of right' provisions under which the holder of a process patent would be forced to license its patents at a royalty not exceeding four per cent.

The JPC met 39 times over the next two years and invited over 50 experts, including bureaucrats, lawyers, and activists, to depose before it. Its final report recommended several changes to the bill.[30] This JPC's most significant contribution was effectively rewriting the provisions on compulsory licensing.

Such rewriting and emphasis on compulsory licensing was deliberate. It had the same policy goals as those of the Doha Declaration on the TRIPS Agreement and Public Health, which was adopted by the WTO at its Ministerial Conference on 14 November 2001, a month before the JPC report was tabled. The Doha Declaration is considered a landmark reaffirmation of the right of WTO members to interpret TRIPS in a manner supportive of public health. Specifically, this Declaration ensured that member states could grant compulsory licences in order to protect public health.[31] This was a hard-won battle, for just before the Declaration was signed, 39 multinational pharmaceutical companies had challenged a provision of patent law in South Africa, which allowed the government to override domestic patent law in a public health emergency. South Africa claimed the provision was necessary because of the unprecedented AIDS epidemic that was killing millions of its citizens. The patent-owning pharmaceutical industry eventually withdrew its challenge after being severely criticized across the world.[32]

The JPC had been thorough in its research, analysis, and recommendations, and as a result, the parliamentary debates that followed had little to add to the content of the bill. Since the Congress party, sitting in opposition, supported this bill, it sailed through both in the Lok Sabha and the Rajya Sabha easily, and became the Patents (Second Amendment) Act, 2002.

The Third Amendment

The last and final Act of India's 10-year journey to amend its patent laws was the Patents (Amendment) Act, 2005. This was the most controversial and most debated legislation because it brought back a full-fledged product patent regime for pharmaceuticals, agrochemicals, and other technologies, after a gap of almost 35 years.

Like 1998, the political pendulum had swung again in 2004. After the general elections that year, for the first time in Indian history, the Left Front, a loose coalition of four communist parties, including the CPI(M), extended 'outside support' to another coalition, the United Progressive Alliance (UPA), led by the Congress party. The UPA did not have a large enough majority to push through legislation in the Lok Sabha without support from the communists. Since the communists had vehemently opposed all previous patent legislation, their presence in the new political dispensation had all the potential to derail India's efforts to comply with TRIPS.

To complicate matters further, India had only a small window of time for compliance. The UPA government headed by Prime Minister Manmohan Singh assumed office in May 2004, and India had to comply with TRIPS by 1 January 2005.

A first draft of the proposed amendments was submitted by the department of industrial policy and promotion (DIPP), ministry of commerce and industry, to the Cabinet, comprising senior ministers of the government, on 25 August 2004. The first draft was identical to the Patents (Third Amendment) Bill, 2003 that had been introduced in Parliament by the then BJP-led government. Parliament had dissolved before that bill could be voted on, and it lapsed. The DIPP presented the same Bill to the new UPA government in 2004. This bill proposed 68 amendments to the Patents Act, most of which were minor, with two substantial exceptions.[33]

The first major amendment was the deletion of Section 5, which prohibited the grant of product patents to inventions in the fields of pharmaceuticals, agrochemicals, and other technologies. This deletion was at the heart of India's compliance with TRIPS. The second was an amendment of the pre-grant opposition mechanism that had existed in India since 1911, a decision that was surprising, because it was not required by TRIPS. Under the existing pre-grant opposition system, the patent office would first examine an application, which, if found in order, would be advertised for a four-month period, within which any 'interested person' could oppose the application. If an opposition was filed, the patent office would postpone its decision to grant the patent until the opposition was disposed of. If no one opposed the application, the patent would be granted and sealed.

Most patentees have had a long-standing grouse against the pre-grant opposition mechanism as it existed in Indian law, for it can substantially delay the grant of a patent, and increase the uncertainty for (prospective) patentees. In fact, the 1950 Patents Enquiry Committee headed by Justice Tek Chand had recommended that this provision be deleted.[34] But Justice Ayyangar, in his 1959 Report on the Revision of the Patents Law, fiercely criticized this recommendation, calling it 'retrograde'.[35] He said that an opposition system increased the quality of patents granted, which is an argument accepted even today. Over-burdened patent offices rarely have the resources or expertise to adequately scrutinize patent applications for cutting-edge technologies. When an industry competitor, who will presumably have a better understanding of the technology, is allowed to file an opposition, there is a good chance that the quality of issued patents may increase dramatically.

The proposed pre-grant opposition mechanism in the new bill significantly watered down the existing mechanism. Interested persons, it was proposed, could file 'representations' at the pre-grant stage, but such persons were not guaranteed the right to be heard. A post-grant opposition mechanism was offered instead, but it could be invoked only after a patent was granted.

Keeping with the practice of the new UPA government, the bill was referred to a Group of Ministers (GoM), a smaller subset of the cabinet. The GoM had to debate the bill and return it to the cabinet with recommendations. The cabinet would then take a final call, before introducing the bill in Parliament. The meetings of the GoM were held on 24 September 2004 and 25 October 2004 in the South Block of the Central Secretariat, which houses most of the important ministries of the Government of India. The GoM consisted of the following ministers and one special invitee: Pranab Mukherjee (holding the portfolio of Defence), Sharad Pawar (Agriculture), Kamal Nath (Commerce and Industry), Ram Vilas Paswan (Chemicals and Fertilisers and Steel), Kapil Sibal (Science and Technology), P. Chidambaram (Finance), Anbumani Ramadoss (Health), Subodh Kant Sahay (Food Processing); and special invitee Montek Singh Ahluwalia (Deputy Chairman of the Planning Commission).[36] The GoM recommended some changes, such as reinstating a compulsory right to hearing in a pre-grant opposition.[37] More importantly, the seriousness with which the bill was taken up signalled the government's intention of fully complying with TRIPS, rather than risking another complaint at the WTO.

The internal discussions within the government were easy. The difficult part would be negotiating with the communists whose support was necessary to move the bill in Parliament. The government first met the CPI(M) on 19 November 2004, when Pranab Mukherjee and Kamal Nath met the communist leaders in Mukherjee's room in Parliament House. In that meeting, the communists said they wanted certain amendments in the bill. On 1 December 2004, Sitaram Yechury, a CPI(M) leader, handed over a document about the amendments to Mukherjee, who forwarded it to commerce minister Nath, with a cover note stating that the proposals be checked for 'WTO compatibility'.[38]

Yechury's document strongly criticized the Patents (Third Amendment) Bill, 2003. It commented that the bill 'was entirely inadequate in addressing domestic concerns relating both to health care and development of the indigenous industry' and that it 'sought to reverse salutary provisions in the original Patents Act of 1970 e.g. by further diluting the provision for "pre-grant opposition"' despite there being no requirement to do so under TRIPS.[39] Appended to the document was a long list of proposed amendments that the communists believed to be 'the minimum that need[ed] to be done to safeguard national interests'.[40]

The most controversial amendment proposed by the CPI(M) was regarding Section 5. The government's bill had simply deleted the provision because it prohibited patenting pharmaceutical and agrochemical products. The CPI(M), however, proposed that Section 5 be retained in a separate form, as follows: '5(1). Patents shall be available for new inventions in all fields of technologies including pharmaceutical substances as defined in Section 2(ta), but excluding inventions stipulated in Section 3, provided that they are new, involve an inventive step and are capable of industrial applications.'[41]

The CPI(M) also proposed that 'pharmaceutical substance' be defined as including a 'new chemical entity or new medical entity involving one or more inventive steps'.

It appeared that the CPI(M) wanted to restrict patenting to only 'new chemical entities', which, in its words, would 'help restrict frivolous claims'. But why did the CPI(M) want such a restriction?

In a standard cycle of drug development, a new chemical entity (NCE) is usually discovered early on, and is the 'breakthrough' moment for the cycle, signifying potential for being developed into a marketable drug for a particular disease or condition. Once identified, an NCE is put through more rigorous testing for toxicity and efficacy. Most NCEs fail toxicity studies, that is, while they may be effective in curing a disease, they may also end up killing the patient because the compound is very toxic. New chemical entities are also put through rigorous clinical trials on human patients to determine efficacy and potential side-effects. Most NCEs fail efficacy studies too, and research on these compounds may be discontinued. At each stage of development, the NCE is modified through incremental innovation to create new formulations that either reduce toxicity or increase solubility or increase stability. A more stable drug can mean easier storage without the need for refrigeration, thus making it easier to deliver the drug to far-flung areas with poor storage facilities. Thus, each of these new formulations developed through the process of incremental innovation can be of tremendous value.[42]

In a given case, a NCE may have been invented in 1995, and patented that year. But the formulation resulting from incremental innovation on the NCE may have been synthesized (and patented) only in 1998. Thus, although the patent on the NCE expired in 2015, competitors would not be able to manufacture generic versions of the drug until 2018, when the patent on the formulation would expire.

The innovator pharmaceutical industry has argued that the process of incremental innovation on a NCE is complicated, and must be protected under law. Public health activists and the generic pharmaceutical industry, however, disagree. They contend that the discovery of the NCE marks the most significant aspect of drug discovery, and most incremental innovation, as claimed by innovator companies is trivial and obvious to a person skilled in the art. They argue that patents sought for such trivial changes merely seek to extend the period of monopoly of the patentee, and that the patent office rarely does a good job of rejecting such applications during the examination process. This practice of extending patent monopolies by claiming trivial changes to existing compounds is called 'evergreening' of patents. An extension of even a few months to the existing patent term could result in millions of dollars of profit. There is some truth to this allegation. The cost of paying a patent lawyer to file applications for trivial inventions is almost negligible when compared to the potential millions that can accrue through the exclusivity conferred if the application converts into a patent. In addition, if a single product is protected by a thicket of patents, it will raise the cost for a generic manufacturer to break through the thicket. Ideally, a competent patent office should be able to draw the line between genuine incremental innovation and frivolous evergreening. But over-worked and underpaid patent examiners are unlikely to conduct such a grueling examination.

The innovator pharmaceutical industry has faced allegations of patenting trivial or frivolous inventions since the 1950s, when US Senator Kefauver, in his capacity as the Chairperson of the Senate Sub-Committee on Antitrust and Monopoly, investigated the American pharmaceutical industry. Kefauver had tried to amend American patent law to ensure that new drugs were granted patents only if such drugs displayed a therapeutic effect 'significantly greater than that of the drug before modification'.[43] His aim was to forbid the patenting of 'me-too' drugs which had only trivial changes, and prevent 'evergreening', but his attempts failed.

By demanding that the amendments in 2005 to Indian patent law be limited to NCEs, the CPI(M) wanted to curb the practice of 'evergreening'. The one problem with the proposal of CPI(M) was that it would also prohibit incremental innovation, and possibly violate TRIPS by denying patents to incremental innovation which otherwise fulfilled the traditional criteria of patentability. The DIPP, which was tasked with examining the TRIPS compatibility of the CPI(M)'s proposal, objected to the CPI(M)'s definition of 'pharmaceutical substance' on the ground that limiting patents to NCEs would restrict 'product patents through the backdoor, and would be TRIPS violative'. There was merit in the DIPP's objection. A central feature of TRIPS was Article 27, which prohibited member states from discriminating against any specific technology sector in their national patent laws. Restricting patents to NCEs, the DIPP thought, could be viewed as discriminating against pharmaceutical inventions since several incremental innovations arising from research on NCEs would not be patentable. The DIPP specifically noted that:

Novelty, inventive step and industrial application form the internationally accepted premise of patentability of an invention. The TRIPS Agreement does not provide for exclusion of any technology, which meets these criteria of patentability. Since modification and improvement which enhance efficacy of products can also meet the criteria of patentability, it is not possible to restrict product patents to new chemical entity only.[44]

Commerce minister Kamal Nath conveyed the DIPP's objections in a letter dated 10 December 2004 to Pranab Mukherjee, the UPA's chief interlocutor with the CPI(M), in which he wrote:[45]

You will recall that during the discussions with the Left Parties it was clarified that two broad parameters would guide our approach to the draft Amendment: (a) the amendment should make the Act TRIPS compliant in a credible manner; and (b) matters that had been discussed and decided upon by the Joint Parliamentary Committee while dealing with the Second Amendment to the Bill in 2002, would not be re-opened... Of the 9 areas of concern we have been able to accommodate 4 ½ in a slightly modified form. It is, therefore proposed to incorporate suitable changes to the draft Bill which would substantially address these concerns.

Among the 4 ½ issues rejected was the CPI(M)'s demand to restrict patenting to NCEs. The CPI(M) stuck to its demand in its next round of correspondence with the government, in the form of a letter from Harkishan Singh Surjeet, the party's General Secretary, to Pranab Mukherjee, on 20 December 2004.[46] After this letter, all lines of communication between the government and the CPI(M) went silent, until the bill was introduced in Parliament.

In the meanwhile, since the 1 January 2005 deadline was drawing close, the government once again issued an ordinance, called the Patents (Amendment) Ordinance, 2004, to ensure compliance with TRIPS. This ordinance, called the Patents (Amendment) Ordinance, 2004, was in effect a copy of the Patents (Amendment) Bill, 2003, and served only to increase the woes of the government. Internationally, the ordinance was most prominently criticized by the *New York Times*, on 18 January 2005, in an editorial titled 'India's Choice',[47] where it singled out specific provisions:

Industry lobbyists managed to insert two noxious provisions in the decree that go well beyond the W.T.O. rules. The decree would limit efforts to challenge patents before they take effect. Also, it is uncomfortably vague about whether companies could engage in 'evergreening'—extending their patents by switching from a capsule to tablet, for example, or finding a new use for the product. This practice, a problem in America and elsewhere, extends monopolies and discourages innovation.

This editorial drew the attention, most unusually, of Hardeep Puri, the Ambassador to the Permanent Mission of India (PMI) at the United Nations (UN), and a diplomat who had no role to play in India's intellectual property (IP) policy. In a remarkably well-articulated letter of 1 February 2005, addressed to the DIPP Secretary, Ambassador Puri warned, '[c]riticism of the Ordinance by what is arguably the most influential western newspaper—the *New York Times*—has to be taken seriously'. He discussed two issues identified by the editorial.[48] The *first* issue was the deletion of the pre-grant opposition mechanism. Pointing out that 'possession was nine-tenths of the law', Puri explained the importance of stopping innovator companies from getting frivolous patents in the first place, rather than providing for only a post-grant opposition, where a patent could be opposed only after already being granted. The *second* issue he highlighted was the dangers of 'evergreening' by the innovator industry. Puri informed the DIPP that 'evergreening' enables pharmaceutical patent holders to extend their patents 'by switching from a capsule to tablet, for example, or finding a new use for the product'. He concurred with the *New York Times* in claiming that the law did not do enough to combat the threat of 'evergreening'. Illustrating with an example, Puri wrote:

> A system that allows Novartis to obtain a patent in India that will guarantee Glivec an exclusive market until almost 30 years after a patent was first filed for the active ingredient in Switzerland, clearly is in need of rectification. If we include clear patentability criteria we should be able to prevent such exploitative use of our laws by the big Western pharmaceutical companies.

Offering a solution to tackle the 'evergreening' issue, Ambassador Puri recommended, '[a] clear stipulation prohibiting the patenting of different salts, hydrates, isomers, metabolites, and polymorphs, would prevent our patent system being tied up endlessly by litigation on grounds of patentability'. This recommendation was suspiciously similar to the campaign by the CPI(M) to limit patentability to only NCEs.

A few months earlier, Puri's colleague, the Indian Ambassador to the US, Ronen Sen, was passing on anonymous notes to the Cabinet Secretariat from lobbies in the US with recommendations that seemed to favour the innovator pharmaceutical industry. One such undated anonymous note from Ambassador Sen stated 'Papers left for Cabinet Secretary by Shri Ronen Sen, Indian Ambassador to the U.S.'. File notings suggest that the note was left with the Cabinet Secretariat in the last week of November, that is, before the government and the CPI(M) began negotiations on the new patent amendments.[49] The recommendations in the forwarded note called for India to allow 'second-use' patents, ensure that compulsory licensing was TRIPS compliant, clarify that importation would amount to working of a patent (that is, foreign patentees would not be penalized for not manufacturing their patented inventions in India), eliminate price as a trigger for the grant of compulsory licences, ensure data exclusivity for pharmaceuticals and agrochemicals, and finally, do away with the pre-grant opposition mechanism.[50] These demands read ominously like the wish list of the Western pharmaceutical industry. It is not clear why Ambassador Sen was pushing this agenda directly with the Cabinet Secretary without revealing the source of the note in writing.

The issue of 'importation as working' was also taken up by Montek Singh Ahluwalia, the Deputy Chairperson of the Planning Commission, again unusually so, because the Planning Commission was never deeply engaged in IP policy. Before joining the Planning Commission, Ahluwalia had worked with the International Monetary Fund (IMF) and the World Bank. He had also worked in the Indian government in the crucial years of 1990–2, when India initiated major reforms and opened its economy to international trade. Ahluwalia raised the issue of working of patents in a note to the Prime Minister's Office (PMO) on 23 November 2004 stating:[51]

> Ambassador Sen was concerned to know whether we would meet our obligations of being TRIPS compliant by January, 2005. I mentioned that while we are working to bring in legislative changes before January 1, 2005 to extend product patents to areas presently excluded, there was one important aspect in which what is currently being contemplated will not be TRIPS compliant. This is because our law allows for compulsory licensing in a situation where the patent is not being 'worked', but importation is not treated as working the patent. This is contrary to

the explicit provision in the TRIPS Agreement where importation is
regarded as working [a] patent.

Ahluwalia's conclusion was contrary to the Indian government's
negotiating position. During depositions made before the Parliamentary
Standing Committee on Commerce in 1993, with regard to the proposed
Dunkel Draft—the final negotiating text of TRIPS—India's chief
negotiator at the Uruguay Round of multilateral talks, A.V. Ganesan,
said that India would not budge from its position, that 'importation'
would not constitute working under patent law.[52] India's opposition on
the issue had its roots in the 1959 Ayyangar Committee report.[53] India
had made importation of a patented invention a ground for issuing a
compulsory licence for a patent, because most patentees were merely
importing their inventions into India, and the government wanted
to encourage domestic manufacture of such inventions. The threat
of compulsory licences was meant to encourage patentees to locally
manufacture products within India rather than in their home countries.
As was evident from the statements by India's chief negotiator before
the Parliamentary Standing Committee, this policy had not changed
even during the TRIPS negotiations, over three decades on.

Interestingly, Ahluwalia also seemed to have been unaware of a
WTO dispute that the US had initiated against Brazil on this same
question of local working requirements years ago in 2000. Both parties
settled that dispute in 2001.[54] It is speculated that the settlement took
place because the Brazilians pointed to Americans laws having the
same requirement for federally funded inventions.[55]

The negotiations with the CPI(M), the lobbying by Ambassadors
Sen and Puri, and Ahluwalia's unsolicited advice illustrate how
different powers were attempting to influence Indian IP policy. In each
case, however, bureaucrats inside the DIPP took the final call. The
only mystery that remains to be explained is the manner in which
Section 3(d) was enacted.

The Birth of Section 3(d)

The DIPP files reveal there was very little communication after
the deadlock with the CPI(M) over the inclusion of NCEs, until the

government introduced the Patents (Amendment) Bill, 2005 in the Lok Sabha on 18 March 2005. The government was under pressure to pass the bill in the budget session of Parliament because the Patents Ordinance, 2004 would lapse within six weeks from the date that Parliament reconvened, and India would once again be in violation of TRIPS.

On 17 March 2005, a day before the bill was introduced, a Director at the DIPP sent a letter to the secretary of the legislative department, ministry of law and justice, informing him that a bill to amend India's patent law has been circulated, and that 'after consultations with the concerned groups/organizations, some draft modifications are proposed in the said bill'.[56] The note concluded with a request for the Legislative Department to draft official amendments to the bill.[57]

The appended note covered six broad areas including provisions on the scope of patentability, strengthening the pre-grant opposition mechanism, and compulsory licensing. The present version of Section 3(d) as exists in the law today was included under the head of 'patentability'. The note did not bear the name of its author, and the DIPP official too had remained silent, in his accompanying note to the law ministry, on the identity of the person or entity that had presented this note. However, the portion on Section 3(d) clearly stated that it was based on a formulation suggested by Justice V.R. Krishna Iyer, 'in order to incorporate the intention of restricting the scope of patentability particularly for pharmaceutical inventions'.[58]

The revelation that Justice V.R. Krishna Iyer, a retired judge of the Supreme Court, was responsible for drafting such a provision was rather surprising, since he was a vehement critic of pharmaceutical patents. In an article published in the *Frontline* of 14–27 October 2000, Justice Iyer had stridently argued against any amendments to Indian patent law for the purpose of complying with TRIPS. He wrote:

> To manufacture cheap outside, import and sell at any price in our market *preventing by law* indigenous producers is almost a definition of colonisation by a foreign power entering India, forbid Indians making the goods but offer a monopoly market. Why concede this dog-in-the-manger strategy? This is a textbook case of the violation of Article 19(1) g and 19(6) of the Constitution. This stratagem, if legislatively approved, is a shock and shame and proof of *conquest by patent*. Articles 14 (equal

protection of the law), 19 (right to any trade or business) and 21 (right to life in good health) stand stultified if such glaring inequality between Indian products (denied patent) and foreign import of any commodity granted exclusive selling rights with no special benefit to the Indian consumer.[59]

To argue that such patents were unconstitutional in 2000, and then to draft a provision which legitimized pharmaceutical patents in 2005 was paradoxical, and raises doubts about whether Justice Iyer was the author of this draft at all. Perhaps the note credited Justice Iyer because it might have been easier to use the name of a former Supreme Court judge to convince a reluctant bureaucrat about the importance of a certain recommendation.

Admittedly, though, the revised wording of Section 3(d) was useful in curbing 'evergreening'. The revised provision created a presumption in law that all derivatives of a substance would be the same as the substance from which they were derived, unless they differed 'significantly in efficacy'. The provision also said that all salts, esters, metabolites, and isomers would be considered the same as the substance from which they were derived, unless the patent applicant could prove that such derivatives demonstrated more efficacy than the known substance. The policy imperative behind this conclusion was simple: Making derivatives of known substances and predicting their properties would be routine for a person skilled in the art, and they should not be patented unless the applicant could show that the derivative would be more efficacious than the known substance from which it was derived. Without Section 3(d), the onus would have been on the patent office to demonstrate why such derivatives were not patentable. This would have increased the workload of the patent office. With Section 3(d), the onus was on the patent applicant to establish that the derivative differed significantly with regard to efficacy, after which the application could be examined on the remaining criteria under the law.

By linking patenting to efficacy, the provision also placed a high burden on pharmaceutical patent applicants to demonstrate to the patent office the increased efficacy of their inventions. As mentioned earlier, the attempt to co-opt 'efficacy' into patent law was not without precedent. United States Senator Kefauver had tried to reform American patent law in the early 1960s, by linking the patenting of pharmaceutical inventions to efficacy demonstrated by the medication. Kefauver failed, but somebody in India had borrowed his formulation while proposing the new version of Section 3(d).

In many ways, Section 3(d) struck a balance between the demands of TRIPS and the counter-demand by domestic lobbies to restrict patenting to NCEs. As interpreted by the Supreme Court eight years later in the Novartis case, incremental innovation was allowed under Section 3(d).[60]

The law ministry replied to the DIPP on 17 March 2005, the same day it received the note, with a draft of the amendments to be introduced in Parliament. The law ministry merely cast the recommendations of the note into the proper format, and presented it to the DIPP, with the warning that the Amendment Bill contained some definitions like that of 'new invention' and 'pharmaceutical substance' despite not being used anywhere in the law.[61] It turned out that the DIPP had made an error because the CPI(M)'s recommendation for defining 'pharmaceutical substances' in Section 2 was tied to its earlier recommendation to amend Section 5 in a manner that restricted patenting to 'pharmaceutical substances'. Since the amendment to Section 5 was rejected, the DIPP should not have inserted the definition of 'pharmaceutical substance'.

That the DIPP retained both definitions, of 'pharmaceutical substance' and 'new invention' even after the law ministry pointed out the errors, is indication enough of the tearing hurry in which the government passed the Patents (Amendment) Bill, 2005. In fact, the government was in such a hurry that it invoked emergency provisions to bypass normal administrative procedures. Ordinarily, the Cabinet should have approved the DIPP's last-minute amendments to the pending legislation, but given the urgency, the DIPP wrote to the PMO seeking an exemption from this process, and the amendments were rushed directly to Parliament.[62]

The Patents (Amendment) Bill, 2005 was debated in the Lok Sabha on two days in March 2005. This debate marked a historical turnaround for both the Congress and the communist parties, both of whom had voted in 1970 for abolishing product patents for pharmaceuticals and agrochemicals, among other technologies. In 2005, the Congress was the ruling party, and the CPI(M) was supporting it in Parliament. The

BJP, now sitting on the other side, was completely opposed to the Patents (Amendment) Bill, 2005, arguing that it would raise the prices of drugs and adversely affect the Indian pharmaceutical industry.[63] The BJP's stand was baffling because it was a BJP-led Parliament that had enacted the amending patent laws in 1999 and 2002. In fact, even the Patents (Amendment) Bill, 2005 was a substantial copy of the Patents (Amendment) Bill, 2003, which was introduced in the Parliament by the BJP-led government at the time.

The CPI(M)'s decision to vote in support of the bill was particularly interesting because unlike the Congress, it had been a staunch critic of the earlier amendments and was opposed to the WTO's policies. Explaining its new stance in the Lok Sabha, CPI(M) MP Roopchand Pal said, '[w]e cannot wish away WTO. We cannot wish away TRIPS. But, our endeavour, struggle and position have all along been to derive as much benefit as possible using the flexibility clauses of the TRIPS.'[64] He then went on to highlight the demands of the CPI(M) which were accepted by the government during negotiations over the new patent amendments. Amongst the accepted amendments listed by Pal were the definitions of 'new step' and 'new invention', and stronger systems of compulsory licensing and pre-grant opposition. There was, of course, no mention of the fact that the phrase 'new invention' was not used anywhere else in the Act. The sore points that remained were the restriction of patenting to NCEs, and the prohibition of patents on microorganisms.

Commerce minister Kamal Nath informed the Parliament that the government was worried that these demands would be construed as incompatible with TRIPS. But, to reassure the CPI(M), Nath said that he would refer the issue to a group of experts.

The last-minute introduction of the amendments to Section 3(d) meant that the new avatar of the provision was hardly debated, apart from references by Nath. Reacting to concerns about the 'evergreening' of pharmaceutical patents, Nath pointed to Section 3(d), and said, '[t]here is no question of evergreening'. He did not offer any more details.[65]

Since Section 3(d) was in effect drawing a balance between the demands of TRIPS and the demand to limit patents to NCEs, it was not unrealistic to expect a detailed debate on this provision. Could it be possible that both the CPI(M) and the BJP had no understanding about the true impact of this provision? Given the haphazard manner in which Section 3(d) was rushed into Indian law, it is entirely possible that none of the MPs were aware of the true implications of this provision.

Nath's solution to create an expert committee worked, because the CPI(M) supported the bill, and it was passed by the Lok Sabha, despite protests and a walkout by members of the BJP-led National Democratic Alliance (NDA) on the ground that the bill should have been referred to a Parliamentary Standing Committee for further debate and examination.[66]

The next day, the bill was debated in the Rajya Sabha. Again, the BJP objected to the bill that they had drafted themselves, recommending that it be referred to a Parliamentary Standing Committee. When the government refused to accede to this demand, the NDA again staged a walkout in protest.[67] But the bill was passed by a majority of the remaining members, and received Presidential assent as well. (Years later, in 2009, an Expert Committee headed by the scientist Dr R.A. Mashelkar, concluded that India would have been in breach of its obligations under TRIPS if it had restricted patenting to only NCEs, and if it had prohibited patents for microorganisms. The government accepted the Committee's report.[68])

The enactment of the Patents (Amendment) Act, 2005, ended a remarkable and unprecedented era in the history of India's patent law. Patents for pharmaceutical products were back in India after 35 years. Unlike 1970, though, when India first abolished such patents, by 2005, India had a thriving generic pharmaceutical industry, which was not going to let the foreign pharmaceutical industry assert their newly minted Indian patents without fighting them out in the courtrooms.

Notes

1. Section 3 of the Patents (Amendment) Ordinance, 1994.
2. Article 123 of the Constitution provides that an ordinance is valid for six weeks from the day Parliament reconvenes after the ordinance is promulgated. Article 85 of the Constitution requires that a Parliament

session must be convened at least every six months, ordinances will ordinarily expire within seven-and-a-half months.

3. India, Rajya Sabha, *Written Answers to Government's Reaction on Dunkel's Proposals* (25 February 1992), at 90.

4. Lok Sabha, *Debate on the Patents (Amendment) Bill, 1995*, (21 March 1995), at 292.

5. Press Information Bureau (Government of India), *Intellectual Property Rights*, available at http://pib.nic.in/feature/fe0199/f2001993.html (Last visited on 26 March 2015).

6. See generally World Trade Organization, *Understanding the WTO: Settling Disputes*, available at https://www.wto.org/english/thewto_e/whatis_e/tif_e/disp1_e.htm (Last visited on 26 March 2015).

7. See World Trade Organization, *Chronological List of Disputes Cases*, available at https://www.wto.org/english/tratop_e/dispu_e/dispu_status_e.htm (Last visited on 26 March 2015).

8. World Trade Organization, *India—Patent Protection for Pharmaceutical and Agricultural Chemical Products*, WT/DS50/1, available at https://www.wto.org/english/tratop_e/dispu_e/cases_e/ds50_e.htm (Last visited on 26 March 2015) (request for consultation made by the US on 2 July 1996).

9. The Patents (Amendment) Ordinance, 1994 (Preamble).

10. Panel Report, *India—Patent Protection for Pharmaceutical and Agricultural Chemical Products*, WT/DS79/R (*circulated* 5 September 1997).

11. Appellate Body Report, *India—Patent Protection for Pharmaceutical and Agricultural Chemical Products*, WT/DS50/AB/R (*adopted* 16 January 1998).

12. World Trade Organization, *India—Patent Protection for Pharmaceutical and Agricultural Chemical Products*, DS79, available at https://www.wto.org/english/tratop_e/dispu_e/cases_e/ds79_e.htm (Last visited on 26 March 2015) (request for consultation made by the European Communities 28 April 1997).

13. Dispute Settlement Body, *India—Patent Protection for Pharmaceutical and Agricultural Chemical Products—Reasonable Period of Time for Implementation of the DSB's Recommendations*, WT/DSB/M/45 (10 June 1998), at 16.

14. Parliamentary Standing Committee on Commerce, India and the World Trade Organization, ¶ 21 (4 December 1998).

15. Parliamentary Standing Committee on Commerce, ¶ 21.

16. Parliamentary Standing Committee on Commerce, ¶ 22.

17. Lok Sabha, Report of the Joint Committee on the Patents Bill, 1967 28–9 (27 February 1970).

18. *U.S. Imposes Sanctions on India,* CNN, 13 May 1998, available at http:// edition.cnn.com/WORLD/asiapcf/9805/13/india.us/ (Last visited on 26 March 2015).

19. India, Rajya Sabha, *Debate on the Patents (Amendment) Bill, 1998* (22 December 1998), at 308.

20. Rajya Sabha, *Debate, 1998,* at 301.

21. Rajya Sabha, *Debate, 1998,* at 457–65 (the results of the motion on whether the bill should be sent to a Select Committee).

22. Rajya Sabha, *Debate, 1998,* at 335–49.

23. Rajya Sabha, *Debate, 1998,* at 335–49.

24. Rajya Sabha, *Debate, 1998,* at 349–62.

25. *Ordinance Gives Effect to Patents Bill Provisions,* Business Standard, 15 January 1999.

26. India, Lok Sabha, *Debate on the Disapproval of Patents (Amendment) Ordinance, 1999 and Motion for Consideration of the Patents (Amendment) Bill, 1998* (10 March 1999).

27. Lok Sabha, *Debate on the Disapproval of Patents, 1999 and Motion for Consideration, 1998* (9 March 1999).

28. Lok Sabha, *Debate on the Disapproval of Patents, 1999 and Motion for Consideration, 1998* (10 March 1999).

29. Rajya Sabha, Report of the Joint Committee on the Patents (Second Amendment) Bill, 1999 i–ii (19 December 2001).

30. Rajya Sabha, Report of the Joint Committee on the Patents (Second Amendment) Bill.

31. World Trade Organization, Ministerial Declaration of 14 November 2001, WT/MIN(01)/DEC/2, 41 I.L.M. 746 (2002) (The Doha Declaration).

32. Karen Birmingham, *South Africa vs. Big Pharma,* 7 Nature Medicine 390 (2001).

33. Government of India, Ministry of Commerce and Industry (Department of Industrial Policy and Promotion), *Note for the Group of Ministers (Proposals for Strengthening of Patents Regime and Amendments to the Patent Act, 1970)* (September 2004), available at http://www.spicyip. com/docs/GMO.pdf (Last visited on 26 March 2015).

34. Ministry of Industry and Supply, Report of the Patents Enquiry Committee, *Recommendations for Improving the Law of Patents in India,* ¶154, at 70 (1948–50).

35. Justice N. Rajagopala Ayyangar, Report on the Revision of the Patents Law 78–84 (September 1959).

36. Government of India, *Record of the Discussion of the Meetings of the Group of Ministers* (24 September 2004 and 25 October 2004), available at

http://www.spicyip.com/docs/GMO.pdf (Last visited on 26 March 2015), at 1.

37. Government of India, *Record of the Discussion of the Meetings of the Group of Ministers*, ¶6.

38. Letter Addressed to Kamal Nath (Minister of Commerce and Industry), signed by Pranab Mukherjee (Minister of Defence) (2 December 2004).

39. Letter Addressed to Kamal Nath, at 3.

40. Letter Addressed to Kamal Nath, at 3.

41. Letter Addressed to Kamal Nath, at 7.

42. See generally World Intellectual Property Organization, *Follow–on Innovation and Intellectual Property*, available at http://www.wipo.int/export/sites/www/policy/en/global_health/pdf/who_wipo.pdf (Last visited on 26 March 2015).

43. Jeremy A. Greene, *Reform, Regulation, and Pharmaceuticals: The Kefauver–Harris Amendments at 50*, 367(16) N. ENGL. J. MED. 1481 (2012).

44. Letter Addressed from Kamal Nath (Minister of Commerce and Industry) to Pranab Mukherjee (Minister of Defence) (2 December 2004), at 16.

45. Letter from Kamal Nath to Pranab Mukherjee, at 14.

46. Letter Addressed to Pranab Mukherjee, signed by Harkishan Singh Surjeet (General Secretary, Communist Party of India (Marxist)) (20 December 2004).

47. *India's Choice*, THE NEW YORK TIMES, 18 January 2005, available at http://www.nytimes.com/2005/01/18/opinion/18tues2.html (Last visited on 26 March 2015).

48. Letter Addressed to Ashok Jha (Secretary, Department of Industrial Policy and Promotion, Government of India), signed by H.S. Puri (Ambassador to the Permanent Mission of India) (1 February 2005); Prashant Reddy, *Pages from History: The Influence of the New York Times on Indian Patent Policy in 2005*, SPICYIP, 5 November 2011, available at http://spicyip.com/2011/11/pages-from-history-influence-of-new.html (Last visited on 26 March 2015).

49. Letter addressed to S.N. Menon, Secretary, Department of Commerce from Pravir Krishn, Director, Cabinet Secretariat, (December 2004), available at http://www.spicyip.com/docs/12.pdf (Last visited on 26 March 2015).

50. Prashant Reddy, *Pages from History: Ambassador Sen's Contributions to the Debate on India's New Patent Law in the Year 2005*, SPICYIP, 7 November 2011, available at http://spicyip.com/2011/11/pages-form-history-ambassador-sens.html (Last visited on 26 March 2015); Government of India, Cabinet Secretariat, *TRIPS Obligations for India:*

Third Set of Patent Act Amendments (December 2004), available at http://www.spicyip.com/docs/12.pdf (Last visited on 26 March 2015).

51. Reddy, *Pages from History: Ambassador Sen's Contributions*; Government of India, Prime Minister's Office, *Note to Secretary, Department of Industrial Policy & Promotion*, PMO.UO.No.300/1/C/1/2004-ES.I (1 December 2004), available at http://www.spicyip.com/docs/123.pdf (Last visited on 29 March 2015).

52. PARLIAMENTARY STANDING COMMITTEE ON COMMERCE, DRAFT DUNKEL PROPOSALS 35(14 December 1994).

53. AYYANGAR, REPORT, at 17.

54. World Trade Organization, *Brazil—Measures Affecting Patent Protection*, DS199, available at https://www.wto.org/english/tratop_e/dispu_e/cases_e/ds199_e.htm (Last visited on 26 March 2015).

55. Gary G. Yerkey and Daniel Pruzin, *United States Drops WTO Case against Brazil Over HIV/AIDS Patent Law*, WTO REPORTER, 26 June 2001, available at http://www.cptech.org/ip/health/c/brazil/bna06262001.html (Last visited on 29 March 2015).

56. Prashant Reddy, *Pages from History: The Mysterious Legislative History of Section 3(d)*, SPICYIP, 9 November 2011, available at http://spicyip.com/2011/11/pages-from-history-mysterious.html (Last visited on 27 March 2015); Note to the Secretary of the Legislative Department from Rajeev Ranjan, Director DIPP, (17 March 2005).

57. Reddy, *Pages from History: The Mysterious Legislative History of Section 3(d)*; Note Addressed to the Secretary of the Legislative Department by Rajeev Ranjan, Director, DIPP, (17 March 2005).

58. Note Addressed to the Secretary of the Legislative Department by Rajeev Ranjan, Director, DIPP.

59. V.R. Krishna Iyer, *Human Health and Patent Law*, FRONTLINE, 14–21 October 2000, available at http://www.frontline.in/static/html/fl1721/17210790.htm (Last visited on 27 March 2015).

60. Novartis AG v. Union of India, AIR 2013 SC 1311.

61. Note to Director, DIPP from N.K. Nampoothiry, Joint Secretary and Legislative Counsel, Ministry of Law and Justice, Legislative Department (17 March 2005).

62. Letter Addressed to B.K. Chaturvedi (Cabinet Secretary), signed by Ashok Jha (Department of Industrial Policy and Promotion) (19 March 2005).

63. Narendra Kaushik, *BJP Attacks the UPA on Patents*, ASIAN TRIBUNE, 26 March 2005, available at http://www.asiantribune.com/news/2005/03/26/bjp-attacks-upa-patents (Last visited on 27 March 2015).

64. Lok Sabha, *Debate on the Statutory Resolution Regarding Disapproval of Patents (Amendment) Ordinance, 2004 (No.7 of 2004) and the Patents (Amendment) Bill, 2005* (22 March 2005).

65. Lok Sabha, *Debate on the Statutory Resolution Regarding Disapproval of Patents (Amendment) Ordinance, 2004 and the Patents (Amendment) Bill, 2005.*

66. *Lok Sabha Passes Patents Bill amid Walkout*, THE HINDU, 23 March 2005, available at http://www.thehindu.com/2005/03/23/stories/2005 032307680100.htm (Last visited on 27 March 2015).

67. *Parliament Approves Patents Bill*, THE HINDU, 24 March 2005, available at http://www.thehindu.com/2005/03/24/stories/2005032408720100. htm (Last visited on 27 March 2015).

68. Amitabh Sinha, *Pharma Patents: Mashelkar Report Gets Centre Approval*, THE INDIAN EXPRESS, 16 August 2009.

4

NOVARTIS TRIPS OVER SECTION 3(D)

The story of Glivec can be traced to the 1960s, when two Philadelphia-based researchers—Peter Nowell and David Hungerford—discovered an abnormality in chromosome 22 in patients diagnosed with chronic myeloid leukaemia (CML). Named the Philadelphia chromosome after the city of its discovery, this was the first step in the quest for a cure for CML. In the 1970s, Janet Rowley, a researcher at the University of Chicago, demonstrated that the abnormal Philadelphia chromosome was a result of a reciprocal translocation between chromosome 9 and chromosome 22, that is, the abnormality was caused by these chromosomes exchanging genetic material with each other. This translocation resulted in the oncogene (a gene with the potential to cause cancer) called Bcr-Abl. By 1986–7, David Baltimore of the Whitehead Institute for Biomedical Research, Massachusetts Institute of Technology, and his associates discovered that Bcr-Abl made a specific tyrosine kinase, an enzyme-like substance, which caused unregulated cell division, leading to a dangerously high count of white blood cells, the main cause of death in CML patients.[1]

Once the cancer-causing enzyme was identified, the challenge was to identify a cure that would act only on the cancer-causing enzyme, without disrupting any surrounding kinases that were necessary for cells to survive and grow. This had never before been achieved in the history of humankind's battle with cancer.

In 1988, Ciba-Geigy Corporation, which would later merge with Sandoz to form Novartis in 1996, had two scientists—Nick Lydon and Alex Matter—leading the company's efforts to find an inhibitor for the tyrosine kinase that caused CML. Matter was the head of Ciba-Geigy's newly created Oncology Unit in Basel. Lydon, who headed the tyrosine kinase programme in Matter's division, met Brian Druker at the Dana-Farber Cancer Institute, while searching for new collaborations. Druker suggested to Lydon that Bcr-Abl would be the ideal target for a new drug. If Lydon's team could inhibit the kinase function in the Bcr-Abl gene, they could possibly have a cure for CML.[2]

Once the decision had been taken to develop a kinase inhibitor that would specifically target the Bcr-Abl gene, the task of screening and testing potential candidates was given to two other scientists at Ciba-Geigy—Jurg Zimmermann, a medicinal chemist and Buchdunger, a cell biologist.[3] Zimmermann was to design potential compounds that would inhibit the Bcr-Abl kinase, and send them to Buchdunger, who would test the compounds in her biological assay laboratory. The task before Zimmermann and Buchdunger was not easy. They had to identify a compound that targeted *only* the Bcr-Abl kinase, and not the other kinases necessary for regulated cell division in the human body. After testing several compounds between 1990 and 1993, the Ciba-Geigy team delivered four compounds in August 1993 to Druker, who went on to perform protein, cell, and animal studies based on certain models that he had developed.[4]

Of the four compounds, Druker informed the team at Ciba-Geigy in February 1994 that STI-571 was the most promising candidate since it had a good inhibitory effect on leukaemia cells without too many side effects on normal cells. This compound eventually came to be known as imatinib. Ciba-Geigy Corporation filed a patent application for this compound and all its known forms in 1994, naming Zimmermann as the sole inventor, with a priority date going back to 1992, meaning that the compound had been identified in 1992.[5]

This was the first step of a very long journey to drug development. Imatinib would still have to go through animal studies, and clinical trials on human beings, before it could be validated for human use. Even before the riskiest stage—that of human clinical trials—could begin, the commercial viability of continuing with the development of the drug had to be assessed. Chronic Myeloid Leukaemia was a relatively rare disease in the United States (US), with approximately 5,000 people diagnosed every year in that country. Would the cost and the risk of the clinical trials of this drug be justified by potential future sales? At this stage, Druker appeared to have convinced Ciba-Geigy to go ahead with clinical trials on human beings.[6]

Several changes and modifications later, the beta crystalline form of imatinib mesylate was finally identified as the preferred candidate for clinical trials. This version was christened Glivec, and Novartis filed a patent application on 18 July 1998, with a priority date of 18 July 1997, for this form of the drug, naming Zimmermann and two others as its inventors.[7] Phase III clinical trials on patients with CML began towards the end of 1998. Phase III clinical trials are usually the most difficult phase of clinical trials because the drugs are tested on patients suffering from the disease that the drug is supposed to cure. A majority of potential drug candidates fail at this stage.

The clinical trials of Glivec on CML patients, led by Druker, were a spectacular success: Out of 54 patients, 53 showed complete hematologic response within the first four weeks of therapy, that is, the white blood cell count had returned to normal in all but one patient. The first five-year survival rate study of the drug published in 2006 showed that after 60 months, 89 per cent of Glivec's patients had survived, a dramatic increase from the 30 per cent five-year survival rate of CML patients before Glivec was available. Side effects were also reported to be minimal when compared to other therapies.[8] Glivec was clearly a stunning breakthrough in the centuries-old battle against cancer.

For the first time ever, a dangerous cancer like CML had been transformed into a manageable chronic disease. Glivec gave several thousand patients worldwide a new lease of life. *Time* magazine carried 'Glivec' on its cover, calling the drug a 'bullet' in the war against cancer.[9] It marked a revolutionary new approach to cancer therapy, where a treatment had succeeded in 'switching off' the faulty enzyme causing cancer.

Such innovation, though, always comes with a price tag. In Glivec's case, the pricing issue invited criticism even from Druker, a key person responsible for its success.[10] The question that bothered many was simple: How do you place a price-tag on a life-saving drug?

Like other businesses, drug companies do not always price a new drug in relation to the cost of its manufacture or research; instead, they peg it to the price that a consumer (that is, a patient), is willing to pay to enjoy the drug's benefits. For a life-saving drug like Glivec, essential for all patients diagnosed with CML, Novartis thought that a fair price would be USD 90,000 for a year's worth of treatment. It marked the beginning of a new age of cancer drugs that would be priced at astronomical rates. Pharmaceutical companies said these prices were justified because research was expensive and risky, and successful drugs paid for not only the cost incurred for their development, but also the cost of failed drugs. Patient groups, obviously, thought otherwise. They argued that prices charged by companies like Novartis were unethical, immoral, and unrealistic, especially in poorer countries.[11]

In developing countries like India, the lack of medical insurance coupled with Novartis' disinclination to reduce the drug price in proportion to Indian per capita income denied any praise of Novartis for its contribution in the development of Glivec. Instead, the pricing controversy fuelled a 10-year long patent battle that would test the boundaries of India's newly minted patent law. Novartis faced-off with the Indian government, and also India's largest generic pharmaceutical companies like Cipla, Ranbaxy, Natco, and Hetero, all of which sold the generic version of Glivec at a fraction of the cost. Alongside the generic manufacturers was the Cancer Patients Aid Association (CPAA), a non-governmental organization (NGO) representing the community of cancer patients, which would play just as important a role as the generic pharmaceutical industry in taking on pharmaceutical patents and protecting vital drugs like Glivec.

The First Round of Litigation

India's obligation under the Agreement on Trade-Related Aspects of Intellectual Property Rights (TRIPS) to recognize pharmaceutical inventions began in 1995. As a result, India was not required to extend patent protection to imatinib, which was a new chemical entity (NCE) discovered in 1992. Any generic drug manufacturer could have manufactured imatinib, except that it would have been of no use since imatinib itself could not be administered to patients. The drug sold to patients as Glivec was a derivative of imatinib, in the beta crystalline polymorphic form of imatinib mesylate. Since this crystalline form was discovered in 1997, India was obliged under TRIPS to protect this form of the drug, so long as it met the requirements of Indian patent law. India had introduced a system of exclusive marketing rights (EMRs) to provide transitional protection until it completely abolished prohibitions against the patenting of pharmaceutical products in 2005. Exclusive marketing rights were patent-like rights that the Government of India had been forced to create, after it lost a legal dispute before the World Trade Organization (WTO) on complaints filed by the US and the European Communities (EC). This complaint, discussed in detail in Chapter 3 of this volume, was regarding India's failure to enact transitional measures as required by Article 70 of TRIPS. The EMR system would exist only till 2005, after which the same patent application would be examined under India's new patent law, which would be enacted that year.

In 2003, the Indian Patent Office examined patent application number 1602/MAS/1998 filed by Novartis for the beta crystalline form of imatinib mesylate, that is, Glivec, and decided to grant Novartis an EMR for Glivec. This did not stop India's generic pharmaceutical industry from manufacturing generic versions of Glivec. Before long, the market was flooded with generic versions of Glivec being sold at a fraction of the cost charged by Novartis. A legal showdown in Indian courts between Novartis and the generic industry was inevitable. Novartis sued the Indian generics in the High Courts of Madras and Bombay.

A judge of the Madras High Court granted Novartis an ex parte interim injunction against six generic pharmaceutical companies (Ranbaxy, Cipla, Sun, Intas, Hetero, and Emcure). In other words, he restrained the generics from infringing the EMR for Glivec, without giving these companies an opportunity to defend themselves. (It is disturbing to note that some Indian high courts, especially the Delhi High Court and Madras High Court, are in the habit of regularly meting out interim injunctions without giving the other side a hearing.[12]) The first ex parte injunction was granted on 20 January 2004. The generics later requested the court to 'vacate', or remove, the injunction, but this did not work out in their favour. After hearing both parties, the judge passed another order in April 2004, making absolute the interim injunction against the six generic pharmaceutical companies.[13]

This meant that the generics companies could not manufacture the drug until the trial concluded.

On appeal, a Division Bench of the Madras High Court upheld the order in December 2004. Appearing before the Division Bench, Novartis gave an undertaking that it would supply Glivec free to any Indian citizen earning less than Rs 336,000 per month, under its charitable programme called Glivec International Patient Access Program (GIPAP). This undertaking significantly influenced the decision of the Madras High Court, because the strongest argument put forth by the generics was that patients would be adversely affected if they did not have access to the cheaper generic versions.[14]

The second infringement suit filed by Novartis against Natco and Meher Pharma before the Bombay High Court did not go as smoothly. Unlike the Madras High Court, the Bombay High Court did not grant an ex parte interim injunction and instead heard both the parties. Here too, Novartis tried to convince the Bombay High Court that the GIPAP would take care of 'public interest'. But the generics successfully argued that there were substantial doubts about the validity of the EMR granted to Novartis for Glivec. They referred to a Canadian patent application filed by Novartis in 1993 for imatinib, which had allegedly also claimed its various salt forms, and argued that there was no invention after 1995. As a result, the Bombay High Court, in a judgment dated 23 December 2004, declined to grant an injunction and allowed the matter to proceed to trial.[15]

Two judges in different high courts had come to completely opposite conclusions on the same facts. This was a sign of the difficulty being faced by Indian courts in handling this relatively new area of law.

The Novartis Patent Application for Glivec

A few months after the judgments of the Bombay and Madras High Courts, the Patents (Amendment) Act, 2005 was enacted. This amendment reinstated a product patent regime for pharmaceuticals. Section 5 of the older law, which prohibited the grant of product patents for certain technologies, was deleted. This amendment also introduced the present avatar of Section 3(d), which, as discussed in

Chapter 3 of this volume, was the result of a last minute amendment. It was introduced as a safeguard against 'evergreening', a rent-seeking practice by which pharmaceutical companies extend their patent monopolies over already-patented drugs by claiming protection for frivolous or trivial changes to existing formulations. The new Section 3(d) prohibited the patenting of derivatives of known substances, unless the new form demonstrated more 'efficacy' than the original substance from which it was derived. The provision also came with an 'explanation', clarifying that certain forms such as esters, isomers, polymorphs, etc., would, by default, be regarded as the same as the known substance itself, unless they demonstrated improved 'efficacy'.

The word 'efficacy' in Section 3(d) caused panic in the innovator pharmaceutical industry, especially amongst the Americans who had fought against the inclusion of the same word in US patent law by Senator Kefauver in the 1960s.[16] A key concern was that 'efficacy' was a concept associated with regulatory law. In the regulatory sense, a drug cannot be sold in the market unless it clears safety and efficacy requirements mandated by drug safety laws. Such approval is usually granted only after several rounds of clinical trials provided the drug has cured a disease. Patent law, as practiced then and now in most developed countries, does not require an assessment of the 'efficacy' of a drug in the regulatory sense. A patent applicant is not expected to demonstrate to the patent office that the drug it claims is safe and effective on human beings. Instead, the practice is to grant patents to any invention that has passed the three-step test of novelty, inventive step, and industrial applicability. The third step, of judging industrial applicability, does require the patent office to determine whether the claimed invention can be used by industry, but the threshold to meet this requirement is quite low. Most pharmaceutical patentees usually submit some data generated in a laboratory demonstrating the expected effect of the drug in laboratory tests, but this data is not comparable to the clinical trial data submitted to a drug regulator for approval. Indian courts were left to grapple with the interpretation of efficacy in patent law, with no equivalent concept in any other patent law system in the world.

Besides these concerns, the innovator pharmaceutical lobby also flagged the TRIPS compatibility of Section 3(d), contending that an 'efficacy' requirement would go beyond Article 27 of TRIPS. This provision of TRIPS defined the patentability criteria in terms of novelty, inventive step, and industrial application. By prescribing 'efficacy' as an additional ground, it was argued, Section 3(d) ran the risk of violating TRIPS.

There were also practical issues with the requirement to demonstrate 'efficacy', because patent applications are typically filed much before any 'efficacy' data (in the regulatory sense of Phase III clinical trials) is generated. In the case of Glivec, the patent application was filed in 1997 for the beta crystalline form of imatinib mesylate, but the clinical trials concluded only in 2001.

Despite being poorly drafted, Section 3(d) is a clever provision. It draws a fine line between 'evergreening' which is an undesirable practice, and 'incremental innovation' which is how most innovations take place in the pharmaceutical industry. Typically, pharmaceutical companies first patent a NCE, and then patent every derivative of that NCE on the ground that each derivative was the result of incremental innovation that required investment and effort by the innovator. The resulting drug could be protected by a thicket of patents, one for the NCE and several more for each derivative. Each extra patent could push the period of exclusivity over the final drug and make it more expensive for generics to break through the patent thicket.

In Glivec's case, the NCE was imatinib, which was not patentable in India because it was invented in 1993, two years before the cut-off date for TRIPS. Since the beta crystalline form of imatinib mesylate (the only form in which it could be administered on patients) was invented only in 1997, Novartis filed a patent application for it only in 1998, and once granted, the term of the patent would have extended till 2018.

Public health activists and generic companies argue that derivatives of NCEs, such as polymorphs or salt forms, are trivial inventions not worthy of patent protection since they are obvious to a person skilled in the art. To these critics, the patent over the beta crystalline form was a classic attempt by Novartis to 'evergreen' its patent exclusivity over Glivec. On the other hand, innovator pharmaceutical companies, like Novartis, reason that making many of these derivatives involves incremental innovation that is not obvious to a person skilled in the art. The derivatives emerge as a result of innovation aimed at optimizing a drug, after it has shown basic efficacy in treating a disease. Examples of incremental innovation would be modifications to reduce the toxicity of a drug, or to increase its bioavailability, that is, the solubility of the drug in the bloodstream. A failure on either front could make it difficult to administer the drug on patients. Similarly, derivatives can result from incremental innovation aimed at ensuring better stability or hygroscopicity of drugs; both these factors determine the ability to manufacture and store drugs, and easier manufacturing or better storage can lower the costs of the final product.

Both sides of the debate make valid arguments. While pharmaceutical companies are correct in claiming that there is value in incremental innovation, it can also not be denied that some companies also claim patents for frivolous derivatives merely to extend their monopolies. The cost of paying a patent lawyer to file applications for such frivolous derivatives is negligible compared with the potential benefits of an extended monopoly over the drug. Strategically, therefore, in order to maximize profits most pharmaceutical companies will attempt to evergreen their patents.

Section 3(d) was inserted into the law precisely to make it difficult to patent such derivatives. It did so by creating a presumption under law that the derivatives of a known substance would also be known, and would therefore be unpatentable. The 'explanation' contained in Section 3(d) creates a legal fiction that salts, esters, polymorphs, etc., of a known form would be presumed to be the same as the known form and therefore, would be unpatentable. A patent applicant can refute this presumption by proving that the 'new form of the known substance' has demonstrated a significant difference in efficacy when compared to a 'known substance'. Section 3(d) effectively reversed the burden of proof, since in all other cases, the initial burden of proof to demonstrate lack of patentability lies on the patent office. To complicate matters further, Section 3(d) was conveniently vague on the contours of the various phrases used in the provision, such as 'efficacy', 'known substance', and 'differ significantly in properties with regard to efficacy'. By raising the threshold for patenting derivatives, Section 3(d) hoped to curtail 'evergreening' and make it easier for generics to enter the market faster, thus offering more competition, and reducing the prices of these medicines.

In many ways, patent application number 1602/MAS/1998 for Glivec, or to be more precise, the beta crystalline polymorphic form of imatinib mesylate, was a perfect test-case for evaluating the impact of Section 3(d). At first glance, the beta crystalline polymorphic form of imatinib mesylate—the claimed crystalline form—appeared to fall within the 'explanation' contained in Section 3(d), which clarified that 'polymorphs' of a 'known substance' would be presumed to be the same as the 'known substance'. Thus, the burden fell on Novartis to prove that the new form demonstrated a significant difference in efficacy in comparison to the 'known form' from which it was derived. This application became the first test case for Section 3(d) when it was taken up for examination by the patent office.

The Pre-grant Oppositions

The EMR system did not allow for any pre-grant opposition. But, by 2005, when the Glivec patent application came up for consideration, Parliament had reintroduced the pre-grant opposition system via the Patents (Amendment) Act, 2005. Since the EMR for Glivec had already led to litigation between Novartis and India's generic pharmaceutical companies, it was no surprise when leading generics like Cipla, Natco, Ranbaxy, and Hetero filed pre-grant oppositions against patent application number 1602/MAS/1998. A fifth opposition was filed by the patient group, the CPAA, which marked the beginning of a concerted engagement by NGOs with the patent system. All these oppositions were filed between May and September 2005.

The opponents challenged the patent application on several grounds including anticipation or lack of novelty, lack of inventive step, and the lack of increase in efficacy under Section 3(d). The first two concepts are as old as patent law itself. 'Anticipation' means that the claimed invention is not new or novel as of the priority date, because it has either been disclosed in prior art or has been publicly used; and a 'lack of inventive step' means that the claimed invention is obvious to a person skilled in the art as of the priority date.

After conducting hearings on 14 October 2005 and 15 December 2005, the Assistant Controller of Patents and Designs at the Indian Patent Office in Chennai passed near-identical six-page orders on 25 January 2006 in each pre-grant opposition, rejecting Novartis' patent application on the grounds of anticipation, obviousness, and lack of efficacy under Section 3(d).[17] The orders, however, were poorly reasoned. To be fair to the patent office, this was the first pharmaceutical product patent application that it was examining in more than 35 years, and it was hardly equipped to handle such complex questions, especially since most of the staff, including Controllers who take the decision to grant or reject patents, lacked legal training. For Novartis and the rest of the innovator pharmaceutical industry, the most alarming part of the decision was the ruling on Section 3(d).

The opponents had argued that the patent application was hit by Section 3(d) since the beta crystalline polymorph of imatinib mesylate was a derivative of a known substance, which had failed to demonstrate increased efficacy when compared to the known substance. On the other hand, Novartis defended its invention as being more efficacious than its known forms since it demonstrated 30 per cent more bioavailability than the imatinib free base. As mentioned earlier, bioavailability refers to the ability of a medicine to dissolve in the bloodstream. The better the bioavailability of a medicine, the lesser the quantity required to be administered on a patient. As the amount of medicine administered to a patient is reduced, its side-effects are also likely to be reduced, although reduced side-effects are not always guaranteed.

From the Controller's orders, though, it was not clear if Novartis had made the logical extension that increased bioavailability would lead to an increase in efficacy. In any case, the Controller was not satisfied with the explanation offered by Novartis, noting that the company did not give any proof of significant enhancement of known efficacy. Strangely, the Controller did not explain this further. For example, why was a 30 per cent increase in bioavailability not an increase in efficacy; what would qualify as an increase in efficacy; or how much of an increase in bioavailability would qualify as an increase in efficacy? The Controller's order, not being well-reasoned, gave Novartis a strong ground to appeal.

The Aftermath of the Rejection

After being rejected by the patent office, Novartis had a right under law to file an appeal before the Intellectual Property Appellate

Board (IPAB). But there was a slight problem. The IPAB had been created under the Trade Marks Act, 1999, with its primary purpose being to hear cases pertaining to trademark law. In 2002, the patent law amendment required the IPAB to hear appeals from the patent office. But the government still had to publish an official notification authorizing the IPAB to hear such cases, and also provide the IPAB with the staff to start hearing such cases. The administrative unpreparedness of the central government was alarming. As a result, Novartis filed its appeals before the Madras High Court whose judges prodded the central government to notify the IPAB for hearing appeals from the patent office. Once the notification was published, the appeal by Novartis was transferred to the IPAB.

While the appeal against the Controller's decision was expected, Novartis, unexpectedly, also filed a writ petition challenging the constitutionality of Section 3(d) before the Madras High Court. The petition asked the court to declare the provision to be inconsistent with India's requirements under TRIPS, and violative of the Constitution of India. The decision to challenge the constitutionality of Section 3(d) was a monumental public relations blunder. It was perhaps similar to a fatal move made by a group of 39 pharmaceutical companies in South Africa, challenging the constitutionality of that country's new patent law in 1997. The South African challenge was eventually withdrawn, and universally acknowledged to be a public relations disaster for the innovator pharmaceutical industry often referred to as 'Big PhRMA', which expands into Pharmaceutical Research and Manufacturers of America.[18]

Novartis' constitutional challenge angered public health activists. They portrayed the challenge as the desperate gambit of a greedy multinational company which wanted to overturn a law enacted by a sovereign Indian Parliament with the intent of protecting public health.[19]

The Constitutional Challenge before the Madras High Court

Under Indian constitutional law, a parliamentary law can be struck down for one of two reasons—if it violates the fundamental rights assured under Part III of the Constitution, or if the legislature that made the law lacked the competence to enact the law under the constitution. Here, there was no question of Parliament not having the competence to enact a patent law, since the Seventh Schedule to the Constitution, which demarcates the legislative fields of Parliament and the state legislatures, clearly allocates the subject of patents to Parliament. Instead, Novartis argued that Section 3(d) violated the right to equality under Article 14 of the Constitution of India for being vague, arbitrary, and conferring unfettered powers on the patent office. Under the Indian law, whenever Parliament delegates certain decision-making powers to the executive (in this case, the patent office), it must provide the executive with the parameters to exercise the power. If a law delegates unfettered powers to the patent office, it is in effect delegating legislative functions to the patent office.[20] In addition, Novartis made the novel argument that Section 3(d) violated India's obligations under TRIPS, by prescribing criteria over and above the minimum patentability requirements in Article 27 of TRIPS.

The Article 14 Challenge against Section 3(d)

Article 14 is arguably the most important provision of the Constitution of India since it guarantees the fundamental right to equality. It ensures that the State shall not deny any person 'equality before the law or the equal protection of the laws within the territory of India'.[21]

Traditionally, the Supreme Court of India has used the test of 'reasonable classification' to determine whether a law or executive action violates Article 14. Under the 'reasonable classification' test, the State can apply the law differently to different classes of persons, provided there is a reasonable basis to distinguish between the two classes of persons, and at the same time, there is a rational nexus between the classification and the aim of the law or executive action. Take, for example, the reservation policy, mandated for historically discriminated classes of persons, in government jobs or public educational institutions. The reservation policy survives the reasonable classification test since there is a rational basis for the classification, that is, some classes of people are socially and economically disadvantaged, and also because the classification bears direct nexus to the aim of the State to uplift the social and economic status of historically disadvantaged persons. With time, the Supreme Court's interpretation of the right to equality under Article 14 has evolved considerably. In the landmark case of *E.P. Royappa* v. *State of Tamil Nadu*[22] decided by the Supreme Court in 1974, the concept of equality was described by Justice Bhagwati in the following, oft quoted lines:

> Equality is a dynamic concept with many aspects and dimensions and it cannot be 'cribbed cabined and confined' within traditional and doctrinaire limits. From a positivistic point of view, equality is antithetic to arbitrariness. In fact equality and arbitrariness are sworn enemies; one belongs to the rule of law in a republic while the other, to the whim and caprice of an absolute monarch. Where an act is arbitrary it is implicit in it that it is unequal both according to political logic and constitutional law and is therefore violative of Art. 14.

This interpretation allowed the Supreme Court to strike down arbitrary actions of the State on the ground that it violated the right to equality under Article 14. Eminent jurists like H.M. Seervai have criticized this interpretation, arguing that it has no basis in the language of Article 14 and that it 'hangs in the air'.[23]

When Novartis decided to challenge Section 3(d), therefore, two interpretations of Article 14 were on offer—the reasonable classification test, and the arbitrariness test. Of the two, Novartis had almost no hope of succeeding under the traditional 'reasonable classification' doctrine because the State would have convincingly argued that there was a reasonable basis for treating pharmaceutical inventions differently from other inventions. Instead, Novartis contended that the wording of Section 3(d) was so vague that it was arbitrary and thus violative of Article 14. This contention pivoted on the use of 'efficacy', and significant difference in efficacy. Since both phrases were undefined in the law, Novartis said that the law granted unfettered discretion to the patent office, and opened the door to arbitrary application of Section 3(d).[24]

In its final judgment, the Madras High Court refused to strike down Section 3(d) as unconstitutional. On the lack of legislative guidance regarding the interpretation of 'efficacy', the court ruled that the principles of statutory interpretation allowed courts and other authorities to depend on dictionaries to interpret terms not otherwise defined in the law. The High Court then referred to Dorland's Medical Dictionary, which defined 'efficacy' in the field of medicine as essentially therapeutic efficacy, that is, the ability of the drug to cure a disease. On the lack of guidelines to quantify a significant difference in efficacy, the Government of India told the court that it was impossible for Parliament to provide any specific formula, and that it was better to provide the patent office with some amount of discretion to interpret Section 3(d). The High Court accepted this argument, and held that Section 3(d) provided the patent office with enough guidance to exercise its powers in a non-arbitrary fashion.

The TRIPS Compliance of Section 3(d)

The other issue raised by Novartis was whether Section 3(d) was compliant with TRIPS. The question of TRIPS compatibility should ordinarily have been brought before the Dispute Settlement Body (DSB) of the WTO. But under WTO law, only a member state can file such a challenge. In this case, the Government of Switzerland (the parent country of Novartis) did not take India to the WTO over Section 3(d). Novartis then pursued this challenge under Indian law itself.

Novartis argued that Article 51(c) and Article 253 of the Indian Constitution required Parliament to ensure that Indian law complied with its international obligations, and that a parliamentary legislation which violated the country's international obligations could be declared unconstitutional. Novartis said that Section 3(d) was incompatible with India's obligations under TRIPS, because the provision prescribed a test of 'efficacy', which was over and above the three-step patentability test (of novelty, inventive step, and utility) prescribed by Article 27.1 of TRIPS.[25]

This argument was creative, but was also doomed to fail, because the Supreme Court had, in the past, held that national law enacted by Parliament was always superior to international law.[26] In the event of a conflict, the Supreme Court required a harmonious construction between national and international law. If the conflict were irreconcilable, national law would prevail. The justification for this is fairly straightforward: The political executive can sign international treaties on India's behalf, but the elected representatives in Parliament, who are the ultimate source of power in a democracy, can overrule the international commitments made by the political executive. TRIPS was a textbook example of such a scenario. The Indian government had signed TRIPS as part of the WTO package without the prior authorization of Parliament, so when Parliament enacted Section 3(d) as part of the Patents (Amendment) Act, 2005, logically, parliamentary law would overrule any international commitments made by the political executive.

The Madras High Court took a simpler approach towards this aspect of the Novartis challenge, based on principles of contract law. It compared TRIPS to an international contract, and since the contract mandated a dispute resolution mechanism in the form of the DSB, the Madras High Court concluded that the DSB was the appropriate forum for Novartis to approach. As a result, the Madras High Court refused to examine the issue of TRIPS compatibility.[27]

The Impact of the Madras High Court's Ruling

The generic industry and public health activists cheered the Madras High Court's judgment, delivered on 6 August 2007 dismissing the constitutional challenge to Section 3(d).[28] Reacting to the High Court's judgment, the Director of the Médecins Sans Frontières' (MSF) Campaign for Access to Essential Medicines, Tido von Schoen-Angerer said, '[t]he court's decision now makes Indian patents on the medicines that we desperately need less likely. We call upon multinational drug companies and wealthy countries to leave the Indian Patents Act alone and stop pushing for ever stricter patent regimes in developing countries'.[29] Paul Herrling, Head of Corporate Research at Novartis, on the other hand, expressed his disappointment at the High Court's ruling: 'It is clear there are inadequacies in Indian patent law that will have negative consequences for patients and public health in India... Medical progress occurs through incremental innovation. If Indian patent law does not recognise these important advances, patients will be denied new and better medicines.'[30]

In a sense, Novartis had exited the constitutional challenge worse off than they were before, since the Madras High Court expressly defined 'efficacy' in Section 3(d) as 'therapeutic efficacy'—an interpretation that would prohibit patents for those forms of incremental innovation, which, though inventive, did not increase 'therapeutic efficacy'. An example of such an invention would be a new salt form that is more stable or that demonstrates other properties, which make it easier to manufacture the drug in question.

The IPAB Judgment

Although Novartis lost the constitutional challenge before the Madras High Court, it was yet to argue its appeal against the decision of the patent office to reject its patent application over the beta crystalline form of imatinib mesylate. As explained earlier, the appeal was originally filed before the Madras High Court, since the IPAB had not been notified to hear appeals under the Patents Act, 1970. Reprimanded by the High Court, the Government of India moved quickly to ready the IPAB for hearing patent appeals. The former Controller General of Patents was appointed as a member of the IPAB bench designated to hear this appeal. He was appointed because the Patents Act required the appointment of a technical member, who was either a former Controller of Patents or a Patent Agent, to sit on a bench with a judicial member. Novartis objected to the appointment of the former Controller General of Patents since it feared bias,[31] because he headed the patent office when its patent application was rejected in the pre-grant opposition. After a series of petitions and appeals all the way up to the Supreme Court, Novartis and the government reached a compromise under which a serving Controller from the Kolkata Patent Office was temporarily deputed to the IPAB for hearing only the appeal filed by Novartis.[32] This arrangement flew in the face of constitutional propriety, especially the fundamental principles of separation of powers and judicial independence, as a serving member of the executive was being deputed to what was meant to be an independent judicial tribunal. But Novartis agreed to this arrangement and argued its appeal before this bench of the IPAB. The IPAB delivered its judgment on 26 June 2009.

Unlike the Controller of Patents who delivered six-page orders in each of the five pre-grant oppositions, the IPAB delivered an elaborate consolidated judgment of over 143 pages with detailed reasoning.[33] On three issues—anticipation, obviousness, and the dispute over the priority date—the IPAB ruled in favour of Novartis, overruling the Controller's findings in the pre-grant opposition. On two other issues, the IPAB ruled against Novartis—the contentious Section 3(d), and a last-minute surprise, Section 3(b).

With regard to Section 3(d), borrowing from the Madras High Court's judgment, the IPAB used the same Dorland's Medical Dictionary to interpret 'efficacy' to mean only 'therapeutic efficacy'. It then concluded that the beta crystalline polymorph of imatinib mesylate was the same as imatinib mesylate and that both forms demonstrated the same efficacy. Novartis' argument that the beta crystalline form demonstrated 30 per cent more bioavailability was also rejected by the IPAB on the ground that bioavailability was different from therapeutic efficacy.

The 'surprise' sprung upon Novartis was Section 3(b) of the Patents Act. This section prohibits the grant of patents for inventions whose use or commercial exploitation would be contrary to public order or morality. This provision is found in patent laws around the world, but is rarely used. The Indian Patent Office reportedly once used this provision to refuse a patent for an invention making medicinal powder from the skeletal remains of dead bodies dug up within a week of burial.[34] In that case, the patent office had said that digging graves for commercial profit was highly objectionable and against public morality. In Europe, this morality clause has been used to refuse patents for stem-cell related inventions, since they would have been created through the destruction of human embryos.[35] The IPAB used this provision to refuse a patent for Glivec citing the high cost of the drug, which, according to the IPAB, the poor in India could not afford. The IPAB reasoned: 'Thus, we also observe that a grant of product patent on this application can create havoc to the lives of poor people and their families affected with the cancer for which this drug is effective. This will have disastrous effect on the society as well.'[36] This reasoning was fundamentally flawed, because the public order and morality clause was never meant to prohibit patents for inventions on account of being too expensive. If this were the intention of Section 3(b), it would be practically impossible to grant a patent for any expensive invention.

The Appeals to the Supreme Court of India

Judgments from tribunals like the IPAB are usually appealed to the high court that has supervisory jurisdiction over that tribunal. In rare cases, the Supreme Court allows direct appeals to itself against orders of tribunals, without a high court first having heard the appeal. The IPAB's order in the Glivec case was the first-ever judicial interpretation of Section 3(d), and the case was anyway destined for the Supreme Court, because of its seminal importance. So Novartis decided to skip the appeal to the Madras High Court, and directly approached the Supreme Court through a special leave petition (SLP). The gamble paid off when the Supreme Court admitted the appeal. At the same time, Natco and the CPAA filed a series of counter-appeals before the Supreme Court against those aspects of the IPAB's order which went in favour of Novartis.

Early in the matter, there was the mysterious recusal of two Supreme Court judges from the bench designated to hear the appeals. The first recusal was that of Justice Markandey Katju, an outspoken judge, on 31 August 2009, just as the arguments began. The recusal was made without any reasons (it is customary for judges to cite a reason for recusing themselves, but not mandatory). Usually, a recusal occurs if there is a conflict of interest, or if a judge has publicly expressed views on issues that are to be decided. In this case, Justice Katju had written an article on pharmaceutical patents titled 'Intellectual Property Rights and the Challenges Faced by the Pharmaceutical Industry' in the articles section of a court publication called the 'Supreme Court Cases' in 2004.[37] The article commented on the upcoming transition to a TRIPS regime in India, and the need to balance intellectual property rights (IPRs) with the need to make drugs available to Indians at an affordable price. He had also written on the possibility of excluding certain products from patentability on grounds of being against public morality and order, noting: 'India cannot unilaterally say that it will not accept patent in a particular product or process on the ground that acceptance of the patent will be prejudicial to morality, order or the health of the Indian masses. Only if majority of other countries also make this exclusion can it do so.'[38] Effectively, Justice Katju had already publicly expressed his views on one of the issues in dispute, that is, the IPAB's interpretation of Section 3(b) holding the grant of pharmaceutical patents for expensive drugs to be against public order. This was possibly the reason for this judge's recusal from the Glivec case.[39]

The second recusal was that of Justice Dalveer Bhandari on 6 September 2011, after Novartis had already argued its appeal for several hours. The reason for Justice Bhandari's recusal was perhaps a letter petition made to the law minister on 5 September 2011 by five public health activists—Amit Sengupta of the Delhi Science Forum; B. Ekbal, former Vice Chancellor of Kerala University; M.R. Santosh from the Centre for Trade and Development; K.M. Gopakumar, a lawyer; and Prabir Purkayastha of the Knowledge Commons. This letter petition was made public through a news report in the *Times of India* on 6 September 2011, when the Supreme Court was to continue hearing arguments in the Glivec case.[40] The news article, titled 'SC Judge under Attack from Health Activists', reported that the activists had demanded 'that the government should seek Justice Bhandari's recusal as he had participated in at least two international conferences for judges organized by the US-based Intellectual Property Owners Association (IPOA), whose members include Novartis, among a host of pharmaceutical and IT giants'.[41]

The main complaint of the activists was against four sentences in a paper presented by Justice Bhandari at one of the conferences:

> Majority of pharmaceutical patents holders and IPR holders are from developed countries. They have [the] bounden duty and obligation to educate people regarding the importance of the protection of IP Rights by organizing seminars, symposia, debates on regular interval[s]. They must make all efforts to ensure that all countries are persuaded to enact

proper laws. They must also create awareness about the existing laws to the people.[42]

According to the activists, these statements by Justice Bhandari 'could be held to be in conflict with the intent and letter of the Indian Patent Act, which tries to balance the rights of patent holders (mainly from developed countries as the said paper clearly acknowledges) with the larger interests of people who are not able to access health care for economic reasons'.[43] The activists argued that since Justice Bhandari had already publicly expressed his opinion on IP, he should withdraw from the case, saying 'we ask that the government take up the matter of recusal with Hon'ble Justice Bhandari to avoid any room for questions to be raised once the judgment is given in light of the already expressed opinions on IP discussed above'.[44]

Neither the *Times of India* article nor the letter by the public health activists made a single reference to the 'Restatement of Values of Judicial Life'—a code of judicial ethics adopted by the Supreme Court on 7 May 1997.[45] This code of ethics does not bar Supreme Court judges from attending conferences funded by private parties. On the issue of expressing public opinion, the code says that, '[a] Judge shall not enter into a public debate or express his views in public on political matters or on matters that are pending or are likely to arise for judicial determination'. The paper presented by Justice Bhandari, however, was absolutely silent on the Glivec case or the possible interpretation of Section 3(d). The three sentences cited by the activists did not refer to any of the issues before the Supreme Court in the Glivec case. Justice Bhandari had merely stressed upon the importance of IP owners educating people on IP law. This statement was more axiomatic than a substantial argument, since IP literacy is poor in most countries, with many fundamentally misunderstanding even the basics of IP law. But the news report had already cast Justice Bhandari in poor light, and he withdrew from hearing the case on the same day as the article was published.[46]

With the second recusal, the Glivec case was re-assigned to a different bench of the Supreme Court, consisting of Justice Aftab Alam and Justice Ranjana Desai. This bench finally heard and rejected the Novartis appeal against the IPAB's judgment.

The Judgment and the Media Verdict

On 1 April 2013, seven years after the Glivec patent application was rejected by the patent office, the Supreme Court delivered its judgment dismissing the Novartis appeal, primarily on the ground that the claimed invention had failed to demonstrate increased efficacy as required by Section 3(d). This judgment, written by Justice Aftab Alam, ran into a hefty 112 pages.

Given the ramifications of the judgment on India's status as the 'pharmacy of the world', almost every national and international newspaper reported the judgment on its front pages. The *Hindu* ran a story under the headline 'Landmark Verdict Gives Big Boost to Cancer Patients' while the *New York Times* reported it as a victory for poor patients around the world in a front-page news item titled 'Low-cost Drugs in Poor Nations Get a Lift in Indian Court'.[47] A flood of commentary followed the media blitz, with innovators, generics, academics, bloggers, and public health activists, among many others, praising, criticizing, and critiquing the judgment. The pro-innovator lobby criticized the judgment for adopting a protectionist interpretation of Section 3(d), while jubilant public health activists praised the Supreme Court for protecting the interests of poor patients across the world by curbing evergreening of pharmaceutical patents in India.[48] *The Hindu*'s editorial titled 'A Just Order' claimed that the judgment was a 'landmark' and that '[i]t will greatly strengthen the quest for access to affordable medicines in India'.[49] An editorial in the *New York Times* described the judgment as an 'important ruling' that operated as a 'limited precedent'.[50] This meant that several issues remained open to interpretation by future courts. In other words, the future will see a lot of litigation that could have been avoided by a better-reasoned judgment from the Supreme Court.

Analysing the Supreme Court's Judgment

The Supreme Court tackled three issues in its judgment.[51]

The first issue was whether the beta crystalline form of imatinib mesylate was 'anticipated', that is, not new, in light of prior art.

In patent law, if a patent is 'anticipated', it means that the entire invention was disclosed either by publication, or by use, that predates the priority date of the patent application. The Court decided that the claimed form 'may be accepted to be new, in the sense that it is not known from the Zimmermann patent'.[52]

The second issue was whether section 3(d) applied to the facts of this case. In pertinent part, Novartis had argued that Section 3(d) required a comparison of the derivative with a known substance with known efficacy and that neither imatinib nor imatinib mesylate (which were known substances) had any known efficacy. The Supreme Court disagreed with Novartis on the grounds that prior art such as the Zimmermann patent of 1993 and an article in *Cancer Research* had established that both imatinib and imatinib mesylate had the potential to treat tumours. Thus the court held that Section 3(d) did apply to the facts of the case.

The third and last issue pertained to the interpretation of Section 3(d). (Strangely, the judgment is silent on the IPAB's interpretation of Section 3(b).) To begin with, it was necessary to identify the 'known substance' from which the beta crystalline form of imatinib mesylate was derived. This analysis was important because Section 3(d) required the court to compare the 'efficacy' of the claimed invention (in this case, the beta crystalline form of imatinib mesylate) with that of the 'known substance'. The claimed invention would pass the test contained in Section 3(d) only if the difference in 'efficacy' between the 'known substance' and the claimed invention was 'significant'.

In the case of Glivec, the dispute was whether imatinib or imatinib mesylate would be the 'known substance'. Novartis argued that imatinib should be the 'known substance', while its opponents argued that imatinib mesylate should be considered as the 'known substance'. Both sides obviously chose the substance that made it easier for them to prove or disprove increased efficacy.

Novartis argued that the imatinib free base should be presumed to be the 'known substance' because the beta crystalline form of imatinib mesylate could be derived directly from imatinib. But the Supreme Court went the other way, and held that the comparison should be between the claimed invention and imatinib mesylate. The Supreme Court justified this conclusion because Novartis had earlier 'contended that the subject product, in terms of invention, is two stages removed from Imatinib in free base, and the substance immediately preceding the subject product is Imatinib Mesylate (non-crystalline)'.[53]

When confronted with two differing arguments put forth by the same litigant, the court should have given a reason for choosing between them. Such an analysis would have helped identify an appropriate principle to interpret the phrase 'known substance' for an analysis under Section 3(d). Should 'known substance' be understood in terms of the manufacturing process, or in the sequence of innovation leading to the derived substance? Or should it be determined according to the purported legislative intent of the provision? In other words, since the provision sought to curb 'evergreening' by increasing patent terms, should the known substance always be a compound that has been claimed by a previously granted patent? Unfortunately, no such principles for identifying the 'known substance' were laid down, leaving future courts with no binding precedent to guide them on this issue.

The case should have ideally ended with this conclusion of the Supreme Court that imatinib mesylate was the known substance, since Novartis had not provided any data to compare the efficacy of imatinib mesylate with that of the claimed invention.

The Court, however, decided to also consider a scenario where imatinib was the known substance, and assess whether the claimed invention, that is, the beta crystalline form of imatinib mesylate, demonstrated more efficacy when compared with imatinib. Novartis had submitted efficacy data in this regard.

The first challenge before the court was interpreting the phrase 'efficacy'. Both the Madras High Court and the IPAB had used a medical dictionary to interpret 'efficacy' as only 'therapeutic efficacy'. The Supreme Court however used the Oxford English Dictionary to interpret 'efficacy' as follows:

> What is 'efficacy'? ... 'the ability to produce a desired or intended result'. Hence, the test of efficacy in the context of section 3(d) would be different, depending upon the result the product under consideration is desired or intended to produce. In other words, the test of efficacy would depend upon the function, utility or the purpose of the product under consideration. Therefore, in the case of a medicine that claims to cure a disease, the test of efficacy can only be 'therapeutic efficacy'.[54]

The Supreme Court's interpretation, unlike the IPAB's, links efficacy to the utility or function of the invention. In doing so, it avoids a situation where the patent office would have to judge the 'therapeutic efficacy' of other chemical inventions which would fall under the purview of Section 3(d) but which were never intended to cure diseases. Therefore, if the chemical invention in question were a pesticide, the patent office would be required to judge the efficacy regarding the utility of the pesticide. In the case of medicines, the Supreme Court was clear that utility, and by extension, efficacy, meant only therapeutic efficacy. The disadvantage of this interpretation is that it discounts all other forms of non-therapeutic efficacy. As discussed earlier, a new form may demonstrate better stability or other features which aid in storage or manufacture of pharmaceuticals. If such features are inventive, why should the patenting of such inventions be prohibited?

In this case, the question was whether an increase in 'bioavailability' would increase the 'therapeutic efficacy' of the drug. The court chose not to refer to any arguments made by Novartis or the generics, preferring instead to refer to arguments made by two other persons— Shamnad Basheer and Anand Grover, the Senior Advocate representing the CPAA. Basheer was a well-respected academic and the founder of the SpicyIP blog, a website known for tracking matters related to Indian IP and innovation, with which the authors have also been closely associated. Basheer intervened in the case as an amicus curiae, or friend of the court, to provide the Supreme Court with an academic perspective of the various complex issues of patent law. The CPAA was a group representing cancer patients. The lawyer representing the CPAA, Anand Grover, was a personality in his own right. Appointed by the United Nations (UN) as the Special Rapporteur on the right to health, Grover is best known as one of the founders of Lawyer's Collective, an NGO with a well-known history of representing marginalized communities. Appearing for several different patient groups in various patent cases, Grover had developed a reputation as a 'patent-slayer'.

Unlike Novartis and the generics companies, both Basheer and the CPAA were not interested in the manufacturing of Glivec. Basheer wanted to settle the law, while the CPAA wanted to ensure the strictest possible interpretation of Section 3(d) to restrict patents and monopolies on future essential medication. Both had differing interpretations of 'efficacy'.

Grover, after referring extensively to medical literature, argued that bioavailability did not contribute to an increase in therapeutic efficacy. Basheer argued, on the basis of relevant authority, that bioavailability had a link to safety and toxicity, both of which are vital parameters to assess the efficacy of a drug. According to him, an increase in bioavailability could result in an increase in therapeutic efficacy depending on the facts of the case. Basheer prefaced this legal argument with the factual conclusion that Novartis had indeed failed to submit any evidence to demonstrate whether bioavailability did in fact lead to an increase in therapeutic efficacy.[55]

Referring to these two sets of arguments, and without once mentioning the arguments put forth by Novartis and the generics, the Supreme Court seemed open to consider that increased bioavailability led to an enhancement of therapeutic efficacy, provided that it was 'specifically claimed and established by research data'. Since Novartis had produced no evidence based on an 'in vivo animal model', the Supreme Court concluded that Novartis had failed to meet the threshold set by the law.[56]

Thus, even though the Supreme Court allowed for a possible reversal of Novartis' fortunes, the possibility quickly faded when it became clear that Novartis had not filed any evidence on the point. The only benefit to the innovator was that the Supreme Court held that data generated from tests on animals would suffice for the purpose of establishing 'efficacy'. This meant that pharmaceutical patent applicants did not have to provide data from clinical trials on human beings. Regardless of these small victories, the Supreme Court ultimately dismissed the appeal. Novartis lost its seven-year battle to patent Glivec in India.

After the failed attempt by Novartis to protect Glivec, Section 3(d) emerged as the poster-child for other developing countries trying to combat 'evergreening' of pharmaceutical patents. Even though it is poorly drafted, the provision is an excellent example of how India used the flexibilities in TRIPS to outwit the innovator pharmaceutical industry. The innovator lobby has consistently maintained that Section 3(d) is in violation of Article 27 of TRIPS, but no country has so far challenged the TRIPS compatibility of the provision, over a decade after India enacted it into law. On its part, the Supreme Court missed an opportunity to clarify some thorny issues, such as the definition of a 'known substance' under Section 3(d), or why 'efficacy' should be confined to only 'therapeutic efficacy'. In the coming years, as India comes under renewed pressure from powerful lobbies to strengthen its IP laws, Section 3(d) will be a rallying point for many, and India's political strength in the international arena will be determined according to the compromises that it is ready to make with regard to its patent law.

Notes

1. *Rowley to Receive Japan Prize for Her Role in the Development of Targeted Cancer Therapy*, EUREKALERT, 24 January 2012, available at http://www.eurekalert.org/pub_releases/2012-01/uocm-rtr012312. php (Last visited on 15 March 2015); Peter C. Nowell, *Discovery of the Philadelphia Chromosome: A Personal Perspective*, 117(8) J. CLIN. INVEST. 2033 (2007).

2. See BENJAMIN YANG, *Executive Summary of a Book: Magic Cancer Bullet*, 2(18) DISCOVERY MEDICINE, 16–19 (2003), available at http://www.discoverymedicine.com/Benjamin-Yang/2009/05/23/executive-summary-of-a-book-magic-cancer-bullet/ (Last visited on 15 October 2016)

3. See The Lasker Foundation, *Clinical Medical Research Award*, available at http://www.laskerfoundation.org/awards/2009_c_description.htm (Last visited on 15 March 2015).

4. See YANG, *Executive Summary of a Book: Magic Cancer Bullet*.

5. U.S. Patent No. 5,521,184.

6. See generally Graham Dutfield, *Who Invented Glivec? Does It Matter Anyway?*, XLVIII(32) EPW 41 (August 2013).

7. U.S. Patent No. 6,894,051.

8. See Lasker Foundation, *Clinical Medical Research Award*.

9. See *There is New Ammunition in the War against Cancer*, TIME, 28 May 2001.

10. Andrew Pollack, *Doctors Denounce Cancer Drug Prices of $100,000 a Year*, THE NEW YORK TIMES, 25 April 2013, available at http://www.nytimes.com/2013/04/26/business/cancer-physicians-attack-high-drug-costs.html (Last visited on 15 March 2015).

11. Matthew Herper, *Is This How We'll Cure Cancer?*, FORBES, 5 July 2014, available at http://www.forbes.com/sites/matthewherper/2014/05/07/is-this-how-well-cure-cancer/ (Last visited on 15 March 2015).

12. Shamnad Basheer, *The Growing Promiscuity of Indian Courts in Granting 'Ex Parte' Injunctions*, SPICYIP, 24 March 2009, available at http://spicyip.com/2009/03/growing-promiscuity-of-indian-courts-in. html (Last visited on 14 May 2016).

13. Novartis AG v. Adarsh Pharma, 2004 (29) PTC 108 Mad.

14. Intas Laboratories Pvt. Ltd. v. Novartis AG, 2005 (1) CTC 27.

15. Novartis AG v. Mehar Pharma, 2005 (30) PTC 160 Bom.

16. Jeremy A. Greene, *Reform, Regulation, and Pharmaceuticals: The Kefauver–Harris Amendments at 50*, 367(16) N. ENGL. J. MED. 1481 (2012).

17. Novartis AG v. CIPLA Ltd., Novartis AG v. Natco Pharma Ltd., Novartis AG v. Ranbaxy Laboratories Ltd., Novartis AG v. Hetero Drugs Ltd., Novartis AG v. Cancer Patients Aid Association, India, before the Patent Office in the matter of pre-grant opposition against Patent Application No. 1602/MAS/98.

18. Rachel L. Swarns, *Drug Makers Drop South Africa Suit Over AIDS Medicine*, THE NEW YORK TIMES, 20 April 2001, available at http://www. nytimes.com/2001/04/20/world/drug-makers-drop-south-africa-suit-over-aids-medicine.html?pagewanted=all (Last visited on 14 May 2016).

19. Kanaga Raja, *India: Former Swiss President Joins Chorus against Novartis' Patent Challenge*, SOUTH-NORTH DEVELOPMENT MONITOR 6192, 16 February 2007, available at http://www.twn.my/title2/health. info/twninfohealth077.htm (Last visited on 29 March 2015); *Madras HC Dismisses Novartis' Patent Plea*, BUSINESS STANDARD, 7 August 2007, available at http://www.business-standard.com/article/economy-policy/ madras-hc-dismisses-novartis-patent-plea-107080701017_1.html (Last visited on 15 March 2015); Savvy Soumya Misra, *Madras HC Dismisses Novartis' Petition*, DOWN TO EARTH, 31 August 2007, available at http:// www.downtoearth.org.in/node/6452 (Last visited on 15 March 2015); *Call to Boycott Novartis Products*, THE HINDU, 3 December 2007, available at http://www.thehindu.com/todays-paper/tp-national/tp-karnataka/ call-to-boycott-novartis-products/article1960531.ece (Last visited on 15 March 2015).

20. See generally M.P. JAIN, INDIAN CONSTITUTIONAL LAW (2010).

21. THE CONSTITUTION OF INDIA, art. 14.

22. AIR 1974 SC 555.

23. H.M. Seervai, Constitutional Law of India: Critical Commentary, Vol. I, 438 (1999).

24. See generally Shamnad Basheer and Prashant Reddy, *The 'Efficacy' of Indian Patent Law: Ironing Out the Creases in Section 3(d)*, 5(2) SCRIPTED 232 (2008).

25. See Shamnad Basheer and Prashant Reddy, *'Ducking' TRIPS in India: A Saga Involving Novartis and the Legality of Section 3(d)*, 20(2) NLSIR 131 (2008).

26. Gramophone Co. v. Birendra Pandey AIR 1984 SC 667.

27. Novartis AG v. Union of India, 2007 (4) MLJ 1153.

28. *Madras High Court Dismisses Novartis' Petitions*, THE HINDU, 7 August 2007, available at http://www.thehindu.com/todays-paper/tp-national/madras-high-court-dismisses-novartis-petitions/article1887489.ece (Last visited on 15 March 2015).

29. *Indian Court Ruling in Novartis case Protects India as the 'Pharmacy of the Developing World'*, Press Release, MEDECINS SANS FRONTIERES, 6 August 2007, available at http://www.doctorswithoutborders.org/news-stories/press-release/indian-court-ruling-novartis-case-protects-india-pharmacy-developing (Last visited on 29 July 2016).

30. Sarah Hiddleston, *Verdict Will Impact Public Health*, THE HINDU, 7 August 2007, available at http://www.thehindu.com/todays-paper/tp-national/verdict-will-impact-public-health/article1887488.ece (Last visited on 15 March 2015).

31. *Intellectual Property Board Bench to Hear Novartis Appeal*, THE HINDU, 17 November 2007, available at http://www.thehindu.com/todays-paper/tp-national/intellectual-property-board-bench-to-hear-novartis-appeal/article1949888.ece (Last visited on 15 March 2015).

32. *Glivec Case: Technical Member Appointed on IPAB*, DNA, 2 October 2008, available at http://www.dnaindia.com/money/report-glivec-case-technical-member-appointed-on-ipab-1194914 (Last visited on 15 March 2015).

33. Novartis A.G. v. Union of India, MIPR 2009 (2) 345.

34. See Shamnad Basheer, *Grave Diggers, 'Immoral' Patents and the NBRA*, SPICYIP, 30 July 2008, available at http://spicyip.com/2008/07/grave-diggers-immoral-patents-and-nbra.html (Last visited on 15 March 2015).

35. James Randerson, *Europe Rejects Patent Governing Use of Embryonic Stem Cells*, THE GUARDIAN, 27 November 2008, available at http://www.theguardian.com/science/2008/nov/27/embryonic-stem-cells-patent (Last visited on 15 March 2015).

36. Novartis A.G. v. Union of India (2009), at 19.

37. Justice Markandey Katju, *Intellectual Property Rights and the Challenges Faced by the Pharmaceutical Industry*, 4 SCC (JOUR) 46 (2004).

38. Katju, *Intellectual Property Rights and the Challenges Faced by the Pharmaceutical Industry*.

39. Manoj Mitta, *How Two SC Judges Recused Themselves from the Case*, THE ECONOMIC TIMES, 2 April 2013, available at http://articles.

economictimes.indiatimes.com/2013-04-02/news/38218028_1_health-activists-justice-markandey-katju-recusal (Last visited on 15 March 2015).

40. Manoj Mitta, *SC Judge Under Attack from Health Activists*, THE TIMES OF INDIA, 6 September 2011, available at http://timesofindia. indiatimes.com/india/SC-judge-under-attack-from-health-activists/ articleshow/9879869.cms?referral=PM (Last visited on 15 March 2015).

41. Mitta, *SC Judge Under Attack*.

42. Amit Sengupta, B. Ekbal, M.R. Santhosh, K.M. Gopakumar, and Prabir Purkayastha, *Full Text of the Letter Asking for Justice Bhandari's Recusal from the Novartis Glivec Dispute*, SPICYIP, 8 September 2011, available at http://spicyip.com/2011/09/full-text-of-letter-asking-for-justice.html (Last visited on 15 March 2015).

43. Sengupta, Ekbal, Santhosh, Gopakumar, and Purkayastha, *Full Text of the Letter Asking for Justice Bhandari's Recusal from the Novartis Glivec Dispute*.

44. Sengupta, Ekbal, Santhosh, Gopakumar, and Purkayastha, *Full Text of the Letter Asking for Justice Bhandari's Recusal from the Novartis Glivec Dispute*.

45. Government of India, Department of Justice, *Restatement of Values of Judicial Life*, available at http://doj.gov.in/?q=node/73&page=5 (Last visited on 16 March 2015).

46. Mitta, *How Two SC Judges Recused Themselves*.

47. Gardiner Harris and Katie Thomas, *Low-cost Drugs in Poor Nations Get a Lift in Indian Court*, THE NEW YORK TIMES, 1 April 2013, available at http://www.nytimes.com/2013/04/02/business/global/top-court-in-india-rejects-novartis-drug-patent.html (Last visited on 15 March 2015).

48. Roger Bate, *New Delhi's Patent Malpractice: A Court Decision against the Inventors of a Cancer Drug Endangers Patients in India and Abroad*, THE WALL STREET JOURNAL, 2 April 2013, available at http://online.wsj. com/news/articles/SB10001424127887323296504578398170339408 826 (Last visited on 15 March 2015); Sarah Boseley, *Novartis Patent Ruling a Victory in Battle for Affordable Medicines*, THE GUARDIAN, 1 April 2013, available at http://www.theguardian.com/world/2013/ apr/01/novartis-patent-ruling-affordable-medicines (Last visited on 15 March 2015).

49. *A Just Order*, THE HINDU, 2 April 2013, available at http://www. thehindu.com/opinion/editorial/a-just-order/article4570090.ece (Last visited on 29 July 2016).

50. *India's Novartis Decision*, THE NEW YORK TIMES, 4 April 2013, available at http://www.nytimes.com/2013/04/05/opinion/the-supreme-court-in-

india-clarifies-law-in-novartis-decision.html?_r=1 (Last visited on 15 March 2015).

51. Novartis AG v. Union of India, AIR 2013 SC 1311.
52. Novartis AG v. Union of India (2013), ¶158.
53. Novartis AG v. Union of India (2013), ¶170.
54. Novartis AG v. Union of India (2013), ¶180.
55. Prashant Reddy, *A Successful Academic Intervention before the Supreme Court in the Novartis–Glivec Patent Case*, SPICYIP, 20 November 2012, available at http://spicyip.com/2012/11/a-successful-academic-intervention.html (Last visited on 16 March 2015) (*see* page 11 of the written submissions (Part I) filed by Shamnad Basheer).
56. Novartis AG v. Union of India (2013), ¶189.

5

NEW DELHI CHALLENGES
THE BERNE CONVENTION

Copyright law in India has for long been an esoteric subject, left to be discussed mostly in the courtrooms. Occasionally, the debate spills out onto the streets and editorials of newspapers, as happened when University of Delhi (DU) and a private photocopy shop on its premises were sued by three leading academic publishing houses, Oxford University Press (OUP), Cambridge University Press (CUP), and Taylor and Francis (T&F). This lawsuit awakened a 'copyright conscience' among DU students and teachers, who vehemently protested against the publishers' attempt to monetize academic course-packs compiled by the photocopy shop's owner from copyrighted content belonging to the publishers. The publishers had proposed to charge for each page of copyrighted content used in the compilation of these course-packs, but the prospect of costlier course-packs led to protests by the academic community. The legal issues raised in this case, namely the breadth of the 'educational use' exceptions and 'fair dealing' limitations in the Copyright Act, 1957, are likely to be debated all the way till the Supreme Court.

Besides complex issues of interpretation of the Copyright Act, the 'DU photocopy case', as it has come to be known, has revived debates on the link between Indian copyright law and access to knowledge. This issue has come up at least twice before, first in the 1950s, while debating independent India's first copyright law that was eventually enacted in 1957, and second in the 1960s and early 1970s, when India led a camp of developing countries to radically alter international copyright law. These two interlinked episodes, which have remained poorly documented until now, provide fascinating insights into the key stakeholders and their influence on copyright law in India.

The first story tells how a newly independent India attempted to break away from the copyright law it had inherited from the British. This breakaway would have also meant violating commitments under the Berne Convention for the Protection of Literary and Artistic Works, 1886 (Berne Convention), an international copyright treaty that India had signed while under British rule. But this effort, between 1955 and 1957, to alter the boundaries of Indian copyright law was defeated by an unusually effective lobby of Indian authors, editors, and poets, who argued that the proposed new law would be in violation of the Berne Convention. The second story is of how India tried to reform the Berne Convention which restricted the ability of developing countries to mould domestic copyright law to suit their specific development agenda. Under the stewardship of its education minister, Justice M.C. Chagla, and the Registrar of Copyrights, T.S. Krishnamurti, India nearly shook the foundations of international copyright law by demanding, along with other newly independent countries, a drastic dilution of the high standards of copyright protection under the Berne Convention. The politics, negotiations, and compromises that led to success and failure in the international arena are relevant because the DU photocopy case is forcing India to face the same issues once again.

A Vote of Allegiance to the Berne Convention

The 1950s marked a period of intense law-making in India, having won independence from the British in 1947, and having only just adopted a new Constitution in 1950. For convenience, and to prevent administrative disruptions, the Constitution recognized laws enacted by the British in previous decades, including the Copyright Act, 1914. But the newly elected Indian government, led by Prime Minister Jawaharlal Nehru, began reforming several of these existing laws to meet the legitimate expectations of a newly independent democracy.

Nehru's pronounced socialist leanings influenced his economic policies in considerable measure. There was still some room for private enterprise, although with several controls. Land reforms included redistribution of land, and abolition of the feudal zamindari system. Reforms of intellectual property (IP) law, too, were on the agenda. A Patents Enquiry Committee, set up in 1948, submitted its report in 1950, recommending a dilution of patent rights by prohibiting patents for some technologies, and by making it easier to issue compulsory licences for patents.

Given this trend of weakening property rights, one would have expected the new Indian republic to follow a similar approach towards copyrights. Surprisingly, this was not the case. In fact, the first discussion on copyright law, in the Rajya Sabha, took place when the Government of India introduced a resolution on 7 August 1952 seeking Parliamentary approval to ratify the latest revisions of the Berne Convention. These revisions had been made at the Brussels Conference in 1948, increasing the already-high standards of the convention.

A brief digression to explain the Berne Convention and its application to India is useful to place the Rajya Sabha debates in proper context. The Berne Convention is an international copyright treaty established by a group of rich and developed European countries like Belgium, France, Germany, Italy, Spain, Switzerland, and the United Kingdom (UK) in 1886.[1] This Convention laid down certain criteria required to be adhered to by member countries in their domestic copyright law, such as a minimum copyright term and the recognition of foreign copyrights. Many colonies of the countries who instituted the convention were made signatories to the treaty by their colonial masters, ignoring the fact that different countries require different standards of copyright protection at different stages of development. India was one such country, which was made a member of the convention in 1887 by Britain;[2] but it also had the option, like other colonies, to walk out of the Berne Convention on attaining Independence. Indonesia exercised this right on gaining independence from the Dutch after the Second World War, and withdrew from the Berne Convention with effect from 19 February 1960.[3] Had India done the same with the intention of no longer recognizing foreign copyrights, it would have kept illustrious company with the United States (US), which had delayed the recognition of foreign copyrights after its independence from the British.

Indeed, the US did not recognize foreign copyrights till 1891, well over a century after its independence, when it enacted the International Copyright Act (also known as the Chace Act).[4] The US had held out until then for purely economic reasons. It was 'overwhelmingly a net importer of books from England', and it made no sense to send royalties out of the country when it could simply publish foreign copyrighted books royalty-free within the US.[5] For example, prior to 1891, American book publishers made a fortune by selling the wildly popular books of the British author, Charles Dickens, without Dickens himself getting a single penny in royalties from the US sales. On a visit to America in 1842, Dickens complained in letters sent home, 'I am the greatest loser alive by the present law'.[6] For the rest of his trip, he publicly advocated for a change in US copyright laws to respect the works of foreign authors. While espousing the benefits of copyright protection in Boston, Dickens said,

> Securing to myself from day to day the means of an honourable subsistence, I would rather have the affectionate regard of my fellow men, than I would have heaps and mines of gold. But the two things do not seem to me incompatible. They cannot be, for nothing good is incompatible with justice; there must be an international arrangement in this respect: England has done her part, and I am confident that the time is not far distant when America will do hers. It becomes the character of a great country; FIRSTLY, because it is justice; SECONDLY, because without it you never can have, and keep, a literature of your own.[7]

Like the US in the eighteenth and nineteenth centuries, India in the mid-twentieth century was a net importer of copyrighted works. Copyright in most advanced scientific research and English literature was owned by the US and countries in Europe. Being party to the Berne Convention meant that Indians could access these works only after paying royalties to foreign copyright owners. But the cost of paper and print combined with the cost of copyrights was leading to a massive shortage of books in India. Malcolm Adiseshiah, an Indian development economist working with the United Nations Educational, Scientific and Cultural Organization (UNESCO) in the 1960s pointed out that while countries in Europe and North America had a book supply of 2,000 pages per person per year, India's book supply ran to only 32 pages per person per year, leading him to famously remark that, 'India as a nation ran the risk of dying intellectually and spiritually if the prevailing book famine was not checked'.[8]

India could partly reduce the cost of accessing foreign-owned copyrighted publications by walking out of the Berne Convention, and thus, ceasing to recognize foreign copyrights. Such a move could have also given a boost to domestic publishing and printing industries, by providing them royalty-free content to publish and sell. Royalty-free content also meant that no publisher could monopolize the publication of a book, leading to increased competition and reduced prices. Walking out of the Berne Convention would hurt Indian authors, though, whose foreign (and most lucrative) market would likely retaliate by not recognizing the copyright of Indian authors. The Indian economic policy of the day eventually placed the greater economic good of the country over and above that of the individual.

Given this context, it was certainly surprising that the Government of India moved a resolution in August 1952 seeking Parliament's approval to ratify the most recent revisions to the Berne Convention as approved at the Brussels Conference in 1948. Among other things, these revisions increased the term of copyright from the existing term of the duration of the life of the author plus 25 years, to the life of the author plus 50 years. When the Rajya Sabha took up this resolution, there was practically no debate, either about India remaining a member of the Berne Convention, or about the higher standards imposed by the revisions. On the contrary, several Members of Parliament (MPs) were upset that the government had not moved faster to ratify the 1948 revisions. Rajagopal Naidu of the Indian National Congress, from Madras, wanted to know 'what this Government has been doing for the last five years without getting this [the Berne Convention] ratified'.[9] Another Madras MP, Rama Rao, took the moral high ground, and lambasted the Americans for not following prevalent international copyright norms. He said,

> I am told, and I think it is true, that I (an author) must get any book of mine separately copyrighted in America also, otherwise there can be any amount of piracy in America and I am helpless ... if what I am saying

is correct, then America must be told that consistent with her 'global strategy,' she must fall in line with us; for there cannot be two copyright laws in the world.[10]

Rama Rao, being an editor and author himself, was an outspoken advocate for strong copyright laws. Disappointed with India's 'weak and defective copyright law',[11] he wanted 'to amend the Copyright Act in order to make authorship more lucrative and worthwhile'.[12] Other MPs backed this demand.

C.C. Biswas, the minister who introduced the resolution as a 'formal matter', had initially said, 'there is nothing very exciting about it'.[13] But, caught off-guard by the turn that the discussion had taken, he said, '[t]o be taken by surprise like this as if I was here to be questioned on every point relating [to] copyright, well, I had not bargained for it'.[14]

Why were parliamentarians supporting higher standards of copyright protections? Personal motivations were perhaps behind this, because Parliament, especially the Rajya Sabha, was filled with authors, editors, and poets, such as poet laureate Ramdhari Singh Dinkar, lawyers Minoo Masani, and W.S. Barlingay, who had authored books, and journalist Rama Rao, the first editor of the National Herald. For these authors and poets, copyright law directly impacted their earnings from the sale of their works, and possibly influenced the decision to support higher standards of copyright protection. It is also possible that political ideologies had a role to play in the decision to support higher standards of copyright protection.

Plotting to Walk Out of the Berne Convention

In 1955, the government introduced the Copyright Bill in the Rajya Sabha, to replace the British-era Copyright Act, 1914. Since Parliament had already approved the ratification of the Berne Convention, it was a reasonable assumption that the new Bill would comply with the latest (1948) revisions to the convention. But a reading of the Bill suggests that somebody within the government wanted to chart a course independent from the Berne Convention, for two key provisions of the 1955 Bill not only departed from the 1948 revisions, but also struck at the very heart of the convention's most sacred principles.

The first departure was regarding the term of copyright. For the duration of the term of copyright, no person can reproduce or perform the work without the permission of the copyright owner. Under the Copyright Act, 1914, which had effectively extended the Imperial Copyright Act, 1911, as it existed in Britain, to India, the term of copyright was the duration of the life of the author plus 50 years.[15] Similarly, the Berne Convention, as revised at Brussels in 1948, required all member states to provide for a copyright term for 50 years after the death of the author for all literary and artistic works.[16] The 1955 Bill, however, reduced the copyright term to only the life of the author plus 25 years for literary, dramatic, musical, or artistic works.[17] For photographs, sound recordings, and cinematograph films, the term was 25 years 'from the beginning of the calendar year next following the year'[18] in which the work is made or published.

The second departure related to the registration of copyrights with the Copyright Office in order to institute legal action for infringement.[19] This went against a founding principle of the Berne Convention, which prohibited any kind of administrative formality (such as registration) as a prerequisite for copyright enforcement.[20] Doing away with registration made it easier for owners to enforce copyrights, since it saved them bureaucratic delays and costs. Foreign authors and copyright owners, especially, would have found such a registration requirement to be onerous, because they would have to register copyrights in different countries. But the lack of a registration requirement also increased administrative costs, since it would be difficult for users of such works to accurately identify the author, the owner, and the term of copyrighted works.

These two changes were strange. Recall that parliamentary approval to ratify the revised Convention was sought in 1952. Now, in 1955, the government had presented a Bill which appeared to backtrack on its earlier resolution to ratify the revised Convention. Why? One possibility is that India was contemplating denouncing the Berne Convention and remaining a member of only the Universal Copyright Convention (UCC). The UCC, which was drafted by UNESCO and promoted primarily by the US, was an alternative for countries that were not signatories to the Berne Convention. The US was reluctant to become a member of the Berne Convention because several provisions in its domestic copyright law were not in conformity with the convention. For instance, US copyright law required copyright registration as a prerequisite for enforcement, and in some cases, also required a copyrighted work to be 'domestically manufactured' in order to enjoy copyright protection.[21]

The UCC's standards of copyright protection were significantly less burdensome than the Berne Convention.[22] The term of a copyright was one such example, a version of which the government had borrowed in its 1955 Bill. Unlike the Berne Convention, which provided for long copyright terms, the UCC allowed its member states to provide a term of only the life of the author plus 25 years, or alternatively, a fixed term of copyright protection which was limited to 25 years from the date of publication.[23] The UCC also allowed its member states to make registration and domestic manufacture mandatory conditions for copyright enforcement. Further, if translations of foreign copyrighted works were not published in the national language of a contracting state, the UCC permitted the issuance of compulsory licences to domestic publishers for publishing such translations. The UCC's copyright regime was perhaps more in tune with the needs of newly independent and developing countries like India. In fact, India was one of the first countries to sign the UCC in September 1952, as soon as it was adopted and opened for signatures.[24] But withdrawing from the Berne Convention and joining the UCC was not an easy task, because a lobby of developed countries that were signatories to the Berne Convention had negotiated a 'Berne Safeguard Clause' into the UCC, which would potentially complicate attempts—like India's—to completely withdraw from one and join the other. This Clause would prohibit countries who denounced the Berne Convention from relying on the UCC in their copyright relations with members of the Berne Union.[25]

Parliament Enacts the Copyright Act, 1957

After its introduction in the Parliament, the 1955 Bill was referred to a 45-member Joint Parliamentary Committee (JPC) consisting of 15 members from the Rajya Sabha and 30 from the Lok Sabha.[26] A JPC has a mandate to examine a bill, invite testimonies from witnesses and experts, and recommend amendments to the bill. The government of the day usually accepts most of the recommendations made by a JPC, although these are not binding.

Both national and international entities came forth to present their views to the JPC. Some prominent and influential author organizations to tender evidence were the Confédération Internationale des Sociétés d'Auteurs et Compositeurs (CISAC), also known as the International Confederation of Societies of Authors and Composers, headquartered in Paris; the British Joint Copyright Council; the All-India Centre of PEN (an acronym for Poets, Essayists, and Novelists, PEN was an international association of writers, founded in London in 1921); and the All-India Hindi Publishers Association, Allahabad.[27] These organizations managed to convince the JPC to recommend undoing the two provisions which would have put India at variance with its commitments under the Berne Convention. In its final report, the JPC recommended that India 'should fall in line with the majority of the Berne Convention countries', and comply with the copyright term of the life of the author and 50 years prescribed by the Berne Convention.[28] Similarly, the JPC recommended doing away with compulsory copyright registration as a necessary prelude to suing for infringement, as it 'would be an undue restriction on the owner of the copyright to exercise his rights'.[29]

When the bill returned to the Rajya Sabha for a vote, the government signalled its willingness to accept the JPC's recommendations. Speaking on 14 May 1957, the minister of state for education, K.L. Shrimali, said that the government had proposed a reduced copyright term because it 'thought that unlimited monopoly right might work adversely against the interests of the general public and that a period of 25 years was enough to safeguard the interests of the author and his family'.[30] But, he said, the government decided to accept the JPC's recommendation to restore the term of copyright to 50 years after death, because Indian authors were strongly opposed to a reduced term.[31] Surely, though, the government ought to have known at the start of the legislative process that authors would be opposed to this reduction in term? The minister's introductory speech was brief, and although he was not entirely forthcoming on the reasons for the backtrack, other loquacious MPs willingly gave the Rajya Sabha a detailed account of why the government had dropped its controversial amendments. One such MP was Ramdhari Singh Dinkar, a freedom fighter and one of the best known Hindi language poets of his time, who would later be awarded the Sahitya Akademi Award (1959), the Padma Bhushan (1959), and the Jnanpith Award (1972).[32] A member of the Indian National Congress party, Dinkar served three terms in the Rajya Sabha.[33] Dinkar was made a member of the JPC examining the 1955 Bill, thus allowing him to influence the proceedings.

In his speech, Dinkar narrated, in Hindi, how authors and authors' organizations of the country were up in arms because the Bill provided for a reduced copyright term.[34] He said, '[w]hen there was a big uproar on this issue in the country, we discussed it in [the] Sahitya Academi and some of us writers, and some members of Parliament met Maulana Saheb'.[35] Maulana Saheb, or Abul Kalam Muhiyuddin Ahmed Azad, better known as Maulana Azad, was one of the most prominent faces of the Indian independence movement and independent India's first minister of education. His ministry was responsible for India's copyright policy and his junior minister, Shrimali, was piloting the Copyright Bill, 1955, through Parliament. In Dinkar's words, Maulana Azad 'didn't even take two minutes to understand what the writers wanted',[36] and asked them [the authors] to submit a report on the amendments they wanted. Dinkar spoke of a committee formed by the authors, consisting of Mama Sahib Warerkar, Humayun Kabir, and others, which submitted a list of recommendations to the government.

Similarly, Dinkar described how the authors lobbied to scrap the requirement to register copyrights as a prerequisite for enforcement. He said, '[w]hen the paper was sent to us the governor of Bihar in a letter to Mr. Maulana had mentioned that the authors will be upset with this issue. The minister then said that it will not be compulsory but will be optional.'[37] Dinkar believed this requirement would seriously disadvantage writers in rural areas, observing, '[a]nother difficulty I foresee is that it will be easy for the writers from cities to register but the rural writers will suffer. All authors are highly impractical. The more practical he becomes, the less creative he gets.'[38]

Dinkar also delivered a memorable speech in Parliament on why copyright was important to him as an author. Speaking in chaste

Hindi, he forewarned that by diluting copyright protection and forcing authors to depend on state patronage, the state would be able to ensure that authors were richly rewarded, but such an approach would most certainly kill their creative instincts. Drawing comparisons with communist states, he said:

> ...you go to any communist country, in a couple of days you will start feeling that the happiest people in that country are poets, dancers, writers, researchers and inventors; this is because the state gives them a lot of concessions. They find it difficult to know how to spend their money. Last time when there was a movement in Russia to introspect then they accused the authors that they had so much wealth that they were buying sea-side villas, leading a luxurious life and that they had lost connect with the people.... What did the authors of communist countries get? They have physical comfort, lot of money and easy life, along with this relaxation in income tax. But what do they have to give away for all this? They have lost their freedom of expression, as they had to fall in line with the government's thinking.... I ask you how many days have passed since the revolution, then why is it that authors like Dostoevsky, Terziev, Djakovo, Tolstoy and Gorky have not been born in communism. They cannot be born again...[39]

Thus, argued Dinkar, copyright law in a democracy was necessary to ensure the independence of writers. In his words:

> if we are serious about democracy in the state then the first thing on our agenda should be to give autonomy to writers and publications. They should be allowed to criticize anybody legitimately and unmask the deeds of anybody. This will enhance our democratic values. If on the one hand, we dilute the copyright laws and on the other hand give them government patronage, this will amount to buying the talent. People have died for the reason of money in the world; this country's writers will also prefer to drown themselves in the sea rather than accept being slaves of the state.[40]

While several MPs backed Dinkar's stand, some also harshly criticized the decision to not reduce the copyright term. The most outspoken of these speakers was Kishen Chand, an MP from Andhra Pradesh. Chand had been cautioning the Rajya Sabha on the perils of an expansive copyright law since 16 February 1956, when the motion to refer the bill to a JPC was being debated, arguing that 'this Bill, the way it has been drafted, is a bit too liberal to the authors'.[41] He said, in the case of property, we do not permit people to charge any rent they like; in the case of any industry, we do not permit the industrialists to make any profit they like. We restrict them. In society, the right of every individual is restricted, and likewise...the rights of the authors, the rights of the painters, the rights of the artists and the rights of the musicians should be restricted.[42]

On 14 May 1957, after the bill returned to Parliament, Chand, who spoke right after Dinkar, sarcastically remarked,

the [honourable] Member who has spoken just before me let the cat out of the bag. He told us that the entire writing public, the authors of this country, rose up against the proposed Bill and they went on a deputation to the [honourable] Education Minister and persuaded him to accept the amendments proposed by them. Sir, if we are going to adopt legislation only on the basis of agitation carried on by persons involved in it, possibly the zamindars of this country also would have carried on their agitation and would have insisted that their rights in the property should be allowed to continue. But Parliament does not go by it.[43]

The reference to zamindars, the feudal landlords who held large tracts of land across the country, was deliberate and apposite. Legislation aimed at abolishing the zamindari system by placing ceilings on individual landholdings, with the State appropriating the excess land, was being discussed around the same time. This law required Parliament to maintain a fine balance between the fundamental rights of individuals, and the policy of ensuring the greatest good for the greatest number by limiting ownership and redistributing land. Extending the utilitarian approach to copyright law would have required Parliament to severely dilute existing copyright law. Why, then, was a majority of the Rajya Sabha supporting a strong copyright law which favoured the individual author over society? Chand bluntly deduced, 'I think when anything touches the pockets of the [honourable] Members, they immediately start arguing that because something is not done elsewhere, it should not be here'.[44] This statement was a reference to all the author–poet–parliamentarians, including Dinkar, who would be affected by falling book earnings because of a diluted copyright law. Imploring the House to follow a socialistic policy even in copyright law, Chand told the Rajya Sabha that if the bill was considered:

on its merits under a socialistic pattern of society and in the interest of advancement of knowledge, especially when our country is going to have compulsory education and adult education and the literary public is going to increase in large numbers, it is very essential that we try to bring down the prices of books and restrict the profits of the authors.[45]

Chand remained in a minority in the Rajya Sabha, which voted instead for retaining the copyright term of the life of the author plus 50 years, and for doing away with the copyright registration requirement. Chand did find partial sympathy from the minister of state, Shrimali, who, in his closing statement said,

I am certainly in full sympathy with the authors but they must take into account the various other interests that are affected and the most important interest is that of the society in general. The author does not exist in a vacuum. The individuality of the genius does not express itself in isolation. In protecting the interests of the authors, we should not forget the interests of the society in general.[46]

When the bill travelled to the Lok Sabha, the debate proceeded on similar lines. Speaking for the government, Shrimali cited 'strong public opinion' for the government's decision to accept the JPC recommendation on restoring the term of copyright to 50 years after death.[47] The star speaker in the Lok Sabha was Minocher Rustom Masani, better remembered as Minoo Masani. A barrister by training, Masani had been jailed by the British during India's struggle for freedom. He was also a member of the Constituent Assembly which drafted the new Indian Constitution, and had co-authored a book titled *India's Constitution at Work*.[48] By 1960, a few years after the debate on the Copyright Bill, Masani would break away from Nehru's Indian National Congress, and found the Swatantra Party.[49] This would be independent India's first political party which openly supported a market-based economy that protected property rights, rather than the socialist-style economy imposed by Nehru. In parliamentary debates in the 1960s on India's patent law, the Swatantra Party, Masani in particular, would be the solitary political voice opposing the move to abolish pharmaceutical patents.[50] Masani had a similar stance on the Copyright Bill, 1955. He argued against the two changes—reducing the copyright term and compulsory registration—on the grounds that such conditions would 'jeopardize' India's membership of the Berne

Convention, and not only adversely impact authors, but also led to India's 'isolation' from the 'world family'.[51] Like in the Rajya Sabha, there were hardly any voices of dissent in the Lok Sabha and the House soon voted in favour of the Copyright Bill, 1955.

Setting the Stage for Revising the Berne Convention

In 1963, India had a new minister of education, Mahommedali Currim Chagla, better known as Justice M.C. Chagla. Previously, he had been the Chief Justice of the Bombay High Court from 1948 to 1958, and had also served as India's Ambassador to the US and the UK. Unlike his predecessor-minister Maulana Azad, who had conceded to the authors' demands for a strong copyright law, Chagla viewed the aims of Indian copyright policy differently, most likely because he faced immense problems in standardizing the quality of textbooks across India. In his autobiography, *Roses in December*, Chagla wrote,

> One serious difficulty in the way of introducing standard text-books, especially in colleges, was the question of copyright. Our ultimate object was that all text-books should be written by Indian authors. At the time such authors were not available, and therefore, we had to translate the standard text-books written in European languages. The stumbling block in our way was the law and conventions relating to copyright... We wanted these Conventions to be amended so as to help textbook production in developing countries.[52]

In a short but impressive speech to the regular joint sessions of the Berne Convention and the UCC being held in New Delhi on 2 December 1963, Chagla spelt out his vision for a new international copyright regime.[53] To him, a copyright law for developing countries had to ensure affordable access to scientific and technological books, which would lead to better education and accelerated development. Chagla told the audience:

> I believe books are the very life-blood of democracy. People must read; people must think; people must be familiar with different ideas, even ideas which are opposed to ours. We must keep our windows open to all opinions and ideas and therefore I am entirely in favour of complete freedom of books coming to this country. But I have got to balance this

with the economic needs of my country and if we can devise some method whereby we can prevent foreign exchange being spent on the import of books, we must think about it because it would, as I said, not merely affect India, but would also affect the African countries.[54]

The diplomat in him knew that India needed support from other developing countries, especially from those in Africa, who had spelt out a similar vision for copyright reform in the African Symposium on Copyright held at Brazzaville in August 1963.[55] His speech, thus, repeatedly highlighted that Africa and India shared the goal of reforming international copyright law, especially the Berne Convention. Previous political debates on copyright law had centred on issues like the duration of the copyright term. Chagla shifted the focus to two other issues: translations (important for India's multilingual society), and the proliferation of costly imports of copyrighted books (rather than domestic publication). While the first dealt with the issue of access to knowledge, the second dealt with bolstering domestic publishing and printing businesses.

Translation rights under Indian copyright law have had a contentious history dating to the nineteenth century. Lionel Bently, in a magnificent academic work, chronicles the reasons behind translation rights being introduced in India for the first time via the 1914 copyright law.[56] Until 1914, translation rights were not considered to be protected under either the Copyright Act, 1847, enacted by the East India Government, or the Literary Copyright Act, 1842, enacted by the British Parliament for the entire UK and colonies of the British Empire. This meant that if a book was written in English and protected under copyright, any person could translate it into another language without the permission of the copyright owner of the English language work. In the Indian case of *Macmillan* v. *Shamsul Ulama M. Zaka*,[57] Bently quotes the judge as saying '[t]ranslations of copyrighted books are not referred to in the Act. It is difficult to understand why they should not be mentioned in the Act if they were intended to be prohibited.'[58] After losing this case in 1895, Macmillan reportedly joined forces with other big English publishing houses, such as the OUP and CUP to lobby for changing copyright law to provide for translation rights as well. The chief motive was financial, since India promised to be a lucrative market for translations.

Indeed, the Indian market was important enough for larger publishing houses like Macmillan and OUP to open offices here by 1912.[59] Expectedly, the publishers justified their demand for expanding copyright law to include translation rights, but masked it as being needed to protect the interests of authors. Macmillan cited the example of the Indian poet and author, Rabindranath Tagore, who had, around that time, been awarded the Nobel Prize for Literature (1913), to defend their demand.[60] Macmillan, who was also Tagore's publisher, argued that the lack of such rights would adversely affect Tagore, whose translated works were in great demand in Europe and elsewhere.[61] Both British administrators in India, and Indians themselves, opposed this demand, because they thought translation rights would either deprive Indians of access to advanced European knowledge, or make access more costly, particularly because a vast majority of Indians could not read in English. But the publishers' lobby was successful, and translation rights were recognized in the new Indian Copyright Act, 1914, subject to an exception for works first published in India.[62] This exception stated that translation rights would cease to exist where such works were not translated into other languages within the first 10 years of publication.[63]

After Independence, during deliberations over the Copyright Bill, 1955, the JPC tried to replicate such an exception, under which any person could publish translations if the copyright owner of an Indian work failed to do so within 10 years from the original publication.[64] But this proposal failed to pass muster in Parliament. During the Rajya Sabha debate, speakers like Dinkar made an impassioned plea for giving authors stronger translation rights. Besides financial reasons, Dinkar said that authors like Tagore had felt that translations of their works would not do justice to the spirit of their writings. In Dinkar's words, 'the government should make sure that respecting the sentiment of the author, if he does not want his/her works to be translated, it should not be done. He should have the right over translation for his entire life, no one should be allowed to translate his works independently'.[65] Even so, the new Copyright Act, 1957, did create a scheme in Section 32, under which anybody could apply for a compulsory licence to translate any literary or dramatic work if its translations had not been published in India, within seven years of the first publication of the work. It is doubtful whether Section 32 was compliant with the Berne Convention because at the time, the convention did not permit compulsory licences to be granted for translations.

For this reason, perhaps, in his speech on 2 December 1963, education minister Chagla floated the idea of diluting translation rights in the Berne Convention, and suggested instead 'a provision similar to what you find in the Universal Convention about the rights of translation'.[66] At the time, the UCC provided for compulsory licensing for translation of works into local languages of member countries if the copyright owner did not make the work available in such language within seven years.[67] The copyright owner was entitled to just compensation for such licences. The Berne Convention had no such provision.

The second issue raised by Chagla in his speech related to the fact that copyright owners, most of whom lived abroad, preferred to publish their books in those countries and then export them to India. As a result, India had to spend valuable foreign exchange on importing such books. Chagla's solution was to allow developing countries to issue compulsory licences for publishing those works that were not domestically published within the first two years of their publication anywhere else in the world. This was during the 1960s, when India was trying hard to build its domestic industry and cut down on imports generally. Other countries, like the US, also had similar policies to placate *their* powerful domestic printing lobbies. For instance, from 1891, when the US first recognized foreign copyrights, all foreign works had to be published and manufactured within the US in order to enjoy copyright protection, subject to minor exceptions.[68] This policy, designed to protect domestic publishing and printing industries from foreign competition, was greatly criticized worldwide.[69] This requirement under American copyright law was diluted when the US became a member of the UCC in 1954, and finally expired on 1 July 1986, paving the way for the US to join the Berne Convention three years later in 1989.[70] India, although arguably entitled to enact a similar protectionist provision, would be in violation of the Berne Convention if it chose to do so.

Although Chagla's term as minister ended in 1966, India would follow his vision and achieve some success at the Stockholm

Diplomatic Conference in 1967 where the Berne Union discussed the demands of developing countries. By then, India had assumed the leadership mantle among developing countries seeking to reform the Berne Convention.[71] An important event preceding the 1967 Stockholm Conference was the East Asian Seminar on Copyright, held in New Delhi, in January that year. This was organized by the Bureaux Internationaux Réunis pour la Protection de la Propriété Intellectuelle (BIRPI) on the invitation of the Indian government. The BIRPI was the predecessor of the World Intellectual Property Organization (WIPO), and was deeply involved in efforts to broker a deal between developing and developed countries on the reform of international copyright law.

At this seminar, speakers from around the world discussed how international copyright law could be recalibrated to meet the demands of developing countries. The speakers also submitted articles, later published by the Government of India as a book in which, quite aptly, it disclaimed copyright. One author in this publication was T.S. Krishnamurti, the then Registrar of Copyrights, and the person who took Chagla's vision to the international platform.[72] Explaining the demand for reform, Krishnamurti wrote, '[t]he most urgent problem for developing countries is the promotion of knowledge and the rapid transfer of knowledge particularly in the fields of science and technology from developed and advanced areas'.[73] Krishnamurti proposed a compulsory licensing model where copyright owners would be *forced* to license their copyright to other parties for the original work or for translation rights, at a royalty fixed under law.[74] He drew parallels with domestic patent laws of developed and developing countries and spoke of how the BIPRI model law on inventions justified a policy to encourage the exploitation of patents.[75] Krishnamurti reminded his audience that even the US retained a domestic manufacturing clause in its copyright law, under which, to enjoy copyright protection, books had to be domestically printed in the US. Assuaging concerns of such a system affecting an author's economic interests, Krishnamurti noted, '[l]imited printing facilities within most countries of the region, acute shortage of paper, high figures of illiteracy, dearth of capital, unsatisfactory means of book-distribution and such other factors are bound to restrict applications for compulsory licences'.[76] He ended with the hope that the Stockholm Conference would take a 'bold step' to make the 'Copyright Union truly international and universal'.[77]

Krishnamurti remained silent, though, on the possibility of India completely walking out of the Berne Convention. A few months before Krishnamurti's speech, on 25 November 1966, two MPs, Banka Behary Das and R. Khandekar, had asked the minister of education two questions in the Rajya Sabha. The first question was regarding 'whether suggestions have recently been made to withdraw India from Copyright Conventions', and the second question followed, 'if so, the reaction of [the] Government in the matter and whether any decision has been taken thereon'.[78] The deputy minister of education, Bhakt Darshan, said: 'This proposal was considered some time ago and it was decided that this issue may be reconsidered only after August 1967, when the revised version of the Berne Convention will become available'.[79] The message from the Government of India was clear: If the Berne Convention was not revised to cater to the interests of developing countries like India, it would actively consider withdrawing from the Berne Convention.

From Victory in Stockholm to Retreat in Paris

By the time Sweden hosted the Stockholm Diplomatic Conference on the Revision of the Berne Convention in 1967, the chorus for reform had grown strong and loud among developing countries, which now constituted 24 out of the 57 member countries.[80] Unlike previous conferences, where countries had more or less unanimously agreed to higher levels of protection, the end of colonialism changed the dynamics of the Berne Union. For the first time, at the Stockholm Conference, the Berne Union faced a demand to downgrade the high levels of copyright protection. The main item on the agenda was a Protocol for Developing Countries, drafted by expert committees of the BIRPI.[81] This protocol would be attached to the convention, and would contain reservations made by developing countries to the text of the convention for a period of 10 years. In legal parlance, a country may make a 'reservation' to certain provisions of a treaty to indicate that it will not be bound by those provisions.

The aim of this protocol, which was applicable only to developing countries, was to revise the Berne Convention to meet the educational and cultural requirements of developing countries. It proposed five major revisions that would significantly dilute the high standards of the Berne Convention. These included reducing the term of copyright to life of the author plus 25 years; extinguishing translation rights if translations were not published within 10 years; allowing developing countries to issue compulsory licences for the publication of translations and reproductions after three years from publication; replacing the existing text on broadcasting rights with language from the Rome Text of the Berne Convention;[82] and special blanket exceptions allowing copyrighted material to be used for educational and scholastic activities.[83] In addition, a common thread to the compulsory licensing proposals was a provision to allow developing countries to impose national currency restrictions. This would mean that even when foreign authors were entitled to royalties under compulsory licences, the remittances of royalties to home countries would be subject to restrictions placed by developing countries.

Expectedly, some developed countries, especially the UK (which had a considerable market in developing countries for its books), baulked at the proposals. Due to the differences between both camps, this was perhaps the only revision conference which threatened to tear apart the Berne Union, since developing countries were prepared to walk out if their demands were not met.[84] At the time, the situation was described by some as a 'Crisis in International Copyright'.[85]

In the negotiations, India led the charge for the developing countries. The country attached considerable importance to the conference, for it was among the few countries to have its delegation headed by an elected politician, that is, its minister of state for education, Sher Singh.[86] Most others were represented by diplomats or bureaucrats, which is the usual practice in negotiations. Explaining India's stance to the conference, India's Registrar of Copyrights, Krishnamurti (who was also a part of the delegation) reminded other members that since Independence, Indians had been clamouring for more and better facilities for education, and that a democratically elected government could not ignore these demands. He expressed his hope that 'the Berne Convention should place no obstacle in the way of the gigantic tasks facing [the Indian Government in] bringing education to the masses'.[87] Reminding the developed world that the 'world was shrinking so that it was no longer possible to have cases of prosperity in a desert of poverty, islands of knowledge in an ocean of ignorance', Krishnamurti told them that they had a responsibility to help meet the demand for educational and scientific literature in the developing world, failing which developing countries would have no option but to drop out of the Berne Convention.[88]

The main opponents to the demands of developing countries were the UK and Mexico. Both had a stake in the international book trade— the UK was the leader in the English language market, and Mexico was a major supplier of Spanish language textbooks.[89] According to one account, between eight British publishers—Longmans, OUP, CUP, Evans Bros., Sweet and Maxwell, Nelson, University of London Press, and Heinemann—the British publishing industry had invested significantly in developing countries, producing 550 new titles specifically for East Africa, 972 for West Africa, 1404 for India and Pakistan, and 696 for the Far East.[90] Most of these titles were sponsored by British publishing houses and written by authors from the countries where the books were to be sold.[91] Given the stakes, the British publishers' reaction to the Stockholm Protocol was described eloquently as one that had 'the startled look of a milkmaid who had just been turned up by her favourite cow'.[92] The UK and Mexico were faced with either submitting to the demands of the developing countries, or having them denounce the Berne Convention. The negotiations reportedly took place in a 'febrile atmosphere of crisis and bitter debate' with most of the real decisions being made 'in camera' between India and the UK.[93]

Only one major concession could be won from the developing countries: It was agreed that authors would be given 'just compensation' even when their works were used for 'teaching, study and research in all fields of education'; unlike the original language of the Protocol, under which copyrighted material could be used for 'educational or scholastic purposes' without giving any compensation to authors.[94] Faced with the prospect of a large group of developing countries walking out of the Berne Convention, the developed countries refrained from blocking the passage of the Stockholm Protocol. Of the 58 member countries, 51 were present at the Stockholm Conference. Eventually, 35 countries signed the Stockholm Act on 14 July 1967, while four more signed before the deadline of 13 January 1968.[95] But no country opposed the protocol.

The UK abstained from voting mainly because it feared that a vote against the convention would lead to a walkout by the developing countries.[96] A secondary reason was an assessment by the British that the protocol was, in reality, unenforceable. The *Financial Times* quoted a source within Whitehall as saying, '[o]ne can make a moral gesture—like saying the Suez Canal must stay open, or whatever it might be—but it is not always wise to make moral gestures if you cannot enforce them'.[97] This appears to be a veiled reference to the complex mechanism for the issuance of compulsory licences under the protocol, its design attributed to efforts of British negotiators. In the words of one British newspaper, 'the agreement which has emerged is so complicated that it could only have been drafted by the British civil service bent on destruction'.[98]

Notwithstanding the criticism by some that the provisions on compulsory licensing were almost unworkable, the UK still had to face the ire of its domestic industry for not voting against the protocol. The Publishers' Association reportedly sent a strongly worded letter to remind the British government that a failure to vote against the protocol would lead to 'willing away' the private property of its citizens as an 'aid' to developing countries. Similarly, the British Copyright Council was furious with the British government for abstaining rather than killing the protocol with just 'one vote'.[99] The council accused its government of cowardice and of admitting 'a delayed-action bomb of dangerous principles into the flagship of Copyright, the Berne Convention'.[100] In a letter to the *Times*, its Chairperson called upon the British government to declare that in no circumstance would the British sign the new act which included the protocol.[101]

For India, the Stockholm Protocol was quite a diplomatic coup, since developing countries rarely won a bout against the developed world in the international arena. But the Indian government had few admirers back home. The lobby of Indian authors had their daggers drawn against their government. In editorial after editorial published in the Indian press, the Indian government was criticized for lowering the standards of international copyright protection offered by the Berne Convention.[102] The censure was very similar to the one faced by the UK government from its authors and publishers for *not* voting against the Stockholm Protocol. A widely published open letter, titled 'Men of Letters Speak Out', signed by prominent contemporary Indian authors and intellectuals, like Nissim Ezekiel, A.G. Noorani, Khushwant Singh, and Minoo Masani, noted with regret 'the growing trend in Government circles to repudiate all moral obligations in the reproduction or translation of books published abroad'.[103] Terming the government's approach towards copyright as 'nothing short of piracy even if it is carried out under the garb of the law', the authors demanded that the publishing of Indian reprints be subsidized, or reasonable time-limits be placed for foreign publishers to bring out Indian editions of books for universities here. The letter also condemned the Protocol for imposing national currency restrictions, terming it as a policy followed only by communist countries. It concluded with asking the government and the public to consider the 'moral propriety' of the Stockholm Protocol, and drew attention to India having received large amounts of aid from various countries, observing that a decision to not pay royalties would be seen as lack of 'practical wisdom', the insinuation being that foreign economic aid would stop if Indians were perceived to be robbing foreign authors of their just rewards.

The burden of defending the Indian government against this onslaught fell once again upon the Registrar of Copyrights, T.S. Krishnamurti. In a reply to an opinion-editorial in the *Statesman*, Krishnamurti reminded critics that the Stockholm Protocol still required the payment of 'just compensation' to copyright owners.[104] Moreover, the Registrar gently reminded the authors that 'however outstanding an author, it should not be forgotten that he stands on the shoulders of others who have preceded him and has certain obligations to posterity'.[105] Countering the moral outrage expressed by the authors, Krishnamurti boldly wrote,

> Looked at impartially, the Stockholm Revision which is bound to be hailed in the future as a brave and understanding measure calculated to spread knowledge and remove illiteracy, safeguards the financial interests of authors without making developing countries subject to cultural exploitation, under the guise of international copyright, by unscrupulous publishers or other agents of authors, who, even when an author is prepared to authorize the dissemination of his works, can act as a bar.[106]

As a finishing touch, he pinned down the entire opposition to the Berne Convention as purely financial rather than moral, since the 'printing and publishing industries of developed countries ... earn more by selling the finished books outside instead of allowing local manufacture on payment of just compensation'.[107] The *Statesman* responded again, in an editorial,[108] noting that 'the Stockholm revision, so far from being a brave and understanding measure seems a prelude to licensed larceny'.

Strangely, despite leading the Stockholm Protocol negotiations, and vociferously defending its decision to a hostile domestic audience of authors and editors, India never actually took advantage of the reservations under the Protocol. In fact, only four developing countries—Bulgaria, Mauritania, Pakistan, and Senegal—deposited instruments of ratification indicating that they would be availing either all or some of the reservations for 10 years.[109] The British assessment, as reported in the *Financial Times*, that the Protocol was too complicated to work was thus likely correct. India's reluctance to not ratify the protocol is not quite clear, even though minister Sher Singh had said, at the Stockholm Conference on 12 July 1967, that the protocol should come into operation as rapidly as possible, within 'the coming two or three months'.[110] One of the other likely reasons for India's non-ratification, was perhaps that it was aware of international efforts already afoot to roll back the protocol.

By 1969, a joint meeting of the Permanent Committee of the Berne Union and the Intergovernmental Copyright Committee of UNESCO decided to form a Joint Study Group to study the needs of developing and developed countries under the existing international copyright regime. In October that year, the Study Group formulated what are known as the 'Washington Recommendations'.[111] These formed the basis of the Paris Conference held from 5 to 24 July 1971, with the express purpose of revising 'the provisions relating to the developing countries contained in the Stockholm Act (1967) of the Convention'.[112]

This time, the Indian delegation to the Paris Conference did not have a single member from the earlier delegation sent in 1967 to Stockholm. Equally strange was the composition of this new delegation. It consisted of the Joint Secretary to the ministry of education, the Joint Secretary to the ministry of home affairs, and the Joint Secretary to the ministry of law. No representative from the Copyright Office was present.[113]

In any event, the Paris Conference which resulted in the Paris Act, 1971, agreed to insert a new Article 34 into the Berne Convention, foreclosing any country from making reservations under the Stockholm Protocol. India, like others, accepted this proposal in favour of concessions offered in a new Appendix to the Berne Convention. Unlike the Stockholm Protocol, this appendix did not include provisions allowing for a reduced copyright term, or a blanket exception allowing developing countries to use copyrighted work for the purposes of teaching or instruction, on the payment of just compensation. Instead, the appendix, which formed a part of the Paris Act, 1971, offered developing countries a compulsory licence system for translations and reproductions of works. But developing countries could issue these compulsory licences only after three years (for works of the natural and physical sciences, including mathematics, and of technology) or seven years (for works of fiction, poetry, drama and music, and for art books), after following several preconditions, including a vague and problematic requirement to determine the 'reasonableness of the price of the book'. Given India's original agenda, the Paris Act of the Berne Convention was certainly a step backwards from the Stockholm Protocol.

Although India amended its law in 1983 to provide for compulsory licences on the lines approved during the Paris Conference, not too many Indian publishers appear to have applied for such compulsory licences. The Copyright Office, in a response to a query by the authors under the Right to Information (RTI) Act, 2005 said that 'no such information are [sic] readily available in this office at present'.[114] There has been no effort since 1971 (Paris) to relook the high standards of copyright protection under the Berne Convention.

The Photocopy Machine Disrupts Book Publishing

One reason for compulsory licences not being issued, or even requested, with any significant frequency is perhaps the advent of large-scale piracy in India. As far back as September and October 1982, local newspapers had reported on widespread book piracy in India, which had reverberations in Parliament. Khushwant Singh and Shrikant Verma, both journalists and renowned authors who were also

MPs in the Rajya Sabha, questioned the government on steps being taken against book piracy.[115] The next month, another MP, M.M.S. Siddhu, moved a motion in the Rajya Sabha on the need to bring a law to control book piracy. He claimed that at least 2,000 titles of well-known authors on popular, academic, and technical subjects, were being pirated in India. He asked the government to respond to demands by 'reputed authors, their delegations, as well as the federation of publishers, booksellers and associates' for amendments to the Copyright Act in order to combat book piracy.[116]

By 1984, the government considered piracy to be such a troublesome issue for both the book publishing and film industry that it introduced the Copyright (Amendment) Bill, 1984 as a major reform in copyright law to provide harsher criminal penalties and action against infringement. In her speech introducing the Copyright (Amendment) Bill, 1984, the minister of state for education Sheila Kaul estimated that 'four hundred to five hundred titles are pirated in India every year'.[117] The amendments sailed through Parliament without much opposition, consequently increasing penalties for copyright infringement, and making it easier for the police to seize pirated books. But the book publishing industry still complained of high levels of piracy in India.

A study commissioned by the ministry of human resource development (HRD) (previously known as the ministry for education) in 1999, 15 years after the 1984 amendments, concluded that 'photocopy piracy' was the second most significant form of book piracy after unauthorized printing and selling of books.[118] The same study also noted that 'large scale photocopying of books relating to medical, engineering and other professional courses is also noticed because being costly such books remained beyond the buying capacity of a large number of students'.[119] The International Intellectual Property Alliance (IIPA), an influential lobby consisting of IP owners, has consistently complained about photocopy piracy in India. In its annual report on India in 2010, the IIPA reported that '[w]holesale copying of entire books is increasingly complemented or replaced by use of unauthorized compilations in the form of course packs, or "self instructional material" (SIM). These are used both for classroom teaching and distance learning, with the materials for the latter sometimes found in electronic form'.[120] The IIPA also reveals in its report that it was pressuring the HRD ministry to fulfil a commitment made in 2006 to issue a circular to all universities and academic institutions to combat illegal photocopying. Such a circular would have had a massive effect, since most Indian universities are still public universities that function under the umbrella of the HRD ministry. But the ministry never issued such a circular. It should not be surprising that the HRD ministry, which is responsible for increasing literacy and education standards in India, disagrees with the publishing industry's views on copyright law. When efforts to lobby the government failed, publishers shifted strategies to monetizing 'photocopy piracy' by suing the photocopiers directly for copyright infringement, the DU photocopy case being the first such attempt. This monetization model required universities or photocopy shops to seek reprographic licences (or licences to create photocopies) from the Indian Reprographic Rights Organisation (IRRO), which is a copyright society. These licences would allow photocopiers to prepare course packs for students on the payment of royalty for each copied page to the IRRO. These royalties would then be distributed to the publisher-members of the IRRO, who may share them onwards with their authors, as per contractual arrangements.

Like most developments in copyright law, this business model was perhaps forced upon the publishing industry by a revolutionary new technology. In this case, the technology was the Xerox 914 photocopier introduced in 1960 by Xerox Corporation. Weighing 648 pounds and measuring 48 inches to the top of the control panel, this machine is credited with revolutionizing photocopying because of the quality of the copies and its simplified operability.[121] At one point, Xerox, in its advertisements, showed a chimp using its machine (to demonstrate how simple and easy it was to use), but had to pull the advertisement off the air, when secretaries and personal assistants who used the 914 in offices complained about how they began to find bananas on photocopy machines.[122] The US publishing industry viewed the photocopy machine as an imminent threat to its business model because it allowed users to make reproductions of any published material with relative ease. In the early 1970s, Williams & Wilkins, a publisher of medical journals, sued the US Government's National Library of Medicine when the Library declined to pay the publisher a sum of two cents for each page that they photocopied, for their patrons, from the publisher's journals.[123] The government lawyers for the Library rejected Wilkin's demand for two cents per page that was photocopied, on the grounds that the photocopying of academic articles for scholarly use was protected under the fair use exception to copyright law, and that there was a long-standing custom of such articles being photocopied in libraries across the country without paying any royalty to the publisher from whom the journal was purchased.[124] The lawsuit caused a furore amongst the library community in the US, with several calls to boycott subscriptions to the entire line of journals owned by Williams & Wilkins.[125]

Williams & Wilkins scored a victory after trial when the Commissioner to the Court of Claims held in favour of the publishers, saying that photocopying by libraries was copyright infringement and not fair use.[126] However, on review, this finding was overturned by the judges of the Court of Claims in 1973, who found photocopying by libraries to be covered by the 'fair use' exception under American law.[127] 'Fair use' or 'fair dealing' as it is also known, is a defence to copyright infringement in most jurisdictions.

There are different explanations for the doctrine of fair dealing in copyright law. From an economic perspective, fair dealing exists because of an inherent market failure in the publishing business. For example, locating, contacting, and negotiating with a publisher for the right to use a mere two pages out of a book of 1,000 pages may cost more than the actual licence being offered by the publisher for those two pages. In such cases, it is more efficient to regard the use of the two pages as a reasonable exception to copyright law since the use of those two pages is not likely to hurt the publisher in any way. Another justification for fair dealing lies in the fact that, unlike tangible property, IP, being *intangible*, can be enjoyed by more than one person at the same time without harming the creator's use of the same. Thus, photocopying a work for archival purposes or reproducing a certain passage for the purposes of parody or criticism, will not affect the financial interests of the copyright owner, nor will it harm the incentives for future creation of IP by the community at large.

The law prevalent at the time of the Williams & Wilkins lawsuit—the US Copyright Act, 1909—did not provide for a fair use defence.

The defence was instead an exception *carved out* of the law by US judges.[128] The four-factor test described by the Court of Claims in this case reflected the economic rationale for fair dealing. The Court held that cases of copyright infringement required an examination of: '(a) the purpose and character of the use, (b) the nature of the copyrighted work, (c) the amount and substantiality of the material used in relation to the copyrighted work as a whole, and (d) the effect of the use on a copyright owner's potential market for and value of his work'.[129]

Williams & Wilkins could not establish that they were losing money because of the photocopying. On the contrary, the evidence on record showed a general increase in net profits over the years. The court also noted that the four journals that were the subject of the lawsuit were profitable for the most part, and that they counted for a very small part of the publisher's overall business. The court said that, '[t]he record is also barren of solid evidence that photocopying has caused economic harm to any other publisher of medical journals'.[130] The Court of Claims added that the publisher 'has never made a detailed study of the actual effect of photocopying on its business, nor has it refuted defendant's figures'.[131] The court went on to point to the lack of any viable licensing mechanism created by the publishing community to cater to the photocopying needs of libraries. Since the evidence overwhelmingly pointed to the lack of any economic damage to the publisher, the Court of Claims ruled in favour of the libraries while lamenting the lack of legislative guidance on the issue of photocopying.[132] This decision was appealed to the US Supreme Court but in an unfortunate anti-climax, one of the nine judges on the US Supreme Court recused himself from the matter and the remaining eight were equally split in their conclusions. This meant that the judgment of the Court of Claims would continue to stand and be treated as good law.[133]

The Williams & Wilkins case was a wake-up call for the publishing community, which now had to face newer challenges, with photocopying technology getting better, and affordable. This case had two consequences. First, US publishers tried to curb the legal limits of photocopying in libraries, so as to force them to purchase licences for photocopying. This effort would bear fruit in

1976, when the US Congress enacted restrictions in Section 108 of the new Copyright Act, which limited photocopies in libraries and archives only to the limited purposes of replacing lost or destroyed copies. This was an emphatic victory for the efforts of publishers like Williams & Wilkins, who had long battled against the right of libraries to photocopying. With the new restrictions in place, libraries would be forced to purchase licences from the publishers to allow patrons to photocopy their books.[134] The second consequence was the creation of the Copyright Clearance Center (CCC) in 1978 by publishers. The CCC would be a collective licensing agency, on the lines of the copyright societies that had already existed in the music industry for several decades. The CCC would issue licences and collect royalties from all institutions which were engaged in large-scale photocopying of journals and books whose copyright was owned by publishing houses that were members of the CCC. By creating a viable licensing mechanism for monetizing such large amounts of photocopying, the publishers were hoping to overcome their most significant weakness in the Williams & Wilkins case, where the court had concluded that the publisher was not losing revenue from photocopying because it did not have a viable licensing mechanism in place to collect such revenues. With the CCC in existence, such an argument would not hold in the future.

The CCC's business model was as audacious as the Williams & Wilkins lawsuit against the libraries since it sought to monetize a practice which had continued for several decades without any claim by copyright owners. However, the CCC had two quick victories in *Basic Books* v. *Kinko's Graphic*[135] (1991) and *Princeton Univ.* v. *Michigan Document Servs.*[136] (1996). Both cases involved photocopied course packs aimed at the student market. The 'fair use' defence was quickly overcome when the publishers were able to establish, as anticipated, that they had a viable mechanism to collect revenues for photocopying of their content, and that they were suffering economic damage due to unlicensed photocopying. Publishers won both cases and photocopying services now had to pay royalties to the publishers for course packs. The challenge of keeping pace with technology continues for the publishing industry. There is an ongoing case in US courts on whether digital course packs made available by universities on their computer networks are within the boundaries of fair use.[137] A final judgment is awaited in this series of litigation.

The DU Photocopy Case

The DU photocopy case filed by three academic publishers, mentioned briefly at the beginning of this chapter, was dismissed in September 2016 by a single judge of the Delhi High Court.[138] The court ruled that photocopying for educational purposes was covered under the exception provided under Section 52(1)(i) of the Copyright Act, 1957. According to the court, this provision (incidentally, introduced before photocopier machines became commercially viable for Indian universities) permits the reproduction of any copyrighted work by a teacher or pupil in the course of instruction. The High Court chose to interpret the provision without placing any restrictions on the amount of work that could be photocopied. In other words, the court appears to have now permitted any copyrighted work to be used for any educational uses without payment of any royalty. Recall that India had demanded a similar provision in the Stockholm Protocol for any work that was being used for educational or scholastic activities. After opposition from the developed countries, especially the UK, this demand was toned down, and the Stockholm Protocol, 1967, was worded to permit developing countries to make a reservation allowing the use of copyrighted works for 'teaching, study and research in all fields of education', provided the copyright owners were paid 'just compensation'. In 1971 at the Paris Revision Conference, the Stockholm Protocol was replaced with a complicated compulsory licensing regime which was incorporated into Sections 32, 32A, and 32B of the Copyright Act in 1983. Some of these provisions were directed at 'systematic instructional activities'. These compulsory licensing provisions, unlike an exception in the form of Section 52(1)(i), ensure that the copyright owner is paid a royalty for the use of the work. The Delhi High Court's decision appears to make these compulsory licensing provisions redundant since it has allowed works to be photocopied for educational purposes without requiring either a compulsory licence from the Copyright Board or permission from the copyright owner. There is a general presumption in law against interpreting a legislation in a manner which renders any individual provision of that legislation otiose. The Delhi High Court's judgment appears to ignore this principle of statutory interpretation. In all fairness, however, it is not clear whether the publishers pursued this line of argument before the Delhi High Court.

This judgment is currently under appeal before a Division Bench of the Delhi High Court. While this decision of the High Court was welcomed by the students and academics involved in the case, the question remains whether this decision will adversely affect the incentives of publishers to invest more resources into publishing Indian scholarship.

Notes

1. Paul Goldstein, International Intellectual Property Law: Cases and Materials 158 (2008).

2. *List of Contracting Parties to the Berne Convention*, available at http://www.wipo.int/treaties/en/remarks.jsp?cnty_id=969C (Last visited on 9 March 2015).

3. Sam Ricketson and Jane C. Ginsburg, International Copyright and Neighboring Rights, ¶ 14.05, at 885 (2005).

4. Goldstein, International Intellectual Property Law, at 159.

5. Paul Goldstein, Copyright's Highway: From Gutenberg to the Celestial Jukebox 149 (2003).

6. *When Charles Dickens Fell out with America*, BBC NEWS, 14 February 2012, available at http://www.bbc.com/news/magazine-17017791 (Last visited on 9 March 2015).

7. Charles Dickens, *Speech Given at a Dinner in Boston* (February 1842), available at https://ebooks.adelaide.edu.au/d/dickens/charles/d54sls/chapter3.html (Last visited on 9 March 2015).

8. World Intellectual Property Organization, *Records of the Intellectual Property Conference in Stockholm, June 11 to July 14, 1967* Vol. II, at 948 (1993.3) (1971); See also Eva Hemmungs Wirtén, *Colonial Copyright, Postcolonial Publics: The Berne Convention and the 1967 Stockholm Diplomatic Conference Revisited*, 7(3) Scripted, 532–50 (2010).

9. Rajya Sabha, *Debate on the Resolution re Approval and Ratification of the Berne Convention* (7 August 1952), at 3396.
10. Rajya Sabha, *Debate on the Berne Convention*, at 3387.
11. Rajya Sabha, *Debate on the Berne Convention*, at 3387.
12. Rajya Sabha, *Debate on the Berne Convention*, at 3391.
13. Rajya Sabha, *Debate on the Berne Convention*, at 3379–80.
14. Rajya Sabha, *Debate on the Berne Convention*, at 3399.
15. Copyright Act, 1911, as contained in the First Schedule, Indian Copyright Act, 1914, available at http://www.wipo.int/edocs/lexdocs/laws/en/il/il013en.pdf (Last visited on 9 March 2015).
16. Brussels Act, 1948, art. 7 (Article 7(1) states: 'The term of protection granted by this Convention shall be the life of the author and fifty years after his death.')
17. The Copyright Bill, 1955, clause 21.
18. The Copyright Bill, 1955, clauses 23, 24, and 25.
19. The Copyright Bill, 1955, clause 65(2).
20. Berne Convention for the Protection of Literary and Artistic Works, 1886, art. 5(2).
21. Barbara Ringer, *The Role of the United States in International Copyright: Past, Present, and Future*, 56 GEO. L. J. 1050, 1059 (1967–1968).
22. Ringer, *The Role of the United States in International Copyright*, at 1060–1.
23. Universal Copyright Convention, 1952, art. IV.
24. *India ratified the UCC on 21 October 1957*, available at http://www.wipo.int/wipolex/en/other_treaties/parties.jsp?treaty_id=208&group_id=22 (Last visited on 9 March 2015).
25. Ringer, *The Role of the United States in International Copyright*, at 1068.
26. Rajya Sabha, *Debate on the Copyright Bill 1955* (16 February 1956).
27. REPORT OF THE JOINT COMMITTEE OF THE HOUSES ON THE COPYRIGHT BILL, 1955 (Parliament of India), THE GAZETTE OF INDIA, EXTRAORDINARY, Part II, Sec. 2 968 (1956).
28. REPORT OF THE JOINT COMMITTEE OF THE HOUSES ON THE COPYRIGHT BILL, 1955, at 911.
29. REPORT OF THE JOINT COMMITTEE OF THE HOUSES ON THE COPYRIGHT BILL, 1955, at 915–16.
30. Rajya Sabha, *Debate on the Copyright Bill 1955* (14 May 1957), at 88–9.
31. Rajya Sabha, *Debate on the Copyright Bill 1955* (14 May 1957), at 88–9.
32. See Rajya Sabha, *General Information about Members*, available at http://rajyasabha.nic.in/rsnew/pre_member/1952_2003/d.pdf (Last visited on 9 March 2015).

33. See Rajya Sabha, *List of Former Members of Rajya Sabha (Term Wise)*, available at http://164.100.47.5/Newmembers/mpterms.aspx (Last visited on 9 March 2015).

34. Rajya Sabha, *Debate on the Copyright Bill 1955* (14 May 1957), at 120–34.

35. Rajya Sabha, *Debate on the Copyright Bill 1955* (14 May 1957), at 120–34.

36. Rajya Sabha, *Debate on the Copyright Bill 1955* (14 May 1957), at 120–34.

37. Rajya Sabha, *Debate on the Copyright Bill 1955* (14 May 1957), at 120–34.

38. Rajya Sabha, *Debate on the Copyright Bill 1955* (14 May 1957), at 120–34.

39. Rajya Sabha, *Debate on the Copyright Bill 1955* (14 May 1957), at 120–34.

40. Rajya Sabha, *Debate on the Copyright Bill 1955* (14 May 1957).

41. Rajya Sabha, *Debate on the Copyright Bill 1955* (16 February 1956), at 74. (The motion for this debate was titled 'the Bill to amend and consolidate the law relating to copyright is referred to a Joint Committee of the Houses consisting of 45 members').

42. Rajya Sabha, *Debate on the Copyright Bill 1955* (16 February 1956), at 74.

43. Rajya Sabha, *Debate on the Copyright Bill 1955* (14 May 1957), at 134–46.

44. Rajya Sabha, *Debate on the Copyright Bill 1955* (14 May 1957), at 145–6.

45. Rajya Sabha, *Debate on the Copyright Bill 1955* (14 May 1957), at 146.

46. Rajya Sabha, *Debate on the Copyright Bill 1955* (15 May 1957), at 228.

47. Lok Sabha, *Debate on the Copyright Bill 1955* (27 May 1957), at 2168.

48. See Parliament of India, *List of Members of the Constituent Assembly (as in November 1949)*, available at http://rajyasabha.nic.in/rsnew/constituent_assembly/constituent_assembly_mem.asp (Last visited on 9 March 2015); SIR CHIRRAVOORI YAJNESWARA CHINTAMANI AND MINOCHEHER RUSTOM MASANI, INDIA'S CONSTITUTION AT WORK (1940).

49. See generally Howard L. Erdman, *India's Swatantra Party*, 36(4) PUBLIC AFFAIRS 394 (Winter 1963–1964).

50. As discussed in Chapter 1, 'Indian Patent Law Declares Independence', in this volume.

51. Lok Sabha, *Debate on the Copyright Bill 1955* (27 May 1957), at 2172.

52. M.C. CHAGLA, ROSES IN DECEMBER 365 (1973).

53. Address by Shri M.C. Chagla, Minister of Education, Government of India, at the inauguration of the Eleventh Session of the Permanent Committee of the International Union for the Protection of Literary and Artistic Works (Berne Union) and the Seventh Session of the Inter-Governmental Copyright Committee held in New Delhi on 2 December 1963 as published in INTERNATIONAL COPYRIGHT: NEEDS OF DEVELOPING COUNTRIES: A SYMPOSIUM HELD BY THE MINISTRY OF EDUCATION, GOVERNMENT OF INDIA 4 (1967).

54. Address by Shri M.C. Chagla at the inauguration of the Eleventh Session of the Berne Union and the Seventh Session of the Inter-Governmental Copyright Committee, INTERNATIONAL COPYRIGHT, at 2–3.

55. Charles F. Johnson, *The Origins of the Stockholm Protocol*, 18 BULL. COPYRIGHT SOC'Y U.S.A. 91, 103–8 (1970–1971).

56. Lionel Bently, *Copyright Translations and Relations between Britain and India*, 82(3) CHI.-KENT L. REV. 1181 (2007).

57. (1895) 19 ILR (Bom) 557, at 567.

58. Bently, *Copyright Translations*, at 1208.

59. Bently, *Copyright Translations*, at 1201.

60. Bently, *Copyright Translations*, at 1230.

61. Bently, *Copyright Translations*, at 1237.

62. Bently, *Copyright Translations*.

63. Copyright Act, 1914, § 4.

64. REPORT OF THE JOINT COMMITTEE OF THE HOUSES ON THE COPYRIGHT BILL, 1955, at 914.

65. Rajya Sabha, *Debate on the Copyright Bill 1955* (14 May 1957).

66. Address by Shri M.C. Chagla at the inauguration of the Eleventh Session of the Berne Union and the Seventh Session of the Inter-Governmental Copyright Committee, at 3.

67. Universal Copyright Convention, 1952, art. V.

68. See generally Robert N. Herman, *The Manufacturing Clause: A History and Critique of Sophism in the Copyright Act*, 17(2) IDEA 9 (1975).

69. Herman, *The Manufacturing Clause*, at 21.

70. Marshall A. Leaffer, *International Copyright from an American Perspective*, 43 ARK. L. REV. 373, 400 (1990).

71. Johnson, *Origins of the Stockholm Protocol*, at 158–9.

72. T.S. Krishnamurti, *Needs of Developing Countries in the Field of International Copyright*, in INTERNATIONAL COPYRIGHT: NEEDS OF DEVELOPING COUNTRIES: A SYMPOSIUM HELD BY THE MINISTRY OF EDUCATION, GOVERNMENT OF INDIA 25 (1967).

73. Krishnamurti, *Needs of Developing Countries*, at 26.

74. Krishnamurti, *Needs of Developing Countries*, at 28.

75. Krishnamurti, *Needs of Developing Countries*, at 32.

76. Krishnamurti, *Needs of Developing Countries*, at 34.

77. Krishnamurti, *Needs of Developing Countries*, at 38.

78. Rajya Sabha, *Written Answers to the Reactions of the Government on Suggestions to Withdraw from Copyright Conventions* (25 November 1966), at 2803–4.

79. Rajya Sabha, *Written Answers to the Reactions of the Government on Suggestions to Withdraw from Copyright Conventions*, at 2803–4.

80. RICKETSON AND GINSBURG, INTERNATIONAL COPYRIGHT, ¶ 14.05, at 885.

81. RICKETSON AND GINSBURG, INTERNATIONAL COPYRIGHT, ¶ 14.13, at 885.

82. The Berne Convention for the Protection of Literary and Artistic Works of 9 September 1886, revised at Rome on 2 June 1928.

83. Johnson, *Origins of the Stockholm Protocol*, at 123. Ricketson and Ginsburg, International Copyright, ¶ 14.10, at 891.

84. RICKETSON AND GINSBURG, INTERNATIONAL COPYRIGHT, ¶ 14.34, at 915.

85. H.D. Sacks, *Crisis in International Copyright: The Protocol Regarding Developing Countries*, 26 JOURNAL OF BUSINESS LAW, 128 (1969).

86. COPYRIGHT: Monthly Review of the United International Bureaux for the Protection of Intellectual Property (BIPRI), 3rd Year (No. 11) 258 (November 1967).

87. World Intellectual Property Organization, *Records of the Intellectual Property Conference in Stockholm*, Vol. II, ¶ 2, at 947 (1993).

88. World Intellectual Property Organization, *Records of the Intellectual Property Conference in Stockholm*, Vol. II, ¶ 12, at 947 (1993).

89. Ken Gofton, *Copyright and Developing Countries, in* COPYRIGHT: LEGALIZED PIRACY? 16, 18 (N.N. Gidwani ed., 1968) (this article is a newspaper article that was originally printed in the Financial Times and the Economic Times (Bombay) on 5 August 1967).

90. Gofton, *Copyright and Developing Countries*, at 18.

91. Gofton, *Copyright and Developing Countries*, at 19.

92. Gofton, *Copyright and Developing Countries*, at 18.

93. Ringer, *The Role of the United States in International Copyright*, at 1070.

94. Ricketson and Ginsburg, International Copyright , ¶ 14.25, at 907.

95. Ringer, *The Role of the United States in International Copyright*, at 1074.

96. Gofton, *Copyright and Developing Countries*, at 18.

97. Gofton, *Copyright and Developing Countries*, at 16.

98. A report in the *Sunday Times* in July 1967 titled 'Books Row by Insight' provided the following analysis of the role played by the British civil service in obfuscating the provisions of the Protocol:

> The Stockholm conference emerges as a minor classic in the annals of the British civil service. Britain's role at Stockholm was to wreck the new proposals without incurring the odium of actually voting against them. It proved to be a task uniquely suited to the talents of Whitehall. The negotiations themselves were a patient rearguard action strategically derived from years of careful committeemanship. And the agreement which has emerged is so complicated that it could only have been drafted by the British civil service bent on destruction.

> Quoted in Jaman H. Shah, *India and International Copyright Conventions*, VIII (13) EPW 645, 647 (31 March 1973).

99. A.P. Herbert, *Britain's Role in Copyright Decision, in* COPYRIGHT: LEGALIZED PIRACY? 21, 22 (N.N. Gidwani ed., 1968) (this article is a

newspaper article that has been reprinted from the Times (London), 3 August 1967).

100. Herbert, *Britain's Role in Copyright Decision*, at 22.

101. Herbert, *Britain's Role in Copyright Decision*, at 22.

102. See COPYRIGHT: LEGALIZED PIRACY? (N.N. Gidwani ed., 1968).

103. Nirad C. Chaudhuri, Anant Kanekar, G.V. Desani, D.F. Karaka, P.L. Deshpande, M.R. Masani, Nissim Ezekiel, R.K. Narayan, R.E. Hawkins, A.G. Noorani, P.S. Jayasinghe, Prabhakar Padhye, Khushwant Singh, *Men of Letters Speak Out, in* COPYRIGHT: LEGALIZED PIRACY? 39–40 (N.N. Gidwani ed., 1968) (this article is a newspaper article that has been reprinted from the Times of India (Bombay), 21 September 1967).

104. T.S. Krishnamurti, *Official View, in* COPYRIGHT: LEGALIZED PIRACY? 30 (N.N. Gidwani ed., 1968) (this article is a newspaper article that has been reprinted from the Statesman (Calcutta), 8 September 1967).

105. Krishnamurti, *Official View*, at 31.

106. Krishnamurti, *Official View*, at 31–2.

107. Krishnamurti, *Official View*, at 32.

108. *Licensed Larceny, in* COPYRIGHT: LEGALIZED PIRACY? 33 (N.N. Gidwani ed., 1968) (this article is a newspaper article that has been reprinted from the Statesman (Calcutta), 11 September 1967).

109. *List of Contracting Parties to the Berne Convention (Stockholm Act, 1967)*, available at http://www.wipo.int/treaties/en/ActResults.jsp?act_id=23 (Last visited on 9 March 2015).

110. World Intellectual Property Organization, *Records of the Intellectual Property Conference in Stockholm*, Vol. II, at 810 (¶ 202.7—Summary Minutes—Plenary).

111. World Intellectual Property Organization, *Records of the Diplomatic Conference for the Revision of the Berne Convention July 5 to July 24, 1971* 35 (¶ 21—Conference Documents) (1974).

112. World Intellectual Property Organization, *Records of the Diplomatic Conference*, at 165 (¶ 2—General Report).

113. World Intellectual Property Organization, *Records of the Diplomatic Conference*, at 21.

114. F. No. 11 – 78/2015 –CRB/RTI – dated 11 September 2015, Reply from the Central Public Information Officer, Copyright Office.

115. Rajya Sabha, *Written Answers to Questions Raised by Khushwant Singh and Shrikant Verma on the Issue of Piracy of Books* (8 October 1982), at 83–4.

116. Rajya Sabha, *Motion: 'Calling Attention of the Rajya Sabha on the Need to Bring a Bill to Control Book Piracy'* (4 November 1982), at 375–6.

117. Rajya Sabha, *Debate on the Copyright (Amendment) Bill, 1984* (23 August 1984), at 201.

118. MINISTRY OF HUMAN RESOURCE DEVELOPMENT, GOVERNMENT OF INDIA, STUDY ON COPYRIGHT PIRACY IN INDIA 48 (1999).

119. MINISTRY OF HUMAN RESOURCE DEVELOPMENT, STUDY ON COPYRIGHT PIRACY IN INDIA, at 69–70.

120. International Intellectual Property Alliance, *Annual Submission to the USTR* (30 April 2010), at 39 (piracy and enforcement updates in India); International Intellectual Property Alliance, *Annual Submission to the USTR* (10 February 2012), at 68 (piracy and enforcement updates in India).

121. Clyde H. Farnsworth, *Happy Birthday, Xerox 914*, THE NEW YORK TIMES, 9 August 1985, available at http://www.nytimes.com/1985/08/09/us/happy-birthday-xerox-914.html (Last visited on 15 March 2015).

122. EVA HEMMUNGS WIRTÉN, NO TRESPASSING: AUTHORSHIP, INTELLECTUAL PROPERTY RIGHTS, AND THE BOUNDARIES OF GLOBALIZATION, Chap. 3, at 62 (2004).

123. See GOLDSTEIN, COPYRIGHT'S HIGHWAY, Chap. 3.

124. See GOLDSTEIN, COPYRIGHT'S HIGHWAY, Chap. 3.

125. See GOLDSTEIN, COPYRIGHT'S HIGHWAY, Chap. 3.

126. Williams & Wilkins Co. v. United States, 172 U.S.P.Q. 670 (Ct.Cl. 1972).

127. Williams & Wilkins Company v. The United States, 487 F.2d 1345 (Ct.Cl. 1973).

128. Williams & Wilkins Company v. The United States (1973).

129. Williams & Wilkins Company v. The United States (1973).

130. Williams & Wilkins Company v. The United States (1973).

131. Williams & Wilkins Company v. The United States (1973).

132. Williams & Wilkins Company v. The United States (1973).

133. See GOLDSTEIN, COPYRIGHT'S HIGHWAY, Chap. 3.

134. GOLDSTEIN, COPYRIGHT'S HIGHWAY, at 114–15.

135. 758 F. Supp. 1522 (S.D. N.Y. 1991).

136. 99 F.3d 1381 (6th Cir. 1996).

137. Cambridge University Press et al. v. Patton et al., 863 F.Supp.2d 1190 (N.D. Ga. 11 May 2012).

138. The Chancellor, Masters & Scholars of the University of Oxford & Ors. v. Rameshwari Photocopy Services & Anr. CS(OS) No. 2439 of 2012 before the High Court of Delhi decided on 16 September 2016.

6

THE MOVING PICTURE

The movies first arrived in India in 1896, when a representative of the Lumière brothers screened a film at the Watson Hotel in the city then known as Bombay. The first full-length Indian feature films were made later (Dadasaheb Phalke's *Raja Harishchandra* (1913), the first silent feature, and Ardeshir Irani's *Alam Ara* (1931), the first talkie), which breathed life into a nascent industry, and changed the way the world looked at Indian cinema forever. Intellectual property (IP) issues in Indian cinema are nearly as old as the industry itself, focusing mainly on copyright, occasionally drifting towards trademarks in film titles. A 1928 committee on films referred to problems of 'piracy' in the country;[1] and a handful of cases reached the courts before Independence. The first major decision in copyright in cinema came many decades later, in 1978,[2] where the Supreme Court of India laid down the tests and principles to determine the infringement of a copyright, setting precedents that impact the law and the industry even today. Since then, the film industry has been tested by a range of questions in IP, compelling courts to devise newer principles to tackle newer generations of filmmakers.

Intellectual Property in Early Indian Cinema

The first copyright law was brought into India in 1847 'for the encouragement of learning'. Later, the Indian Copyright Act, 1914, co-opted the Imperial Copyright Act, 1911, into British India. The

1914 legislation extended copyright protection to four classes of works: literary, dramatic, musical, and artistic. At the time, 'copyright' was defined to mean the sole right to produce or reproduce the work or any substantial part in any material form.[3] In the specific case of 'literary, dramatic or musical works', copyright also extended to the right to make any record or 'cinematograph film or other contrivance by which the work may be mechanically performed or delivered'.[4] To explain further, if X made a movie similar or even identical to an original movie made by Y, the latter could not sue the former for copyright infringement in the film by itself as the law did not recognize films as a separate class of works. But Y could possibly sue X for copyright infringement in the underlying literary work (for example, the script) or dramatic work (for example, choreography or scenic arrangement), because the copyright in the literary or dramatic work gave the copyright owner the sole right to perform or reproduce the work in public. Thus, although the Copyright Act, 1914, did not expressly protect cinematograph films as a separate class, it still gave film producers the right to sue for copyright infringement of the underlying literary or dramatic works. It was only later that the Copyright Act, 1957, recognized cinematograph films as a separate class of works. Indian policymakers were, however, grappling with the issue of copyright protection of cinematograph films as early as the 1920s.

One of the earliest bodies to express concerns on IP law in cinema was the 1928 Indian Cinematograph Committee, constituted even before the talkies took off. Its views on copyright issues, though, were limited, and were, by no means, exhaustive.

Established by the Governor-General of India, the Cinematograph Committee was headed by a Madras-based lawyer, Diwan Bahadur T. Rangachariar. Its primary task was to 'examine and report on the system of censorship of cinematograph films in India'.[5] The committee faced many challenges—the film industry was just over a decade old, there was no data or reliable information about films, and none of the members of the committee were knowledgeable about the industry. It concluded that the Indian film industry could develop only with government support, and among other things, recommended a liberal censorship of films.

The committee was also asked to 'survey the organisation for the exhibition of cinematograph films and the film-production industry in India',[6] for which it examined the copyright issue of piracy of films. Film exhibitors complained that the exclusive rights they obtained through contracts with producers or owners of films elsewhere were 'infringed by the free introduction of pirated copies of such films by other exhibitors'.[7] In other words, importers/exhibitors in India would obtain exclusive rights to exhibit foreign films in India, but simultaneously, other foreigners would make copies of the same films, and sell it to other persons in India at cheaper rates. In theory, the importers/exhibitors could be assigned the copyright in the script or dramatic work underlying the film, and sue for infringement subsequently.[8] But no precedent for a solution existed. The committee suggested other remedies to address this concern. First, importers could, by contract, require their foreign (mainly American) suppliers to indemnify the importers against losses from such practices followed by others. Second, individual films intended for exhibition in India could be compulsorily registered, along the lines of the registration system followed in England under their Cinematograph Act, 1927. The committee recommended that following such registration, no licence to exhibit any copy of such films should be granted to anyone but the registered persons.[9] But, like most of the committee's recommendations, this was never taken up or implemented.

Another copyright issue before the committee was brought by the Director of the Bombay Circle of Madan Theatres, Ardeshir Bilimoria, who raised the question of jurisdiction of the Copyright Act in India. The Copyright Act, 1914, which co-opted the British Copyright Act, 1911, into India, was applicable only to 'British India', leaving out many areas of the subcontinent. Bilimoria argued that copyright law should apply to 'Indian Native States' as well.[10] In fact, this did happen, but much later, with the extra-provincial jurisdiction law[11] that came into force when India became independent. The legal scholar Upendra Baxi contends[12] that there was limited knowledge about copyright law in the princely states of the subcontinent that were not a part of British India. The State of Hyderabad, though, had its own version of copyright law. The Portuguese and French enclaves in India, which remained separate for some years after the Republic of India came into being, also likely had different systems of protection. These remain interesting and as yet insufficiently explored areas of discussion.

The 1928 committee admitted that the existing copyright law was 'very complicated'.[13] The evidence of Motiram Vallicha, Manager of the Empire Film Company, was particularly illuminating:

> All pictures are copyrighted by producers. There are two kinds of copyrights. One is the copyright for the scenario or the plot, and the other is the copyright for a negative. Both copyrights are necessary to safeguard one's interests. If you have a copyright for a scenario and do not possess a copyright for the negative, your interests are not so fully safeguarded... I had a dispute in connection with one of the pictures recently, and I find that law says that unless and until the pictures or the publication of any book or novel or stage play is copyrighted in London and New York simultaneously, the British Empire does not recognise the American copyright. Very many times it so happens that copyrights have not been effected simultaneously in London and New York, and thus exclusive rights are not granted to us.[14]

Although there were a few cases to guide the committee,[15] it made only a passing reference to the idea–expression debate in copyright law by drawing attention to the lack of originality in the Indian films. Specifically, the committee pointed to the tendency of borrowing 'plots and incidents' from novels, and the habit of imitating Western films 'both in action and treatment'.[16]

The more obvious question of authorship and originality in films was ubiquitous but latent for a long time. The notion that authors of works could have exclusive rights over their creations was an eighteenth-century formulation (the Copyright Act of 1710 passed in the reign of Queen Anne of England), although its origins are attributed earlier still to charters granted to printers of books in the mid-sixteenth century.[17] The requirement that works protected by copyright must be 'original' was recognized by the English copyright law of 1911.[18] In order to claim copyright over a work, an author usually has to demonstrate that the work is the original *expression* of a thought or idea, rather than an original thought or idea itself. This disparity is frequently referred to as the 'idea–expression dichotomy' or the 'idea-expression divide', in copyright law.[19] Over the years, Indian law has interpreted the *expression* of the idea as bearing testimony to the 'investment by the author of mental faculties, skills, competence, craftsmanship, knowledge, labour and capital in the production of any work'.[20] By extension, the requirement of originality has come to mean that a work should not be substantially a copy of another work, or 'should not amount to a piracy ... of another's skill, competence, craftsmanship, labour and capital'.[21]

Copyright in films became a major subject of judicial scrutiny in India only in the middle of the twentieth century, which was a period of tumultuous change for the film industry the world over. By the 1950s, India had grown to become one of the biggest film producing countries in the world, second only to the United States (US).[22] However, the country was still reeling from the effects of partition of 1947, and struggling to find its own distinctive cinematic language so as to stand out amongst its global peers.

In 1951, more than two decades after the Rangachariar Committee, a Film Enquiry Committee was set up to report on the Indian film industry. The 1951 report discussed the need for industry reform, and discussed copyright briefly, but offered no ideas for reforming the law itself. It merely pointed out that, at the time, a film was not regarded as a form of original work as such, and could only be protected as a combination of literary, artistic, and dramatic works.[23] But India had recently signed the Brussels Act of 1948 revising the Berne Convention for the Protection of Literary and Artistic Works (Berne Convention), under which cinematograph films were recognized as a separate class of work protectable under copyright.[24] In order to meet treaty obligations, India had to now expand the definition of copyrightable works under law. This it did only in 1957.

Until the law clearly included cinematograph films as a separate form of copyright, rights in film content had to be protected in some other manner. The 1951 report disregarded the recommendation of the 1928 committee on the registration of films, for being impractical in modern times (it had recommended creating a register of film titles, containing a description of the work and photographs taken from each scene of the film.)[25] Instead, the 1951 report said, 'a complete copy of the film must be ... deposited with a central authority, who could produce it in court in case of disputes'.[26]

The 1951 report also referred to prevalent practices of 'plagiarism' in the film industry: Indian producers were routinely 'plagiarizing' material from literary works. Without an association of authors and playwrights in the country, affected authors could not defend themselves. At the same time, writers also submitted material to filmmakers, claiming originality, but in fact, copied content themselves. Studios were also accused of stealing ideas and themes from unpublished material submitted to them. Some industry representatives suggested that authors should run a story bureau to deal with producers on copyright issues.[27] The idea of a 'story bureau' was to create a 'register' for scripts, similar to the register for films suggested by the 1928 committee. It is interesting that both the 1928 and 1951 committees were faced with the choice between industry self-regulation and formal copyright law as methods of protection. But the 1951 report concentrated more on film certification and censorship, and was a precursor to the Cinematograph Act passed the following year.

By 1957, a new copyright law was enacted in India. No story bureaus or registers for film scripts were created, although films would now be works entitled to protection separate from literary, artistic, or dramatic works.[28] But the first major court case in Indian cinema came before the 1957 Act came into existence, testing, therefore, the older version of copyright law. The fact that a cinematograph film was not separately protectable under the older law did not prevent the court from laying down principles of copyright law that have been invoked by the film industry for decades since.

The Movies Meet the Supreme Court

The films made in the early post-Independence years were harbingers of the 'golden era' of Indian cinema. A minor hit, the Hindi-language film called *New Delhi* (1956), a black-and-white romantic comedy starring Kishore Kumar and Vyjayanthimala, became the subject of a landmark decision in India's copyright and cinematic history, *R.G. Anand* v. *Delux Films*.[29] The case laid down the tests and principles to determine the infringement of a copyright, setting precedents that impact the law and the industry even today.

The history of the case began with a play entitled 'Hum Hindustani' (not to be confused with the 1960 movie of the same name) written by R.G. Anand, an architect by training, and also a playwright and theatrical producer. Written in Hindi in 1953, the play was first staged in February 1954 at Wavell theatre, a former cultural landmark of the Indian capital city, once situated on the modern-day shopping street, Janpath.

The play was built around the theme of provincialism, showing the prejudice between persons belonging to different states, depicted through relations between two families, one each from north and south India. The 'boy' from one family falls in love with the 'girl' from the other, to the displeasure of both families, which then decide to find suitable alliances for their children within their own communities. The two broker a suicide pact, but a good samaritan in the form of the marriage broker (coincidentally) hired by both families intervenes. The parents, however, believe their children to have killed themselves, and realize their mistake. Eventually, the two young people appear on stage, now apparently married to each other, with the rites performed by the marriage broker, and the two families reconcile.

In 1955, filmmaker Mohan Sehgal announced the production of a film called *New Delhi* under his own banner, Delux Films. The film, like the play, was about two families, one each from north and south India, where the 'boy' from one family, played by Kishore Kumar, and the 'girl' from the other, played by Vyjayanthimala, meet and fall in love. The film dealt with questions of provincialism, dowry, and caste, with many sub-plots in between, including marriage pacts and suicide attempts. Eventually, both groups shed their prejudices and the original couples unite.

Anand, after watching the film upon its release in 1956, filed a suit for violation of copyright under the Indian Copyright Act, 1914, against Sehgal and the production house, for making a film that was 'entirely based' on his play. Anand claimed that Sehgal had 'dishonestly imitated' the story of the play in the film, which Anand had allegedly narrated to Sehgal during a brief meeting earlier.

The defendants—Delux Films and Sehgal, among others—had their own version of the story. Sehgal claimed that he had been interested in making a film on 'provincialism', that is, the attitudes of people from the provinces. Balwant Gargi, the renowned Punjabi dramatist and short-story writer, apparently suggested to Sehgal that he might be interested in a play called 'Hum Hindustani' along similar lines. After meetings that allegedly took place between all the parties, Sehgal apparently informed the playwright, 'though the play might have been all right for the amateur stage, it [is] too inadequate for the purpose of making a full length commercial motion picture'.[30] The trial court and the Delhi High Court both held that there was no violation of copyright in the play, after which the matter reached the Supreme Court.

That the subject matter of both the play and the film was provincialism was a fact to which the parties as well as the court conceded. This was a sentiment reverberating throughout contemporary Indian social and political commentary. The magazine *FilmIndia* said that the film 'expose[d] and emphasize[d] the crass and inherent stupidity of that widely prevalent attitude in India which is called provincialism and which makes the people of one linguistic region deride and distrust those of others'.[31]

Producer–director Sehgal, in a 1977 interview, months before the Supreme Court decision, offered further context. *New Delhi*, the first film to be made under his home banner, Delux Films, was apparently inspired by contemporary debates on the reorganization of states:

> This film was originally to be based on the subject of inter-communal marriage. But at that time, the [States] Reorganisation Commission was in session to carve out states into linguistic divisions. At that time, I thought that such divisions may generate an air of provincialism among the people of respective states, so I got a chance to pick up a topical subject of national and social significance. We finalised the subject and made 'New Delhi'.[32]

The States Reorganisation Commission (SRC) came into existence in 1953 after the Telugu-speaking people undertook a spirited and aggressive protest for linguistic autonomy. The SRC was appointed by the Indian government to 'make recommendations in regard to the broad principles which should govern the solution of this problem'.[33] The SRC's recommendations led to the enactment of the States Reorganisation Act, 1956, which reorganized the provinces along the lines of the languages spoken in different parts of the country. The substantial success of the creation of modern Indian states showed that language was 'a more powerful marker of identity than caste or religion', and an indicator of 'provincial pride'.[34]

Both Sehgal's film and Anand's play were artistic representations of the linguistic differences that pervaded Indian society, and to that end, similarities and resemblances between the two were discernible. In assessing whether *copyright infringement* could be established, the Supreme Court identified certain key principles that have been applied time and again in all subsequent matters on the subject. Firstly, there could be no copyright in ideas, subject matter, themes, plots, or historical or legendary facts, and violation of copyright in such cases would be confined to the form, manner, and arrangement and expression of the idea by the author of the work. Secondly, where the source of a work is the same idea, similarities are bound to exist. In such cases, the question is as to whether the copy is fundamentally or substantially similar to the copyrighted work. If a work were a literal imitation of the copyrighted work, with only minor variations, then it would be a copyright violation. Thirdly, the best test to determine a copyright violation lies in the opinion of the reader, spectator, or viewer after having read or seen both works. This can be established if there is 'an unmistakable impression that the subsequent work appears to be a copy of the original'.[35] Fourthly, there can be no infringement where the same theme is presented and treated differently such that the subsequent work becomes a completely new work. Fifthly, there can be no infringement even if there are similarities between the two works, but other material and broad dissimilarities in the works counter the intention to copy the original, and coincidences are clearly incidental. Sixthly, regarding copyrights in stage plays and films, the two modes of expression have very different perspectives, with films having a much wider scope, field, and background than plays. Despite this, however, if after watching a film, a viewer 'gets a totality of impression that the film is by and large a copy of the original play',[36] copyright violation may be said to have been proved.

Applying these tests to the case, the Supreme Court concluded that the film could not be regarded as a substantial copy of the play, observing, 'but for the central idea (provincialism, which is not protected by copyright), from scene to scene, situation to situation, in climax to anti-climax, pathos, bathos, in texture and treatment and purport and presentation, the picture is materially different from the play'.[37]

R.G. Anand had filed his original suit in 1954, under the 1914 copyright law. The Supreme Court decision came only in 1978, twenty-four years on. By then, the Copyright Act, 1957 had come about. Its provisions were borrowed from English law only to some extent, and it introduced some new concepts and principles, although the underlying principles of copyright were substantially the same. Upendra Baxi affords this law much historical significance, noting that this was 'the first truly Indian legislation after well over two centuries of subjection to the "imperial" law', the first time India had its own copyright law 'in contemporary history', which 'represented the law–policy choices made by its independent legislature'.[38]

For the first time, the 1957 law recognized cinematograph films as a separate type of work entitled to copyright protection. The author of a cinematograph work is the producer of the film. To the extent that a film is, among other things, a combination of a script (literary or dramatic work), performance (performers' rights), music (musical work), and lyrics (literary works), the law recognizes that copyrights in a film or a sound recording can exist separate from the copyrights in the underlying works, such as music and lyrics. The rights of the owners of the underlying works remained under a cloud, partly because the law was poorly understood, and partly due to controversial interpretations by courts.

The rights in the underlying works were the subject of a 1977 Supreme Court decision involving the Indian Performing Right Society Ltd. (IPRS) and Eastern India Motion Pictures Association.[39] The debate that followed this judgment eventually fructified into the 2012 Copyright Amendment, discussed in Chapter 7 in this volume. The 1977 case also gave us one of the most florid and oft-quoted definitions of films, provided by Krishna Iyer, J.:

A cinematograph is a felicitous blend, a beautiful totality, a constellation of stars... Cinema is more than long strips of celluloid, more than miracles in photography, more than song, dance and dialogue and indeed, more than dramatic story, exciting plot, gripping situations and marvellous acting. But it is that ensemble which is the finished product of orchestrated performance by each of the several participants, although the components may, sometimes, in themselves be elegant entities. Copyright in a cinema film exists in law, but [the law] preserves the separate survival, in its individuality, of a copyright enjoyed by any 'work' notwithstanding its confluence in the film. This persistence of the aesthetic 'personality' of the intellectual property cannot cut down the copyright of the film qua film.

The 1977 decision discussed the conditions under which a film or record producer could claim ownership over the copyright in the 'elegant entities' such as the music and lyrics used in the film or record. It concluded that when a producer commissioned a person to compose music or lyrics in return 'for reward or valuable consideration', the producer became the 'first owner of the copyright'. The issue of contention was the difference between a musician or lyricist working as an employee of a film producer (under a contract of service) and working on a commission for a specific film (under a contract for service). This is discussed in much greater detail in Chapter 7 in this volume.

The New Wave

If the 1950s and 1960s were the 'golden age' of Indian cinema, the 1970s and 1980s brought to the fore a 'new wave' of filmmakers, who moved away from commercial counterparts in content and picturization. Their films were realistic, drawing inspiration from true incidents. As film critic B.D. Garga says, a 'far cry from the petrified clichés of commercial cinema, they focused on the common man, his socio-economic problems, expectations and frustrations'.[40] These filmmakers sought to show aspects of Indian life that had always been 'glossed over' by mainstream cinema. Two cases involving films made in this era stretched the copyright principles laid out in the 1978 *R.G. Anand* decision to some extent.

The suit between the *Indian Express* newspaper and filmmaker Jagmohan Mundhra was one of these cases, filed and decided in 1984.[41]

On 27 April 1981, the first in a series of articles written by journalist Ashwini Sarin appeared in the *Indian Express*, with these opening lines: 'Yesterday, I bought a short-statured skinny woman, belonging to a village near Shivapuri in Madhya Pradesh for Rs 2,300/-.

Even I find it hard to believe that I have returned to the Capital this morning buying this middle aged woman for half the price one pays for a buffalo in Punjab'.[42] Three more provocative articles appeared subsequently, describing in detail the journalist's investigation into a prostitution racket in the state of Madhya Pradesh. They described his efforts in approaching those concerned, the resistance he faced, the circumstances under which he decided to 'buy' a woman to expose the racket, how the deal was struck, and how the woman—Kamla—was brought to New Delhi and escorted to the journalist's residence.

Some months after the newspaper articles appeared, the eminent playwright Vijay Tendulkar wrote a play titled 'Kamla', which came to be staged over 150 times in seven languages across India. Filmmaker Jagmohan Mundhra made a film version of the play, with the same title, in 1984, with a script authored by Tendulkar. The film's central theme was the purchase of a woman called Kamla by a journalist to draw attention to the flourishing flesh trade in the country. Sarin and the *Indian Express* sued Tendulkar and Mundhra in the Bombay High Court on the grounds that the movie *Kamla* infringed the copyrights in the story and articles published in 1981, and that the movie depicted the journalist and the newspaper in a defamatory situation.[43]

On defamation, the court agreed that the film introduced scenes and characters to highlight how reputed newspaper managements succumbed to political pressure, and directed the filmmaker to remove certain scenes before further distribution of the film.

On copyright violation, the court relied extensively on the principles set by *R.G. Anand*, even though this case had been filed under the newer copyright law. The Bombay High Court dismissed the infringement contentions, observing that there was no copyright in historical facts. Copyright violation in such cases would be confined to the form, manner, arrangement, and expression of the facts in the second work. Here, the movie and the play were not works of pure fiction, as the central character and theme of both were clearly based on the newspaper articles. But, the court observed that the form, manner, or arrangement of a drama and movie are fundamentally and materially different from newspaper articles, and therefore, there is fundamental and substantial dissimilarity in the two modes of expression (that is, in a newspaper article, and in a stage play or movie). Claims of copyright infringement were thus 'misconceived'. Upendra

Baxi identifies this conclusion drawn by the court as a problematic 'nature of media' test: If the nature of the media were to determine infringement, then it would not be necessary to further examine the similarity or dissimilarity between two works. Arguably, this could not have been the intent behind copyright law.[44] Fortunately, this test did not find much favour in subsequent decisions.

Another case related to a documentary film made by Anand Patwardhan, titled *Waves of Revolution* (1975), about a contemporary students' revolt in Bihar led by the freedom fighter and revolutionary, Jayaprakash Narayan. The incident is believed to have led to, and was eventually repressed by, the infamous declaration of Emergency that same year. The state-run television channel, Doordarshan, telecast this film in 1977. Over a quarter of a century later, in 2003, the same channel telecast another film titled *26th June 1975*, made by their own employee, on the same incident. Patwardhan, in a suit filed in 2004 before the Bombay High Court, alleged that the Doordarshan film infringed his copyright by inserting extracts from his 1975 film without his knowledge or permission.[45] The filmmaker, who was eventually awarded damages of Rs 10 lakh or Rs 1 million, also argued that the extracted footage had been twisted and used to fundamentally differ from the viewpoint originally expressed. The 2009 decision offered an opportunity to discuss many points of law relating to copyrights in films previously not addressed by courts.

Doordarshan claimed that its employee had taken excerpts of the film from its archival recordings, without knowledge of it being Patwardhan's documentary. It argued that the archival tape did not mention the origin of the recording, or whether its use would entail a liability. The court said that ignorance of copyright in a work could not apply to a film in which copyright was implicit, and it was for the channel to verify whether the copyright had been assigned to them, or whether the copyright term had expired.

Doordarshan also argued that they had been assigned the rights in the 1975 film. In fact, what the channel thought was an 'assignment to use' was only a 'partial assignment' by way of a licence to telecast Patwardhan's film for a fee of Rs 500 per telecast, with the specific condition that the film must be shown in full. Thus, the terms of the licence completely demolished the channel's claim of having rights to use footage from the documentary.

The channel also claimed that the film was related to historical facts, as the declaration of Emergency was a key event in modern Indian political history, and, therefore, no breach of copyright could be established. But this was not a case of two different films made on the same facts. Instead, here, the *expression* of the facts (the revolt, among others) had been directly copied. In the case of a film, copying includes 'making a photograph of any image' that forms part of the film, and even a single shot taken from a film could potentially constitute copyright infringement, subject to an assessment of the circumstances of the case. Here, the court pointedly said that the channel's 'cut-and-paste' job was clearly an infringement of copyright.

Copyright law allows for the defence of 'fair dealing', where works can be used to a limited extent without having to obtain permission from the copyright owners. This is interpreted differently across jurisdictions. In India, various examples of fair use are codified under law. For instance, it is not considered infringing to include an artistic work only by way of background, or incidental to the principal matters in the film. In this case, Doordarshan claimed that the total duration of the shots taken from the original documentary was only 86 seconds, and hence, could not be considered a substantial reproduction of the original work. But this contention, too, was dismissed by the court, which noted that the fair use exemption extended only to 'artistic' works, which the documentary was not, and that the reproduction was hardly incidental to the film.

In Borrowed Feathers

By the 1990s, Indian commercial cinema was nearly a century old, but had become more jaded in content and character than ever before. Experimentation in filmmaking was risky, as audiences seemed unwilling to accept anything new, and most films were substantially based on, if not entirely copied from, films made elsewhere. This was not a new trend, by any means. The 1928 Rangachariar Committee had also expressed concerns over the lack of originality in Indian films: 'In the social dramas there is frequently a tendency not only to borrow plots and incidents from Western novels, but also to imitate the Western films both in action and treatment. This kind of mimicry is not pleasing or successful. Though much can be learned from the Western films this sort of crude imitation is to be avoided'.[46]

Film critic B.D. Garga, too, said that with rare exceptions, this was a period of cinematic history that would 'go down as a barren period, devoid of any social concern or creative impulse, and catering to the lowest common denominator'.[47] In 2002, another film critic raised the same issue,[48] estimating that that year had seen a landmark number of Hindi films inspired by Hollywood films. Borrowing was rampant across all aspects of filmmaking. But the courts got involved only in a few cases, mainly dealing with stories, titles, and songs.

Borrowed Stories

Despite the lack of originality in Indian cinema being an open secret, there were no big-ticket copyright infringement suits by foreigners against Indian filmmakers until the turn of the twenty-first century. It was not that foreigners could *not* sue Indians for infringement. On the contrary, foreign works have always had the same rights of copyright protection as Indian works under law. Ordinarily, intellectual property rights (IPRs) are protected only within the jurisdictions where they are registered. Copyrights are different from other types of IP because many countries offer domestic protection for copyrights of works from foreign countries under certain conditions elaborated by international conventions.[49] In India, the Copyright Act contains a separate chapter dealing exclusively with international copyright. The law, read with the International Copyright Order, 1999—which is an executive order issued by the central government—allows India to extend copyright protection to works from those countries that reciprocate such protection for Indian citizens. Foreign copyright owners, including film producers, can enforce their rights in India through this order and the corresponding law.[50] This right was available since the first International Copyright Order was passed in 1958 (since replaced).[51] *Reciprocity* of protection is the key factor. While India has offered reciprocal protection, and permitted foreign rights-holders to pursue enforcement actions here, it has been criticized for not carefully examining whether Indian copyrighted works are afforded an equivalent degree of protection abroad.[52]

So, if foreigners were not prevented from initiating legal action in India, why were they not suing Indian producers for infringing their copyrights in movies? Hollywood film producer and former Indian tennis player Ashok Amritraj suggested that this was because Indian movies were too 'far under the radar' and Hollywood studios were unaware of allegations.[53] Interestingly, litigation was begun, not by the film industry, but by the television industry; and not by a big-ticket Hollywood producer, but by a romance novelist in the United Kingdom (UK).[54]

In the summer of 2003, Barbara Taylor Bradford alleged that her best-selling novel, *A Woman of Substance*, was being made, without her consent, into a television serial called *Karishma: Miracles of Destiny*. Both the novel and the serial tell a rags-to-riches tale of a servant who rises to become a businesswoman. After much forum-hopping (the Bombay and Calcutta High Courts, and the Supreme Court), the novelist's claims were dismissed, and pleas to stay the serial's telecast by Sahara Media Entertainment (the financier, producer, and broadcaster) were 'unhesitatingly and emphatically turned down', with the Calcutta High Court observing: 'Copyright Law does not protect basic plots and stock characters. If it granted such protection, four or five writers writing 15 or 20 novels with stock characters and stock plots could stop all writers of pop literature from writing anything thenceforth.'[55]

After the *R.G. Anand* and *Indian Performing Right Society* cases, the Indian movie industry had not seen any major reported decisions in copyright actions, but *this* case signalled renewed interest in the area, with several hundreds of crores of rupees at stake each time.

The American film studio, Twentieth Century Fox was involved in two major cases concerned with both film and television. The first was a 2010 case relating to its hit thriller *Phone Booth* (2002), about a man held hostage in a telephone booth by a sniper. The Bombay High Court was convinced that the unreleased Hindi film, *Knock Out*, was substantially a copy of *Phone Booth*.[56] Reiterating principles of the idea–expression debate, the court said, 'whilst the idea may not be unique to the author, the image portrayed or the expression made is essentially unique to the author [and if] such an expression in the shots of a film is copied, lifted from an earlier film, the infringement is complete'.[57] The court offered two tests to determine whether the second work is a copy of the original: First, the impression of the average viewer was necessary to determine infringement; and second, if the allegedly infringing parts were removed from the copied work, would the remainder have become meaningless. That the Hindi film had apparently been sent out for release in theatres did not help the Indian defendants, and the court decided in favour of the Hollywood production house, and the film's release was temporarily stalled. The defendants appealed, and the injunction was lifted, but the matter was eventually settled.[58]

The second major case involving Twentieth Century Fox dealt with its successful television series, named *24*, filmed on the fictional character of counter-terrorist agent Jack Bauer. Each season, across 24 episodes, covered a day (24 hours) in the agent's life, and used a real-time method of narration. In 2005, the Indian media conglomerate Zee Telefilms and its head Subhash Chandra were sued for making a television serial titled *Time Bomb*, which appeared to have many similarities with 24. The main pivot of the case was the format—spread over an hour, depicted in real time, with a clock counting down the seconds (including during commercial breaks), and multiple screens portraying simultaneous events. The content was also allegedly similar, dealing with terrorism, assassination attempts, and secret service agents. Zee relentlessly argued that there was no copyright in formats or presentation techniques, saying that both real-time and multiple screen formats were well-known and established methods. The Delhi High Court took eight years to arrive at its decision in 2012.[59] The court agreed that there could be no copyright in the manner and format of presentation. By now, Zee had already telecast episodes of its serial, which worked in the channel's favour. The court also offered some insights into the complex question of distinguishing between idea and expression, suggesting that it would always remain a subjective exercise:

> Where does idea end and expression begin? These are the questions which are the most difficult to answer or even to explain at the interim stage. These are situations for legal assessment after parties lead exhaustive

> evidence. Just as there is no mathematical formula for finding out when
> it is just and convenient to appoint a receiver, similarly ... there is no
> final and exact way of determining what is a copy, or what is a copy of
> the expression, or what is a copy of the idea, or what is a copy of the
> idea only.[60]

Eventually, *Time Bomb* ran only from June to December 2005. Anil
Kapoor Films formally acquired the Indian rights to *24* in 2011,[61] and
his adaptation of the American series was aired subsequently.

Litigation between Indian and foreign film industries was not a
one-way street. In 2004, a Karnataka-based film production house,
NRI Film Production Associates, ambitiously tried to sue Twentieth
Century Fox, claiming that the latter's movie, *Independence Day*
(1996) infringed the copyright in the former's film script titled
'Extra Terrestrial Mission'.[62] The Indian company claimed to have
registered the copyright for the film script in 1986, and had engaged
a US lawyer in 1993 to find a co-producer to make the film. (Under
Indian law, registration is not necessary for either acquiring or
enforcing a copyright, but merely creates the presumption that the
person in whose name the work is registered is the actual author or
owner of the work.) The Indian company alleged that the Hollywood
production house had unlawfully accessed the film script through the
US lawyer. But the Karnataka High Court believed that the differences
between the two were sufficiently stark to defeat the Indian case.
The court also ignored the allegations of illegal access of the film
material. In doing so, an opportunity was lost to build jurisprudence
on questions of access and confidentiality, which could have been very
useful to the film industry. The decision was interesting for making
a minor but important reference to the concept of 'scène à faire',
literally translated from the French as 'scene to be made' or 'scene
that must be done'. According to this concept, there are certain logical
scenes, actions, or sequences of events that are standard to general
themes or topics, for example, a depiction of a robbery will invariably
be followed by a chase sequence. Here, objection was raised about
depictions of traffic jams, disrupted communications, and effects of
nuclear missiles as a result of the alien invasion. The court concurred
with the Hollywood production house that, these being 'hackneyed
subjects' of science fiction, no novelty or uniqueness existed either

in their idea or expression, and therefore, they could be afforded no copyright.

Both issues of access and protecting 'scènes à faire' came up again in a case involving *Dhoom 3* (2013), the third in a popular series of heist films in Hindi. Mansoob Haider, a professional film scriptwriter, alleged that *Dhoom 3* infringed his rights in a script he allegedly delivered to Yashraj Films, the producers of the Dhoom franchise some years previously. He sued in 2014, many months after the film was released, and just before it was to be premiered on satellite television, claiming only credit in the film, and no damages. The Bombay High Court, in its 2014 judgment,[63] concluded that the two narratives unfolded in completely different ways, and decided in favour of Yashraj. The central question was whether, after removing all unoriginal scenes, such as all 'scènes à faire', would the film and the script still be substantially similar? And had the film copied a substantial part of the script? The court offered a three-step test to determine such cases: First, could it be proved that the other party had access to the original work?; second, would an ordinary person inevitably conclude that the work was copied?; third, was there substantial and material overlapping or commonality with the original elements? The court held that merely using well-established and commonly-used motifs, themes, or elements, or even coincidentally placing these in a certain order, gave a person no infringement rights. A token cost of one rupee was awarded against the complainant, to discourage persons from 'taking their chances' in making frivolous claims of this kind, which the film production house generously waived.

In recent years, instead of looking only to foreign shores, filmmakers are finding inspiration from other films in India itself. As a result, suits are flying across the country. For instance, the makers of the Tamil film *Naan Avanillai* (2007) alleged that Yash Raj Chopra's *Ladies v. Ricky Bahl* (2011) infringed their copyright.[64] The court appointed six lawyers to see both films to determine similarities and dissimilarities. The lawyers, being nominated by either side, unsurprisingly reported in favour of the side they were nominated by, and their accounts were inconclusive. Eventually, the Madras High Court, which heard the lawsuit just a day before the scheduled worldwide theatrical release of the Hindi film, went with Chopra's arguments and refused to stay its release.

Another subject that emerges in the debate surrounding cinema and copyright is that of remakes, where old movies are made again with a new set of artists, and released as new works. Remakes tend to be formally authorized by the original filmmakers, or those who own the rights through succession or assignment. But it is not always smooth sailing. Films capture the zeitgeist of their times. A film becomes successful usually because it resonates with its audience, either through its storyline, its selection of actors, or its music, or all of these together. The chances of replicating successes in a completely different environment, when catering to a different audience, are limited. Therefore, those undertaking remakes also experiment with the original film, for example, by fiddling with characterizations or dialogue. Executing these changes is a delicate exercise, and depends on the permissions received from the original filmmakers.

Sai Paranjape, the playwright, director, and scriptwriter of the classic, *Chashme Buddoor* (1981), was appalled at the new (2013) version of her film, and claimed that the remake 'was a complete distortion' of her work, being 'sleazy, vulgar, obscene and repulsive'.[65] She tried to prevent its release, alleging that her copyright in the script, and her 'moral rights' had been violated, and demanded Rs one crore by way of 'settlement'. But the production house submitted a contract dating to 1980, claiming Paranjape had assigned the copyright in the film script to the production house (which was unsuccessfully contested). Another claim in favour of the makers of the new film was the delay in filing the lawsuit. The intention to issue a remake was publicized in 2007, and the new movie was advertised for months before release. But Paranjape approached the High Court only a few days before its release in 2013. In light of the publicity the movie had received since 2007, the court concluded that Paranjape would have had prior knowledge of the movie, and decided against her.[66]

Films are also remade, or reissued, in dubbed form, in multiple languages, catering to different parts of the country. These films offer a different set of copyright challenges. Thiagarajan Kumararaja, the scriptwriter and director of a 'neo-noir' Tamil film, *Aaranya Kaandam* (2011), convinced the Madras High Court to prevent Capital Film Works (India) Limited (the producers of his film) from releasing dubbed versions of the film in Telugu and Hindi. Kumararaja claimed to have consented to the production of his film only in Tamil, and had refused to assign all his rights in the script to the film producers. Thus, although the producers owned the copyright in the Tamil film, they did not own the rights to the script. Under copyright law, a film script is entitled to protection as a work separate from the film it is incorporated into. This meant that the producers would require Kumararaja's permission each time they wanted to remake the film. The court agreed that there was irrefutable evidence that the dubbed films were about to be released, and that Kumararaja would suffer irreparable injury if a stay were not granted.[67]

The *Chashme Buddoor* and the *Aaranya Kaandam* lawsuits are in stark contrast to each other, for one important reason. Sai Paranjape, the filmmaker–scriptwriter of the first case, was perhaps not fully aware of the rights she was handing over when she signed the agreement in 1980 with her film producers. Kumararaja, though, was more astute when signing agreements around his film. When the other side tried to exploit the agreements and reissue dubbed versions, Kumararaja was quick to enforce his rights, which were clearly enumerated in the agreements. As cultural and linguistic cross-pollination increases over time, more such cases will emerge. Hopefully, the experience of their predecessors would have taught future filmmakers a lesson or two in assigning their copyrights onwards.

Borrowed Songs

Indian cinema is incomplete without its music, and the soundtrack accompanying a film has spawned an industry of its own, creating its own subculture of superstars, hits, and misses, which are often separate from the films they are associated with. Not surprisingly, the film music industry has its share of IP issues as well, particularly involving the issue of copyrights in songs. Every film song comprises at least three separate elements—melody, lyrics, and performance. These elements are actually three separate works that can be protected under copyright law: the musical work, that is, the melody, authored by the music composer; the literary work, that is, the lyrics, authored by the lyricist; and the performance, which is the right of the singer or the instrumentalist. Further, the film producer can separately claim the rights to the entire song recording itself, in the form that it is used in a film or in a soundtrack. Copyrights in film songs, just as in films, are a complex bundle of rights, and their enforceability is equally tricky. Most publicized claims of copyright infringement in film songs have dealt with sound recordings, but in fact relate to the underlying musical work (the melody), and for that reason, the words 'song' and 'melody' are used interchangeably in this chapter.

Entire websites are dedicated to the exercise of meticulously keeping track of original and 'lifted' pieces across films made in various Indian languages.[68] But music is a gentle language, and few such cases of inspiration ended in acrimony.

Two cases of copyright infringement took place, unusually, in the US, involving Indian musicians or music companies suing their peers there. Both cases involved hip-hop artistes and the practice of 'sampling', where a portion, or 'sample', of one recording is reused in a different song. Sampling is popular with disc jockeys, who 'mix' multiple sounds by playing different recordings simultaneously, or at different speeds, or in other ways. Sampling has been around for decades, but became a legally contentious issue when musicians began to make profit from recordings that used samples from others' music.

The first case was a copyright claim by music director Bappi Lahiri, also known as India's 'disco king', and Saregama, the music company, in the song *'Thoda Resham Lagta Hai'*, from the film *Jyoti* (1981). In 2002, Lahiri and Saregama filed two separate lawsuits in the district court of Los Angeles, alleging that a contemporary hip-hop hit single, 'Addictive', by Truth Hurts featuring Rakim, had used samples from 'Thoda...' without permission. The main defendant in the lawsuit was the rapper and music entrepreneur Andre Young, better known as Dr Dre.

Lahiri had written 'Thoda...' after signing a two-page agreement with Pramod Films, the film's producers, who in turn assigned the music copyrights in *Jyoti* to Saregama India Limited. In 2002, Lahiri discovered his song 'had been sampled and used as the "hook" and the main musical track' in 'Addictive'. He obtained a US copyright registration for the composition in April 2003. Two weeks later, Saregama also registered a US copyright in the sound recording and the musical composition. Lahiri and Saregama then filed separate complaints, which were consolidated into a single action. The US courts delved into Indian law and judicial precedent more than ordinarily expected in such matters, because Young and his co-defendants raised questions about the ownership of the original copyrights in the Hindi film song.

An early US court decision said there was 'genuine issue' of copyright in the song between Lahiri and Saregama, since both held US copyright registrations, and they had agreed that they were co-owners of such copyrights. Actually, the Lahiri–Saregama agreement was to split, in a ratio of 30:70, any recovery in the lawsuit (Saregama had claimed damages of USD 500 million), and the agreement spoke of co-ownership only for these consolidated cases. The court, misled by Lahiri's lawyers, had incorrectly construed the agreement to amount to full co-ownership.[69] Young argued that Lahiri and Saregama had conflicting claims for copyright ownership, and that Lahiri, in fact, had no copyrights to the song under Indian law. Further, he said that the music director and the company should clarify the ownership issue separately in an Indian court before taking any action in the US. In its 2007 decision, the US court agreed that Lahiri never owned, and certainly did not own at the time of filing the suit, the copyright in 'Thoda...', because Pramod Films had hired him to compose and produce the song. Under their contract, Lahiri had agreed 'to work as Music Director in any one of [Pramod's] forthcoming films' and to 'compose music for the said film [Jyoti] including background music', in consideration for which, Pramod agreed to pay Lahiri Rs 30,000 and credit him as the music director.[70] The US court relied heavily on the interpretation of the Indian Supreme Court in *Indian Performing Right Society Ltd.* v. *Eastern India Motion Pictures Association*,[71] and concluded that existing and future rights of music composers or lyricists could be defeated by a film producer (this is discussed in more detail in Chapter 7 in this volume).

Based on the *Indian Performing Right Society* case, and provisions of Indian copyright law, the US court decided that Lahiri did not own the copyright in the song. (The court's decision came in response to an application by Universal [the defendants] claiming that Lahiri did not own copyright in the song, and instead the copyright lay with Saregama). Usually, a copyright registration creates a presumption that the ownership of the copyright is valid, but here, ownership would be determined according to Indian copyright law.

The second US case also involved Saregama, which brought an infringement action against American rapper and music producer Timbaland, for sampling the song, 'Baghon Mein Bahar Hai' from the film *Aradhana* (1969) in his hip-hop song, 'Put You on the Game'. Saregama claimed ownership in the sound recording of the song under a 1967 agreement between the film producer, Shakti Films and Saregama's predecessor-in-interest, Gramophone Company of India Limited. Both the US district and appellate courts discussed a single question: Did the agreement grant Saregama a copyright in the sound recording? Both courts closely analysed the agreement, and concluded that according to that document, Saregama had only a two-year exclusive right, or copyright, to re-record any pre-recorded song covered by the agreement, after which this right no longer existed. The courts did not examine whether this song was covered by the agreement, but merely said that Saregama could not file a lawsuit, because it had no rights.[72]

In 2004, a Bangladeshi band, Miles, sued music director Anu Malik and others for copying the melody (and theme) from their song 'Phiriye Dao Amar Prem', which was so popular, that '[j]ust as Santana cannot leave a concert without performing "Black Magic Woman", [the band could not] conclude a concert without performing "Phiriye Dao"'. They alleged that Malik had copied the song in his song, 'Jana Jane Jana', from the film *Murder* (2004). The Calcutta High Court agreed with the Bangladeshi band, and directed that the song be removed from the film soundtrack.[73]

In 2008, the Punjabi musician Rabbi Shergill claimed that the song 'Jalte Hain' from the movie *Sorry Bhai* (2008) was a copy of his own 'Ballo' from his album 'Avengi ja Nahin'. As it turned out, Shergill's album had been produced and recorded in the studio run by the film's music director Gaurav Dayal. A Delhi High Court judge heard the two songs in his chamber, concluding that they appeared to be similar, if not identical, and restrained the film's release with the song in its soundtrack.[74] The two judges on the division bench hearing the appeal in this case also listened to the songs. This time, the court observed, '[t]here was some similarity in the use of the guitar, which is ... an acoustic guitar... This apart, there is some difference in the use of the accompanying sounds comprising of instruments and claps in so far as [Dayal's] song is concerned'. It concluded that the main constituent of a song is its melody, and, 'some similarity in the rhythm of the accompanying acoustic guitar cannot be sufficient to infer [copyright infringement]'.[75] The matter, however, did not end there. Upon the suggestion of Shergill's lawyers, the court then referred the matter to an expert, the santoor maestro Bhajan Sopori.[76] Eventually, Dayal acknowledged that his song was 'partly inspired' by Shergill's song.[77] Both parties agreed that neither would malign the other in the media, and as a mediated compromise, a sum of Rs one lakh was donated to a charitable organization.[78]

In 2011, Canadian singer Loreena McKennitt, sued music composer Deepak Dev, and the producers and distributors of the Malayalam movie *Urumi* (2011), one of the most expensive films ever made in that language.[79] McKennitt alleged that two of her songs were rearranged in the Malayalam film song 'Aaro nee aaro'. The Delhi High Court, in its 2011 order,[80] agreed, and restrained the Indian filmmakers from using the song in forthcoming versions of the film in Tamil, Telugu, Hindi, and English, but did not pass an order against the song already included in the Malayalam film. Attempts to reach a negotiated agreement failed, and the case remains pending before the court.[81]

What Lies Ahead

Several IP issues relating to films remain unexplored in this chapter. For instance, courts and tribunals in India have issued fascinating decisions on broadcasting rights and distribution. Piracy is another such issue. The 1928 Cinematograph Committee was the first to discuss the question of piracy in films, but filmmaking and the information age have transformed the concerns of 1928 into issues they would not have recognized today. Films are stored, distributed, broadcast, and shared in a manner radically different from even the 1980s. That was around the time Indian legislators tried to fashion an amended copyright law (1984) to curb video piracy (when sharing meant sharing *physical* copies of films embedded on videotapes). Addressing piracy challenges in the twenty-first century requires a nuanced understanding of how technology and the law intersect, and foresight of how the areas of filmmaking and technology are likely to evolve. Another issue is how states have developed enforcement mechanisms of their own to address unauthorized sharing. Legislatures of states such as Kerala, Tamil Nadu, and Maharashtra, have passed laws for preventive detention to combat allegedly increasing rates of piracy in their states.[82] Other states contemplate similar changes, but the constitutionality of such legislation remains questionable.[83] Several rights in existing copyright law also remain untested as yet. Perhaps the years to come will give us more insight into these questions, and more stories to tell.

Notes

1. INDIA, REPORT OF THE INDIAN CINEMATOGRAPH COMMITTEE (1927–1928).
2. R.G. Anand v. Delux Films, AIR 1978 SC 1613.
3. Section 1(2), Copyright Act, 1911, as contained in the First Schedule, Indian Copyright Act, 1914.
4. Section 1(2)(d), Copyright Act, 1911, as contained in the First Schedule, Indian Copyright Act, 1914.
5. INDIA, REPORT OF THE INDIAN CINEMATOGRAPH COMMITTEE, *Resolution of the Government of India, Home Department, (Political), Dated Simla, 6 October 1927, No. D.-4169* xii.
6. INDIA, REPORT OF THE INDIAN CINEMATOGRAPH COMMITTEE, *Resolution*, at xii.
7. INDIA, REPORT OF THE INDIAN CINEMATOGRAPH COMMITTEE, *Distribution and Exhibition (Piracy)*, at 85.
8. INDIA, REPORT OF THE INDIAN CINEMATOGRAPH COMMITTEE, *Chairman's Note on 'Copyright in Cinema Films—Foreign Films Piracy in India—Prevention Legislative Requirements' (Appendix H)*, at 219.
9. INDIA, REPORT OF THE INDIAN CINEMATOGRAPH COMMITTEE, *Chairman's Note*, at 219.
10. THE INDIAN CINEMATOGRAPH COMMITTEE, EVIDENCE, *Oral Evidence of Mr. Ardeshir Bilimoria, Director, Madan Theatres Ltd. (Bombay Circle) on 14 November 1927*, Vol. I, at 342.
11. INDIA, REPORT OF THE FILM ENQUIRY COMMITTEE, *Chapter III: The Film Under the Law* 36 (1951).
12. Upendra Baxi, *Copyright Law and Justice in India*, 28(4) JILI 497, 499 (1986).

13. THE INDIAN CINEMATOGRAPH COMMITTEE, EVIDENCE, *Oral Evidence of Mr. Rustomji Dorabji, Proprietor, Wellington, West End and Venus Cinemas on 15 November 1927*, Vol. I, at 363.

14. THE INDIAN CINEMATOGRAPH COMMITTEE, EVIDENCE, *Oral Evidence of Mr. Motiram Vallicha, Manager of Empire Film Company on 22 November 1927*, Vol. I, at 716.

15. The Committee mentioned a contemporary case in Bombay where 'a piece from a foreign film was taken over into an Indian film', which was apparently followed by a 'police court proceeding'. However, no further information was provided. As recounted in THE INDIAN CINEMATOGRAPH COMMITTEE, EVIDENCE, *Oral Evidence of Mr. Karamchand Bulchand, Director, 'Educational Kinematograph' on 22 November 1927*, Vol. I, at 689.

16. INDIA, REPORT OF THE INDIAN CINEMATOGRAPH COMMITTEE, *Production (The Types of Films Produced)*, at 34.

17. W. Cornish and D. Llewellyn, *Range and Aims of Copyright, in* INTELLECTUAL PROPERTY: PATENTS, COPYRIGHTS, TRADEMARKS AND ALLIED RIGHTS 375–9 (2008).

18. W. Cornish and D. Llewellyn, *Subsistence of Copyright, in* INTELLECTUAL PROPERTY: PATENTS, COPYRIGHTS, TRADEMARKS AND ALLIED RIGHTS 422 (2008).

19. University of London Press, Limited v. University Tutorial Press, Limited, [1916] 2 Ch. 601. The 'idea–expression' divide was expounded in detail here:

    The word 'original' does not in this connection mean that the work must be the expression of original or inventive thought. Copyright Acts are not concerned with the originality of ideas, but with the expression of thought, and, in the case of 'literary work,' with the expression of thought in print or writing. The originality which is required relates to the expression of the thought. But the Act does not require that the expression must be in an original or novel form, but that the work must not be copied from another work—that it should originate from the author.

20. Baxi, *Copyright Law and Justice in India*, at 508.

21. Baxi, *Copyright Law and Justice in India*, at 508.

22. MIHIR BOSE, BOLLYWOOD: A HISTORY 164 (2007).

23. INDIA, REPORT OF THE FILM ENQUIRY COMMITTEE, *Chapter III*, at 36–8.

24. INDIA, REPORT OF THE FILM ENQUIRY COMMITTEE, *Chapter III*, at 36.

25. INDIA, REPORT OF THE INDIAN CINEMATOGRAPH COMMITTEE.

26. INDIA, REPORT OF THE FILM ENQUIRY COMMITTEE, *Chapter III*, at 36.

27. INDIA, REPORT OF THE FILM ENQUIRY COMMITTEE, *Chapter III*, at 37.

28. Sections 2(f) and 14(d), Copyright Act, 1957.

29. R.G. Anand v. Delux Films.

30. R.G. Anand v. Delux Films, ¶ 8.

31. As cited in NANDINI BHATTACHARYA, HINDI CINEMA: REPEATING THE SUBJECT 94 (2012).

32. Indian Film Information, *From the Archive of IFI: We Bring You an Exclusive Interview of Director, Producer Mohan Segal (1977)*, available at http://www.indianfilminformation.com/index.php/bollywood-flashback/1384-from-the-archive-of-ifi-we-bring-you-an-exclusive-interview-of-director-producer-mohan-segal-1977 (Last visited on 3 February 2015).

33. See REPORT OF THE STATES REORGANISATION COMMISSION (1955), available at http://www.prsindia.org/uploads/media/SRC%201953%20-%20Part%20I.pdf (Last visited on 4 February 2015).

34. RAMACHANDRA GUHA, INDIA AFTER GANDHI 198–200 (2008).

35. R.G. Anand v. Delux Films, AIR 1978 SC 1613, ¶ 46.

36. R.G. Anand v. Delux Films, AIR 1978 SC 1613, ¶ 46.

37. R.G. Anand v. Delux Films, AIR 1978 SC 1613, ¶ 62.

38. Baxi, *Copyright Law and Justice in India*, at 503.

39. Indian Performing Right Society Ltd. v. Eastern India Motion Pictures Association, AIR 1977 SC 1443: 1977 SCR (3) 206.

40. B.D. GARGA, SO MANY CINEMAS: THE MOTION PICTURE IN INDIA 242 (2006).

41. Indian Express Newspapers v. Jagmohan Mundhra and Anr., AIR 1985 Bom 229.

42. Indian Express Newspapers v. Jagmohan Mundhra and Anr., ¶ 2.

43. Indian Express Newspapers v. Jagmohan Mundhra and Anr.

44. Baxi, *Copyright Law and Justice in India*, at 533.

45. Shri Anand Patwardhan v. The Director General, Directorate General of Doordarshan and Ors., Suit No. 2259 of 2004 (Bombay High Court) (unreported), (order passed on 31 March 2009).

46. INDIA, REPORT OF THE INDIAN CINEMATOGRAPH COMMITTEE, *Production*, at 34.

47. GARGA, SO MANY CINEMAS, at 205.

48. Aseem Chhabra, *How Original is Bollywood?*, REDIFF MOVIES, 31 October 2002, available at http://www.rediff.com/entertai/2002/oct/31bolly.htm (Last visited on 3 February 2015).

49. These include the Berne Convention, the Universal Copyright Convention (UCC), the Agreement on Trade-Related Aspects of Intellectual Property Rights (TRIPS), and the Convention for the Protection of Producers of Phonograms against Unauthorised Duplication of their Phonograms (1971).

50. The Copyright Office claims to have lost the file pertaining to the International Copyright Order, 1999, in a response to an application filed by the authors under the Right to Information (RTI) Act, 2005, which did not permit the authors to analyse the reasons for which Indian copyright protection has been extended to foreign works. The Copyright Office said, 'the file pertaining to the International Copyright Order, 1999 is not readily available and seems to be misplaced due to shifting of our office from Curzon Road Barracks to Parliament Street, New Delhi. The efforts are being made to trace the file and the documents will be sent ... as and when the file is transferred.' See Prashant Reddy, *Copyright Office Loses the File Pertaining to the International Copyright Order, 1999*, SPICYIP, 14 August 2011, available at http://spicyip.com/2011/08/copyright-office-loses-file-pertaining.html (Last visited on 3 February 2015).

51. D.C. Gabriel, *Note on Copyright*, available at http://www.nalsarpro.org/PL/Articles/DCGabriel.pdf (Last visited on 3 February 2015).

52. See Shamnad Basheer, *Changing Our Tune*, THE INDIAN EXPRESS, 15 January 2011, available at http://archive.indianexpress.com/news/changing-our-tune/737681/0 (Last visited on 3 February 2015).

53. Chhabra, *How Original is Bollywood?*.

54. Rachana Desai, *Copyright Infringement in the Film Industry*, 7(2) VAND. J. ENT. LAW & PRACT. 259 (Spring 2005).

55. Barbara Taylor Bradford v. Sahara Media Entertainment Ltd., 2004 (28) PTC 474 Cal.

56. Twentieth Century Fox Film Corporation v. Sohail Maklai Entertainment Pvt. Ltd., 2010 (112) BOMLR 4216.

57. Twentieth Century Fox Film Corporation v. Sohail Maklai Entertainment Pvt. Ltd., at 17.

58. Prashant Reddy, *A Clarification on the Fox–'Knockout' Copyright Dispute*, SPICYIP, 20 March 2013, available at http://spicyip.com/2013/03/a-clarification-on-fox-knockout.html (Last visited on 3 February 2015).

59. Twentieth Century Fox Film Corporation v. Zee Telefilms Ltd., 2012 (51) PTC 465 Del.

60. Twentieth Century Fox Film Corporation v. Zee Telefilms Ltd., at 108.

61. Meenakshi Verma Ambwani, *Anil Kapoor's Production House Bags Rs 100 cr Deal to Adapt 24 Series*, THE ECONOMIC TIMES, 9 November 2011, available at http://articles.economictimes.indiatimes.com/2011-11-09/news/30377957_1_indian-television-major-hollywood-emmy (Last visited on 3 February 2015).

62. NRI Film Production Associates v. Twentieth Century Fox Film Corporation, ILR 2004 Kar 4530.

63. Mansoob Haider v. Yashraj Films Pvt. Ltd., 2014 (59) PTC 292 Bom.

64. See Nemichand Jhabak v. Yash Raj Films Pvt. Ltd., C.S. No. 756 of 2011 (Madras High Court) (unreported), (order passed on 25 January 2012).

65. Sai Paranjpaye v. PLA Entertainment Pvt. Ltd. and others, Notice of Motion No. (L) 764 of 2013 in Suit No. (L) 280 OF 2013, ¶ 2, (Bombay High Court) (unreported), (order passed on 4 April 2013).

66. Prashant Reddy, *Bombay High Court Paves the Way for the Release of 'Chashme Budoor'*, SPICYIP, 5 April 2013, available at http://spicyip.com/2013/04/bombay-high-court-paves-way-for-release.html (Last visited on 3 February 2015).

67. Prashant Reddy, *Producers of 'Hit' Tamil Movie 'Aaranya Kaandam' Face an Ex-parte Injunction for Alleged Copyright Infringement*, SPICYIP, 6 March 2012, available at http://spicyip.com/2012/03/producers-of-hit-tamil-movie-aaranya.html (Last visited on 3 February 2015); Thiagarajan Kumararaja v. M/s Capital Film Works (India) Pvt. Ltd. and S.P. Charan, OA No. 96 of 2012 in CS No. 93 of 2012 (Madras High Court) (unreported), (order passed on 29 February 2012).

68. See, for example, http://www.itwofs.com/ (Last visited on 4 February 2015).

69. Bappi Lahiri and Anr. v. Universal Music and Video Distribution, Inc. and Ors., United States Court of Appeals for the Ninth Circuit, 2010 (Opinion by Judge Conlon), available at http://cdn.ca9.uscourts.gov/datastore/opinions/2010/06/07/09-55111.pdf (Last visited on 4 February 2015).

70. Bappi Lahiri v. Universal Music & Video Distribution, Inc., et al.; Saregama India Limited v. Andre Young pka Dr. Dre, et al., United States District Court, C.D. California, Western Division, 513 F.Supp.2d 1172 (2007), Order Granting Defendants' Motion for Summary Judgement, 9 August 2007 (Order by Otis D. Wright II), available at http://www.leagle.com/decision/20071685513FSupp2d1172_11599/LAHIRI%20v.%20UNIVERSAL%20MUSIC%20&%20VIDEO%20DISTRIBUTION (Last visited on 25 January 2015).

71. AIR 1977 SC 1443: 1977 SCR (3) 206.

72. See Saregama India Ltd. v. Mosley, 687 F. Supp. 2d 1325 (S.D. Fla. 2009), available at http://www.ipinbrief.com/wp-content/uploads/2011/08/Saregama-music-sampling-case-Florida.pdf (Last visited on 4 February 2015); Saregama India Ltd. v. Mosley, United States Court of Appeals for the Eleventh Circuit, Case No. 10-10626, March 2011, available at http://www.gpo.gov/fdsys/pkg/USCOURTS-ca11-10-10626/pdf/USCOURTS-ca11-10-10626-0.pdf (Last visited on 4 February 2015).

73. Abul Kalam Azad, *Rock 'n Roll in Bangladesh: Protecting Intellectual Property Rights in Music*, WORLD TRADE ORGANIZATION, Case Study 3, Managing the challenges of WTO participation: 45 Case Studies, (2005), available at http://www.wto.org/english/res_e/booksp_e/casestudies_e/case3_e.htm (Last visited on 4 February 2015).

74. Rabbi Shergill v. Puja Entertainment (India) Ltd. and Ors., CS (OS) No. 2473 of 2008 (Delhi High Court) (unreported), (order passed on 26 November 2008).

75. Gaurav Dayal **v.** Rabbi Shergil and Ors., 2009 (39) PTC 205 Del.

76. Gaurav Dayal v. Rabbi Shergil and Ors., FAO (OS) No. 464 of 2008 (Delhi High Court) (unreported), (order passed on 15 December 2008).

77. Gaurav Dayal v. Rabbi Shergil and Ors., FAO (OS) No. 464 of 2008 (Delhi High Court) (unreported), (order passed on 18 December 2008).

78. Gaurav Dayal v. Rabbi Shergil and Ors., FAO (OS) No. 464 of 2008 (Delhi High Court) (unreported), (order passed on 9 January 2009).

79. MATHRUBHUMI, *Santosh Sivan's 'Urumi' for Busan Film Fest*, 11 September 2011, available at http://www.mathrubhumi.com/english/movies/malayalam/113995/ (Last visited on 4 February 2015).

80. Loreena Mckinnitt and Ors. v. Deepak Dev and Ors., CS(OS) No. 2349 of 2011 (Delhi High Court) (unreported), (order passed on 21 November 2011).

81. Loreena Mckinnitt and Ors. v. Deepak Dev and Ors., CS(OS) No. 2349 of 2011 (Delhi High Court) (unreported), (order passed on 31 July 2014).

82. For example, the Maharashtra Prevention of Dangerous Activities of Slumlords, Bootleggers, Drug-Offenders, Dangerous Persons and Video Pirates Act, 1981 (as amended), and the Tamil Nadu Prevention of Dangerous Activities of Bootleggers, Drug Offenders, Forest Offenders, Goondas, Immoral Traffic Offenders, Slum Grabbers and Video Pirates Act, 1982 (as amended).

83. T. Prashant Reddy and N. Sai Vinod, *The Constitutionality of Preventing 'Video Piracy' through Preventive Detention in Indian States*, 7(3) J. INTELLECTUAL PROPERTY LAW & PRAC. 194 (2012).

7

AKHTAR RESCRIPTS COPYRIGHT LAW[*]

On 24 August 2012, the Parliament of India hosted a 'shukrana'—a concert of gratitude—by a group of musicians associated with the Indian film industry. The concert was a 'thank you' from the musicians of Bollywood to the lawmakers in Parliament who had come together to pass the Copyright (Amendment) Act, 2012.

The lobbying and public debate that took place before the enactment of the law were unprecedented in India. Previous amendments to the Copyright Act, 1957 had been tame affairs with little or no public debate. The Copyright (Amendment) Act, 2012, however, drew the battle lines within Bollywood. Playing out like a movie itself, the debate saw the 'small guys', a motley crew of musicians and lyricists, taking on a mighty industry, comprising the largest and wealthiest Indian music labels. The 'small guys' eventually emerged victorious, although, at one point, film producers and heads of music labels had felt so threatened by the proposed amendments that they nearly hit the streets in protest.[1]

Much of the background story to the tensions between the music labels and the lobby of musicians and lyricists has escaped the attention of mainstream media. Like Bollywood, the complexities were simplified for public consumption. This chapter unfolds the

---

[*] This chapter has borrowed extensively from an earlier publication by one of the authors in the *NUJS Law Review*. The citation is Prashant Reddy T., *The Background Score to the Copyright (Amendment) Act, 2012*, 5 NUJS L. REV. 469 (2012).

original background score to the Copyright (Amendment) Act, 2012, and explains the circumstances leading up to the amendments.

Copyright Transactions in Film Music

Unlike other markets, where the music industry exists independent of the movie industry, in India, both these industries are deeply interconnected. Music is usually written, scored, and performed especially for the movies, and the success of the music often depends on the success of the movie. Be it Bollywood or any other regional language cinema, the importance of music associated with a movie cannot be underestimated. Music sales form a large part of the profits of the movie, and are also important for pre-release publicity. Simply put, a good movie with bad music is an oxymoron in India.

The basics of copyright transactions in film music are similar to those in other countries, but the Indian music industry has its own eccentricities. Under the Copyright Act, a music single from a Hindi movie comprises at least three different types of works: a musical work (the melody), a literary work (lyrics), and the sound recording (which emerges from the recording of the performance of the music and lyrics in a studio). Each work is protected by a different copyright. A copyright is not a singular right, but is, in fact, a bundle of rights, such as the right to reproduce the work, the right to communicate the work to the public, or the right to incorporate the work in a sound recording or cinematograph film. These rights can be either packaged together, or can be unbundled from each other. As a result, it is entirely possible that the right to reproduce the work can be assigned to one person, and the right to communicate the work to the public can be assigned to a different person.

By default, under the Copyright Act, the composer of a musical work is the 'author' of the musical work and the person writing the lyrics is the 'author' of the literary work. For example, the author of the musical work could be A.R. Rahman, while the author of the lyrics could be Javed Akhtar. The 'author' of the sound recording could be a producer such as Yash Raj Films. The music label would usually be a company such as Tips or Saregama, which acquires the copyright in the sound recording from the film producer. There is also additionally, a performer's right that vests in the 'performer'—the person who sings the lyrics or plays the music on an instrument. However, the breadth of such rights is still unclear in India, and is not discussed in this chapter.

While the authorship of a work can never change, the *ownership* of the copyrights can change depending on the contractual obligations of the various authors. In film music, the composer, lyricist, and producer may keep all other rights, and license only the right to synchronize their respective works with the film to the film producer. In such a case, the producer can buy only the right to use the music and lyrics with the film, while the authors retain all other rights such as public performance rights in hotels and restaurants, or reproduction rights in ringtones for mobile phones. Before 2012, it was a normal practice in the Indian film industry for the composer and lyricist to assign away the copyright in their works to the film producer for a single lump-sum payment. Alternatively, in cases where there was no contract or assignment, film producers were presumed to be the first owners of the copyrights in the music and lyrics. This default treatment (of producers being presumed owners) was due to a decision of the Supreme Court in 1977 in the case of *Indian Performing Right Society Ltd.* v. *Eastern India Motion Pictures Association*.[2]

As industry practice, film producers rarely market their own sound recordings (in the form of ringtones or compact discs). Instead, they prefer to license or assign the copyrights in these sound recordings to music labels like Saregama, who have marketing and distribution channels to advertise and sell the music. Over the years, some music labels like Tips and T-Series have grown so big that they have entered the movie production business to create an integrated business unit.

Akhtar's Inspiration for Lobbying for the Copyright (Amendment) Act, 2012

Appreciating the history of the Copyright (Amendment) Act, 2012, requires understanding the role played by Javed Akhtar, one of India's best known lyricists and poets, in this story. As the face and voice of the lobbying effort to protect the rights of composers and lyricists, he caused much turmoil in the industry. Several film production houses, including the bigger music labels with integrated production services, threatened to stop working with him, and, indeed, some eventually did.[3] However, during this period, Akhtar was nominated as a member of the Rajya Sabha, the Upper House of Parliament, in recognition of his contributions to the arts.[4] This gave him unrestricted access to lawmakers from across India and to key bureaucrats in the central government responsible for drafting policies, allowing him to charge ahead with the amendments, undaunted by the threats of the film industry.

Akhtar's inspiration to don the mantle of a crusader on behalf of his fellow composers and lyricists can be traced to two specific events. The first event was of 2004, when Akhtar was backed by musicians and lyricists to stand in the elections of the governing council of the Indian Performing Right Society Ltd. (IPRS), a copyright society founded in 1969 by a group of film producers and musicians with the aim to collectively enforce their copyrights. Akhtar had stood for elections to the governing council of IPRS at the request of his fellow musicians and lyricists. They were worried about losing control over IPRS to music labels, which had entered IPRS only a decade ago, that is in 1993. When Akhtar won the elections, the music labels moved swiftly to sue IPRS, on grounds that the annual general meeting (AGM) which elected Akhtar did not comply with the requirements of Indian company law. A civil judge, sitting 2,000 kilometres away from the Mumbai film industry, in Barasat, West Bengal, granted an interim stay, and Akhtar's election to IPRS was set aside. From here on, the music labels drew Akhtar into a bottomless well of litigation. They sued IPRS every year to get a stay on the AGM, which was the only event that gave IPRS members the right to intervene in its functioning. Eventually, IPRS stopped paying Akhtar and his supporters their due royalties because they refused to accept the terms set by the music labels. Perhaps frustrated with the slow progress made before the Barasat court, Akhtar may have decided to focus on lobbying the government for a complete overhaul of copyright law.[5]

The second event that may have influenced Akhtar was a copyright infringement lawsuit filed by him against Magic Mantra Vision, a Bollywood film producer.[6] Akhtar claimed he had assigned to the production house only the rights to synchronize his lyrics with the music of the film *Pyar Ki Dhun*. In other words, he argued that the film producer had only the limited right to play the music along with the movie, and the producer did not have the right to use the music in any other way, independently of the movie. At the time, he claimed to have retained all other rights, such as the right to collect royalties when the music was publicly performed as a standalone track, that is, not as a part of the film but, say, in a hotel or at an event. His suit alleged that the production house, without his authorization, had assigned to Saregama (a music label) even those rights that he had not assigned to the production house in the first place. But the defence was prepared. The producers presented a 'letter' in court, purportedly from Akhtar, assigning to them all the rights in the lyrics, including synchronization and publishing rights. Akhtar acknowledged his signature was on the 'letter' but claimed to have 'had no idea' that he had been made to sign an agreement giving away or assigning or transferring his rights. He withdrew the suit and was fined one lakh rupees for causing 'hardship' to the defendant. This was a typical example of a transaction between a 'legally illiterate' composer or lyricist and a 'legally savvy' production house. Most authors appear to understand little about copyright contracts and rarely appear to have received sound legal advice.

The experience with IPRS and the embarrassing loss of his lawsuit against Magic Mantra proved to be a baptism by fire for Akhtar in his long-drawn battle to reform Indian copyright law. (Interestingly, Akhtar almost never refers to the lawsuit in interviews.) These two events appear to have taught him the nuances, complexities, and the one-sided nature of most negotiations with financially powerful producers and music labels. These events were also symptomatic of deeper problems faced by composers and lyricists, which Akhtar sought to target.

The Problems Faced by Lyricists and Composers

Bollywood lyricists and composers faced four problems in their relationship with music labels. Firstly, there was the issue of first ownership of the copyrights in music and lyrics incorporated in the soundtrack of a movie. Secondly, most of them had relatively weak bargaining powers against Bollywood producers. Thirdly, when composers and lyricists signed contracts assigning away their copyrights, the idea of sharing royalties from the use of the music in newer technologies, such as mobile ringtones, did not exist. Lastly, composers and lyricists were being pushed out of copyright societies by powerful music labels. Each of these issues is discussed below, along with the solutions proposed through the amendments.

Who Owns the 'Music and Lyrics' Used in a Movie?

A classic issue of copyright law across different countries is that of first ownership of copyright for works that are commissioned, or works that are created during employment. Under the Copyright Act, 1957, the author of a work is usually also the first owner of the copyright in the work. But Section 17 alters this principle of 'first ownership' in specific cases where a work is created during employment or for a commission. For example, under Section 17, the copyright in articles written by a journalist employed by a newspaper will ordinarily be owned by the newspaper unless there is a contract to the contrary. Section 17 covers other similar situations where paintings or photographs or cinematograph films are created by a person for a commission. In all these cases, copyright in the final work is owned by the person who paid for the creation of the work, unless the creator or the author has a contract to the contrary.

Two reasons underlie the provisions contained in Section 17. The first reason is that it is a practical commercial solution, especially when a large number of people come together to create a work which is the subject of a copyright. For example, there may be tens or hundreds of people involved in the production of a movie or a sound recording, each one contributing to the final work, and sometimes working on more than one production simultaneously. In such a case, Section 17 creates an automatic presumption of ownership in favour of the producer. This reduces the risk of confusion over ownership of the final work, by pre-empting possible claims from various contributors to the work who might otherwise claim ownership. The practicality of this solution is made clearer in proviso (a) to Section 17. Here, a newspaper is presumed to be the first owner of the copyright in every article published in that newspaper by journalists that it employs. If the default rule of copyright ownership were to apply, journalists would be the first owners of copyright in works they authored. If Section 17 did not exist, every journalist would have to assign the copyright in every article to the newspaper. But, if a journalist is employed by a newspaper, Section 17 presumes that the newspaper is the first owner of the copyright in the articles, and thus, saves both the newspaper and the journalist the trouble of entering into a copyright assignment each time.

The second reason why Section 17 exists is to reward the person who takes a risk and invests financial resources in the creation of goods or ideas. This idea of rewarding the risk-taker is the cornerstone of capitalism, which Indian copyright law embodies by creating a presumption of first ownership in favour of the person who bears the risk. In the context of copyright law, the application of this principle may be questionable because the skill and talent of the author of the work also contributes significantly to the eventual success or failure of the work.

The most significant judgment on the first ownership of copyright in music and lyrics in films was delivered by the Supreme Court in 1977 in *Indian Performing Right Society Ltd.* v. *Eastern India Motion Pictures Association*.[7] In this case, IPRS, whose membership at the time comprised mainly composers and lyricists, had publicly advertised a scheme of licence fees to be charged for the public performance of Indian and foreign musical works and lyrics that were a part of its portfolio. An association of film producers complained to the Copyright Board, a quasi-judicial tribunal, that composers and lyricists owned no copyright or associated public performance rights in music and lyrics incorporated into films. The film producers argued that, because of Section 17, *they* owned all the copyrights in the music and lyrics created for a film. Their logic ran thus: Since producers commissioned authors to create music and lyrics for films, the resulting works would necessarily be owned by the commissioning producer, and not by the composers or lyricists. On the other hand, IPRS (representing the authors, that is, composers and lyricists) argued that their members owned all the public performance rights to the music, and that anybody publicly performing the music would require a licence from IPRS. In effect, IPRS was arguing that the various authors had only assigned synchronization rights to film producers, that is, the right to use the music along with the films, but retained all remaining rights in the bundle that constitute a copyright. This argument was put forward by the authors, most probably, because they wanted to collect royalties every time their music was publicly performed at a restaurant or an event.

The question of law that followed was this: Who owned the right to public performance, in such cases? Was it the producers who foot the bill for creating and marketing the music, or was it the authors who actually created the music and lyrics? This question was argued all the way from the Copyright Board to the Supreme Court.

The authors won the first round before the Copyright Board, but lost the next two before the Calcutta High Court and the Supreme Court. The Supreme Court referred to two provisos of Section 17 to arrive at its decision that the copyright was owned entirely by the film producers. Under proviso (b), a person who commissions the creation of a cinematographic film, photograph, painting, portrait, or engraving, owns the copyright in the resulting work. Under proviso (c), any work created during the course of employment is deemed to be owned by the employer, unless otherwise provided in the contract. In the absence of a contract to the contrary, the Supreme Court concluded:

> [W]hen a cinematograph film producer commissions a composer of music or a lyricist for reward or valuable consideration for the purpose of making his cinematograph film, or composing music or lyric there-fore i.e. the sounds for incorporation or absorption in the sound track associated with the film, which ... are included in a cinematograph film, he becomes the first owner of the copyright therein and no copyright subsists in the composer of the lyric or music so composed unless there is a contract to the contrary... The same result follows ... if the composer ... is employed under a contract of service or apprenticeship to compose the work.[8]

This judgment has been debated for decades now. It has been criticized for expanding the scope of proviso (b) to include the music and lyrics of a soundtrack, when the provision covers only four categories of works: photograph taken, painting or portrait drawn, an engraving, or a cinematograph film. One interpretation suggests that the proviso extends only to films, and not the music and lyrics that are created separately, and incorporated into the film at a later stage. This leads to another controversial legal issue. At the time, the Copyright Act, 1957 defined 'cinematograph work' to include 'soundtrack if any'.[9] 'Soundtrack' itself was undefined in the law, but the Supreme Court appears to have presumed that the term included music and lyrics (as opposed to merely the dialogue of the movie), and that both would be covered by proviso (b).[10] The Court's reading of proviso (c) is equally contentious. It accepted the argument that all the musical and literary works were made during the course of employment under contracts of service.[11] But composers and lyricists in the film industry compose music and lyrics for a number of producers, and are rarely 'employed' by any single producer. An employment contract would typically restrict an employee to only one employer, who would pay a monthly salary and provide all benefits under employment law. Under a commissioning contract, a contractor would be paid a fixed sum for the job to be completed, and could simultaneously work on multiple jobs for other clients. But the Supreme Court arrived at its decision without explaining the difference between 'employment contracts' and 'commissioning contracts'. In contrast, the United States (US) Supreme Court, when dealing with a similar case, laid down certain criteria, such as mode of payment, tax treatment, and other factual grounds, to determine whether a person was an employee or an independent contractor.[12]

After the 1977 judgment, all producers who commissioned authors to create musical or literary works for their films would be the first owners of copyrights in those works, unless there was evidence of a contract to the contrary. The Supreme Court judgment, in fact, gave composers and lyricists the right to retain ownership of copyright in their works by specifying ownership rights in their contracts. But most composers and lyricists lacked the bargaining power to negotiate such contracts, and instead tended to assign away their copyrights for a single lump-sum payment.

The only way to circumvent the 1977 Supreme Court judgment was to get Parliament to amend the law. That is exactly what Akhtar did when he got the government to introduce the Copyright (Amendment) Bill in Parliament in 2010. The Amendment Bill sought to insert the following proviso in Section 17: 'Provided that in case of any work incorporated in a cinematograph work, nothing contained in clauses (b) and (c) shall affect the right of the author in the work referred to in clause (a) of sub-section (1) of section 13'.[13]

The 'works' referred to in Section 13(1)(a) are 'original literary, dramatic, musical and artistic works'. The Parliamentary Standing Committee, to which the Amendment Bill was referred, endorsed this particular amendment thus:

> The Committee also takes note of the fact that independent rights of authors of literary and musical works in cinematograph films are being wrongfully exploited by the producers and music companies by virtue of [the] Supreme Court judgment in Indian Performing Rights Society v. Eastern India Motion Pictures Association which held that [the] film producer is the first owner of the copyright and authors and music composers do not have separate rights.[14]

The amendment was retained in its original form in the final version of the law passed by Parliament two years later as the Copyright (Amendment) Act, 2012. As a result, authors would now own their rights in the music and lyrics even if they were created for a cinematograph film.

Mandatory Royalty-Sharing

Parliament's decision to overrule the Supreme Court decision in the IPRS case (1977) was a revolutionary moment for composers and lyricists. But music labels could still compel composers and lyricists to assign all their rights for a one-time payment. In fact, this was the practice for most composers and lyricists who lacked the bargaining power to negotiate with music labels. Akhtar wanted to change this equation permanently by ensuring that composers and lyricists had a mandatory, unassignable *lifetime right* to an equal share of royalties earned by the producer or music label while they commercially exploited the music and lyrics.

Deposing before the Parliamentary Standing Committee that was examining the amendments, Akhtar, flanked by his lawyers Ameet Datta and Sai Krishna Rajagopal, explained to the Members of Parliament (MPs) the reason behind the demand for mandatory royalty-sharing:

> We demand that the royalty should be non-assignable because that is the only way artists can save their right. This demand is from Pandit Ravi Shankar to anyone that it should be non-assignable... Let us be fair. We don't want to swindle, destroy or harm the other party, the producer or the film company. Obviously, we have to survive together and cooperate with each other. We said that as long as the song is in the film, we have no claim whatsoever. But, if the song is taken out of the film and is used as ring-tone or used in a hotel, restaurant, aircraft, FM, etc., then, royalty should come and we should have our share of royalty. It is not that we want all the royalty but, our share should come to us.[15]

Datta buttressed Akhtar's submissions by explaining to the Committee that most of the music in India was 'concentrated in 15 companies', and by 'logical deduction', contracts were 'foisted and forced' on artists who had no choice but to deal with these companies.[16]

Supporting the demand of Indian composers and authors was the International Confederation of Societies of Authors and Composers, known by its French acronym, CISAC, an influential body abroad. CISAC's Indian representative, Achille Forler, a Frenchman and an experienced hand in the Indian music industry, impressed upon the Committee the importance of the proposed amendments. He said, '[w]e are talking, of course, about money. But we are not talking only about money... [T]he product of a human mind is the most sacred of all properties and it is the duty of the state to protect that property.'[17] For effect, Forler linked the importance of creativity and the arts to the idea of India as a nation, saying, '[i]f India were not to manufacture tyres or cars, India would still be India. But what would India be without its film industry, without the Ramayan, without the Mahabharat, without the Upanishads, without the Sufi traditions. It would not be the same India.'[18]

The demand to retain mandatory royalty-sharing in the amendments was the most contentious negotiating point between Akhtar and the music industry. So far, the music industry had been governed by the rules of the free market: Composers and lyricists, depending on their standing in the market, would either assign away their rights for a one-time payment or enter into a royalty-sharing agreement. Only a few popular composers like A.R. Rahman had the power to negotiate a royalty-sharing agreement with music labels. It was no surprise that Akhtar's proposal to ensure lifetime mandatory royalty-sharing for all authors was met with fierce resistance from film producers and music labels. Akhtar was disrupting an age-old business model, and powerful music labels did not like such sweeping changes.

On their part, music labels and film producers had valid reasons to oppose such a provision. After all, it was they, along with film producers, who assumed the most risk with any new music being released in the market. Composers or lyricists typically had nothing to lose because they received a one-time payment regardless of the success or failure of the music. According to the music industry, only a small proportion of the music released every year would succeed while the remaining would inevitably fail. Similarly, they argued that the popularity (and success) of the music would often depend on the success of the film itself. A big-budget movie with a popular star lip-synching a foot-tapping number would draw a lot of attention. *This* investment by film producers in star actors, and related publicity, would also impact the success of the music. The music label marketing the music on behalf of the producer would also spend considerable sums on promotion and advertising the music. As explained to the Parliamentary Standing Committee by moviemaker Yash Chopra:

> [W]e spend crores of rupees on one song. Who creates the song? It is the producer. The producer tells the music director or the writer that this is the situation and I want this type of a song. Then a song is created. The producer spends crores of rupees on artists, on sets, on locations and on that song. On that song or on that writer, has he no right?[19]

Criticizing the non-assignability clause, Chopra warned the committee against aping foreign laws, since the structure of the Indian music industry was fundamentally different from elsewhere, where the music industry was disconnected from the movie industry.

Neel Mason, the lawyer for the IPRS, explained this difference between the Indian and Western music industry to the committee:

> One must understand that the Indian music industry is highly synergised with the Indian film industry. Therefore, whenever we look at a parallel between the Indian music industry and the Western music industry, one

must understand that the very fibre is different. In the West you have the music recording done, you have the music available in the market, people buy the music, subsequently a film [maker] may or may not want to incorporate a song in a film. Therefore, they may take a licence for that. However, that is not the case in India. In India, most of the music is film-driven.[20]

This was an important argument, because the authors had told the Committee that they were seeking the same rights enjoyed in the West, without really explaining the context of such rights.

Bollywood, or the Hindi film industry, was not the only movie industry opposing the amendments. The South Indian Film Chamber of Commerce sent a delegation headed by sitting MP and movie director Dasari Narayana Rao to depose before the committee. Like Chopra, Rao told the committee:

[The] Producer is the man who invests the money. The first man to invest the money for the production is the producer and he is the last man to receive the last pie. The stake is of the producer. A director or a lyrics writer or a writer or an actor or whoever may be, is paid according to consideration. They will take their money. They don't have any responsibility. The loss and profit goes to the producer only. Within this industry, there are only 5–8 percent successful films and 85–90 per cent is failure.[21]

The depositions by the movie industry and music labels repeatedly belaboured the fact that both film producers and music labels invested large sums of money in the music, and as a result, they also assumed a larger portion of the risk. To share royalties equally with the composer and lyricist in these circumstances was unfair, they argued.

The mandatory royalty-sharing provisions proposed by Akhtar are quite rare in the English model of copyright law followed by India. But they can be found in the European system of copyright law, in the form of *droit d'auteur*, literally 'author's rights'. The end effect of copyright law and *droit d'auteur* is very similar but their philosophical underpinnings are quite different.

The model of copyright law that originated in Britain with the Statute of Anne in 1710, regarded copyright as a property right that could be transferred between different persons for a certain consideration.[22] In contrast, *droit d'auteur* regards a creative work to be an extension of an author's personality.[23] It borrows from the philosophy of natural rights. For example, in Germany, an author can never waive ownership of rights,[24] although the author can license the right to use the work to other persons in exchange for royalties.[25] Germany also has a law entitling authors to receive adequate remuneration,[26] and if an author believes that adequate remuneration has not been received, the author can approach a court to make such a determination.[27] The standard of adequate remuneration is pegged to the rates negotiated between authors' associations and the industry, but courts also play a significant role.[28] German copyright law also has a 'bestseller provision', under which authors can claim a share in profits if a work generates profits completely disproportionate to initial expectations.[29]

The specific European law which might have influenced the government's proposal is the 1992 European Communities Rental Rights Directive (ECRRD), which is also rooted in the *droit d'auteur* system.[30] Although directed at rental royalties, the author of this model, Professor Silke von Lewinski, acknowledges that it can be applied to other sectors.[31] The amendments that eventually became a part of the Copyright (Amendment) Act, 2012 in India were very similar to the ECRRD. Under the new amendments incorporated in Sections 18 and 19 of the Copyright Act, 1957, composers or lyricists could now transfer copyrights in their works but not their rights to receive an equal share of the royalties. This right to receive royalties could be assigned only to a copyright society or a legal heir. Any contract to the contrary was deemed void by the amendment.

Despite stiff resistance from the music industry, film producers, and several others, the mandatory royalty-sharing provisions put forth by the government and blessed by Akhtar were enacted into law as a part of the Copyright (Amendment) Act, 2012.

Assigning Copyright in New Technology

Another revolutionary and controversial reform was a clause which would deem void any contracts that made composers and lyricists assign away rights in all future technologies that had not yet been invented at the time the copyright was assigned. This was prompted by the booming success of mobile ringtone music in India. The growth of mobile telephony had increased the demand for music, especially in the form of ringtones. Indians were ready to pay for not only the music that *they* would hear on receiving a call, but also for the music that a *caller* would hear.[32] Even a small percentage of the nearly 700 million mobile phone subscribers in India downloading ringtones would mean an entirely new revenue stream for copyright owners, and all this was possible with insignificant additional investment.[33] For one copyright society, revenues from this category zoomed by almost 2239 per cent in a span of seven years.[34]

With all this money floating around, authors wondered where their share from these sales had vanished. It turned out that many authors had contracted away all their rights, including benefits accruing from the use of their works in future technological media. In other words, a contract signed when only compact discs (CDs) were in vogue would have also included an assignment of rights in any technology developed in the future.[35] This is exactly what had happened with contracts signed before the mobile technology boom took place in India. Consequently, the authors had lost a fortune.

Therefore, the amendments had a clause which would render void any contracts that required composers and lyricists to assign away rights in future technological media. This meant that film producers and music labels would have to renegotiate contracts with composers and lyricists every time a new technological medium was invented.

Unsurprisingly, this provision was extremely controversial. Opponents included not only music labels but also members of the book publishing industry.[36] They were worried that since technology was rapidly changing, an assignee (for example, a producer or a publisher), who had contracted for only a particular technology could be completely upended by the emergence of a new technology.[37] But the provision was retained as drafted, and became a part of the Copyright (Amendment) Act, 2012.

The Takeover of the Indian Performing Right Society and the Attempt to Reform Copyright Societies

Of the several factors which inspired Akhtar to lobby for the reform of Indian copyright law, the most influential factor was perhaps his experience with the music labels at IPRS. When asked to narrate his journey, Akhtar often starts with how, in 2004, the IPRS boardroom became the scene of a battle between composers and lyricists on the one hand, and music labels on the other.[38] IPRS story is a complicated one, involving deft legal manoeuvring over several years by music labels which surreptitiously took over the copyright society. Eventually, IPRS stopped repatriating royalties to Akhtar and his supporters, an act which cemented Akhtar's resolve to lobby for a reform of Indian copyright law.

Incorporated in 1969 by a group of film producers, authors, and composers, IPRS is a company limited by guarantee. Its incorporation documents show that IPRS sought to be a copyright society for mainly music, lyrics, and other underlying works in a soundtrack.[39] Other copyright societies, like Phonographic Performance Limited (PPL), dealt only with the licensing of sound recordings. A copyright society helps in the 'trading' of music. Copyright owners, as members of a copyright society, jointly license and collect music royalties to reduce transaction costs and make their works more affordable to content users.[40] This business model benefits end-users like radio stations or restaurants, who have to negotiate with only one entity for a licence, instead of each copyright owner. Most copyright societies offer such users a blanket licence, under which they can play any music owned by the society for a fixed fee. These fees are divided amongst members of the copyright society according to a previously agreed formula. Given the complexities of administration of copyright licences and distribution of royalties, copyright societies are required to function with the utmost degree of transparency.

In 1993, the then management of IPRS headed by music director Naushad Ali signed a memorandum of understanding (MoU) with the Indian Music Industry (IMI) and PPL, both of which were associations of music labels.[41] The MoU set a roadmap for allowing music labels to become members of IPRS. The MoU made three key changes to the way IPRS had functioned in the past. First, IPRS would terminate the membership of film producers, and replace them with music labels from PPL and IMI. Second, the society's future earnings would be redistributed as follows: 50 per cent would go to members who were music publishers (that is, music labels from PPL), 30 per cent to composers, and 20 per cent to author members (that is, lyricists). The

MoU says that the 'appropriation of 50% of the revenue for composers/authors [would be] in the interests of giving encouragement to the composers/authors'.[42] Third, the society's governing council would have equal representation from composers, lyricists, and music labels.

Why was IPRS so ready and willing to welcome outsiders into its fold? Perhaps, with signs that the Indian popular music industry was about to take off after the 1991 economic liberalization wave, IPRS too wanted to enter the big league of copyright societies, for which it needed resources. Music labels were most likely willing investors, provided they were promised a share in the profits. Separately, amendments to the copyright law were also afoot (they were eventually passed in 1994) that required all copyright societies to be registered with the Registrar of Copyrights to carry out the business of licensing copyrights. The language of the amendments suggested that not more than one society per class of works would be allowed. Could it be that IPRS was strategizing to monopolize copyright licensing in music and lyrics?

In order to be implemented, the MoU required an amendment to the articles of association (Articles) of IPRS. For this, composers and lyricists who were members of IPRS would have to vote and ratify the MoU signed by its management. But even before that, IPRS had to be registered with the Registrar of Copyrights. By now, the tougher regulatory regime introduced by the Copyright (Amendment) Act, 1994, was in place. Under this new law, in ordinary circumstances, the Registrar of Copyrights would register only one copyright society in each class of works.[43] To obtain registration, a copyright society had to meet many new requirements: They should be managed by copyright owners, and not spend more than 15 per cent of revenue on administration.[44] If a copyright society was found violating these terms, its registration could be cancelled after due inquiry.[45]

The registration of IPRS as a copyright society is a classic tale of negligence and bureaucratic tardiness. It filed its application for registration on 1 February 1996.[46] A key registration requirement was that IPRS had to be in the control of copyright owners of works administered by the society.[47] But the Registrar of Copyrights failed to recognize that the governing laws of IPRS linked membership not to *ownership* of copyright in music or lyrics but to *authorship*.[48]

Under the copyright law, authorship and ownership are entirely different concepts, and the Registrar of Copyrights should have denied registration right away until IPRS amended its Articles appropriately. In fact, during the registration process, a junior bureaucrat did point out that IPRS had not submitted a list of owners—the Register of Owners—as required under law.[49] The Register of Owners would have a list of all the copyright owners who were members of IPRS along with a list of the works owned by these persons. But a superior officer swept aside these objections with the following reasons:

> During the hearing, Shri Tandon explained that the composer-members have copyright over all their compositions and the songwriters have copyright over all their songs. These members include leading lights in Indian film music like Naushad Ali (who incidentally, is the current Chairman of the IPRS), Bappi Lahiri, Anup Jalota, Hemant Kumar, Ilaiya Raja, and M.B. Srinivasan. Shri Tandon said that the list of their works would be voluminous. Since it is well known that these reputed composers and songwriters have a large number of compositions and songs to their credit, it may not be necessary to have on file a list of their works, and we may not insist on that.[50]

Thus, instead of requiring the Register of Owners to be submitted, the Copyright Office (wrongly) concluded that authors were also owners of copyrights. Had it insisted on the Register of Owners along with an amendment to the Articles of IPRS in 1996 itself, the issue of whether copyright owners were in control of IPRS would have been clarified right away. The issue of control over a copyright society is vital because those in control will determine crucial issues like membership criteria, royalty distribution, and tariff structure. When the Copyright Office registered IPRS as a copyright society without determining the question of control properly, it created a fertile ground for a dispute, the effects of which can be felt till this day in the music industry.

Under pressure from music labels, IPRS began the process of amending its governing laws to comply with the 1993 MoU that it had signed with the labels. These amendments gave the music labels more representation on the Governing Council, and a greater say in the affairs of IPRS. At no point of time did IPRS carry out amendments to give control to copyright owners. In 2004, at the 34th AGM of IPRS, Akhtar and his allies stood for the elections of the governing council and won. As Akhtar recounted in an interview, he had been asked to stand for the elections by a group of composers and lyricists who were dissatisfied with the manner in which IPRS was being administered by the representatives of the music labels.[51]

The music labels were clearly unhappy with the composition of the new governing council after the 34th AGM because they reacted by suing IPRS in two different judicial forums. One litigation was launched before the Company Law Board (CLB) by Universal and another music label.[52] But that litigation did not progress much, for procedural reasons (the labels lacked the mandatory numbers to contest a petition for oppression and mismanagement before the CLB). The second legal action, filed by Saregama, was a shareholders' derivative lawsuit before a civil court in a town called Barasat, on the outskirts of Kolkata, and 2,000 kilometres from Mumbai where Akhtar and his allies resided. The venue was chosen perhaps because Saregama was located in the neighbourhood, and was likely very influential in and around Kolkata, as it was a part of the billion-dollar RPG Group that has its roots in Kolkata.

A shareholders' derivative lawsuit allows minority shareholders to sue the company's management before a civil court (instead of approaching the CLB) on behalf of the remaining shareholders, on grounds that the company is being mismanaged. In its lawsuit, Saregama argued that the 'Register of Owners' had never been created by IPRS despite the fact that the terms of its registration as a copyright society required it to be governed only by owners. Saregama also argued that since only copyright owners could vote at AGMs, no elections should be held until such a 'Register of Owners' was created. It also requested the court to appoint a receiver for the purpose of creating such a register.[53] Through this lawsuit, the implementation of the results of the 2004 elections was temporarily stayed, thus keeping Akhtar and his supporters away from any management control of IPRS. The progress of such lawsuits before lower courts can be tortuously slow, especially if one of the parties deliberately delay proceedings. Similar shareholders' derivative lawsuits were filed in 2005, 2006, and 2007 by Saregama to ensure IPRS did not hold an AGM, as such a meeting would give authors the opportunity to regain control of IPRS.

An AGM is a critical event for a company, since it is the main forum where shareholders can hold the management of a company accountable for its performance. With no AGMs, IPRS members could ask no questions of the management. An especially problematic issue at IPRS was the collection of royalties for the licensing of mobile ringtones. As explained earlier, ringtone royalties were a new and lucrative source of revenue for the music industry since it did not require much additional investment and the telecom market was growing by leaps and bounds. After initially collecting mobile ringtone royalties for some time, in 2004, IPRS abruptly informed licencees that it would no longer administer ringtone royalties.[54] This decision made no financial sense since ringtone royalties (Rs 36.5 million in 2003–4) constituted 30 per cent of IPRS's earnings that year, which was likely to exponentially rise in the future.[55] The category of 'ringtone royalties' disappeared completely from IPRS balance sheets in 2006–7.[56] Mysteriously, while IPRS's ringtone royalties dwindled, the ringtone royalties of PPL, a different copyright society which would collect royalties for sound recordings (as opposed to IPRS which collected royalties for the underlying music and lyrics), rose enormously (Rs 70.6 million in 2004–5 to Rs 1.65 billion in 2010–11).[57] Cumulatively, PPL earned over Rs 5 billion between 2004 and 2011 from ringtone royalties.[58]

Logically, PPL's successes should have resulted in a proportional increase in royalty income for IPRS. This is because a ringtone contains both music and lyrics and a 'sound recording' which incorporates the music and lyrics. Therefore, a telecom company wanting to sell ringtones would have to obtain licences from both PPL and IPRS, since the former had the right to administer only 'sound recordings' while the latter had the same rights over 'music and lyrics'. Intriguingly, while PPL's annual report for 2008–9 said that it was collecting ringtone royalties on behalf of IPRS,[59] the balance sheets of IPRS did not reflect this inflow of mobile ringtone royalties. IPRS was not objecting either. Why? This was probably because IPRS governing council was controlled by the same music labels that controlled PPL.[60] In fact, even the representatives to both societies were the same for most music labels.

Composers and lyricists like Akhtar were probably aware of the move by IPRS to surrender ringtone royalties to the PPL. Initially,

Akhtar and his allies had tried contesting the lawsuits pending before the Barasat court, but after more than 100 adjournments, all of them seem to have given up.[61]

Once it became clear that nobody would defend the Barasat lawsuit, the music labels moved swiftly to get IPRS to hold an AGM in January 2008 under the receivership (supervision) of the Barasat court. Since the IPRS management was still under the control of the music labels, this was easy to accomplish. This AGM was attended only by seven music labels: Saregama India Ltd., Tips Industries Ltd., Universal Music India Ltd., Venus Records and Tapes Ltd., Sony Music Entertainment Ltd., Virgin India Ltd., and Krunal Music Ltd.[62] Normally, notice of an AGM should be sent to all members before the meeting. Members of IPRS included over 1,500 composers and lyricists, but none of them turned up at this AGM. Their absence was linked to another story. In the intervening years, IPRS had been fighting another case before the CLB, having been sued by the music label Universal for not maintaining a Register of Owners.[63] When the CLB deputed its officials to oversee the creation of a Register of Owners, the management at IPRS (arguably under the influence of music labels) agreed with Universal's contention that only music labels owned the musical and literary works of IPRS. As a result, the Register of Owners mentioned only music labels. Of all these music labels, only seven music labels eventually attended the AGM in January 2008.[64]

The agenda for this AGM was to replace the governing laws of IPRS to ensure that only music labels, as opposed to authors, would remain in control. Conducting the AGM under the receivership of the Barasat court gave the process an aura of legitimacy. With no opposition, the music labels easily succeeded in replacing the governing laws of IPRS.[65] The new governing laws required that IPRS be under the control of copyright owners. The Register of Owners already drafted under the supervision of CLB officials mentioned only music labels as owners, so this requirement just completed the circle. After replacing the governing laws, the music labels became more assertive in imposing their will on composers and lyricists. For example, the new IPRS management required all composers and lyricists to sign a standard-format letter, accepting the new governing laws acknowledging that the music labels owned the copyright in all their works, and to accept the terms of the 1993 MoU. Those who did not sign the letter were not paid annual royalties. Since royalties from IPRS were a substantial portion of income for smaller composers and authors, at least 1,473 of them (which was nearly all of them) did sign.[66] Those who chose to fight and not sign the letter—like Akhtar and his allies—were denied royalties. This non-payment of royalties was likely the last straw, and Akhtar and his allies responded by filing complaints with the Registrar of Companies.

In March 2008,[67] Akhtar and his supporters asked the central government to take over the administration of IPRS and ensure that royalty payments were made to all the composers and lyricists. In January 2009, a complaint was filed by Ravi Shankar Sharma, better known as 'Bombay Ravi', the composer of *Chaudhvin ka Chand* (1960), *Gharana* (1961), and *Nikaah* (1982).[68] Ravi's complaint said that composers and lyricists were being 'harassed and tortured' by the music labels of IPRS, including through withheld royalties. He died three years later, possibly without receiving any of his dues.[69] The Registrar of Copyrights did initiate inquiries against these complaints, but with little result.[70]

IPRS did everything in its power to stall the inquiries. Most audaciously, Saregama made the Registrar of Copyrights, who sits at New Delhi, a party in one of the lawsuits pending before the Barasat court, and sought an interim injunction against the Registrar from carrying out further inquiries or directing IPRS to repatriate money to authors and composers.[71] Ordinarily, civil courts cannot pass orders against the central government without giving a chance to be heard, unless there is urgency to waive the requirement.[72] But the Barasat court issued a 'status-quo' order against the Registrar even before hearing him.[73]

Another complaint was filed in December 2011 before the then minister for human resource development (HRD), Kapil Sibal, by four leading industry personalities—Jagjit Singh, Shankar Mahadevan, Vishal Bhardwaj, and Javed Akhtar.[74] By now, the lobbying efforts to change the law had gained traction, and the Copyright (Amendment) Bill, 2010, was already in the Parliament. This complaint again asked the central government to take over IPRS and appoint an administrator to look into its affairs.[75]

This time, the management of IPRS, already under the spotlight after scathing observations against it in a Parliamentary Report, cooperated with the Registrar to some extent, by replying to the complaint.[76] However, its replies were full of legal contradictions. For example, the IPRS Chairperson claimed that the society was not collecting any ringtone royalties, and had not assigned the right to collect these royalties to anyone.[77] But a statement in PPL's Annual Report confirmed that *it* was collecting ringtone royalties on behalf of IPRS: 'Tariff same as last year—25% of end-user-price, subject to a minimum of Rs. 2.50 per tone (inclusive of performance royalty to IPRS Society, as this is licensed as a single window)'.[78] Other such contradictions warranted a more in-depth enquiry by the Registrar of Copyrights, but the Registrar does not seem to have attempted such an inquiry.

Since the mismanagement at IPRS was key to Akhtar's push for reforming copyright law, the originally tabled version of the Copyright (Amendment) Bill, 2010, proposed that copyright societies would only be under the control of authors and not owners. This proposal was opposed by copyright owners who said that it would be extremely unfair to them, having invested capital and assumed risk by purchasing the title to copyrighted works. The Parliamentary Standing Committee, in acknowledgement, recommended to the government to follow a system of joint management where the governing council of a copyright society would have an equal number of authors and owners. This recommendation was accepted in the final version of the law enacted by Parliament, although it remains to be seen how an equally divided governing council will deal with contentious issues where authors and owners are unable to see eye to eye.

Parliamentary Debates before the Vote on the Copyright (Amendment) Act, 2012

The Copyright (Amendment) Bill, 2010, was introduced in Parliament in a turbulent phase of Indian politics. The central government, under the leadership of the Congress-led United Progressive Alliance (UPA), had been accused of massive corruption by the opposition led by the Bharatiya Janata Party (BJP). With the leadership reluctant to announce fair and transparent probes into various scandals its officials were accused of, the opposition frequently stalled the functioning of Parliament. These frequent disruptions made it more difficult for the government to push through its legislative agenda.

To add to Akhtar's woes, a personality issue emerged early on. The minister in charge of the Bill, Kapil Sibal, handling the human resource development (HRD) portfolio, was not the most well-liked minister in the Cabinet, perhaps because he was simultaneously trying to make unpopular reforms in the Indian education system.[79] An early attempt to pass the Copyright Bill was aborted after the opposition accused Sibal of an alleged conflict of interest: His son, a leading lawyer, represented a music label that would allegedly benefit from one provision in the law, dealing with version recordings.[80] Differences were eventually set aside successfully when the Bill was taken up for debate in May 2012. This time, opposition participation was positive, and even appreciative of Sibal's efforts to ensure the Bill's passage.[81]

Speaking in support of the Bill during the Parliamentary debate, M.P. Achuthan, an MP belong to the Communist Party of India (Marxist) (CPI(M)), in the Rajya Sabha, said, 'I support this Bill. Generally, we do not get an opportunity to support a Bill piloted by Mr. Kapil Sibal. Now, after some changes, he has brought the Bill. Apart from the suggestions given by the Standing Committee, he has made so many amendments, which I support'.[82]

Nearly every MP who participated in the debate, regardless of political affiliation, spoke of the starving authors and composers.[83] The fact that there was not a single statement defending the music labels showed how effective Akhtar and his allies had been in their lobbying efforts. The parliamentary debate skipped the finer nuances of the law and concentrated on the larger political issues of the weakening rights of authors.

When both Houses of Parliament voted unanimously to enact the Copyright (Amendment) Act, 2012, it marked a rare exception in a Parliament which was otherwise divided on almost every issue. Months after its enactment, the constitutionality of the Copyright (Amendment) Act, 2012, was challenged by film producers, music labels, copyright societies, and authors before the Delhi High Court. These petitions, which are yet to conclude, challenge the amendments and the new rules as violative of the fundamental rights of the petitioners. Most of these challenges may fail, since the standards for testing the constitutionality of parliamentary law are set very high.

∗∗∗

More than four years after the amendments to the Copyright Act, there have been few changes in the manner in which the music industry functions. The key roadblock for the authors is that they still lack an effective copyright society which will protect their rights. IPRS is currently the subject of two investigations: The first is a Commission of Inquiry ordered by the central government under the Copyright Act, while the second investigation is being carried out by the Enforcement Directorate (ED), under the Prevention of Money Laundering Act, 2002.[84] IPRS is yet to be re-registered as a copyright society under the new law. Without an effective copyright society, individual authors and composers are likely to find it difficult to administer their rights in India.

On other issues, there has been little public discussion on whether composers and lyricists have been getting their equal share of royalties. In a case involving a movie co-produced by Abhay Deol and Viacom 18, there was a public breakdown in negotiations with the music label T-Series because the composers Shankar–Ehsaan–Loy refused to sign an 'illegal contract'. While precise details of the dispute are not available, T-Series later withdrew from the deal and was replaced by two smaller music labels.[85] It is likely that the mandatory royalty-sharing provisions and the first ownership of copyright were at the core of the dispute. Lawyers involved in negotiating such contracts report that not much has changed for smaller composers and lyricists, as producers and music labels use backdated agreements and advance royalties to circumvent mandatory royalty-sharing provisions.[86] Smaller lyricists and composers are unlikely to sue music labels over such contracts for fear of losing future opportunities. It would have been very different if composers and lyricists had a strong copyright society protecting their rights through collective bargaining. But such a society is yet to see the light of day. These failures are largely attributable to a policy paralysis in the Copyright Office.

The last chapter of this epic dispute between Akhtar and the music industry is yet to be written. The Copyright (Amendment) Act, 2012 is by no means a perfect piece of legislation, and it may not have helped empower smaller composers and lyricists. But the lobbying and debate that led to this law provided an opportunity to educate composers and lyricists of their intellectual property rights, which is perhaps the most valuable contribution of this new law.

———————

Notes

1. Shabana Ansari, *Copyright Act: Film-makers Decide to Take Protest Ahead*, DNA, 25 December 2010, available at http://www.dnaindia. com/mumbai/report-copyright-act-filmmakers-decide-to-take-protest-ahead-1485842 (Last visited on 22 April 2016).
2. AIR 1977 SC 1443: 1977 SCR (3) 206.
3. Subhash K. Jha, *The Film Industry has Boycotted Me*, MID DAY (Mumbai), 2 May 2012, available at http://www.mid-day.com/entertainment/2012/may/270512-The-film-industry-has-boycotted-me.htm (Last visited on 22 April 2016).
4. ET Bureau, *Mani Shankar, Javed Akhtar Nominated to Rajya Sabha*, THE ECONOMIC TIMES, 20 March 2010, available at http://articles. economictimes.indiatimes.com/2010-03-20/news/27627121_1_theatre-personality-rajya-sabha-javed-akhtar (Last visited on 22 April 2016).
5. See generally Prashant Reddy T., *The Background Score to the Copyright (Amendment) Act, 2012*, 5 NUJS L. REV. , 469 (2012).
6. Javed Akhtar v. Magic Mantra Vision, CS (OS) No. 1743/2005 (Delhi High Court) (unreported), (order passed on 21 August 2006).
7. AIR 1977 SC 1443: 1977 SCR (3) 206.
8. Indian Performing Right Society Ltd. v. Eastern India Motion Pictures Association, 1977 SCR (3) 206.
9. The Copyright Act, 1957, § 2(f) ('"cinematograph film" includes the sound track, if any, and "cinematograph" shall be construed as including any work produced by any process analogous to cinematography"') (un-amended 1957 Act).
10. See generally Nikhil Krishnamurthy, *IPRS v. Eimpa, Performing Right or Wrong?*, 1 MIPR 169 (2007), which provides an excellent critique of the Supreme Court judgment.

11. Indian Performing Right Society Ltd. v. Eastern India Motion Pictures Association, SCR at 222.

12. Community for Creative Non-Violence v. Reid, 490 U.S. 730 (1989).

13. Clause 5 of the Copyright (Amendment) Bill, 2010.

14. INDIA, PARLIAMENTARY STANDING COMMITTEE ON HUMAN RESOURCE DEVELOPMENT, TWO HUNDRED TWENTY-SEVENTH REPORT ON THE COPYRIGHT (AMENDMENT) BILL, 2010, ¶ 9.14 (23 November 2010), available at http://164.100.47.5/newcommittee/reports/EnglishCommittees/ Committee%20on%20HRD/227.pdf (Last visited on 17 August 2016).

15. INDIA, PARLIAMENTARY STANDING COMMITTEE ON HUMAN RESOURCE DEVELOPMENT, TWO HUNDRED TWENTY-SEVENTH REPORT ON THE COPYRIGHT (AMENDMENT) BILL, 2010, *Minutes of Evidence*, at 25 (XIX Meeting of the Committee, 4 June 2010).

16. PARLIAMENTARY STANDING COMMITTEE ON HUMAN RESOURCE DEVELOPMENT, TWO HUNDRED TWENTY-SEVENTH REPORT, *Minutes of Evidence*, at 25 (XIX Meeting).

17. INDIA, PARLIAMENTARY STANDING COMMITTEE ON HUMAN RESOURCE DEVELOPMENT, TWO HUNDRED TWENTY-SEVENTH REPORT ON THE COPYRIGHT (AMENDMENT) BILL, 2010, *Minutes of Evidence*, at 70–1(XXI Meeting of the Committee, 22 June 2010).

18. PARLIAMENTARY STANDING COMMITTEE ON HUMAN RESOURCE DEVELOPMENT, TWO HUNDRED TWENTY-SEVENTH REPORT, *Minutes of Evidence*, at 70–1 (XXI Meeting).

19. INDIA, PARLIAMENTARY STANDING COMMITTEE ON HUMAN RESOURCE DEVELOPMENT, TWO HUNDRED TWENTY-SEVENTH REPORT ON THE COPYRIGHT (AMENDMENT) BILL, 2010, *Minutes of Evidence*, at 72–3 (XX Meeting of the Committee, 15 June 2010).

20. INDIA, PARLIAMENTARY STANDING COMMITTEE ON HUMAN RESOURCE DEVELOPMENT, TWO HUNDRED TWENTY-SEVENTH REPORT ON THE COPYRIGHT (AMENDMENT) BILL, 2010, *Minutes of Evidence*, at 83–4 (XXIII Meeting of the Committee, 15 July 2010).

21. PARLIAMENTARY STANDING COMMITTEE ON HUMAN RESOURCE DEVELOPMENT, TWO HUNDRED TWENTY-SEVENTH REPORT, *Minutes of Evidence*, at 83–4 (XXIII Meeting).

22. See PAUL GOLDSTEIN, COPYRIGHT'S HIGHWAY: FROM GUTENBERG TO THE CELESTIAL JUKEBOX (2nd edn, 2003), for an excellent history of copyright law.

23. WILLIAM F. PATRY, PATRY ON COPYRIGHT, Chap 3 § 3: 19 (2012).

24. DOROTHEE THUM, COPYRIGHT THROUGHOUT THE WORLD Chap 16: 16:29 (a) (Silke von Lewinski ed., 2011).

25. THUM, COPYRIGHT THROUGHOUT THE WORLD, Chap 16: 16:29 (a).

26. Thum, Copyright Throughout the World, Chap 16: 16:32 (a).

27. Thum, Copyright Throughout the World, Chap 16: 16:29 (a).

28. Thum, Copyright Throughout the World, Chap 16: 16:29 (a).

29. Thum, Copyright Throughout the World, Chap 16: 16:32 (b).

30. Council Directive 92/100/EEC of 19 November 1992 on Rental Right and Lending Right and on Certain Rights related to Copyright in the Field of Intellectual Property, O.J.L 346/61 of 27 November 1992.

31. Silke von Lewinski, *Collectivism and Individual Contracts, in* Individualism and Collectiveness In Intellectual Property Law 122–3 (Jan Rosen ed., 2012).

32. Arindam Mukherjee, *Music, Games to Drive Mobile VAS Growth,* The Economic Times, 2 February 2007, available at http://articles. economictimes.indiatimes.com/2007-02-02/news/28415854_1_mobile-music-mobile-subscribers-vas (Last visited on 22 April 2015).

33. See Rajeev Mantri, *The Story of India's Telecom Revolution,* MINT, 8 January 2013, available at http://www.livemint.com/Opinion/ biNfQImaeobXxOPV6pFxqI/The-story-of-Indias-telecom-revolution. html?facet=print (Last visited on 22 April 2015).

34. See Phonographic Performance Ltd., *Auditor's Report* (30 August 2011), available at http://www.spicyip.com/docs/ppl8.pdf (Last visited on 22 April 2015); See also Prashant Reddy, *The 'Numbers' Continue to Talk—PPL's Revenues from Mobile Ringtones Has Zoomed Up by 1857% in 6 Years from Rs. 7 Crores to Rs. 137 Crores,* SPICYIP, 12 February 2011, available at http://spicyipindia.blogspot.com/2011/02/ numbers-continue-to-talk-ppls-revenues.html (Last visited on 22 April 2015).

35. Rahul Bhatia, *The Quiet Royalties Heist,* OPEN, 29 March 2011, available at http://www.openthemagazine.com/article/art-culture/the-quiet-royalties-heist (Last visited on 22 April 2015).

36. Parliamentary Standing Committee on Human Resource Development, Two Hundred Twenty-Seventh Report, at 22–5.

37. Parliamentary Standing Committee on Human Resource Development, Two Hundred Twenty-Seventh Report, at 22–5.

38. See Aparna Joshi, *Interview with Javed Akhtar, Lyricist,* 1(7) Sound Box 20 (February 2011).

39. Memorandum of Association, Indian Performing Right Society, 1969.

40. Memorandum of Association, Indian Performing Right Society, 1969.

41. The Indian Performing Right Society, *Memorandum of Understanding between IPRS, PPL and IMI,* ¶ 2, ¶3, and ¶5 (12 November 1993), available at http://spicyip.com/docs/IPRS%20MoU.pdf (Last visited on 22 April 2015).

42. The Indian Performing Right Society, *Memorandum of Understanding between IPRS, PPL and IMI*, ¶ 3.

43. The Copyright Act, 1957, § 33 (after the 1994 amendment).

44. The Copyright Act, 1957, § 34, § 35 (after the 1994 amendment); Copyright Rules, 1958, Rule 14H (after the 1994 amendment but prior to the 2012 amendment).

45. The Copyright Act, 1957, § 34, § 35 (after the 1994 amendment).

46. Government of India, Ministry of Human Resource Development, *Application Under Section 33(2) of the Copyright Act, 1957 by IPRS for Registration as a Copyright Society* (1 February 1996), available at http://www.spicyip.com/docs/partb1.pdf (Last visited on 28 April 2014).

47. The Copyright Act, 1957, § 35 (after the 1994 amendment).

48. Articles of Association, Indian Performing Right Society.

49. Copyright Rules, 1958, Rule 14(I) (after the 1994 amendment).

50. Ministry of Human Resource Development, *Application by IPRS for Registration as a Copyright Society in Musical Works*, F. NO. 4-1/ 96 – I. C., ¶ 2 (I), available at http://www.spicyip.com/docs/partb1.pdf (Last visited on 28 April 2014).

51. See Joshi, *Interview with Javed Akhtar*.

52. See Reddy, *The Background Score*, for a more detailed history of this case.

53. Reddy, *The Background Score*, at 496.

54. See Reddy, *The Background Score*, for a more detailed history of the administration of royalties.

55. See The Indian Performing Right Society, *Director's Report for the Year Ended March 31, 2004*, available at http://spicyip.com/docs/Annual%20 Report%202003.pdf (Last visited on 28 April 2014).

56. See The Indian Performing Right Society, *Income and Expenditure Account for the Year Ended March 31, 2007*.

57. See Phonographic Performance Ltd., *Auditor's Report* (30 August 2011); See also Reddy, *The 'Numbers' Continue to Talk*, for a detailed analysis of the annual reports of PPL, showing a massive increase in revenues from ringtone royalties.

58. See, for example, GOVERNMENT OF INDIA, MINISTRY OF HUMAN RESOURCE DEVELOPMENT, ANNUAL RETURNS 2008–09 PPL (7 February 2011), available at http://spicyip.com/docs/ppl3.pdf (Last visited on 28 April 2014).

59. Phonographic Performance Ltd., *Annual Return 2008–09*, 18, available at http://spicyip.com/docs/ppl3.pdf (Last visited on 28 April 2014).

60. Phonographic Performance Ltd., *Annual Return 2008–09*, 3; Hasan Kamal (Chairman), *Minutes of the 39th Annual General Meeting of*

Owner Members, 4 (30 September 2009), available at http://spicyip.com/docs/iprs1.pdf (Last visited on 28 April 2014); See also Phonographic Performance Ltd., *Annual Report 2005–06*, available at http://spicyip.com/docs/ppl1.pdf (Last visited on 30 April 2014); The Indian Performing Right Society, *Annual Report 2009–10*, available at http://iprs.org/agm0910.asp (Last visited on 30 April 2014).

61. See Reddy, *The Background Score*, for a more detailed history of the administration of royalties.
62. See Reddy, *The Background Score*, for a more detailed history of the administration of royalties.
63. See Reddy, *The Background Score*, for a more detailed history of the administration of royalties.
64. See Reddy, *The Background Score*, for a more detailed history of the administration of royalties.
65. See Reddy, *The Background Score*, for a more detailed history of the administration of royalties.
66. See Reddy, *The Background Score*, for a more detailed history of the administration of royalties.
67. See Letter to Arjun Singh, Minister of Human Resource Development (26 March 2008), in the matter of illegalities in administration of IPRS (on file with authors).
68. Letter from Ravi Shankar Sharma, Music Director to Amit Khare, Joint Secretary, Ministry of Human Resource Development (24 January 2009), in the matter regarding harassment of composers and authors by publishers (on file with authors).
69. See Ajith Kumar, *Bombay Ravi Dead*, THE HINDU (Kozhikode), 8 March 2012, available at http://www.thehindu.com/arts/music/article2971806.ece (Last visited on 22 April 2016).
70. See Reddy, *The Background Score*.
71. Saregama India Ltd. v. Indian Performing Right Society and Ors. (Application for Interim Injunction), T.S. 124 of 2006, Before the Court of the Second Civil Judge (Sr.- Div.), Barasat, ¶ 41, ¶ 49.
72. Civil Procedure Code, 1908, § 80.
73. See Saregama India Ltd. v. Indian Performing Right Society and Ors., Order, T.S. 124 of 2006, Before the Court of the Second Civil Judge (Sr.-Div.), Barasat, 45–8 (6 November 2011), available at http://spicyip.com/docs/iprs4.pdf (Last visited on 24 December 2012).
74. See Letter from Jagjit Singh, Shankar Mahadevan, Vishal Bhardwaj, and Javed Akhtar to the Minister for Human Resource Development (20 December 2011), in the matter regarding illegalities with respect to administration of IPRS (2) (on file with authors).

75. See Letter from Jagjit Singh, Shankar Mahadevan, Vishal Bhardwaj, and Javed Akhtar.

76. Parliamentary Standing Committee on Human Resource Development, Two Hundred Twenty-Seventh Report, ¶ 21.4 to ¶ 21.6; See letters from Hasan Kamal, Chairman, IPRS to Raghavender, Director and Registrar of Copyrights (3 February 2011 and 11 February 2011) (on file with authors).

77. See Letters from Hasan Kamal, Chairman, IPRS to Raghavender, Director and Registrar of Copyrights (3 February 2011 and 11 February 2011), (on file with authors).

78. Phonographic Performance Ltd., *Annual Return* 2008–09, 18, available at http://spicyip.com/docs/ppl3.pdf (Last visited on 28 April 2014).

79. ET Bureau, *Kapil Sibal Blames Opposition for Lack of Progress in Reforms in Education*, The Economic Times, 25 September 2012, available at http://articles.economictimes.indiatimes.com/2012-09-25/news/34082826_1_accreditation-bill-education-bills-education-sector (Last visited on 22 April 2015); See also ET Bureau, *Education Tribunal Bill: Sibal Shoots Himself in the Foot*, The Economic Times, 2 September 2010, available at http://articles.economictimes.indiatimes.com/2010-09-02/news/27598552_1_education-tribunal-bill-minister-congress (Last visited on 22 April 2015).

80. Sumathi Chandrashekaran, *Copyright Bill Interrupted by 'Conflict of Interest'*, SPICYIP, 13 December 2011, available at http://spicyipindia.blogspot.in/2011/12/copyright-bill-interrupted-by-conflict.html (Last visited on 22 April 2015).

81. See Lok Sabha, *Debate on the Copyright Amendment Bill 2010* (17 May 2012), available at http://164.100.47.5/newdebate/225/17052012/20.00pmTo21.00pm.pdf (Last visited on 28 April 2014).

82. See Rajya Sabha, *Debate on the Copyright Amendment Bill 2010* (17 May 2012) available at http://rsdebate.nic.in/bitstream/123456789/603476/2/PD_225_17052012_p443_p496_25.pdf (Last visited on 17 August 2016).

83. See Lok Sabha, *Debate on the Copyright Amendment Bill 2010* (22 May 2012), available at http://164.100.47.132/newdebate/15/10/22052012/Fullday.pdf (Last visited on 28 April 2014).

84. Kiran George, Dr. Y.P.C. *Dangey Appointed Inquiry Officer in IPRS Investigation*, SPICYIP, 11 December 2015, available at http://spicyip.com/2015/12/spicyip-tidbit-ypc-dangey-appointed-inquiry-officer-in-iprs-investigation.html (Last visited on 3 May 2016); Thomas J. Vallianeth, *ED Attaches IPRS Assets: What Next for Royalty Administration?*, SPICYIP, 24 October 2015, available at http://spicyip.com/2015/10/

ed-attaches-iprs-assets-what-next-for-royalty-administration.html (Last visited on 3 May 2016).

85. *Music of Abhay Deol's 'One by Two' Released,* THE INDIAN EXPRESS, 27 January 2014, available at http://indianexpress.com/article/entertainment/bollywood/music-of-abhay-deols-one-by-two-released/ (Last visited on 28 April 2014).

86. *Ghost Post: Myriad Ways in Which the Copyright (Amendment) Act, 2012* is Being Circumvented, SPICYIP, 18 January 2014, available at http://spicyip.com/2014/01/ghost-post-the-myriad-ways-in-which-the-copyright-amendment-act-2012-is-being-circumvented.html (Last visited on 28 April 2014).

8

DIGITAL INDIA SEEKS 'SAFE HARBOUR'

In 2006, two graduates of the Indian Institute of Technology, Delhi—Anurag Dod and Gaurav Mishra—launched a unique Internet search engine called Guruji.com from Bengaluru (then known as Bangalore). Using proprietary algorithms, Guruji.com sought to provide better search results in the Indian context. The search engine soon became extremely popular, especially for its 'music search', which allowed users to locate and play music from different sites, including 'pirate' sites that hosted copyright-infringing content. From the time of its launch, there were murmurs of how Guruji could be the first Indian 'Google'. Like Google, Guruji was founded by two young graduates from an elite engineering college, and like Google, Guruji had received funding from reputed venture capital firms like Sequoia Capital and Sandstone Capital. Here was a company that had everything necessary to succeed as one of the first *desi* Internet giants.[1] Would it succeed?

The Bengaluru Police answered that question in April 2010 when it raided Guruji.com's office and arrested its chief executive officer (CEO), Anurag Dod, on charges of copyright infringement. The arrest took place on the basis of a complaint under the Copyright Act made by Super Cassettes Industries Ltd. (SCIL), also known as T-Series. T-Series had alleged that Guruji.com had infringed its copyright in songs from the movies *Om Shanti Om*, *All the Best*, *Bhool Bhulaiya*, *Aap kaa Suroor*, and *Aashiq Banaya Aapne* and had demanded the arrest of the website's CEO. Dod's arrest was shocking because until then, arresting people for copyright infringement had been restricted to roadside vendors or small-time shopkeepers. Dod's arrest led to

Guruji.com wrapping up its music search engine and eventually shutting down the website; it is no longer active.[2]

The most important question received very little media attention at the time. Was Guruji.com truly guilty of copyright infringement? *Medianama*, a news portal covering the Internet and digital space in India, wrote, '[w]as Guruji in the know of, and abetting copyright violation? We don't know. Is exploiting a loophole against the law? We don't think so. All across Guruji's website, the emphasis is on music search. It doesn't host or license the content, and repeatedly informs its users that it holds no responsibility for the content it links to.'[3] The news report concluded with the hope that an eventual court ruling would cast light on intermediary liability for search engines and websites which acted as platforms for third parties to host their content, an issue that was in much need of clarification. For reasons not clear, it appears that there was no court ruling in the Guruji case. While these unanswered questions were addressed in subsequent cases and policy debates, the Guruji case highlighted why it was so important to have clarity on Internet intermediary liability, especially in a country like India, where the powers of the police can have the drastic effect of shutting down a company with billion-dollar potential.

The debate on intermediary liability is not about whether anyone should have a free pass to violate copyright law online. Instead, the debate is about correctly apportioning the liability between the person who uploads infringing content and the intermediary who offers the service through which the infringing content is disseminated. An intermediary could either be Google, which is a search engine that indexes the Internet; or YouTube, which is an online service provider (OSP) that stores and publicly shares the content of third parties; or Internet service providers (ISPs) like Airtel or BSNL, which provide Internet connections through which services like Google are accessed and who may have the capability to block the infringers. In other words, any online service which merely acts as a conduit for information can be classified as an intermediary.[4]

Under traditional publishing models, content was distributed only through books or journals where editors would curate content. Since editors had prior knowledge of all the content getting published, it was easier to hold publishers liable for it. But the Internet changed things.

It presented a radically different publishing model where individuals could self-publish their content on platforms provided by third-party intermediaries like Blogger or YouTube or Facebook. The question now was whether the intermediaries hosting such content could be held liable for infringing material uploaded by their users? Similar issues arise in the context of ISPs who facilitate access to such infringing content through Internet services: Should ISPs have an obligation to monitor possibly infringing activity by their users?

Liability under the law in these cases arises only if the law imposes on intermediaries a duty to actively monitor the content being uploaded by their users. In principle, there is a strong argument to impose such a duty on Internet intermediaries because they earn advertising revenue directly linked to the type of content that is shared or accessed. The argument is that if they profit from infringing material, they should be liable for such content hosted on their websites.

However, imposing a duty on intermediaries to actively pre-screen all content to protect against copyright infringement, would make the business of running an OSP, or even a simple search engine, very expensive, since massive resources would be required to pre-screen all content that is made available. Similarly, if an ISP had a duty to monitor all activity of users, it could make the cost of accessing the internet more expensive. Thus, there is an equally strong argument to offer limited immunity to intermediaries for the actions of their users, provided the intermediaries act fast to take down copyright-infringing content once they are informed. Requiring copyright owners to screen vast database like YouTube and issue takedown notices for infringing content, however, remains tremendously expensive for copyright owners, and there is a risk that small entities or individual copyright owners may not be able to afford an extensive monitoring network of all Internet databases. All in all, the question of liability for Internet intermediaries is complicated.

So how did Indian policymakers and judges handle this issue of intermediary liability in cases of copyright infringement? How does it compare with the approach in the United States (US), a jurisdiction which has spawned multiple successful Internet businesses? This chapter tells the story of how music labels and the Internet industry tried to influence India's intermediary liability policy through court battles, government lobbying, and Parliamentary Standing Committees.

From *Netcom* to the Digital Millennium Copyright Act

The US and its legal system have played a pioneering role in shaping global debates on intermediary liability of both ISPs and OSPs for copyright-infringing content transmitted or hosted by their platforms.

An early case was that of *Religious Technology Center* v. *Netcom On-line Communication Services Inc.* ('*Netcom*').[5] The dispute in *Netcom* had to do with the liability of a bulletin board service (BBS) and an ISP for copyright-infringing material posted on the BBS by a user through Internet access provided by the ISP. The copyright-infringing material posted on the BBS comprised the published and unpublished materials of L. Ron Hubbard, the late founder of the Church of Scientology. The copyright of these works was owned by the Religious Technology Center and Bridge Publications Inc., both of whom were the plaintiffs in the case. The user who posted the materials was Dennis Erlich, a former minister of Scientology, and recently turned vocal critic of the Church. Initially, the plaintiffs asked the BBS owner, Thomas Klemesrud, and the ISP, Netcom, to deny Erlich access to the BBS and the Internet, to stop him from posting copyright-infringing material belonging to the plaintiffs. After both Klemesrud and Netcom refused to cooperate, they were named as defendants in a lawsuit for copyright infringement instituted by the plaintiffs.

The plaintiffs argued that Netcom was liable because every time Erlich posted a message on the BBS, a copy would automatically be created on Netcom's computer, from where other users could access the messages for a certain period of time. The fact that copies were created on Netcom's computers was alleged to be an act of copyright infringement by the plaintiffs under different theories such as direct infringement, contributory infringement, and vicarious infringement.

It is useful to distinguish between the different forms of copyright infringement recognized by US courts. Direct infringement is when a person makes copies of a copyrighted work without authorization, and the person making the unauthorized copy can be held responsible for copyright infringement. Contributory infringement takes place when one person knowingly assists or induces another to commit direct copyright infringement. A person can also be held vicariously liable for copyright infringement, even if that person has no knowledge of infringing activity carried out by a person who operates under his authority provided he derives financial benefit from such activity. The key to distinguishing between different forms of copyright infringement in the US is the degree of knowledge and control exercised over the infringing activity.[6]

Since the US had not enacted any special laws to protect Internet intermediaries in 1995, District Judge Ronald M. Whyte who was hearing the *Netcom* case faced the challenge of applying existing copyright law to the Internet. The stakes for the blossoming Internet industry in the US were high. If the ISP and the BBS were held to be directly liable for copyright-infringing content posted by their users, they would have to pay damages and also invest in resources to pre-screen content hosted or routed through them.

Judge Whyte's summary judgment on 21 November 1995 was mostly a victory for the Internet industry. He dismissed the claim of direct infringement with remarkably commonsensical arguments. He reasoned that where the infringing subscriber was clearly directly liable for the same act, it made no sense to adopt a rule that could make countless parties liable, when their role in the infringement was nothing more than setting up and operating a system that was necessary to keep the Internet functioning. He also said that it was not workable to have 'a theory of infringement that would hold the entire Internet liable for activities that cannot reasonably be deterred. Billions of bits of data flow through the Internet and are necessarily stored on servers throughout the network and it is thus practically impossible to screen out infringing bits from non-infringing bits.'[7] No summary judgment was issued on the remaining issues, such as contributory infringement, because questions of facts were involved, and summary judgments can be issued only on questions of law. However, Judge Whyte did hold that it was fair, 'if Netcom is able to take simple measures to prevent further damage to plaintiff's copyrighted works, to hold Netcom liable for contributory infringement where Netcom has knowledge of Erlich's infringing postings yet continues to aid in the accomplishment of Erlich's purpose of publicly distributing the postings.'[8] In other words, Internet intermediaries would have to move fast to remove infringing content, once they were notified of the same.

Judge Whyte's judgment is important because it became the foundation for the 'safe harbour' provisions for intermediaries in Section 512 of the US Copyright Act, which provided limited immunity to Internet intermediaries. This provision was inserted into US law by the Digital Millennium Copyright Act (DMCA), which is a collection of different laws enacted by the US Congress in 1998 to tackle the issue of copyrights in the digital age. In particular, Section 512 was the result of the Online Copyright Infringement Liability Limitation Act (OCILLA) which is in Title II of the DMCA. The provision was the result of a demand by OSPs such as America Online (AOL) and Yahoo!, who warned of the Internet economy being impeded due to the lack of immunity for intermediaries from possible liability.[9]

Report 105–551 of the Committee on the Judiciary in the US House of Representatives in 1998, which examined the OCILLA, traces the lineage of the 'safe harbour' provision to Judge Whyte's judgment. The Report states that:

> ... the bill essentially codifies the result in the leading and most thoughtful judicial decision to date: *[Netcom]*. In doing so, it overrules those aspects of *Playboy Enterprises, Inc.* v. *Frena*, 839 F. Supp. 1552 (M.D. Fla.1993), to the extent that case suggests that such acts by service providers could constitute direct infringement, and provides certainty that *Netcom* and its progeny (so far, only a few district court cases), will be the law of the land.[10]

As explained by the Report, under the new law, 'direct infringement liability is ruled out for passive, automatic acts engaged in through a technological process initiated by another'.[11] However, although the law exempts Internet intermediaries from monetary liability, that is, damages, they are still required to comply with injunctions granted by court. This could mean either taking down infringing content, blocking access to such content, or shutting down accounts of subscribers.

Similarly, with regard to liability for contributory infringement, that is, liability for the acts of users, Section 512 ensured that no monetary damages could be claimed against the Internet intermediary for automatic acts, provided that the service providers fulfilled certain criteria such as putting in place a mechanism for allowing copyright owners to notify service providers of infringing activity and subsequently removing such infringing content expeditiously. This was designed to protect intermediaries who were unaware of the infringing activity of their users. But if these intermediaries failed to remove or block copyright-infringing material even after being informed, they could be liable for contributory infringement and asked to pay damages.

Judge Whyte's ruling and its subsequent codification were a testament to the ability of both US judges and policymakers to understand the nature and potential of the Internet even in its early days. The DMCA's 'safe harbour' provisions have proven successful in balancing public interest with the commercial interests of the American entertainment and Internet industries.

The First Round: The Information Technology Bill, 1999

By the end of the twentieth century, the world had come to recognize India as something of an information technology superpower. Realizing the Internet's potential, the Government of India set up an Inter-ministerial Standing Committee in 1997 to draft a new law to tackle what it referred to as 'information technology'.[12] The Committee drafted the Information Technology Bill ('IT Bill') which was introduced in Parliament in 1999. The legislation was wide-ranging, and sought to amend several existing laws to ensure e-commerce transactions were properly governed under the law. Intermediary liability was one of the issues that the IT Bill dealt with, in its Clause 78. This provision provided qualified immunity to intermediaries. The provision is reproduced as follows:

Network Service Providers Not to be Liable in Certain Cases

78. For the removal of doubts, it is hereby declared that no person providing any service as a network service provider shall be liable under this Act, rules or regulations made thereunder for any third party information or data made available by him if he proves that the offence or contravention was committed without his knowledge or that he had exercised all due diligence to prevent the commission of such offence or contravention.

Explanation.—For the purposes of this section,—

(a) 'network service provider' means an intermediary;
(b) 'third party information' means any information dealt with by a network service provider in his capacity as an intermediary.

'Intermediary' was defined in Clause 2(1)(v) as: '"intermediary" with respect to any particular electronic message means any person who on behalf of another person receives, stores or transmits that message or provides any service with respect to that message.'

This provision (Clause 78) exempted Internet intermediaries from liability for any act committed without their knowledge, or in cases where they had exercised all due diligence to prevent the commission of a contravention of the law. Neither 'knowledge' nor 'due diligence', were defined terms, and it would be up to Indian judges to interpret both phrases. A liberal interpretation of both phrases by Indian judges would have resulted in a conclusion similar to the ruling of Judge Whyte in *Netcom* and would have relieved intermediaries of actively monitoring content provided through their services. On the other hand, a strict interpretation of both phrases would require intermediaries to actively monitor and pre-screen the content made available on their websites.

After its introduction in Parliament, the IT Bill was sent for scrutiny to a Parliamentary Standing Committee. Not surprisingly, Clause 78 and the issue of intermediary liability was a subject of much debate. In particular, this provision had rung alarm bells within the Indian Music Industry (IMI). The Internet was already perceived as a hotbed of piracy of music in the West. For content owners like the music industry, the only way to curb rising online piracy was by putting the onus of monitoring and pre-screening content on Internet intermediaries who allowed users to search or access pirated content through their websites. On 3 May 2000, IMI, lobbying for the music industry, sent a delegation to appear before the Parliamentary Standing Committee examining the IT Bill.[13]

While depositions made before the Standing Committee are not available (because the Parliament library was not able to locate the same in its records, as was informed to the authors in response to an RTI application[14]), its final report sheds some light on the hearings. It appears that IMI tried very hard to convince the Standing Committee to delete Clause 78 on grounds that it would conflict with the Copyright Act, 1957. In the words of the Committee,

> [IMI] submitted that the tests of lack of knowledge or of due diligence as stipulated in clause 78 of the IT Bill were not precise and objective and a Network Service Provider (NSP) or intermediary could rely upon clause 78 of the Bill and by way [of] a defence, resist proceedings initiated against him, under section 51 of the Copyright Act.[15]

This submission by IMI may not have been entirely accurate. As pointed out by some commentators, this provision appears to immunize an intermediary from liability for offences committed by third parties only under the Information Technology Act (IT Act) and not other laws like the Copyright Act.[16] In any case, the Standing Committee debated the possibility of amending Clause 78 to dilute the degree of immunity it offered but refrained from doing so.[17]

Clause 78 in its original form was eventually enacted into law as Section 79 of the IT Act.

The Second Round: The Information Technology (Amendment) Bill, 2006

In 2004, a pornographic video clipping of two high school students shot with a mobile phone went on sale on baazee.com, a website that connected buyers and sellers directly. The video involved students of a prominent school in New Delhi, and the matter got widespread attention throughout the country. When the Delhi Police was informed that an individual was selling a compact disc (CD) containing the video clip on an online marketplace, it arrested the person selling the clip on charges of distributing pornographic material. The police also arrested Avnish Bajaj, the CEO of baazee.com, the platform on which the CD was sold.[18] The case against Bajaj was quashed only several years later by the Supreme Court, on principles of corporate criminal liability rather than intermediary liability.[19] But this incident may have turned public perception against online intermediaries.

In 2005, the Government of India constituted an expert committee to relook certain provisions of the IT Act, 2000, in light of recent developments, such as the baazee.com incident.[20] The issue of intermediary liability was also re-examined by the committee, which comprised bureaucrats, legal experts, and industry representatives, including the President of the National Association of Software and Services Companies (NASSCOM). In its final report, this committee recommended, without substantiating reasons, that India follow the European approach on intermediary liability, and in particular, the European Union Directives on E-Commerce, 2000/31/EC issued on 8 June 2000.[21]

The committee also suggested a new draft of Section 79. This redrafted provision proposed a blanket rule exempting intermediaries from any liability for information routed through the intermediary or made available on the intermediary's website. There was one exception to this rule, to address cases where the intermediary 'conspired' or 'abetted' in the commission of an unlawful act. Both these phrases require an element of intent, which would be difficult to prove in a court of law, thus offering a higher degree of immunity to intermediaries. Intermediaries would still have to expeditiously remove or disable access to offensive content once they were informed by the central government or its agencies. The key change between the proposed Section 79 and the existing Section 79 was the deletion of the phrase 'due diligence' along with the provision of immunity against violations under all laws and not just the IT Act.

The government accepted most recommendations of the Expert Committee, and introduced the Information Technology (Amendment) Bill, 2006, in Parliament on 15 December 2006, recommending 51 amendments to the IT Act, 2000, including a rewrite of Section 79.[22] Although the amendment to Section 79 was on the lines suggested by the committee, the language was altered by the government. As suggested by the Expert Committee, the 'due diligence' requirement was dropped. Now, the intermediary would lose immunity for acts of users, if it 'conspired' or 'abetted' in the commission of an unlawful act. Further the government also inserted a new provision which would delegate powers to the central government to draft rules which would have to be adhered to by the intermediary, failing which the intermediary would incur liability.

As was the norm, the 2006 IT (Amendment) Bill was referred to a Parliamentary Standing Committee. The testimony that the Standing Committee received has been declared privileged information,[23] but its final report gives insights into the deliberations on Section 79.[24] When the issue of intermediary liability first came up for discussion during the drafting of the IT Bill, 2000 it was the music industry that had demanded diluting the immunity for online intermediaries. This time, the Central Bureau of Investigation (CBI) objected to the proposed dilution of liability of online intermediaries. The CBI demanded that online marketplaces 'should not be given immunity unless they proved due diligence which might be exercised by them through technical scrutiny of traffic data through filters for removing hate content, obscene material, sale of contraband goods, etc'.[25] The CBI justified this demand on the grounds that 'in the real world some liabilities existed on the owner of a premise for prevention of certain types of criminal offences including sale of contraband goods' and that online marketplaces should be treated the same way.[26] This practice of drawing parallels between the physical and virtual worlds has repeatedly occurred in the Indian context, and has proven to be a major obstacle for judges and policymakers to understand the difference between e-commerce and conventional commerce.

Since the Department of Information Technology (DIT), Government of India, was the department in charge of the tabled version of the 2006 IT (Amendment) Bill, the Standing Committee asked the DIT for its views on the CBI's stand. The DIT explained that the government deleted the phrase 'due diligence' because it felt that the duties and liabilities of the intermediary had to be explicitly defined. The DIT also said that a new provision delegated powers to the government to make rules to govern intermediaries, and that 'due diligence' could be included in those rules. The Standing Committee was not impressed with this explanation.[27] Instead, it backed the CBI's recommendation of retaining 'due diligence' in the text of the provision itself. It also said that 'if the intermediaries can block/eliminate the alleged objectionable and obscene contents with the help of technical mechanisms like filters and inbuilt storage intelligence, then they should invariably do it'.[28] In other words, the Standing Committee wanted intermediaries to actively monitor and perhaps even pre-screen content hosted on their websites.

When the report was made public, it came under withering criticism from several quarters. An article in the *Times of India* titled 'Recipe for Killing Internet in India', warned that if these recommendations were to go through, 'you might as well pull the shutters down on the net in the country, because the committee seeks to raise the liability of Internet service providers for any third party content in a manner that it will become difficult to run the service and stay away from jail'.[29] The article attacked the Standing Committee for failing to understand the very nature of the Internet by 'proposing this insanity'. The article suggested that 'there's no difference between the phone and the postal service and the net—it's just that one delivers voice or post and the other data. Both deal with third party content which is impossible to verify'.[30] This comment was inaccurate in the context of intermediaries like YouTube or Amazon, because unlike postal or telephony services which cannot view or hear the communications of their patrons, the material on YouTube or Amazon can be publicly viewed by the intermediary. Nevertheless, the criticism was valid. Indian policymakers had failed to understand the nature of the Internet, or how it was different from conventional marketplaces.

The main difference between an online marketplace and the real world is the fact that the medium of the Internet facilitates so many more transactions than the real world that it is unreasonable to expect the owner of an online marketplace to be aware of all the content on a website. Similarly, there is a huge difference between the traditional broadcast industry and websites like YouTube. Unlike the traditional broadcast industry, YouTube is a platform that allows self-publishing, and the volume of content uploaded on YouTube makes it impossible to have a water-tight pre-screening process. Policymakers must recognize that the rules of liability need to be reinvented if newer models of doing business on the Internet are to be encouraged. If traditional rules of liability remain, in the fear that somebody somewhere will misuse the Internet, there is a real risk that business model innovation will stagnate. The rules of liability have been rewritten time and again, over centuries, in order to encourage innovation and facilitate business which will benefit the general public. The creation of the limited liability company, limiting liability on carriers for lost or damaged goods, and limits on liability of airlines for lost baggage or accidental deaths are all examples where traditional rules of liability have been recast to encourage new technologies or businesses.

A practical way of tackling Internet intermediary liability could have been to consider providing intermediaries with *limited* immunity, which exempted them from actively monitoring content but which still required them to remove infringing content after being notified of the same. Unfortunately, the Parliamentary Standing Committee prescribed a formula which required all intermediaries to actively monitor their websites. It examined only the downside of limiting intermediary liability without looking at the benefits of limiting their liability. Would the Standing Committee's conclusions have been any different had it known that by December 2013, over 100 hours of video would be uploaded on YouTube *every minute* and that Amazon would be selling 426 items *per second*?[31] If both these websites were required to actively monitor or pre-screen all content, YouTube and Amazon would have faced the task of verifying every video or every item before making it available for public viewing. To an extent, websites like YouTube do run filtering software (like ContentID) to actively screen copyright-infringing content, but this software is hardly foolproof. For example, it cannot determine whether content possibly falls foul of the several Indian laws which criminalize speech that may be seditious, defamatory, or potentially hurt religious sentiments. Making such determinations would require human intervention. The cost of instituting a foolproof pre-screening mechanism staffed by humans would be prohibitive, and would also require the companies to determine, subjectively, whether online content was defamatory, obscene, inflammatory, or infringing copyright. Such subjective determinations would increase risk and cause significant instability in the companies' overall business models.

It is certainly possible that some people will violate the law by selling prohibited goods or uploading defamatory or inflammatory videos on platforms hosted by Internet intermediaries. But, assuming that these transactions are conducted by a miniscule minority, it would have been better to opt for a policy framework that benefits the majority of the law-abiding public. Unfortunately, there was no attempt to conduct a broader cost–benefit analysis of the policy implications for all stakeholders and the Parliamentary Standing Committee's policy calculations appear to have been dominated by security concerns expressed by agencies like the CBI.

The recommendation of the Parliamentary Standing Committee to re-introduce a 'due-diligence' requirement, was accepted by the government which introduced amendments to the existing IT (Amendment) Bill, 2006 in Parliament. The Information Technology (Amendment) Act, 2008 as eventually enacted by Parliament retained the 'due diligence' requirement in Section 79. Parliament also delegated to the government, via Section 79, the power to make rules to govern the conduct of intermediaries. These rules, eventually called the Information Technology (Intermediaries Guidelines) Rules, 2011, created a system of takedowns whereby intermediaries would have to act within 36 hours of being notified of certain classes of content, described in the rules, in order to maintain their immunity.[32] However, since the problematic phrase 'due diligence' was never defined in the IT Act, its interpretation was left to the judiciary. Unfortunately for the Internet industry, at least one judgment of the Delhi High Court, delivered in a case of copyright infringement, has specifically interpreted 'due diligence' to mean pre-screening of content.[33]

The Music Industry versus the Internet

From 2007, Indian music labels launched a global anti-piracy campaign against websites hosting copyrighted content belonging to the labels. Like their counterparts abroad, the Indian music industry recognized the threat posed by the Internet to their existing business model. Their first target was Guruji.com.

At the time of Guruji.com's launch, the technology-related website Gigaom reported that the Indian search engine claimed to have indexed songs from all major Indian languages from 1932 till 2008. The report also explained that Guruji.com was only indexing existing websites on the Internet rather than hosting any content itself. So, if a user searched for a particular song, Guruji.com would throw up a list of hyperlinks to websites where the song was available and the user could click on that hyperlink to access the song. It was possible that Guruji.com was displaying hyperlinks to websites which hosted pirated music. The question, therefore, from a copyright perspective was whether displaying hyperlinks to pirate websites amounted to copyright infringement, or whether such an action would be protected under Section 79 of the IT Act, 2000.[34] But when a start-up is faced with criminal arrest and seizure of equipment, they are more likely to fold up business than engage with India's snail-paced criminal justice system. That is exactly what happened with Guruji when the Bengaluru Police arrested the company's founders for copyright infringement, as explained earlier in the beginning of this chapter. This website got shuttered, and its founder went on to start new businesses.[35]

Separate from the criminal actions, Section 79 and intermediary protection came up in civil lawsuits filed by T-Series before the Delhi High Court against websites like YouTube, MySpace, and Yahoo!, all of which allowed users to upload music and videos on their websites.[36] Once uploaded, this content could be streamed by other users. Some of the uploaded material was innocuous, like a video of cats playing with a ball of yarn, or a cat playing with another cat. But a lot of content was copyrighted, owned by third parties, and certainly not owned by the users who were uploading it. As one of India's largest music labels, a lot of content owned by T-Series was being uploaded on YouTube. T-Series eventually settled the litigation against YouTube by entering into licensing agreements where the music label would get a share of the advertising revenue earned by YouTube every time its content was played by a user.[37] It was the litigation by T-Series against MySpace, a social networking site with a focus on music, that resulted in the first (although interim) judgment on the issue of whether Internet intermediaries could be held liable for copyright infringement committed by their users.[38] MySpace suffered a comprehensive defeat at this interim stage, and was restrained from continuing to infringe music owned by T-Series. This interim judgment against MySpace delivered by Justice Manmohan Singh in 2011 came in for significant criticism from several quarters for his interpretation of both copyright law and intermediary liability law under the IT Act.[39]

The first issue in the case was whether intermediaries like MySpace had violated copyright law by allowing users to post copyright-infringing content on their websites. In its defence, MySpace argued that it did not have knowledge of the infringing content at the time of its posting, and that its terms and conditions required users to not post copyright-infringing content. Further, MySpace said that if it was informed of any copyright-infringing content, it would swiftly takedown such content. The facts of the case and the arguments by MySpace bear similarity to the *Netcom* case decided by Judge Whyte in 1995. Although there are strong similarities between copyright law in the US and India, Justice Manmohan Singh arrived at an entirely different conclusion from Judge Whyte. This divergence lay mainly in the interpretation of Section 51 of the Copyright Act in the *MySpace* case.

Under Section 51, a person can be liable for copyright infringement, if that person reproduces or transmits, among others, any copyrighted content without the prior permission of the copyright owner; or if that person permits the use of a place for profit to communicate works to the public, where the communication constitutes copyright infringement, unless the person was not aware and had no reasonable ground to believe that such communication would infringe copyright.

The latter prohibition against 'the use of a place for profit to communicate works to the public' has existed in the Indian Copyright Act since it was enacted in 1957, many years before the Internet was invented. In 1957, this provision was most likely targeted at owners of marketplaces, where infringing content was openly sold, or establishments like hotels, where music was openly performed without a licence. Thus, the law could reasonably hold such establishments liable for infringing activities conducted by third parties. 'Knowledge' of the infringing activity is the key requirement for infringement, since Section 51 exempts 'owners of a place' from liability, if they did not have any reasonable ground for believing that infringing activity was taking place on their premises. Such a provision was clearly designed for real-world transactions. But could this be easily or logically extended and applied to the Internet, where websites deal in terabytes of information and millions of users? Can the owner of a website like MySpace practically have knowledge of the activities of its millions of users? Justice Manmohan Singh answered both questions in the affirmative when he found MySpace liable for copyright infringement. He said websites would fall under the definition of 'any place' and that MySpace had knowledge of the infringing activities on its website for four reasons:

(a) MySpace had a takedown mechanism for infringing content, thus indicating that it was aware that infringing content was being uploaded. (The logical and somewhat absurd corollary to this conclusion is that websites like MySpace should not have a takedown mechanism, if they want to prove that they were not aware that infringing content was being uploaded. Surely, this only hurts the copyright owner.)

(b) T-Series had already made available its entire catalogue to MySpace, thus giving MySpace knowledge of the copyrighted content in question.

(c) MySpace took a licence from all users to host the content and also modify it for inserting advertisements.

(d) MySpace had an India-centric office to conduct business in India, apprise Indian copyright owners of its takedown procedures, take licences from Indian users who uploaded content, and also add Indian language advertisements to the content that it was streaming.

Besides arguments under the Copyright Act, MySpace also claimed immunity offered to intermediaries under Section 79 of the IT Act. Justice Singh's ruling on this point was confused. He first held that Section 79 would not apply to copyright cases because of Section 81 of the IT Act, which says that nothing contained in the IT Act would restrict any person from exercising any right conferred under the Copyright Act, 1957. After concluding that Section 79 would not apply, Justice Singh still went ahead to assess whether Section

79 would shield MySpace from liability for copyright infringement, concluding in the negative because MySpace failed to fulfil the criteria laid down in that provision.

Justice Singh's analysis was most worrisome for intermediaries because he interpreted 'due diligence' to necessarily mean pre-screening. Specifically, his judgment stated,

> if the defendants are put to notice about the rights of the plaintiff in certain works, the defendants should do preliminary check in all the cinematograph works relating Indian titles before communicating the works to the public rather than falling back on post infringement measures. The due diligence is also not satisfied when the defendant uploads the contents of the user on their server and then modify the same as per the limited licence to amend from users. This means that the defendants have the chances to keep a check on the works which defendants avoid so to the reasons best known to them.[40]

In other words, MySpace was required to actively pre-screen content.

This analysis was, in spirit, very similar to the conclusions of the Parliamentary Standing Committee examining the IT (Amendment) Bill, 2006. In its report, the Standing Committee had disagreed with the government's proposal to drop the 'due diligence' requirement from Section 79, and had instead recommended that intermediaries be required to observe 'due diligence' by actively pre-screening content.

The Delhi High Court judgment and the Parliamentary Standing Committee report are strikingly different from the judicial and legislative approach in the US. When Judge Whyte declined to hold Netcom liable for copyright infringement in 1995, he reasoned that '[b]illions of bits of data flow through the Internet and are necessarily stored on servers throughout the network and it is thus practically impossible to screen out infringing bits from non-infringing bits'. The US Congress wholeheartedly endorsed Judge Whyte's view, when it codified his judgment into the DMCA. These views on intermediary liability were expressed in the 1990s, when the Internet was still in its infancy, and when the entertainment business was much more powerful than the Internet industry in financial and political muscle. In contrast, the Parliamentary Standing Committee report and the Delhi High Court *MySpace* decision took much more conservative views in 2008 and 2011, respectively, by when the Internet was pervasive in

India, and when the world had already learnt from the US experience that a liberal intermediary liability policy did not necessarily harm the interests of copyright owners. Had the Internet been invented in India, it might well have died a premature death due to views like those that led to the IT Act, 2008 and the *MySpace* judgment.

Internet Service Providers as Copyright Cops

Besides content-hosting websites like YouTube and MySpace, owned and operated by multinational corporations, there are much smaller websites located both in India and abroad, which either stream (like YouTube) or offer content for download. Many of these websites have been targeted by the Indian entertainment and sports broadcast industry for hosting copyrighted content without the permission of the copyright owner. Unlike YouTube or MySpace, these smaller websites rarely offer lucrative monetization options to copyright owners, and are, therefore, targeted by large copyright owners for shutdown.

The primary weapon of copyright owners in the war against these alleged pirate websites located outside India was to seek a 'blocking order' against a list of known websites and also unknown defendants called 'John Does' or 'Ashok Kumars'. These blocking orders were to be necessarily implemented by ISPs who provided Internet connections to customers. The question is whether John Doe injunctions are the most appropriate remedy for the Internet.

One of the first John Doe injunctions, in the context of intellectual property (IP) law, was granted by a US district court in a lawsuit filed by the American pop rock star Billy Joel against unknown defendants selling merchandise bearing Joel's name or photograph outside his concert venues.[41] The order restrained the sale and directed the seizure of such merchandise. The presiding judge, Chief Judge Reynolds, noted that it was an 'extraordinary' order since a court would ordinarily not grant such orders in civil cases against persons not identified by the plaintiff. But he also said that the lack of such an order would cause irreparable injury to the plaintiff, presumably because there was no way to track down these foot-vendors who did not have a fixed location (unlike those who had shops). He also ruled that vendors whose goods were seized would have the right to be named as defendants and present their defence in court.

This order was the principal inspiration behind the first John Doe injunction granted in India by Justice Dalveer Bhandari, in the Delhi High Court, in 2003 in *Taj Television* v. *Rajan Mandal*.[42] This lawsuit was filed by Taj Television, a company which had exclusive broadcast rights for the FIFA World Cup. When these broadcasters approached leading IP lawyer Pravin Anand for a solution, the concept of John Doe injunctions did not exist in India. Arguing before the Delhi High Court, Anand said John Doe orders were needed for time-bound events like the FIFA World Cup, where it was difficult to approach courts for relief after an infringement had occurred. He argued that this was especially so since rogue cable operators could very easily destroy the incriminating evidence. Justice Bhandari was convinced, and granted a sweeping John Doe order against unknown cable operators. He also appointed a court-appointed commissioner to enter and search the premises of suspected cable operators and seize broadcasting equipment.

There was no justification, unfortunately, in Justice Bhandari's order, as to how cable operators, who were registered with the government, and who had heavy transmission equipment, could be equated with the foot-vendors in the *Billy Joel* case. Further, transmissions of pirated signals could be viewed by all subscribers of the operator, and could have been recorded as evidence, unlike the foot-vendors who could destroy the evidence once notice was issued to them by a court. Also, unlike the foot vendors in the *Billy Joel* case, cable operators did not enjoy any anonymity. If an infringer has no anonymity, a John Doe order makes no sense, as such orders need to be issued only where it is not possible to identify the infringer without the aid of a judicial order. The powers given to the broadcaster to seize the cable operator's equipment were also questionable. Such powers could be abused to extort disproportionately high licence fees from an infringer on the threat that the cable-operator's business could be shut down. The practicality of seizing transmission equipment, which would otherwise be used to broadcast non-infringing content, was also not addressed. For example, if a cable network broadcasts 25 different channels of which one is possibly infringing, should the rights-holder of the content on that one channel be allowed to seize all the transmission equipment of the cable operator, or would it more equitable to compensate the rights-holder with damages for the losses it has suffered? Justice Bhandari's order, unlike Chief Judge Reynolds' order (confined to one particular venue where Joel performed), applied to cable operators across India, and set a precedent for vaguely worded orders obtained later that decade, initially by sports broadcasters, and subsequently by movie studios, seeking to restrain cable operators from broadcasting new releases.[43]

As Internet piracy became a greater threat, movie studios began to use this same strategy against pirate websites by securing John Doe orders directing ISPs to block infringing content. These orders remained vaguely worded and poorly reasoned. For example, in 2011, the Delhi High Court issued the following John Doe injunction prohibiting unknown persons from exhibiting the movie 'Singham':

> defendants and other unnamed and undisclosed persons, are restrained from communicating or making available or distributing, or duplicating, or displaying, or releasing, or showing, or uploading, or downloading, or exhibiting, or playing, and/or defraying the movie 'Singham' in any manner without proper license from the plaintiff or in any other manner which would violate/infringe the plaintiff's copyright in the said cinematograph film 'Singham' through different mediums like CD, DVD, Blue-ray, VCD, Cable TV, DTH, Internet, MMS, Tapes, Conditional Access System or in any other like manner.[44]

It is very likely that the judge issuing the injunction had missed the significance of words like 'uploading', or 'downloading', or the 'Internet', and included them only because Reliance Big Entertainment, the producer of the film and its copyright owner, had mentioned these words in its plaint. The chaotic consequences of such a poorly worded order were made obvious when Reliance Big Entertainment served the order on all major ISPs, asking them to proactively block access to all infringing content.

By shifting the onus of monitoring Internet traffic from the copyright owner to the ISPs, the strategic genius of the John Doe order in the Internet age was revealed. In order to strictly comply with this order, ISPs would have to proactively invest in resources to monitor for infringing content, even though Section 79 did not explicitly impose such a duty on ISPs. The ISPs had technology which allowed them to inspect content being accessed or downloaded by users, but monitoring all user activity in real-time and in perpetuity would be near-impossible, given the number of users, besides invading user privacy.

How did the ISPs actually enforce this order in the *Singham* case? Most ISPs simply blocked access to all major file-sharing websites like Megaupload, Rapidshare, Mediafire, DepositFiles in the fear that one movie would be pirated.[45] The blockage left Internet users in India indignant. File-sharing websites have substantial non-infringing uses, and many used them for sharing non-pirated content. Should entire sites be blocked because one copyright owner obtained a John Doe injunction for one movie? This question was highlighted again when the Bombay and Madras High Courts issued similarly worded John Doe injunctions.[46] In the next two years, over two dozen such injunctions were issued by the High Courts of Delhi, Bombay, and Madras—it was now routine for big movie studios to apply for relief even before a movie was released. Each injunction caused more chaos for Internet users in India, because popular websites like Vimeo, Dailymotion, and Github were blocked by overcautious ISPs who did not want to fall foul of vaguely worded injunctions and risk being hauled to court for contempt of court.[47]

Inevitably, both ISPs and users began to push back against these John Doe orders. For instance, anonymous hackers staged an 'online dharna' by hacking the websites of the Supreme Court, the Madras High Court, the ruling Congress Party, and ISPs like Airtel and Reliance Communications.[48] These 'hacktivists' claimed that their only grouse was against the blocking of entire websites, rather than the specific blocking of pirated content. The hacking of these prominent websites was widely reported and made the issue public. One affected ISP, Vodafone, finally appealed against a John Doe injunction of the Madras High Court. The appellate court modified the initial order to require ISPs to block only specific uniform resource locators (URLs) on file-sharing websites offering infringing content.[49] By blocking only a URL, access would be blocked to only the one infringing file rather than the entire website. Thus, entire file-sharing websites would no longer be blocked and the onus shifted back to the copyright owner to monitor the Internet and provide ISPs with details of infringing URLs. Later in 2012, ISPs also tried to use Section 79 to avoid being named defendants in such lawsuits. The Madras High Court, however, fell back on the *MySpace* judgment of the Delhi High Court and said that ISPs could not claim immunity in cases of copyright infringement.[50]

There was a lesser-known litigation in 2012 before the Calcutta High Court in a lawsuit filed by Saregama and others against 104 named websites, offering streaming services or downloads of music without requisite licences.[51] The defendants in this lawsuit, like in the Madras High Court, were ISPs. At the first hearing, the Calcutta High Court directed 387 ISPs to block access to all 104 websites. A second lawsuit in 2013 followed, for blocking another 162 suspected pirate websites.[52] Although these orders were not open-ended John Doe orders, since they specifically identified the websites that required to be blocked, there was still the issue of analysing the contents of the websites. It appears that the Calcutta High Court had taken the music industry at its word, without verifying the contents of the targeted websites, by either going through the content themselves or through experts, and passed an interim injunction even before it heard the proprietors of the targeted websites.

In subsequent hearings, though, the Calcutta High Court took a sympathetic view of the role of ISPs. Justice I.P. Mukherjee, who had issued the earlier blocking order against the 104 websites, noted in an order in April 2014 that the counsel for the ISPs 'seems to be right when he submits that his client is in no position to do policing activity of screening materials being broadcast through myriad websites. He also points out that blocking a website could also tantamount to blocking access to other materials, which are not infringing and yet part of a website.'[53] Justice Mukherjee further pointed to the difficulty in restraining the publication of copyright-infringing content on the Internet. Eventually, he recorded that the onus of implementing the Court's injunction would fall on the Computer Emergency Response Team, India (CERT-IN), a body set up under the IT Act, operating under the Department of Telecommunications.[54] The CERT-IN has the power to block websites under the IT Act, and Justice Mukherjee delegated to CERT-IN complete authority on such blocking. For instance, CERT-IN could either shut down an infringing website or partially block an infringing website.[55] The onus of spotting infringing songs and URLs was squarely on the music owners. Now ISPs only had to follow directions of CERT-IN, and did not have to independently determine implementation methods. This relieved ISPs of the duty of making determinations on which content qualified as infringing content.

However, delegating the issue of how much infringement is 'sufficient' to block a website to bureaucrats at CERT-IN was perhaps not the best idea because this involved legal determination, a task that ought to be in the hands of judges trained in the law. In any case, this arrangement failed because it came to light that CERT-IN was a defunct agency, and had not been functioning since 2010 (the court order came in April 2014)! Thus, in August 2014, the Calcutta High Court shifted the onus back on to ISPs, who now had to block URLs identified by the music owner.[56] The new judge who passed this order failed to explain how ISPs would deal with websites hosting only partially infringing content.

At present, websites continue to be randomly blocked in India at the behest of copyright holders because judges usually pass ex parte orders (without hearing the other side, that is, proprietors of allegedly infringing websites). As a result, ISPs are routinely directed to block all URLs provided by copyright owners, instead of the more practical situation where a judge evaluates the URLs or websites in question, after hearing both sides, and makes an independent determination of whether or not this is a case of infringement of a valid copyright.

The one silver lining for Internet intermediaries in India in the last decade has been the enactment of a 'safe harbour' provision in the Copyright (Amendment) Act, 2012, an inclusion which was lobbied for by the Internet industry.

A Safe Harbour Provision in the New Copyright Law

In 2010, the Government of India introduced the Copyright (Amendment) Bill in Parliament. The legislation had been several years in the making and proposed a wide range of amendments to Indian copyright law. The Copyright Bill proposed two safe harbour provisions for Internet intermediaries. The first safe harbour provision sought to insulate ISPs from liability under copyright law in cases of 'transient or incidental storage of a work or performance purely in the technical process of electronic transmission or communication to the public'. The second safe harbour provision was designed to insulate online intermediaries like Google and MySpace from liability in copyright infringement cases, by requiring them to take down infringing content identified by a copyright owner temporarily for a period of 14 days, within which time the copyright owner had to produce a court order preventing the continued hosting of such content. If no such order was produced within 14 days, the intermediary could continue to host such content.

In many ways, this safe harbour provision proposed by the 2010 Bill for online intermediaries was much stronger than that provided in Section 512 of the US Copyright Act. United States law requires intermediaries to take down infringing content 'expeditiously' once notice is received from the copyright owner. There is no requirement for any kind of judicial determination as a precursor to permanently take down infringing content.

The requirement of court orders in such cases of copyright infringement was introduced, most likely, because private inter-mediaries, if left to do the job themselves, would tend to *over-censor* (as happened in the file-sharing cases) in order to retain immunity and not fall foul of the law. In other words, private intermediaries would not attempt to determine whether copyright infringement had actually taken place, and would prefer instead to implement a copyright owner's takedown notices.[57]

By requiring judicial determination before a takedown notice, these amendments placed a significant burden on copyright owners. Now, they would have to go to court each time infringement took place on the Internet. Expectedly, the main players in the entertainment industry, like Saregama, the South Indian Music Companies Association (SIMCA), the Indian Motion Picture Producers Association, and IMI, opposed this requirement before the Parliamentary Standing Committee examining the Copyright (Amendment) Bill, 2010.[58] Approaching a court of law every time infringing content was noticed on a website was too onerous a responsibility on copyright owners, they said, besides involving spending on lawyers, court fees, and hoping that a judge would provide an order within 14 days.

On the other side of the table, there were some of the biggest Internet companies in the world, like Google, Yahoo!, and Ebay, arguing for robust safe harbour provisions in copyright law before the Standing Committee.[59] Shailesh Rao, chairman of the Internet and Mobile Association of India (and also the managing director of Google India at the time), deposed on the importance of finding the 'right balance between protecting the rights of copyright owners as well as the promotion of inclusive growth through access to knowledge and the spurring of innovation'.[60] His pitch to the Standing Committee was that the Indian economy would enjoy substantial benefits by balancing copyright protection with fair dealing exceptions.[61]

Raman Jit Singh Chima, policy analyst at Google India, sold the story of YouTube being used as a tool to spread education in the country, and of how Google would not be able to continue to effectively provide such services if the Standing Committee did not strengthen the safe harbour principles along the lines proposed by Google. His testimony was as follows:

> We have had people using products that depend upon the copyright law; like, Google, YouTube, and there are companies which post user content like videos, blogs, etc. These allow people to learn languages. For example, we have people learning complex languages like Tamil and Kannada through services like YouTube. We have the Indira Gandhi National Open University teaching students through YouTube. We have lots of other organizations working through online services. If the copyright law is not changed sufficiently enough to cover safeguards that we have proposed in our submission, these very services will be at risk. A free and an open Internet has protected these services, and if the changes that we have recommended are not considered, we might suffer seriously.[62]

So what was this 'model' of safe harbour protection that Google India proposed to the Standing Committee? As explained to the Standing Committee by Google's in-house counsel, Gitanjali Duggal, Google had two specific demands. The first was that the new law must specifically recognize different kinds of intermediaries operating on the Internet, and specifically provide for safe harbour protection for each class of intermediaries. For example, the DMCA provides specific limitations for 'transitory digital network communications', 'information location tools', and so on, recognizing that ISPs and search engines are separately covered under the safe harbour provisions. The second was for the creation of a specific 'notice and take-down' requirement, outlining the information to be submitted by copyright owners to intermediaries to take down content. As explained by Duggal, 'generic talk about availability of certain content on a certain platform should not constitute adequate notice. The notice should be written, directed to the service provider, should specify the contents and specify the right that is being infringed.'[63] This demand was made because intermediaries had faced instances where notice and takedown provisions were vague or abused by copyright owners.

The Standing Committee's report was silent on both points made by Google. However, after the bill was voted into law as the Copyright (Amendment) Act, 2012, the Government of India did notify a 'notice and takedown' procedure in the Copyright Rules, 2013 (this was, however, unusual, since Parliament had not expressly delegated the power to the central government to enact rules on this specific aspect).[64]

For the Internet industry, the Copyright (Amendment) Act, 2012, proved to be a major victory. Even the US does not offer such strong protection for intermediaries. But the question remains as to whether the rights of copyright owners, especially smaller copyright owners, have been whittled down to protect the interests of the Internet industry. Is it realistic to expect small-time copyright owners to invest resources in approaching courts of law to take down obviously infringing content on a website like Youtube? Moreover, are Indian courts, already burdened with existing ills of pendency and delays, equipped to make an assessment for infringement within 21 days (the Standing Committee having extended the 14-day period to 21 days)?

The most pressing problem is a prominent bias amongst judges towards copyright owners, and a persistent failure of courts to grant proprietors of allegedly offending websites a hearing, before ordering them to be blocked. For example, in November 2014, Justice Manmohan Singh of the Delhi High Court ordered 150 websites to be blocked for allegedly webcasting certain cricket matches, the broadcast rights of which were owned by Star India Pvt. Ltd.[65] Nowhere in the order did

Justice Singh state that he had seen the content of the 150 websites. Several other judges have made similar mistakes of failing to view the websites they block. Once such blocking orders are granted, it takes considerable time, effort, and money to get the website unblocked. As a result, legitimate websites also run a real risk of being blocked. Such orders reflect the inability of many Indian judges to apply even the basic principles of justice and equity.

A Fair Bargain?

The issue of intermediary liability in India has come a long way since the arrest of the founders of Guruji.com in 2010. The 'safe harbour' provisions contained in the Copyright (Amendment) Act, 2012, provide intermediaries with relatively strong immunity against claims for copyright infringement. It would not be far-fetched to speculate that a service like Guruji.com would be legal today under the new safe harbours provided for under the Copyright (Amendment) Act, 2012. Although the issue of intermediary liability in cases of copyright infringement is squarely covered under the 2012 amendments to the copyright law, the IT Act continues to be relevant since it determines the immunity of Internet intermediaries for acts committed under other laws. Section 79 of this legislation was significantly strengthened by the judgment of the Supreme Court in the case of *Shreya Singhal* v. *Union of India*,[66] where it was held that an intermediary would be required to take down content only on an order of the government or a court, but the ambiguity regarding the scope of the 'due diligence' requirement remains in the law.

The success or failure of any law is only as good as the judges who sit in our courtrooms. As demonstrated time and again in this chapter, many Indian judges fail to apply basic principles of natural justice, such as providing the proprietor of a website the chance to be heard before the website is blocked in India, and they continue to indiscriminately direct the blocking of websites, merely on the word of copyright owners. Unless a judge views a website and understands the manner of its working, how can that judge understand whether the website qualifies for 'safe harbour' protection?

There is also the question of whether the existing intermediary liability provisions place an unreasonable burden on a copyright owner to monitor the Internet for infringing content. Bigger and more powerful copyright owners have the money and the muscle to monitor such content, but what of smaller copyright owners? Will they ever have the resources to check for infringement on a medium that is as challenging as the Internet?

————

Notes

1. Sahad P.V., *Sequoia Capital India Backs Local Search Engine Guruji.com*, GIGAOM, 12 October 2006, available at https://gigaom.com/2006/10/12/sequoia-capital-india-backs-local-search-engine-gurujicom/ (Last visited on 29 March 2015).
2. Nikhil Pahwa, *Execs of Sequoia Funded Guruji.com Arrested Over Alleged Copyright Violation in India*, MEDIANAMA, 20 April 2010, available at http://www.medianama.com/2010/04/223-execs-of-sequoia-funded-guruji-com-arrested-over-copyright-violation-in-india/ (Last visited on 29 March 2015); *Guruji.com CEO Arrested for Music Piracy*, RADIOANDMUSIC.COM, 30 April 2010, available at http://www.radioandmusic.com/content/editorial/news/gurujicom-ceo-arrested-music-piracy (Last visited on 29 March 2015); Nikhil Pahwa, *Guruji Shuts Music Search*, MEDIANAMA, 9 March 2011, available at http://www.medianama.com/2011/03/223-guruji-shuts-music-search/ (Last visited on 29 March 2015).
3. Pahwa, *Execs of Sequoia Funded Guruji.com Arrested*.
4. Intermediary is currently defined in Section 2(w) of the IT Act as 'any person who on behalf of another person receives, stores or transmits that record or provides any service with respect to that record and includes telecom service providers, network service providers, internet service providers, web-hosting service providers, search engines, online payment sites, online-auction sites, online-market places and cyber cafes'.
5. 907 F.Supp. 1361 (N.D.Cal. 1995).
6. Religious Technology Center v. Netcom On-line Communication Services Inc., at ¶ 24–36.
7. Religious Technology Center v. Netcom On-line Communication Services Inc., at ¶ 23.

8. Religious Technology Center v. Netcom On-line Communication Services Inc., at ¶ 31.

9. Robert P. Merges, Peter S. Menell, and Mark A. Lemley, INTELLECTUAL PROPERTY IN THE NEW TECHNOLOGICAL ERA 667 (2007).

10. COMMITTEE ON THE JUDICIARY, REPORT ON THE WIPO COPYRIGHT TREATIES IMPLEMENTATION AND ON-LINE COPYRIGHT INFRINGEMENT LIABILITY LIMITATION, 105th Congress (2nd Session), Rept. 105–551, 11 (22 May 1998).

11. COMMITTEE ON THE JUDICIARY, REPORT ON THE WIPO COPYRIGHT TREATIES IMPLEMENTATION AND ON-LINE COPYRIGHT INFRINGEMENT LIABILITY LIMITATION, at 11.

12. INDIA, PARLIAMENTARY STANDING COMMITTEE ON SCIENCE & TECHNOLOGY, ENVIRONMENT & FORESTS, SEVENTY NINTH REPORT ON THE INFORMATION TECHNOLOGY BILL, 1999 ¶ 9 (12 May 2000).

13. PARLIAMENTARY STANDING COMMITTEE ON SCIENCE & TECHNOLOGY, ENVIRONMENT & FORESTS, SEVENTY NINTH REPORT, at 18.

14. No.1 (1614)/AA/IC/2015 – Letter dated 13.01.2016 from the Additional Secretary, Lok Sabha Secretariat.

15. PARLIAMENTARY STANDING COMMITTEE ON SCIENCE & TECHNOLOGY, ENVIRONMENT & FORESTS, SEVENTY NINTH REPORT, ¶ 15.

16. Chinmayi Arun, *Gatekeeper Liability and Article 19(1)(a)*, 7 NUJS L. REV. 73, 81 (2014).

17. INDIA, PARLIAMENTARY STANDING COMMITTEE ON SCIENCE & TECHNOLOGY, ENVIRONMENT & FORESTS, SEVENTY NINTH REPORT ON THE INFORMATION TECHNOLOGY BILL, 1999, *Minutes of the XXII Meeting* 28 (12 May 2000).

18. *Lewd MMS Row: Baazee CEO Arrested*, REDIFF, 18 December 2004, available at http://www.rediff.com/news/2004/dec/17bazee.htm (Last visited on 29 March 2015).

19. Avnish Bajaj and Ors. v. State and Ors., (2012) 5 SCC 661.

20. GOVERNMENT OF INDIA, MINISTRY OF COMMUNICATIONS & INFORMATION TECHNOLOGY, REPORT OF THE EXPERT COMMITTEE ON AMENDMENTS TO THE IT ACT 2000 (August 2005).

21. Press Information Bureau (Government of India), *Expert Committee on Amendments to IT Act 2000 Submits Its Report*, 29 August 2005, available at http://deity.gov.in/content/report-expert-committee-amend-ments-it-act-2000-3 (Last visited on 29 March 2015); MINISTRY OF COMMUNICATIONS & INFORMATION TECHNOLOGY, REPORT OF THE EXPERT COMMITTEE, at 46.

22. Information Technology (Amendment) Bill, 2006.

23. No.1 (1483)/IC/14 – RTI Application filed by Sumathi Chandrashekaran.

24. PARLIAMENTARY STANDING COMMITTEE ON INFORMATION TECHNOLOGY, (AMENDMENT) BILL, 2006 (31 AUGUST 2007).

25. PARLIAMENTARY STANDING COMMITTEE ON INFORMATION TECHNOLOGY, (AMENDMENT) BILL, 2006, at 18 ¶ 57.

26. PARLIAMENTARY STANDING COMMITTEE ON INFORMATION TECHNOLOGY, (AMENDMENT) BILL, 2006, ¶ 57.

27. PARLIAMENTARY STANDING COMMITTEE ON INFORMATION TECHNOLOGY, (AMENDMENT) BILL, 2006, ¶ 57 at 18.

28. PARLIAMENTARY STANDING COMMITTEE ON INFORMATION TECHNOLOGY, (AMENDMENT) BILL, 2006, ¶10.

29. Manoj Mitta, *Recipe for Killing Internet in India*, THE TIMES OF INDIA, 17 October 2007, available at http://timesofindia.indiatimes.com/india/ Recipe-for-killing-Internet-in-India/articleshow/2464971.cms   (Last visited on 29 March 2015).

30. Mitta, *Recipe for Killing Internet in India*.

31. *Record-setting Holiday Season for Amazon Prime*, BUSINESS WIRE, 26 December 2013, available at http://www.businesswire.com/news/ home/20131226005066/en/Record-Setting-Holiday-Season-Amazon-Prime#.VKOd-SuUdKg (Last visited on 29 March 2015); Youtube, *Statistics*, available at https://www.youtube.com/yt/press/statistics.html (Last visited on 29 March 2015).

32. The 36-hours requirement was clarified in a subsequent notification to mean that the intermediary was only required to acknowledge receipt of the complaint within 36 hours and that it could take up to a month to redress the complaint. *Clarification on the Information Technology (Intermediaries Guidelines) Rules, 2011 Under Section 79 of the Information Technology Act, 2000, Department of Electronics & Information Technology, Ministry of Communications and Information Technology, Government of India* (18 March 2013), available at deity. gov.in/sites/upload_files/dit/files/Clarification%2079rules%281%29.pdf (Last visited on 29 March 2015).

33. Super Cassettes Industries Limited (SCIL) v. MySpace Inc., 2011(48) PTC 49 Del.

34. Cerius Shah, *Guruji Launches Music Search; Days Without Incident*, GIGAOM, 14 July 2008, available at https://gigaom.com/2008/07/14/419-guruji-launches-music-search-days-since-incident-1/ (Last visited on 29 March 2015).

35. Sonam Gulati, *Mobile Ad Firm Adiquity Publishing 15B Ads Per Month; Learning from Past Venture Guruji.com Helps, Says CEO Anurag Dod*, TECHCIRCLE.IN, 8 January 2013, available at http://techcircle.vccircle. com/2013/01/08/adiquity-publishing-15b-ads-per-month-learning-

from-past-venture-guruji-com-helps-says-ceo/ (Last visited on 29 March 2015).

36. Super Cassettes Industries Ltd. v. Youtube LLC and Ors., CS(OS) 2192 of 2007 (Delhi High Court).

37. Nikhil Pahwa, *YouTube & Music Label T-Series Reach Out of Court Settlement*, MEDIANAMA, 24 February 2011, available at http://www.medianama.com/2011/02/223-youtube-music-label-t-series-reach-out-of-court-settlement/ (Last visited on 29 March 2015).

38. Super Cassettes Industries Limited (SCIL) v. MySpace Inc.

39. Ananth Padmanabhan, *Give Me My Space and Take Down His*, 9 IJLT (2013); Amlan Mohanty, *The Death of Safe Harbour for Intermediaries in India for Copyright Infringement?*, SPICYIP, 6 August 2011, available at http://spicyip.com/2011/08/death-of-safe-harbour-for.html (Last visited on 29 March 2015).

40. Super Cassettes Industries Limited (SCIL) v. MySpace Inc., ¶ 66.

41. Billy Joel v. Various John Does, 1980 U.S.Dist. LEXIS 12841.

42. [2003] FSR 22.

43. UTV Software Communications Ltd. v. Home Cable Network Ltd. and Anr., CS (OS) No. 821 of 2011 (Delhi High Court)(unreported) (order passed on 4 April 2011); Viacom 18 Motion Pictures v. Jyoti Cable Network and Ors. CS (OS) No. 1373 of 2012 (Delhi High Court) (unreported) (order passed on 14 May 2012).

44. Reliance Big Entertainment Pvt. Ltd. v. Jyothi Cable Network and Ors., CS (OS) No. 1724 of 2011 (Delhi High Court) (unreported) (order passed on 20 July 2011).

45. Anant Rangaswami, *Singham Anti-piracy Order Shows Law is an Ass Without Meaning to Be*, FIRST POST, 23 July 2011, available at http://www.firstpost.com/business/singham-anti-piracy-order-shows-law-is-an-ass-without-meaning-to-be-46817.html (Last visited on 29 March 2015).

46. Devika Agarwal, *SpicyIP Tidbit: Happy New Year Granted John Doe Order Ahead of Its Release*, SPICYIP, 18 October 2014, available at http://spicyip.com/2014/10/spicyip-tidbit-happy-new-year-granted-john-doe-order-ahead-of-its-release.html (Last visited on 29 March 2015); Prashant Reddy, *Madras High Court Passes Its First-ever 'John Doe' Order*, SPICYIP, 29 March 2012, available at http://spicyip.com/2012/03/madras-high-court-passes-its-first-ever.html (Last visited on 29 March 2015).

47. Yuvraj Gurung, *Indian Government Orders ISPs to Block Vimeo, Github, and 30 Other Sites (Update: A Few Websites Unblocked)*, TECH IN ASIA, 1 January 2015, available at https://www.techinasia.com/india-orders-blocking-32-websites/ (Last visited on 29 March 2015).

48. R. Krishna, *Anonymous Hacks ISP to Protest Blocking of Sites*, DNA, 27 May 2012, available at http://www.dnaindia.com/india/report-anonymous-hacks-isp-to-protest-blocking-of-sites-1694273 (Last visited on 29 March 2015).

49. Nikhil Pahwa, *No More John Doe Orders? Indian ISPs Get Court Order for Specificity in URL Blocks*, MEDIANAMA, 20 June 2012, available at http://www.medianama.com/2012/06/223-no-more-john-doe-orders-indian-isps-get-court-order-for-specificity-in-urls/ (Last visited on 29 March 2015).

50. R.K. Productions v. Vodafone, C.S. No. 294 of 2012 (Madras High Court) (unreported) (order passed on 30 October 2012).

51. Sagarika Music Pvt. Ltd. and Ors. v. Dishnet Wireless Ltd. and Ors., CS(OS) No. 23 of 2012 (Calcutta High Court) (unreported), (order passed on 27 January 2012); *104 Music Sites to be Blocked on 387 ISPs across India*, TECHITIN, 17 March 2012, available at http://www.techit.in/2012/03/104-music-sites-to-be-blocked-on-387-isps-across-india/ (Last visited on 29 March 2015).

52. *Indian Music Industry's Fight against Piracy Continues*, RADIOANDMUSIC. COM, 5 April 2013, available at http://www.radioandmusic.com/content/editorial/news/indian-music-industrys-fight-against-piracy-continues (Last visited on 29 March 2015).

53. Saregama India Ltd. and Ors. v. Dishnet Wireless Ltd. and Ors., CS. No. 85 of 2012 (Calcutta High Court) (unreported), (order passed on 7 April 2014).

54. Saregama India Ltd. and Ors. v. Dishnet Wireless Ltd. and Ors., (order passed on 7 April 2014).

55. Saregama India Ltd. and Ors. v. Dishnet Wireless Ltd. and Ors., (order passed on 7 April 2014).

56. Saregama India Ltd. and Ors. v. Dishnet Wireless Ltd. and Ors., CS. No. 85 of 2012 (Calcutta High Court) (unreported), (order passed on 20 August 2014).

57. Meta, *Intermediary Liability in India: Chilling Effects on Free Expression on the Internet*, THE CENTRE FOR INTERNET AND SOCIETY, 27 April 2012, available at http://cis-india.org/internet-governance/chilling-effects-on-free-expression-on-internet (Last visited on 29 March 2015).

58. INDIA, PARLIAMENTARY STANDING COMMITTEE ON HUMAN RESOURCE DEVELOPMENT, TWO HUNDRED TWENTY-SEVENTH REPORT ON THE COPYRIGHT (AMENDMENT) BILL, 2010, ¶ 19.3 (23 November 2010).

59. PARLIAMENTARY STANDING COMMITTEE ON HUMAN RESOURCE DEVE-LOPMENT, TWO HUNDRED TWENTY-SEVENTH REPORT, ¶ 19.4.

60. INDIA, PARLIAMENTARY STANDING COMMITTEE ON HUMAN RESOURCE DEVELOPMENT, TWO HUNDRED TWENTY-SEVENTH REPORT ON THE COPYRIGHT (AMENDMENT) BILL, 2010, *Minutes of Evidence*, (XXII Meeting of the Committee, 29 June 2010).

61. PARLIAMENTARY STANDING COMMITTEE ON HUMAN RESOURCE DEVELOPMENT, TWO HUNDRED TWENTY-SEVENTH REPORT, *Minutes of Evidence*, at 64–8 (XXII Meeting).

62. PARLIAMENTARY STANDING COMMITTEE ON HUMAN RESOURCE DEVELOPMENT, TWO HUNDRED TWENTY-SEVENTH REPORT, *Minutes of Evidence*, at 81–2 (XXII Meeting).

63. PARLIAMENTARY STANDING COMMITTEE ON HUMAN RESOURCE DEVELOPMENT, TWO HUNDRED TWENTY-SEVENTH REPORT, *Minutes of Evidence*, at 84–7 (XXII Meeting).

64. The Copyright Rules, 2013, Rule 75.

65. Star India Pvt. Ltd. and Ors. v. Roy Ma and Ors., CS (OS) 3319/2014 (Delhi High Court) (unreported), (order passed on 5 November 2014).

66. (2015) 5 SCC 1.

9

THE TRADITIONAL KNOWLEDGE TRILOGY

'When an elder dies, a library burns', goes an old African proverb, alluding to the infinite volumes of knowledge that vanish with every passing generation of humankind. In the intellectual property (IP) business in India, this proverb brings to mind, literally, a library—the Traditional Knowledge Digital Library (TKDL). Pitched as a database of over 250,000 formulations used in Indian systems of traditional medicine—ayurveda, unani, and siddha—the TKDL was created by the Indian scientific bureaucracy in response to a series of controversies that beset the global patent arena in the 1990s and early 2000s. The spotlight was on patents filed in connection with neem, basmati, and turmeric. Private and public players in India co-opted these patents as symbolic transgressions of national heritage, and used the opportunity to rustle up mass fury in opposition. The patents were fought on the international stage, but saw mixed results. The TKDL was created to prevent any such attempted transgressions in future, with the lofty objective to 'prevent misappropriation of Indian traditional knowledge'.[1] It did this by allowing patent examining offices around the world to test whether a proposed formulation was truly novel and inventive, or, instead, merely repackaged that which was already known. In this sense, the TKDL has always been a defensive database. Its objective has been to *prevent* certain types of formulations from being patented. Any philanthropic disposition towards permitting modern medical science an insight into the history of medicine is entirely absent.

The three cases that led to the creation of the TKDL show that neither India nor its people were under threat—financial or otherwise—from any of the patents. The contentions were that the patents had been examined improperly, or had been granted incorrectly, or both. If either of these allegations (improper examination or incorrect grant) were true, the culpable parties would be the respective patent offices of the countries where these patents were granted, and by extension, their respective governments. It would be impossible to pin the blame on anyone in India for the grant of a bad patent in a foreign jurisdiction. Further, since patents are limited by jurisdiction, the countries most affected would be those where the patents were granted. In other words, patents are enforceable only in countries where they have been granted, and not anywhere else. India did not fall in this category, as none of the patents were granted in India. But significant sums of money were spent on fighting these patents to defend what some regarded as India's wounded pride. This chapter tells the story of how these patent cases were fought, won, and lost in international forums, and examines whether the TKDL, as designed and used today, was truly a necessary and efficient response to these cases.

The Neem Case

Patents have been used as a form of IP protection in India since 1856,[2] although the present Indian law on patents dates to 1970, and has been amended a few times since to meet obligations prescribed under the Agreement on Trade-Related Aspects of Intellectual Property Rights (TRIPS). But international developments in the past two decades have given patents some bad press in the country. One of the first controversies that made patents unfashionable in India involved patents granted to a company, W.R. Grace (or 'Grace'), in the United States (US) and the European Union (EU) for an invention related to the neem plant. This story was steeped in classic anti-globalization speak, propagated by activists protesting against multilateral treaties signed under the aegis of the World Trade Organization (WTO).

Grace, a Maryland-based chemicals conglomerate, was granted patents in the US and the EU for a formulation that helped in the stable storage of *azadirachtin*, the active ingredient in the neem plant. The company planned to use *azadirachtin* for its pesticidal properties. Years after their grant, a group of activists vociferously protested against the patents, claiming it was 'biopiracy'. According to them, the patents 'stole' the knowledge of the Indian farming community that had used neem as a pesticide for several generations. The activists also speculated that the patents would affect the ability of farmers in India to use neem as a pesticide in the future. Petitions were filed before the United States Patent and Trademark Office (USPTO) and the European Patent Office (EPO) to revoke Grace's patents. The international press was fascinated by this debate, tracking developments with furious enthusiasm. In the Indian Parliament, democratically-elected representatives, too, expressed outrage over Indian knowledge having been 'stolen' by foreign multinational corporations.

Even today, the neem patents controversy continues to be referenced each time someone in India wants to emphasize the evils of a patent system. But was the controversy and outrage over the neem patents justified, or did its opponents just misunderstand patent law?

The Wonder Plant is Discovered by the World

In Sanskrit, the neem tree is regarded as *sarva roga nivarini*, or the 'curer of all ailments'. Traditional systems of medicine such as Ayurveda and Unani are familiar with the properties of neem, and prescribe it for treating skin diseases because of its antibacterial and antiviral properties. Besides its medicinal application, neem has also been used as a natural pesticide. Although its pesticidal properties were well known in India, neem did not attract much attention outside the country until the 1970s.

According to an article[3] published in 1992 in *Science*, a leading journal of original scientific research and news brought out by the American Association for the Advancement of Science, the hunt for natural pesticides in the 1970s directed researchers in the US and Europe towards neem. By 1980, interest had peaked sufficiently to warrant holding a conference in Germany to discuss the properties of the plant, by when the researchers had also learnt about neem oil. Neem, it turned out, had a class of chemicals called limonoids, which were known to be detrimental to insects. Researchers were particularly interested in the effects of *azadirachtin*, which was derived from neem oil. *Azadirachtin* appeared to inhibit the growth hormones of some insects, thus 'preventing them from shedding external skeletons and maturing'.[4] This could potentially kill off an entire generation of insects. Neem also affected insects by disrupting their mating patterns and causing sterility. According to the *Science* article, researchers were 'amazed' by neem's potency as a pesticide and termed it as one of the 'best' natural pesticides they had ever worked with. With so much excitement generated, it was hardly surprising that international companies became interested in commercializing the technology.

The first neem-based biopesticide to receive approval from the Environmental Protection Agency (EPA), the environmental safety regulator in the US, was Margosan-O.[5] It was granted initial approval in 1985 for non-agricultural uses, which meant it could be used in greenhouses, commercial nurseries, forests, and homes. The rights for the technology underlying Margosan-O were sold to Grace in 1988, which planned to seek wider approvals for use even in food crops. Since neem grew most abundantly in India, Grace also invested in a factory in India, employing about 60 people, to ensure a constant supply of neem.

Simultaneously, Grace worked on improving the technology, especially relating to its long-term storage. It filed patent applications for these improvements before the USPTO and the EPO, covering broadly the same invention, and naming four co-inventors, one of whom was of Indian origin. Patents were eventually granted in both jurisdictions—in 1992 in the US,[6] and 1994 in the EU.[7]

A patent, by definition, is granted for technology that is novel and non-obvious and has some utility. The patent application filed by Grace, while conceding that the pesticidal uses of neem were known, pointed to the difficulty in storing *azadirachtin* over a long duration. The specific invention claimed was a 'storage-stable' formulation that ensured that *azadirachtin* would have a shelf-life of over two years without any substantial degradation. The US patent eventually granted, numbered 5,124,349, covered a very limited invention. It granted Grace *not* the right to use neem as a biopesticide, but only the exclusive right to use *azadirachtin* in the particular storage solution described in the patent. Since this was a patent granted in the US, its applicability was limited to the territorial boundaries of the US, and could not be enforced in India.

The Protest Petition against the US Neem Patent

One of the first petitions against US patent 5,124,349 was filed by a loosely-organized global coalition of several (some claim up to two hundred) non-governmental organizations (NGOs). Spearheaded by well-known names such as Jeremy Rifkin, Vandana Shiva, Martin Khor, M.D. Nanjundaswamy, and Linda Bullard, the thread uniting these NGOs was a deep-rooted suspicion of globalization and the international trade system.[8]

By the time the petition was filed, Shiva and Nanjundaswamy were already familiar critics of India's decision to sign TRIPS, having challenged (and lost) the issue before the Delhi High Court.[9] Shiva was known as an environmental activist with anti-globalization leanings, and was the founder of the Research Foundation for Science, Technology and Ecology (RFSTE), as well as Navdanya, a movement to protect native seeds, and promote organic farming and fair trade. Nanjundaswamy was another Indian anti-globalization activist whose supporters, angry about the rising prices of seeds, had once ransacked the Indian offices of Cargill, an American seed corporation.[10] The US activist and author, Rifkin, had filed multiple protest petitions on the environment, and science and technology policy, and was particularly known for his opposition to patents granted for genes and microorganisms. Khor was the director of the Third World Network (TWN), a Malaysia-based conglomeration of international NGOs, and a public sceptic of institutions like the WTO, the World Bank, and the International Monetary Fund (IMF). Bullard was the vice-president of the Brussels-based International Federation of Organic Agricultural Movements (IFOAM), an organization known for its campaigns for organic food, and protests against genetically modified food.

Projecting the protest as a battle between the native people of the south and the multinational corporations of the north, the petition claimed that 'WR Grace's patent [had] sparked an outcry among

Indian farmers, scientists and political activists' because it was an 'accumulation of centuries' worth of Indian knowledge and effort'.[11] The petition alleged that, 'Indian citizens are very concerned that WR Grace's patent will deprive local farmers of their ability to produce and use neem-based pesticides by altering the price and availability of the neem seeds themselves. There is already evidence that WR Grace's patent has forced many Indian farmers out of the market for this locally-developed technology'.[12] Pointing to national sentiment, the petition warned that, '[t]here have been numerous protests—involving hundreds of thousands of Indian citizens—against the patenting of indigenous plants like the neem tree. It is important to remember and indicative of the country's sentiments that several Indian manufacturers vehemently refused to participate in WR Grace's initial patenting plans'.[13] On legal issues, the petition said that the patent was obvious in light of the prior art available in India, 'because Indian researchers had already developed the knowledge and technology necessary to make storage-stable *azadirachtin* formulations possible'.[14] On this basis, the petitioners threatened to challenge the validity of the patent through re-examination proceedings before the USPTO.[15]

The petition had its desired effect. Several meetings and seminars were held in India. George Fernandes, a left-wing parliamentarian with strong anti-capitalist credentials, reportedly said, '[p]atenting neem is like patenting cowdung'.[16]

The Response from Grace

The allegations in the petition seemed to have caught Grace by surprise, with one news report describing the company to have been 'flabbergasted'.[17] In a press release[18] denying all the allegations, Grace clarified that '[t]he patent issued to Grace in no way provides exclusive use of the neem seeds or extracts—not even for pesticides. In fact, patents cannot be given to the natural active pesticide ingredient, *azadirachtin*. The Indian farmers can continue to produce and distribute their neem-based pesticides, as they have in the past'.

On the scope of its patents and the invention, Grace confirmed that its 'patent narrowly focuses on a formula which extends the shelf life and effectiveness of the neem-based pesticide. The patent held by Grace applies neither to the extraction nor the processing of the neem extract'.[19]

Grace then pointed out that,

> There are approximately 40 different patents issued on various extraction, process and formulation processes related to the neem extract, *azadirachtin*. These patents are owned by 22 different companies or groups, three of which are Indian. In addition to Grace's joint venture neem-pesticide manufacturing operation in India, there are five other neem extraction plants in operation or under construction in that country. Six Indian companies are currently selling neem-based pesticides, as well as two companies in the United States. Grace holds no neem pesticide patent in India and does not intend to seek a patent there.[20]

Much of this was true. One such neem-related patent was US patent number 5,298,247 granted to the Indian company Godrej Soaps, for an invention titled 'Neem oil fatty acid distillation residue based pesticide' in 1994. (In fact, applications for neem-related patents by Indian entities, including government bodies, have been made for many years since. One notable example is European patent number EP0834254, granted to the Council of Scientific and Industrial Research (CSIR) for 'Azadirachtin formulations and a process for preparing them from neem seed/kernel' in 2003. The CSIR is a network of publicly-funded laboratories meant to promote industrial research in India and is also in charge of the TKDL project. A German company later opposed this patent, and although the patent survived the opposition proceedings, the CSIR lost in appeal, and the patent was revoked.[21])

Responding to allegations of disrupting India's local market for neem, Grace claimed that it bought the seed 'on the open market and has purchased less than three percent of the neem crop harvested since the Company received the patent in 1992'.[22] Since the petition by the NGOs failed to mention any figures or sources, it is impossible to verify which statement was true.

The media spotlight on the dispute continued. Experts quoted in various publications weighed in favour of Grace's defence, arguing that the patent was valid, and that it would have no impact on the use of neem as a pesticide in India. *Time* magazine wrote, '[t]he truth is that Grace's patent has no effect in India, whose laws prohibit the patenting of agricultural products; Indian farmers are free to use neem seeds as they always have. Beyond that, Grace's patent may be upheld', because it found a way to treat the neem extract in a way which 'increased its shelf life from weeks to years'.[23] Similarly, *Science* reported that, '[s]ome independent experts in patent law also question the soundness of Rifkin's legal arguments and the significance of the patent for the Indian farmer'.[24] The *Associated Press* quoted an American patent lawyer who termed the entire controversy a 'red-herring'.[25]

One Indian expert was less charitable to the protesters against Grace. Professor Anil Gupta, at the Indian Institute of Management, Ahmedabad, closely involved with innovation and IP strategies, was quoted by the magazine *Down to Earth* as saying, '[f]irst of all, it is being made out as if Grace has obtained a patent on neem. This is absolute nonsense. No one can claim exclusive rights over a product of nature'.[26] Gupta also asked the all-important question, which almost everyone else in India seemed to have missed, '[w]hat are they fighting for? Grace is not encroaching on anyone else's territory. Indian farmers can continue to produce their pesticides in their traditional way and sell them as they did before.'[27] In his article in the same magazine, Gupta called out the intelligentsia as well, remarking, 'social and intellectual inertia [had] generated a good market in India for halfbaked theories and populist slogans ... based on grossly inaccurate information'.[28]

So, what exactly was the protest about? From the petition, it appears that the NGO collective may have misunderstood the scope of patent law and its impact on Indian farmers (or conspiratorially, deliberately misrepresented the scope of patent law to push forward other hidden agendas). They could still challenge the patents granted in the US and the EU, but what purpose would that serve when the patents did not affect any Indian exports? No immediate benefit awaited either India or its farmers even if the patents were revoked in their respective jurisdictions. Interviews suggest that the protestors might have been more interested in making a statement about 'genetic colonialism'. As Shiva explained to the international science and medical journal *Nature*, 'American people have only heard of software piracy. What they don't know is that their companies are engaged in piracy of the worst kind in trying to profit from the traditional knowledge of India's farmers, who have been using neem as a pesticide for generations'.[29]

On this argument, the protestors received a sympathetic hearing from some quarters. There were genuine concerns about Western companies using biological resources from resource-rich developing countries, and then selling the value-added products onwards for several times their original price without sharing the profits proportionately with the original populations that had identified the unique properties of the biological resources in the first place. Neem was one example of this conundrum. In the *Times of India*, the economist Arvind Panagariya, while dismissing the effects of Grace's patent on Indian farmers, described the issue of sharing benefits derived from the world's biological resources as a 'fundamental but thorny issue'.[30]

In 1992, most countries, including India, had signed the Convention on Biological Diversity, recognizing national sovereignty over biological resources. With this treaty, international law recognized the rights of individual nations to control access to genetic material within their national territory. At the time of the neem dispute, though, India did not have a domestic law that brought the Convention into force. That happened only in 2002, with the Biological Diversity Act. This law required any foreigner accessing biological material within India to necessarily first approach the National Biological Authority for permission to do so. The Authority could set the terms for access, including fees and royalty-sharing agreements, if research related to the material generated IP and value-added products. While fair in theory, this law has proven difficult to implement in practice. Moreover, it has put even resource-rich countries like India on a slippery slope. After all, successful commercial crops such as tea and potato, which many regard today as being near-native to India, were originally brought in from other parts of the world. Such cross-continental breeding took place because biological resources were regarded as the 'common heritage of mankind', with no one nation controlling the right to access such material. However, the Convention on Biological Diversity changed this approach forever.

The Challenges to Grace's US and EU Patents

Shiva followed up on her threat to challenge both the US and European patents granted to Grace. The US patent was challenged through a re-examination proceeding before the USPTO in December 1995. Such a proceeding allowed any person to submit relevant prior art to the patent office with a request that the target patent be re-examined. The patent examiners could then decide whether the patent continued to be valid in light of the new prior art (the re-examination procedure at the USPTO has since been reformed). Shiva's re-examination petition was accompanied by around 40 documents, including scientific articles on neem, mainly from Indian journals. Several of these were, in fact, not relevant prior art since they post-dated Grace's patent application. Under patent law, only documents published *prior* to the patent application, or the date of invention, can be considered valid prior art. The re-examination petition failed, and the USPTO re-issued the patent three years later in October 1998 without any changes.[31]

The attempt to revoke the European patent granted to Grace was relatively more successful. Magda Alvoet, a politician from the Green Party and an elected Member of the European Parliament, initially filed the post-grant opposition proceedings before the EPO.[32] Her opposition was joined by two other parties: the Research Foundation for Science, Technology and Natural Resource Policy, headed by Shiva; and the Brussels-based IFOAM. Eleven others joined them later: Karnataka Rajya Raitha Sangha (KRRS) (India), Third World Network (Malaysia), the Green Group in the European Parliament, the European Coordination No Patents on Life! (Switzerland), Rural Advancement Foundation International (Canada), Cultural Survival Canada (Canada), the Cultural Conservancy (USA), the Edmonds Institute (USA), Institute for Agriculture and Trade Policy (USA), Washington Biotechnology Action Group (USA), and Rio Grande Bioregions Project (USA).

Unlike re-examination proceedings in the US, post-grant opposition proceedings in Europe are adversarial in nature, where both parties must present arguments and evidence before a board of patent examiners.

Most of the grounds of challenge in Europe were similar to those raised before the USPTO. The one additional ground of challenge raised before the EPO was that of morality. In Europe, morality as a ground for denying a patent has been limited to highly controversial inventions, such as embryonic stem-cell research inventions, patents for which were prohibited in the EU by law.[33] Patent offices generally avoid invoking the morality clause because of the inherently subjective nature of such a decision, and to ask a patent office to invoke such a clause usually indicates a weak case on other grounds. The opposition petition filed by Alvoet, Shiva, and the others, argued that morality was an issue because India had shared the knowledge of neem freely with the world community, and that all those who used the knowledge, such as Grace, had the 'unwritten obligation and tradition to share freely'.[34] The petition argued that European culture was based on a principle of mutual respect, and thus, the 'Indian principle' of freely sharing neem would be recognized even in Europe. Since the European principle of mutual respect for other cultures was violated, the petitioners contended, the patent in question deserved to be invalidated. This was an unusual and imaginative argument when compared with conventional patent law arguments, but the Opposition Board constituted by the EPO rejected it. The Board solemnly noted,

> Contrary to the Opponents, the opposition division is of the opinion that no direct connection could be established between the livelihood of a part of the people of India and a method for controlling fungi by a special hydrophobic extract of the neem oil since neither the neem tree or the neem seeds as such nor the neem oil in general is claimed. In addition a European patent does not give to its proprietor any right to prohibit acts done in India, due to the principle of territoriality of patent law.[35]

Although the opponents lost on the ground of morality, the Opposition Board did rule in their favour in 2001 for lack of novelty and inventive step in Grace's patent (the patent had since been bought by Thermo Trilogy Corporation). An appeal was filed, but that too was rejected in 2005, and the patent remains revoked. However, there were no tangible benefits from the revocation of this particular patent, and other neem-related patents continued to exist in Europe. More importantly, there was no evidence that Grace's patent had hurt any Indian interests.

But the case of the neem patent had already caused severe damage to the IP debate in India, and continued to do so for several years after it occurred, because it helped propagate misconceived and false notions of patent law.

The Turmeric Case

Even as the US and European patent offices were re-examining the patents granted to Grace for neem, a similar story was playing out in India. It involved subject matter that was believed to be of Indian origin, like neem, but the players, and the result, were completely different.

The Turmeric Patent and 'National Interest'

The story of the turmeric patent began on 2 July 1996, when N. Subbaram, the head of the Intellectual Property Management Department (IPMD) of the CSIR, and the former Controller General of the Indian Patent Office, sent a note[36] to the Director-General of the CSIR (DG-CSIR) flagging the grant of US patent number 5,401,504 by the USPTO. The patent, granted over a year before, in March 1995, was titled 'Use of turmeric in wound healing', and claimed a method to heal wounds in a patient by administering an 'effective amount' of turmeric. The inventors—two persons of Indian origin—were Suman K. Das, and Hari Har P. Cohly, who had assigned the patent to their employers, the University of Mississippi.

Subbaram felt that the patent should not have been granted because it lacked novelty and was obvious. It lacked novelty, he believed, because the use of turmeric for treating wounds was well-established in traditional medicine in India, centuries before the patent application was filed in December 1993. It was obvious, in his opinion, because the pharmacokinetics of turmeric—or the manner in which turmeric was absorbed, distributed, metabolized, and eliminated by the body—were already well-known. He was also worried that the patent claims were too wide. Patent claims, which define the scope of the monopoly being sought by the patentee, should be clearly stated to allow competitors and the general public to determine the boundaries of the patent. Vaguely-worded patents can be revoked in most jurisdictions.

In his note, Subbaram also expressed surprise that such a patent had been granted by the USPTO, which, in his opinion, was 'reputed for strict examination particularly for determining novelty and more especially in considering the issue of obviousness'.[37] In fact, contrary to Subbaram's views, the USPTO has often been criticized for granting 'bad patents', as it did, for example, for a method of moving a swing side-to-side (that application was filed by a young boy, whose father, a patent attorney, had wanted to teach him about patents and inventions).[38]

Subbaram also, correctly, noted that the turmeric patent was valid only in the US and that the 'rights in the said patent cannot be enforced in India'.[39] Why, then, was a senior functionary of the CSIR spending time conveying such obvious information to the DG-CSIR? The answer to that question lay at the end of Subbaram's note, where he cited reasons of 'national interest' to recommend that the CSIR invoke re-examination proceedings before the USPTO to get the patent invalidated. The re-examination would challenge the novelty of the patent, relying on prior art from India. Prior art is the entire body of knowledge that precedes the filing of a patent application, which is used to establish—or counter—the novelty of an invention. Since the test for novelty under US law included reference to prior art from anywhere in the world, Subbaram felt this attempt could succeed. The re-examination would also attack the lack of inventiveness in the patent, for being obvious in claiming wound-healing properties of turmeric.

But there was a fundamental problem with this line of thought. Since patents vest an economic monopoly in the hands of private players, patents are challenged usually by competing market players. Challenges, therefore, seek to counter the monopoly enjoyed by patentees, so that competitors can enter the market to sell their product or services. National governments do not normally attack the validity of patents for reasons of 'national interest'. Ideally, Subbaram should have assessed whether the grant of such a weak patent would affect Indian economic interests. But no such analysis was contained in his note. Instead, he pointed out that the US patent could not be enforced in India. What was Subbaram's motivation for recommending a challenge to the validity of the patent? Was it to showcase the glory of Indian traditional knowledge? Did anyone stop to consider if it was worth the time, effort, and money for a public-sector institution like the CSIR to chase down a US patent to demonstrate to the world that Indians had known the properties of turmeric for centuries? Subbaram's superiors had to take the final decision, and ideally, they ought to have analysed his recommendation more critically. From the documents made available to the authors under the Right to Information (RTI) Act, 2005, it appears that Subbaram was allowed to go ahead, as indicated by a noting made by the DG-CSIR. The reasons for the DG-CSIR's decision are not recorded in the documents provided to the authors, but soon after this noting, other ministries of the Indian government also got involved in the matter. Three inter-ministerial meetings were held, which were attended by representatives from the ministries of law, industrial development, and external affairs, as also from various scientific research agencies. In the first meeting on 16 July 1996,[40] a second possible line of attack was proposed: The office of the Commissioner of Patents at the USPTO could initiate re-examination proceedings of its own accord, if it was satisfied that matters of public policy were involved. The Indian government could push for this through diplomatic channels. In its next meeting three days later,[41] the inter-ministerial group agreed that once the ministry of law gave its go-ahead, the ministry of external affairs would take it up with the US Commissioner of Patents. Separately, the Indian mission in Washington, DC, could send out a *note verbale*—a form of diplomatic communication—to its host-counterpart. More such inter-ministerial meetings took place. But all through these meetings and communications, none of the bureaucrats involved appear to have asked why the government was looking to expend large amounts of financial, bureaucratic, and diplomatic resources to take down this US turmeric patent which had no consequences for India.

Prior Art and Opposition Strategies

After the decision to initiate the challenge, a wide search of documentation relating to the healing properties of turmeric followed. It was decided that the re-examination request would be filed before 28 October that year, leaving the IPMD team and their lawyers very little time to put all the necessary documentation together. Two leading institutions in the field of traditional medicine were contacted for their expertise—Dabur India and Hamdard University, home to research in ayurveda and unani, respectively. Publications in Hindi, Sanskrit, and Urdu were identified, some dating back several centuries, and formal translations attended to. In truth, though, there was no need for the CSIR to source documents from several centuries ago. Any document prior to 28 December 1993 would have sufficed, as this was the priority date claimed by the patent application.

From the information sourced by the authors on the matter, the documents collected by the CSIR included modern commentaries on classic ayurvedic texts, a book on home remedies titled *Kya Khayein aur Kyun* ('what to eat and why'), popularly referred to as 'Ghar ka Doctor', extracts from the 'Compendium of Indian Medicinal Plants', and nineteenth-century historical texts from the library of Hamdard University. Translators included eminent scholars and practitioners, including the chief physician of the Kerala-based ayurvedic centre Arya Vaidya Sala, a specialist in Sanskrit poetics at University of Delhi (DU), and the dean of the faculty of medicine at Hamdard University.[42]

The prospective fight promised much. There was a swagger in the tone of the attacking side, which said the patentees 'would not have also expected that people from India would have noticed the grant of such [a] patent and even if noticed will not spend the amount involved in such proceedings'.[43]

The Re-examination Process Commences

The formal request for re-examination was filed on the appointed date. Nearly two dozen references were submitted, and it resulted in early success: In January 1997, the USPTO ordered a re-examination. Going against precedent, the USPTO handed over the re-examination proceedings not to the original examiner who had granted the patent, but to someone else in the same department. The new US patent examiner, Shailendra Kumar, evidently also of Indian origin like the inventors, in March 1997, rejected all six claims of the patent on grounds of obviousness and anticipation.[44]

While the proceedings continued, in May 1997, the University of Mississippi, to whom the inventors had assigned their rights in the patent, withdrew from the contest.[45] The university returned the patent rights to the inventors, clarifying that they had nothing to do with the patent, especially in terms of additional cost. In law, an assignment is the legal transfer of a right, property, or a liability. It is fairly common for rights in IP to be assigned from one person to another. In patent and copyright law, for instance, employment contracts usually require employees to transfer rights in any invention made or original work created in the course of employment to their employers. Here, the rights in the patent were originally assigned by the inventors to their employers, but unusually, later returned to the inventors. Presumably, the University of Mississippi felt that it was a fight not worth spending money on. The inventors Das and Cohly, though, chose to continue their defence, and convinced the original attorneys to remain on the case. But the inventors' defence was weak, and in August 1997, the USPTO rejected the patent, as it had been anticipated by the documentation submitted during the proceedings.[46]

The CSIR went to town with this news. In a letter addressed to the minister of state for science and technology, the DG-CSIR Mashelkar boasted that it was 'the first case where the use of the traditional knowledge base of a third world country appropriated through a US patent [was] successfully challenged'.[47] There was a snide reference to the neem case, which had been taken up independently by NGOs and had failed to meet success, in contrast to the CSIR's efforts.[48] The Indian law firm representing the CSIR sounded two warning notes. Firstly, that the final action issued by the USPTO was not equivalent to a final order to reject the case. The patentee could still respond to the examiner's final action, or even appeal against the examiner's decision. Secondly, that about half of the citations were obtained by the lawyers themselves, and not by the CSIR, hinting that the CSIR should perhaps not attempt to take full credit for the proceedings.[49] The CSIR community, however, was already celebrating. Subbaram, who had now shifted from the role of IPMD head to a consultant to the CSIR, was the 'unsung hero', whose 'extraordinary effort' had not been fully grasped by the public.[50]

By September, before a formal rejection was issued, the story was all over the press. *Frontline* called it 'a significant step towards the spread of patent literacy in India'. It quoted the CSIR chief saying that 'the ruling by the [USPTO] has amply demonstrated that India can integrate with the global trade regime pretty much on its own terms'.[51] Meanwhile, an article in *Science* reported that Suman K. Das, the patentee who had spent close to USD 15,000 on the fight to defend his patent, having 'hoped to make turmeric a popular alternative to antibiotics', was a 'dispirited' man.[52] All through, though, nobody asked that fundamental question: What did India gain by having a US patent on turmeric invalidated?

The Basmati Case

After neem and turmeric, another controversy emerged with allegations that an American company called RiceTec had secured a US patent for 'Basmati rice lines and grains', an aromatic variety of rice traditionally grown in India and Pakistan. The panic this time around was much more acute than in the previous instances, because basmati rice was one of the most valuable agricultural exports of India.

The controversy over basmati was a perfect storm. Powerful basmati export lobbies jostled with anti-globalization activists to prove the dangers of biopiracy and IP law. Also, the grant of the RiceTec patent came to light at a time when Americans and Indians were engaged in an intense competition for the high-value European market for premium rice.[53] This was also a very complex controversy, for it involved multiple IP issues, ranging from patent law to the laws on trademarks and geographical indications (GIs). One concern was of the Americans appropriating the name 'basmati' itself. Then, as now, commentators tend to confuse the 'invention-protecting' patent law and the 'name-protecting' trademark law. While the trademark issue was certainly of significance for India, the patent issue was possibly overhyped and fuelled by the controversies over the neem and turmeric patents.

The Discovery of the RiceTec Patent

Patents are dragged into controversy usually when they have to be enforced against a competitor, or when the grant of patents impacts access to the underlying invention. However, like neem and turmeric, the basmati patent, bearing number US 5,663,484, was not discovered because the patent had been enforced against Indians. Instead, it was discovered in 1997, when Indian rice exporters were opposing Texas-based RiceTec's *trademark* for 'Texmati' before the UK trademark office, where the trademark documents apparently referred to a patent recently granted by the USPTO to RiceTec for 'Basmati rice lines and grains'.[54]

The news of the RiceTec patent caused the same outrage in India as earlier, when news of the neem and turmeric patents had reached home. India had already challenged patents before the USPTO, and met with success in the revocation of the turmeric patent.[55] By March 1998, the Indian government had engaged an Indian law firm and appointed 12 scientists from its various scientific establishments, primarily the CSIR and the Indian Council of Agricultural Research (ICAR), to collect evidence establishing that basmati was known to India for several centuries.[56] Simultaneously, Indian activists petitioned Prince Hans Adam of Liechtenstein, the then sole owner of RiceTec Inc., asking him to withdraw the patent for basmati.[57]

On its part, RiceTec claimed it was completely baffled by the accusations being levelled against it by India. In a July 1998 interview to an Indian journalist,[58] the chief executive officer (CEO) of RiceTec, Robin Andrews, said, '[w]e were very surprised by the furore because we still do not believe there is any reason for any legitimate concern. I think the only reason there is such a flap is because of misunderstandings of what RiceTec has done and the difference in the laws between the US and both India and Pakistan.' Defending RiceTec's patent, Andrews explained that,

> There has been tremendous misunderstanding about our patent. The patent is actually for the breeding method RiceTec invented, not for the name or word 'basmati'. We spent more than 10 years developing the variety of rice through this breeding method and our patent protects our investment in the US. Patenting breeding or milling methods is a standard practice in this country.[59]

Most of what Andrews said in his interview was substantiated in the text of the US patent. Like any patent specification, the document described the background to the claimed invention and explained how the claimed invention was a step ahead of existing technology.

RiceTec conceded that, '[g]ood quality basmati rice traditionally has come from northern India and Pakistan'.[60] RiceTec also acknowledged that American-grown long grain rice, often known as 'Basmati type' rice was inferior to actual Basmati rice from India and Pakistan. Its patent application also admitted that the American grown 'Basmati type' rice had 'somewhat less aroma and flavor than premium basmati rice from India and Pakistan. Moreover, they typically elongate only 50% on cooking (which is about the same extent as regular long grain rice), and have cooked textures somewhat different than that of traditional good quality basmati rice'.[61]

RiceTec had experienced difficulties in growing the same Indian and Pakistani basmati rice in the US because of different weather conditions. Therefore, it invested significantly in creating hybrid rice lines which could be grown in the western hemisphere, especially in the US, and which would have characteristics similar to the basmati rice cultivated in India and Pakistan. It did so by trying to cross-breed traditional basmati rice with long-grain rice grown in the US. As explained in RiceTec's specification,

> The rice lines of the invention combine desirable grain traits of basmati rice with desirable plant traits of semi-dwarf, long grain rice. In particular, the combined traits comprise the basmati grain traits of 'popcorn' aroma, long slender grain shape, extreme grain elongation on cooking, and dry, fluffy (or firm) texture of the cooked grain and the semi-dwarf, long grain plant traits of short stature, photoperiod insensitivity, high grain yield, and disease tolerance.[62]

The main invention eventually sought to be patented was limited to rice meeting this description (grain shape, elongation, aroma, among others) capable of being grown in specific geographical regions in the western hemisphere. Along with the admission in the patent application that basmati rice was traditionally from India and Pakistan, this was a sufficient indicator that RiceTec would not be able to enforce its patent against basmati rice exports from the subcontinent.

The Re-examination Process before the USPTO

Possibly realizing the limited potential of the RiceTec patent, the Indian government did not move to have the US patent revoked, despite having put together a group of scientists to study the matter. It is difficult to accurately identify the factors that led to this outcome, because the government agency responsible for the issue— Agricultural and Processed Food Products Export Development Authority (APEDA)—claims that it does not have the relevant files in its possession.[63] In March 1998, a group of activists and Indian rice exporters petitioned the Supreme Court of India seeking directions to the Indian government to challenge the RiceTec patent before the USPTO.[64] The Indian government agreed, and eventually filed a request on 28 April 2000, requesting the USPTO to re-examine the patent assigned to RiceTec.[65] As part of its re-examination request, the Indian government submitted declarations of two scientists, Ankireddypalli Krishna Reddy and Kambadur Nagaraja Rao Gurudutt, along with several publications on basmati rice and the research conducted on such rice in India. One publication by the Indian Agricultural Research Institute (IARI) on 'High Yielding Basmati Rice—Problems, Progress and Prospects'[66] caught the USPTO's attention. This publication, the USPTO felt, 'anticipated' or rendered the core claims of the RiceTec patent 'non-obvious'. On 27 March 2001, the USPTO informed RiceTec that it would revoke 17 of its 20 claims, and invited a rebuttal from the patent holder. In its response of May 2001, RiceTec accepted the USPTO's decision without assigning any specific reasons, and agreed to reduce the 20 claims of its patent to three claims for three different rice lines. RiceTec's decision to not challenge the patent office's decision brought an end to a four-year long dispute over basmati.

A Digital Library for Traditional Knowledge

The controversy and legal battles over the patents granted for neem, turmeric, and basmati generated more heat than light and more passion than reason. The cases clearly show that no financial threat was looming large. Nevertheless, the government and its institutions spent large sums of money to salvage a misguided sense of wounded Indian pride.

The Origins of the Traditional Knowledge Digital Library

In June 1999, the Planning Commission under the Government of India constituted a 'Task Force on Conservation and Sustainable Use of Medicinal Plants', with members drawn from the bureaucratic and scientific establishments in the country. The Task Force was entrusted with an ambitious set of terms relating to medicinal plants, including the identification of measures to facilitate the protection of 'patent rights and IPR of medicinal plants'.[67]

The Task Force pragmatically observed that the 'continued illiteracy and confusion about patents' in India was a 'serious matter', and that a 'weak physical infrastructure, inadequate documentation, poor public awareness and delay in framing and implementing Government policies' would hurt India.[68]

But it also—incorrectly—stated that the USPTO had granted the patent on turmeric for reasons of lack of access to accurate information about prior art:

> [I]t must be understood that patent offices do make mistakes in checking the novelty of an invention because these usually look at their own databases.... The knowledge which may be in public domain in one country may be a new knowledge in another country. Therefore, it is expected that foreign patent offices would make mistakes in granting patents for the inventions based on the traditional knowledge in India and such numbers are to increase with time.[69]

This was an incorrect assumption because most of the prior art information cited by the USPTO while revoking both the turmeric and basmati patents was in the English language, and published in modern scientific journals and books, which would have been presumably available to the USPTO and EPO.

More importantly, the Task Force said that before Indians decided to oppose any such patents which had been mistakenly granted, certain questions needed to be addressed each time: Would Indian trade be affected if the patent were not opposed; how lengthy and costly would such an opposition process be; and had the information required to oppose the patent been established and collated successfully.[70]

Unfortunately, after recommending that these questions must necessarily be addressed before each patent opposition was taken up, the policy recommendations made by the Task Force went the other way, when it recommended the creation of a national TKDL. The TKDL, like similar projects of the CSIR undertaken previously, would have the objective of showing to the world that traditional Indian medicinal knowledge was prior art, and that patent applications on such knowledge would not fulfil the criteria of novelty under patent law. The Task Force stated unambiguously that the TKDL, a web-based library, would help avoid grant of patents in two ways: firstly, it would make available relevant information to examiners during the examination process; and secondly, it could be utilized by the country concerned at the time of opposition proceedings.[71] The previously detailed (and sensible) framework—to necessarily examine the feasibility of opposing patents before actually embarking on the oppositions—appeared to have been conveniently forgotten, and the TKDL was the way forward.

This enthusiasm over defending India's traditional knowledge was followed by an approach paper[72] for establishing the TKDL, which recommended a work plan for making the library a reality, and eventually led to the creation of the TKDL itself.

The TKDL's Mission to Help Patent Offices

The TKDL's mission is to provide 'information on traditional knowledge existing in the country, in languages and format understandable by patent examiners at International patent offices (IPOs) [around the world], so as to prevent the grant of wrong patents. TKDL, thus, acts as a bridge between the traditional knowledge information existing in local languages and the patent examiners at IPOs'.[73] In other words, the Indian scientific establishment believed that the vast repositories of modern science accessed by patent offices outside the country were yet to catch up with discoveries made by ancient Indian traditional knowledge. This issue recurs time and again in Indian scientific and intellectual discourse, one recent example of it being the 102nd

Indian Science Congress held in January 2015. This Congress included a symposium on 'Ancient Science through Sanskrit', organized by a group of Sanskrit scholars and academics, where absurd claims concerning Indian aviation technology were made. A presentation at the symposium referred to four types of 'vimanas' (or vehicles that could fly) from certain 'ancient' books. One of these vimanas, according to the presentation, could fly at around ten times the speed of sound (Mach 10), and another had a base with a diameter of 300 metres. Many decades previously, these vimanas had already been shown to be scientifically unsound, and the 2015 claims were an effort to create 'a false history of Indic science', and a 'spectacularly bad example of the absurd lengths to which attempts at glorification of our past can go'.[74]

The TKDL has helped perpetrate this 'false history of Indic science' in many ways. Apart from the hubris of the assumption on which the TKDL is centred, little evidence is available to support this belief. In each of the three cases that prompted the creation of the TKDL— neem, turmeric, and basmati—the prior art deemed relevant by the examining patent offices were all modern scientific publications, all but one of which were available in English.

In the case of the neem patent, the EPO and its Board of Appeals had relied mainly on witness testimony and an article in *Australian Plant Pathology* to invalidate the neem patent.[75] In the case of the turmeric patent, of the 32 prior art documents cited by the CSIR in the re-examination procedure, all but one were from the twentieth century, and of the remaining 31 documents, only two were older than 1950. Most of the documents, in fact, dated to the 1990s, and had been published in modern scientific journals. The six main references cited by the USPTO to strike down the turmeric patent were (i) an article in the *Journal of Indian Medical Association*, 1950; (ii) a book titled *Ayurvedic Healing*, 1989; (iii) a compilation called *Wealth of India*, 1950; (iv) a book titled *Indian Materia Medica*, 1976; (v) an article in *Economic and Medicinal Plant Research*, 1990; and (vi) a book titled *Home Remedies*, 1958. Of two other references cited, one was a book by the name *Compendium of Indian Medicinal Plants*, 1988, while the second was a book titled *Kya Khayein Aur Kyun* ('What to Eat and Why'), 1979, the latter being the only non-English document cited by the USPTO to invalidate the turmeric patent. In the case of the basmati patent, the main prior art that invalidated the RiceTec patent was a publication of the IARI from 1980.

Without regard to the fact that most relevant prior art was available in English and was accessible to the general public, the TKDL project went ahead. The database was created by scanning and translating scores of books on ancient Indian traditional knowledge systems like Ayurveda, Unani, Siddha, and Yoga. Most of these books were written by Indian authors, and mainly in regional Indian languages.

Agreements were signed with the USPTO, EPO, the Canadian Patent Office (CPO), and the Japanese Patent Office (JPO), granting them free access to the TKDL database. It appears that the Indian government may have invested substantial amounts of money and resources in improving the quality of patents granted by these offices, with little evidence to demonstrate that patents granted by the offices affected Indians or Indian exports in any way. Had the TKDL run on a revenue-generating model, at least some of the monetary investment made in creating the database might have been recovered.

The CSIR also designated its own staff of examiners to trawl through patent applications pending before these foreign patent offices, to file objections against any applications claiming traditional knowledge that might be described in the TKDL. There was no requirement to consider whether the patent applications in question posed a threat to Indian interests, contrary to what the 1999 Planning Commission Task Force had recommended. For instance, the TKDL has made prior art submissions in over a dozen cases involving turmeric. Have any tangible benefits accrued to the Indian turmeric industry as a result of these challenges? Following from that, have the costs incurred in the challenges outweighed the benefits that accrue?

The costs of creating and running the TKDL itself have been significant. According to information disclosed to the authors in response to an RTI application, in the period from 2002 to 2012, about Rs 15.96 crore (approximately USD 3 million) were spent on the TKDL. Around 80 employees were hired to run the database.[76] At the same time, the Indian Patent Office, the counterpart of the USPTO and the EPO, was languishing for lack of resources and staff. The irony of the situation could not have been more stark, for the decisions of the Indian Patent Office, which is responsible for examining patent applications in India, would have a direct impact on the Indian marketplace and economy.

The rerouting of resources in the TKDL debate is relevant not only to the Indian Patent Office, but also to the indigent Indian scientific community. It is challenging, to put it mildly, to develop a scientific temper in an environment beset by poor funding and a misdirected protectionist agenda that hinders innovation. A recent development, though, serves as an interesting, and perhaps even portentous, marker of the discourse around scientific innovation in the country. According to a news report in the *Indian Express*,[77] the ICAR, an autonomous body under the ministry of agriculture, submitted an affidavit before the Supreme Court of India, saying that it believed it was 'not advantageous' to contest certain patents granted to the US company Monsanto for a wheat variety allegedly closely linked to Indian varieties of the crop. (A representative of the ICAR later remarked that after examining the issue through various government committees, it 'was not felt worth the time, effort and money required to contest the case in US/Europe'.[78]) The affidavit was reiterating recommendations made by an expert group in 2007, and crucially, acknowledged that the huge litigation costs that such a patent challenge would incur were not warranted, and that no Indian industry would be adversely affected. Further, it was discovered that during the course of the proceedings, one of the European patents in question had automatically expired with lapse of time, and the writ petition filed before the Supreme Court demanding that the Indian government challenge the wheat patents was no longer valid.[79] It would most certainly have been a waste of resources had the Indian government indeed decided to contest these patents.

This ICAR affidavit was in marked contrast to official Indian responses in the past, where expensive and long-drawn out IP challenges were commenced without any assessment of the likely benefits that would ensue. The basmati and turmeric challenges, for example, not only affected the Indian exchequer, but have also damaged the debate around scientific innovation and IP in India. The ICAR affidavit could well be an indicator that the Indian scientific establishment is revisiting its policy on opposing IP applications filed or rights acquired abroad. As a caveat, though, this bold admission by the ICAR is also probably attributable to its distinct ministerial affiliations, since the ICAR's parent ministry is agriculture, whereas the TKDL and CSIR fall under the ministry of science and technology.

The Cow-milk Patent Application

In the years since its creation, the TKDL has been frequently cited in the press for having defended Indian traditional knowledge by targeting the grant of patents in other countries. European patents appear to have been especially popular targets, since the EPO is one of the few patent offices in the world that allows third parties (that is, those who are neither the inventor/patentee, nor an 'interested person') to intervene during the stage of patent examination.

On closer investigation, however, it appears that some claims of the TKDL might have been greatly exaggerated. An article published in the *Times of India*, titled 'India Foils Swiss MNC's Bio-piracy Bid',[80] suggested that the TKDL was instrumental in invalidating a European patent application filed by the food and beverage multinational Nestlé for the use of cow-milk as a laxative to treat constipation. Quoting an anonymous government source, it said that, '[w]ithin 16 weeks of India [that is, the TKDL] providing evidence, the nearly three-year old attempt by a Swiss multinational company to pirate India's traditional medicinal knowledge was struck down by the European Patent Office'. The evidence submitted by the TKDL included extracts from Indian medicinal texts dating to the fifth century. But a study of the prosecution history of the EU patent by a European patent attorney, David Pearce, who blogs under the nom de plume Tufty the Kat, suggested that even before the TKDL had sent across its centuries-old evidence on the use of cow-milk as a laxative, the EPO examiners had already issued a search report citing 17 prior art documents objecting to the claimed invention. None of those documents were extracted from the TKDL. The TKDL's third-party intervention was filed three months *after* the EPO had already issued its examination report. Claims that the EPO had struck down the patent *because* of the TKDL intervention were also incorrect. As it turned out, Nestlé did not file a response to the EPO's examination report, and was, thus, deemed to have withdrawn its patent application.[81]

The cow-milk story prompted a closer scrutiny of the TKDL's 'kill list' provided on its website where it provided details of patents that had been revoked, rejected, or withdrawn due to its interventions. In a detailed article,[82] Pearce explains that, for the most part, the TKDL appears to have had hardly any impact. Foreign examiners have cited the TKDL only rarely, and mostly when there was modern scientific literature also available.

There also appears to be no rationale for the TKDL's targeting of patent applications. Was the TKDL recklessly spending Indian taxpayer money to attack patent applications without regard to the impact on Indian people or businesses? More troubling was that the TKDL did not intervene before the Indian Patent Office for a long time, despite Indian patents having a direct bearing on the country's economy and its citizens.[83] In fact, while the TKDL routinely objected to patent applications filed in Europe by Indian companies, it remained silent on corresponding patent applications filed in India by the same companies. In one case, the TKDL objected to a patent application filed in Europe by Avesthagen Limited, an Indian company, but did not file a similar objection against the corresponding Indian patent application for the same invention. When the matter came to light a year later,[84] both the TKDL and CSIR were criticized for spending more resources to attack weak patents in Europe rather than India. Subsequent mainstream media coverage on the issue prompted the Indian government to use its extraordinary powers under Section 66 of the Indian Patents Act, 1970, to have the patent revoked.[85]

Other Chinks in the TKDL Armour

There are several other issues with the TKDL that have not as yet been debated sufficiently. The most glaring of these is the location of the TKDL, which highlights questions of institutional design and independence. Should such a database be placed within a scientific institution that is itself in the business of conducting research and patenting the outcomes of its research? Arguably, if the TKDL ought to exist, it deserves its place as a stand-alone database free from institutional biases in its collection and dissemination.

The database remains confidential, and is accessible only by a handful of patent offices with which access agreements have been signed. Even scientists working inside the CSIR system, within which the TKDL is located, do not have access to the database for their research.[86] Only around 1,200 'demonstration formulations' from three disciplines (Ayurveda, Unani, and Siddha) are in the 'open domain'. It is not clear why the TKDL remains confidential, when it is essentially a compilation of information that is already publicly available. The only significant value-addition made by the TKDL is that texts have been digitized, and have been translated into multiple languages. Surely, making the database available to the public, even if for a fee, would be beneficial to the scientific community.

Recent instances of biopiracy have made apparent other chinks in the TKDL armour. For many years, the Indian scientific establishment has bemoaned the fact that foreign scientists were 'stealing' Indian traditional knowledge, and accessing biological resources in contravention of the Biological Diversity Act, 2002. This is supplemented by the Patents Act, 1970, whose Section 3(p) states 'an invention which, in effect, is traditional knowledge or which is an aggregation or duplication of known properties of traditionally known component or components' is not patentable. In a drive to weed out such patent applications, the Indian Patent Office considered all patent applications filed with it for references to traditional knowledge, and sent out objections to applications wherever relevant. Interestingly, patent applicants under the scanner included those of the country's premier scientific laboratories, one of which was the CSIR itself, the home of the TKDL. The Indian Patent Office raised objections to these applications either on grounds that they constituted traditional knowledge or that the laboratories in question were trying to access biological resources without obtaining appropriate permissions from the National Biological Authority (under the Biological Diversity Act, 2002). On the first ground, most objections relied upon information contained in the TKDL, or on other literature regarding traditional knowledge.[87]

There is also a possibility that the TKDL may have copyright issues. The project claims to collate all information relating to traditional knowledge available in India into a single digitized database with translations in several languages. According to its website, most information in the TKDL is sourced from published books. These include 151 books on Ayurveda, 33 books on Unani, 137 books on Siddha, and 38 books on Yoga.[88] Several of these publications are recent, and involve an element of creativity, that is, they are original translations or original compilations of existing information. Both types of works—translations and original compilations—can be protected as literary works under the Copyright Act, 1957. However, there is nothing to suggest that the TKDL's right to use these works was acquired after obtaining permissions from the copyright owners of these books. In fact, when the authors requested for information on this issue, the CSIR replied saying 'TKDL as [the] name suggest[s] refers to traditional knowledge concerning Ayurveda, Unani, Siddha and refers to classical and ancient text[s] of these systems created by respective authors several hundred years back dating to 2500 BC, [and] therefore, are outside the purview of Copyright provisions'.[89] This understanding of copyright law is problematic, for in law, if somebody were to write a book on Ayurveda today, the newly written material could qualify for its own copyright protection if it were original in terms of its expression. Copyrights, unlike patents, protect the expression of an idea, and not the idea itself.

Publicly-funded institutions, like the TKDL's parent-organization CSIR, have the right to pursue the spirit of science independently and without any interference. But, because they are publicly-funded, such institutions also have the duty to be accountable. The difficulty lies in how accountability is measured. In this case, defensive IP protection appears to be a key measure of accountability for the organization. But this protectionist agenda appears to have been constructed without a thorough understanding of IP law. For example, why should India attack foreign patents that do not affect the country or its citizens in any way, or why should India spend large amounts of money to create a database for foreign patent offices, or why should a research institution, designed to focus on cutting-edge industrial and scientific innovation, pursue a mission against biopiracy, instead of creating new knowledge itself? The Indian scientific community has frequently complained about the lack of funding it receives from the government, but surely, it needs to introspect on whether the money it receives is being put to good use.

—— ——

Notes

1. *About TKDL*, available at http://www.tkdl.res.in/tkdl/langdefault/common/Abouttkdl.asp?GL=Eng (Last visited on 21 April 2015).

2. *History of DePenning & DePenning*, available at http://www.depenning.com/history.htm (Last visited on 12 August 2014).

3. Richard Stone, *A Biopesticidal Tree Begins to Blossom*, 255 SCIENCE, 1070 (1992).

4. Stone, *A Biopesticidal Tree Begins to Blossom*, at 1070.

5. Stone, *A Biopesticidal Tree Begins to Blossom*, at 1070.

6. U.S Patent No. 5,124,349 (filed 26 June 1989).

7. European Patent No. 0436257 (filed 20 December 1990).

8. *More Than 200 Organisations from 35 Nations Challenge US Patent on Neem*, THIRD WORLD NETWORK, available at http://twn.my/title/neem-ch.htm (Last visited on 18 August 2016).

9. Vandana Shiva v. Union of India, 1995 (32) DRJ 447, available at http://indiankanoon.org/doc/1110085/ (Last visited on 12 August 2014).

10. Mary Hager and Sudip Mazumdar, *Fight for the Miracle Tree*, NEWSWEEK, 25 September 1995, at 34.

11. *More Than 200 Organisations from 35 Nations Challenge US Patent on Neem*.

12. *More Than 200 Organisations from 35 Nations Challenge US Patent on Neem*.

13. *More Than 200 Organisations from 35 Nations Challenge US Patent on Neem*.

14. *More Than 200 Organisations from 35 Nations Challenge US Patent on Neem*.

15. *More Than 200 Organisations from 35 Nations Challenge US Patent on Neem*.

16. Hager and Mazumdar, *Fight for the Miracle Tree*, at 34.

17. Hager and Mazumdar, *Fight for the Miracle Tree*, at 34.

18. *Grace Issues Statement About Patent for Neem Pesticide*, THE FREE LIBRARY, 14 September 1995, available at http://www.thefreelibrary. com/GRACE+ISSUES+STATEMENT+ABOUT+PATENT+FOR+NEEM+ PESTICIDE-a017422913 (Last visited on 12 August 2014).

19. *Grace Issues Statement About Patent for Neem Pesticide*.

20. *Grace Issues Statement About Patent for Neem Pesticide*.

21. See Status of EP 0834254, European Patent Office, available at https://data. epo.org/gpi/EP0834254B1-Azadirachtin-formulations-and-a-process-for-preparing-them-from-neem-seed-kernel (Last visited on 18 August 2016).

22. *Grace Issues Statement About Patent for Neem Pesticide*.

23. Hannah Bloch and Dick Thompson, *Seeds of Conflict*, TIME, 25 September 1995.

24. Lori Wolfgang, *Patents on Native Technology Challenged*, 269 SCIENCE 1506 (1995).

25. Ralph T. King Jr., *Grace's Patent on a Pesticide Enrages Indians*, ASSOCIATED PRESS, 13 September 1995, available at http://www. apnewsarchive.com/1995/Grace-s-Patent-On-a-Pesticide-Enrages-Indians/id-a359c4a7a2c306d4b5b652f744440947 (Last visited on 12 August 2014).

26. *Bitter Truth*, Indian Environment Portal, 14 October 1995, available at http://www.indiaenvironmentportal.org.in/content/3447/bitter-truth/ (Last visited on 12 August 2014).

27. *Bitter Truth*.

28. *Neemm—Manim, What Else*, DOWN TO EARTH, 30 November 1995, available at http://www.downtoearth.org.in/node/29012 (Last visited on 13 August 2014).

29. David Dickson and K.S. Jayaraman, *Aid Groups Back Challenge to Neem Petition*, NATURE, 14 September 1995, at 95.

30. Arvind Panagariya, *The Myths and Realities of Neem-based Patents*, THE TIMES OF INDIA, 16 January 1996, available at http://www.columbia. edu/~ap2231/ET/toi3-neem%20and%20patents-jan16-96.htm (Last visited on 13 August 2014).

31. United States Department of Commerce, Patent and Trademark Office (USPTO), Request for Reexamination of Patent No. 5,124,349, requested by the Foundation on Economic Trends, Reexamination No. 90/004,050.

32. European Patent Office, Notice of Opposition, Patent Opposed EP0436257, Opponents Magda Alvoet et al., 14 June 1995.

33. Article 53(a), European Patent Convention.

34. European Patent Office, Opposition to European Patent No. 0436257, Statement of Grounds.

35. European Patent Office, Decision of the Opposition Division, Application No. 90250319.2, ¶ 4.2.

36. Letter from N. Subbaram, head of the Intellectual Property Management Department of the Council of Scientific and Industrial Research, to Director-General, Council of Scientific and Industrial Research (2 July 1996) (on file with authors).

37. Letter from N. Subbaram, to Director-General, Council for Scientific and Industrial Research (2 July 1996).

38. Jeff Hecht, *Boy Takes Swing at US Patents*, New Scientist, 17 April 2002, available at https://www.newscientist.com/article/dn2178-boy-takes-swing-at-us-patents/ (Last visited on 15 May 2015).

39. Letter from N. Subbaram, to Director-General, Council for Scientific and Industrial Research (2 July 1996).

40. *Proceedings of the Inter-ministerial Meeting on the Use of Turmeric as a Wound Healing Agent* (16 July 1996) (on file with authors).

41. *Proceedings of the Inter-ministerial Meeting on the Use of Turmeric as a Wound Healing Agent* (19 July 1996) (on file with authors).

42. As detailed in the RTI reply from CSIR to Sumathi Chandrashekaran (18 January 2012) (on file with authors).

43. Note by N. Subbaram, Re-examination proceedings in respect of US Patent No. 5401504: Action Plan, Intellectual Property Management Division, Council of Scientific and Industrial Research (26 July 1996).

44. United States Department of Commerce, Patent and Trademark Office (USPTO), Office Action in Re-examination, Sl. No. 90/004,433, Decision by Shailendra Kumar (Primary Examiner, Group 1200) (March 1997) (as enclosed in a letter from Michael Schuman, Merchant & Gould, to D. Caleb Gabriel, Kumaran & Sagar (7 January 1997) (on file with authors).

45. United States Department of Commerce, Patent and Trademark Office (USPTO), Re examination Interview Summary Form, Sl. No. 90/004,433 (16 May 1997) (as enclosed in a letter from Michael Schuman, Merchant & Gould, to D. Caleb Gabriel, Kumaran & Sagar (10 June 1997) (on file with authors).

46. Letter from Douglas P. Mueller, to N.R. Subbaram, c/o R.A. Mashelkar, Director-General, Council for Scientific and Industrial Research (21 August 1997) (letter reporting examiner's rejection of all the claims) (on file with authors).

47. Note by Dr R.A. Mashelkar, Director-General, CSIR, on Re examination for the Purpose of Revocation of US Patent No. 5401504 for Turmeric Power as 'Wound Healing Agent', No. DG/IPMD/97-RPBD (22 August 1997).

48. Note by Dr R.A. Mashelkar, Director-General, CSIR, on Re examination for the Purpose of Revocation of US Patent No. 5401504 for Turmeric Power as 'Wound Healing Agent', No. DG/IPMD/97-RPBD (22 August 1997).

49. Letter from V. Lakshmikumaran, to R.A. Mashelkar, Director-General, Council of Scientific and Industrial Research (28 August 1997) (on file with authors).

50. Letter from R.A. Mashelkar, Director-General, Council of Scientific and Industrial Research, to J.R. Sharma, Director & Head, C.I.M.A.P (20 September 1997) (on file with authors).

51. Sudha Mahalingam, *Turmeric Triumph*, FRONTLINE, 3 October 1997.

52. E. Marshall and P. Bagla, *India Applauds U.S. Patent Reversal*, 277 SCIENCE 1429 (1997).

53. Shantanu Guha Ray, *The Stealing of Basmati*, REDIFF, 12 March 1998, available at http://www.rediff.com/money/1998/mar/12rice.htm (Last visited on 20 August 2014).

54. R.A. Mashelkar, *Intellectual Property Rights and the Third World*, 81(8) CURRENT SCIENCE 955, 962 (Box 5) (2001), available at http://repository.ias.ac.in/63031/1/30_pub.pdf (Last visited on 20 August 2014).

55. *Basmati Battle in Full Steam*, THE INDIAN EXPRESS, 13 March 1998, available at http://expressindia.indianexpress.com/news/ie/daily/1998 0313/07250114.html (Last visited on 20 August 2014).

56. *Basmati Battle in Full Steam*.

57. *Fight the Aromatic Basmati Rice Patent!*, ETC GROUP, available at http://www.etcgroup.org/content/fight-aromatic-basmati-rice-patent (Last visited on 20 August 2014).

58. Email interview by Amberish K. Diwanji with Robin Andrews, CEO, RiceTec Inc., REDIFF, 7 July 1998, available at http://www.rediff.com/business/1998/jul/07rice.htm (Last visited on 20 August 2014).

59. Email interview by Amberish K. Diwanji with Robin Andrews.

60. US Patent 5,663,484 (filed 8 July 1994) (see under 'Description', 2.3. 'Indian and Pakistan Basmati Rice').

61. US Patent 5,663,484 (filed 8 July 1994) (see under 'Description', 2.5. 'Basmati Rice Breeding Efforts').

62. US Patent 5,663,484 (filed 8 July 1994) (see under 'Description', 5. 'Detailed Description of the Invention'). The UK later refused to recognize the produce of RiceTec's invention as basmati rice.

63. According to the reply provided by APEDA to an RTI application by Sumathi Chandrashekaran (21 February 2012) (on file with authors).

64. *NGO Moves Supreme Court on Basmati Patent Issue*, BUSINESS STANDARD, 11 March 1998, available at http://www.business-standard.

com/article/specials/ngo-moves-supreme-court-on-basmati-patent-issue-198031101102_1.html (Last visited on 20 August 2014).

65. Re-examination Request No. 90/005,709 dated 28 April 2000.

66. *High Yielding Basmati Rice—Problems, Progress and Prospects*, IARI BULLETIN, Research Bulletin No. 30 (1980).

67. GOVERNMENT OF INDIA, PLANNING COMMISSION, REPORT OF THE TASK FORCE ON CONSERVATION & SUSTAINABLE USE OF MEDICINAL PLANTS (March 2000), *Terms of Reference* in Annexure 1, available at http://planningcommission.nic.in/aboutus/taskforce/tsk_medi.pdf (Last visited on 20 August 2014).

68. PLANNING COMMISSION, REPORT OF THE TASK FORCE ON CONSERVATION & SUSTAINABLE USE OF MEDICINAL PLANTS, at 132.

69. PLANNING COMMISSION, REPORT OF THE TASK FORCE ON CONSERVATION & SUSTAINABLE USE OF MEDICINAL PLANTS, at 128.

70. PLANNING COMMISSION, REPORT OF THE TASK FORCE ON CONSERVATION & SUSTAINABLE USE OF MEDICINAL PLANTS, *Terms of Reference* in Annexure 1.

71. PLANNING COMMISSION, REPORT OF THE TASK FORCE ON CONSERVATION & SUSTAINABLE USE OF MEDICINAL PLANTS, at 130.

72. V.K. Gupta, *An Approach for Establishing a Traditional Knowledge Digital Library*, 5 JIPR 307 (2000), available at http://nopr.niscair.res.in/bitstream/123456789/26010/1/JIPR%205%286%29%20307-319.pdf (Last visited on 20 August 2014).

73. *About TKDL*, available at http://www.tkdl.res.in/tkdl/langdefault/common/Abouttkdl.asp?GL=Eng (Last visited on 21 April 2015).

74. See Roddam Narasimha, *The 'Historic' Storm at the Mumbai Science Congress*, 108(4) CURRENT SCIENCE, 471–2 (25 February 2015), available at http://www.currentscience.ac.in/Volumes/108/04/0471.pdf (Last visited on 8 January 2016).

75. European Patent Office, Decision of the Opposition Division, Application No. 90250319.2.

76. RTI reply from Council of Scientific and Industrial Research to Prashant Reddy (7 May 2012), available at https://docs.google.com/file/d/0Bxi2TzVXul5Za3d4cm9xUE9PNG8/edit?pli=1 (Last visited on 20 August 2014); Prashant Reddy, *The Budget for TKDL and Also, Its Focus on Indian Patent Applications*, SPICYIP, 19 May 2012, available at http://spicyip.com/2012/05/budget-of-tkdl-and-also-its-focus-on.html (Last visited on 20 August 2014).

77. Utkarsh Anand, *Centre to SC: No Advantage in Contesting US Patent of Wheat Variety*, THE INDIAN EXPRESS, 8 January 2014, available at http://archive.indianexpress.com/news/centre-to-sc-no-advantage-

in-contesting-us-patent-of-wheat-variety/1216691/ (Last visited on 20 August 2014).

78. See comment by S. Mauria, ICAR, made on 1 March 2016, with regard to Madhulika Vishwanathan, *Evaluating the Veracity of CSIR-TKDL Claims*, SPICYIP, 12 August 2015, available at http://spicyip.com/2015/08/evaluating-the-veracity-of-csir-tkdl-claims.html   (Last visited on 3 March 2016).

79. Research Foundation for Science, Technology & Ecology and Others v. Union of India and Others, Writ Petition (Civil) No. 64 of 2004 (Supreme Court of India) (unreported), (order passed on 16 February 2016).

80. Kounteya Sinha, *India Foils Swiss MNC's Bio-piracy Bid*, THE TIMES OF INDIA, 3 March 2012, available at http://timesofindia.indiatimes.com/business/india-business/India-foils-Swiss-MNCs-bio-piracy-bid/articleshow/12118637.cms (Last visited on 20 August 2014).

81. *Guest Post: The Traditional Knowledge Digital Library and the EPO*, SPICYIP, 19 March 2012, available at http://spicyip.com/2012/03/guest-post-traditional-knowledge.html (Last visited on 20 August 2014) (this article was written on invitation by the authors, on a website that the authors were associated with).

82. *Guest Post: The Traditional Knowledge Digital Library and the EPO.*

83. *About TKDL*, available at http://www.tkdl.res.in/tkdl/langdefault/common/Abouttkdl.asp?GL=Eng (Last visited on 21 April 2015).

84. Prashant Reddy, *Trying to Make Sense of TKDL's Access Policy—Why is the Indian Patent Office Being Ignored?*, SPICYIP, 10 April 2012, available at http://spicyip.com/2012/04/trying-to-make-sense-of-tkdls-access.html (Last visited on 20 August 2014).

85. Sidhartha, *Govt Scraps Patent for Jamun-based Diabetes Drug*, THE TIMES OF INDIA, 27 October 2012, available at http://timesofindia.indiatimes.com/india/Govt-scraps-patent-for-jamun-based-diabetes-drug/articleshow/16975263.cms (Last visited on 20 August 2014).

86. RTI reply from Council of Scientific and Industrial Research to Prashant Reddy (13 March 2012), available at https://docs.google.com/file/d/0Bxi2TzVXul5ZZlFfVnFjYWhTOXFCdUo0SDRlNFdNZw/edit (Last visited on 20 August 2014) (point no. 3 of the reply indicates that CSIR scientists had no access to the TKDL database).

87. Prashant Reddy, *Patent Office Objects to Attempts by CSIR & Co. to Patent Traditional Knowledge and Access Biological Resources Without NBA Approval*, SPICYIP, 9 November 2012, available at http://spicyip.com/2012/11/patent-office-objects-to-attempts-by.html (Last visited on 20 August 2014).

88. *Source of Information*, available at http://www.tkdl.res.in/tkdl/lang-default/common/SourceInfo.asp?GL=Eng (Last visited on 20 August 2014).

89. Prashant Reddy, *Is the TKDL a 'Confidential Database' and is It Compliant with Indian Copyright Law?*, SPICYIP, 29 March 2012, available at http://spicyip.com/2012/03/is-tkdl-confidential-database-and-is-it.html (Last visited on 20 August 2014).

10

THE QUEEN OF ALL RICES

Food connoisseurs will agree that a traditional north Indian meal is incomplete without a bowl of aromatic, long-grained basmati rice, which is so essential to savour the flavour of the accompanying dishes. But few know that every grain of the rice in that bowl tells a story of food and prosperity in India. It is a story of how that rice was meticulously evolved by generations of farmers in the subcontinent over centuries. It is a story of how India has nearly lost those same farmers the right to call it 'basmati' rice (literally meaning 'fragrant' rice), and by extension, the right to reap benefits from their centuries of toil. It is also a story of the intermingling of three distinct forms of intellectual property (IP)—patents, trademarks, and geographical indications (GIs). While Chapter 9 in this volume discusses the basmati patent cases in some detail, this chapter discusses the encounters of basmati with the law on trademarks and GIs in India and the world.

Basmati's Encounters in the World

The greatest threat to the success of basmati rice, traditionally grown in parts of India and Pakistan, as a luxury food product on the international market has been the possibility of competitors selling *any* aromatic, long-grained rice under the name 'basmati'. This risk was especially formidable in the 1990s, because neither the governments of India or Pakistan nor the huge private industry involved took any steps to claim exclusivity over the use of the 'basmati' tag as a trademark or a GI. Unsurprisingly, competitors in the United States (US) and the European Union (EU) challenged the uniqueness of 'basmati' as a trademark, claiming that it was a generic phrase for all aromatic, long-grained rice. Under trademark law, if the exclusivity of a trademark is not rigorously and continuously defended over a long period of time, the trademark risks becoming generic, and anybody may be able to use that trademark. In the case of 'basmati', the word has not been registered either as a trademark or a GI by the basmati industry from India or Pakistan. The 1990s marked the beginning of a series of events in the United Kingdom (UK), India, and the EU attempting to define 'basmati' in legal terms and to protect it as a GI.

The 'Discovery' of Texmati in the United Kingdom

The thought that the identity of basmati could be in danger had probably never crossed anyone's mind in India, until 1995, when Tilda Rice Limited, a UK-based rice-importing company with Indian origins, claimed to have discovered the existence of a trademark for the brand 'Texmati' in the UK trademark registry.[1] Originally owned by an American company called Farms of Texas Company, its corporate successor, RiceTec (which was then a portfolio company owned by the Prince of Liechtenstein), was responsible for the mark at the time. Unlike a GI, which informs the consumer of both the geographical source and quality, a trademark is registered merely as an indicator of the source. In other words, a trademark merely indicates the particular manufacturer or seller who is manufacturing or selling the rice, and not necessarily the geographical source of the goods or the quality of the goods. Thus, registering 'Texmati' as a trademark merely gave RiceTec the exclusive right to prevent others from using the trademark (or any other similar sounding mark) to sell rice. Tilda applied to revoke 'Texmati' in 1995 and apparently met with success the following year when the trademark was removed from the UK register.[2] (The order removing the trademark is presently unavailable, but the authors speculate that Tilda might have argued that 'Texmati' was similar to the word 'basmati', and that consumers were likely to be deceived into believing that the branded rice was basmati rice grown in the Indo-Pak region, whereas it was actually grown in the US.)

Records show that the trademark had existed in the UK since 1977. It is not clear as to why Tilda woke up to challenge the 'Texmati' mark only in 1994, more than 17 years after the trademark was registered. Perhaps, Tilda feared competition from a new variety of aromatic rice (termed 'basmati 867') developed by RiceTec in the 1990s. In a patent application[3] filed by RiceTec in 1994 before the United States Patent and Trademark Office (USPTO), the company claimed to have created 'basmati 867' by crossing a traditional basmati variety from the Indian subcontinent, with other rice varieties grown in the US. In the same application, RiceTec claimed that this development was significant because, for the first time, a basmati line 'equivalent to traditional good quality Indian and Pakistani basmati' had been grown outside the traditional basmati-growing zones in those countries.[4] As a measure of the quality of its new variety, RiceTec commissioned an independent market research company, Research Services of Great Britain (RSGB), to test consumers on how its rice measured up against a leading Indian producer's brand of basmati rice. According to the patent application, test participants, who were all frequent basmati consumers, expressed equal preference for both the varieties, suggesting that the two were indistinguishable. If true, this made RiceTec the first company in the world to successfully grow a high quality basmati crop outside the traditional Indo-Pak region. It also meant that RiceTec could flood lucrative international markets with 'basmati 867' and compete with Tilda's exports of traditional Indian basmati varieties. Tilda's red flags against the 'Texmati' trademark were possibly an attempt to make it difficult for RiceTec to brand its rice in a manner that associated it with 'basmati'. But, despite Tilda's successful revocation of the 'Texmati' trademark, the Indian basmati glasshouse was already showing signs of weakening.

The Risk of Genericization in the United States

A generic trademark is one that began life as a distinctive brand name for a specific product or service before changing in meaning to become synonymous with the entire class of products or services to which it belongs. As a result of this, the trademark loses distinctiveness, and no person can own a genericized mark. Trademarks long declared to have been in the public domain include 'aspirin'[5] and 'cellophane'.[6] The ownership of such marks is prohibited to prevent a monopoly on commonly-used terms. As one commentator puts it: 'Allowing a monopoly on the use of a commonly used term would be ludicrous. No individual should be able to appropriate existing terms in the language for their own commercial advantage when to do so would prevent competitors from using that term to describe their competing products.'[7]

Indians were slow in understanding the dangers of genericization of the 'basmati' mark. Every time a company like RiceTec used a basmati-related name such as Texmati or Kasmati or Jasmati to sell rice that neither had the flavour nor the physical characteristics of basmati grown in the Indian subcontinent, it would increase the chance that consumers would associate the name 'basmati' with any kind of aromatic rice grown anywhere in the world, rather than the specific kind of basmati grown only in particular parts of the Indian subcontinent. Six years after the UK Texmati trademark was 'discovered', a protest was finally lodged against RiceTec's claims of genericization.[8] In 2001, a coalition of Indian and American non-governmental organizations (NGOs) filed a petition with the US Federal Trade Commission (FTC), the American competition regulator mandated to 'prevent fraudulent, deceptive and unfair business practices'.[9] The petition sought to restrict the use of the word 'basmati' to only traditional basmati imported from India, since the unregulated use of the name was likely to mislead consumers. It requested the FTC to 'prohibit advertisers and marketers from using the terms "basmati" [among others] ... to characterize rice grown in the United States'.[10] Effectively, the petition wanted the FTC to declare that the word 'basmati' was not generic, so that the word would remain protected for future use, particularly by Indian farmers. But, in a unanimous 5-0 decision in May 2001, the FTC denied the NGOs' petition because 'there were no agricultural regulations mandating that the use of the term "basmati" be controlled by a rice product's country of origin'.[11] While pointing out that there was no evidence to suggest that 'US grown rice [was] being misrepresented as rice from other parts of the world', the FTC also said that basmati rice was 'included as an example of "aromatic rough rice", and is not limited to rice grown in any particular country'.[12] In other words, and completely contrary to the expectations of the petitioners, the FTC had deemed basmati a generic, non-specific term, which could be used to refer to any and all forms of aromatic rice.

The FTC is not the only US agency that considers basmati rice to be generic. The USPTO, which is responsible for registering trademarks in the US, has routinely directed applicants of trademarks containing 'basmati' to 'disclaim' the use of the word, on grounds that it is descriptive or generic.[13] A 'disclaimer', in trademark practice, is a statement that the applicant does not claim exclusive rights to an unregistrable component of a trademark. In its objections, the USPTO has not usually referred to the FTC decision, but has relied on dictionary definitions of 'basmati' to mean 'aromatic long grain rice from India',[14] or simply, 'aromatic rice'.[15] These decisions lend credence to the worry that basmati has become entrenched as a term of common use in the US, and it is likely that there will be no turning back.

Under Article 24.6 of the Agreement on Trade-Related Aspects of Intellectual Property Rights (TRIPS), a country need not accord GI protection for 'goods or services for which the relevant indication is identical with the term customary in common language as the common name for such goods or services'. In light of the FTC decision, and the various observations by the USPTO, there is a real danger that basmati rice could be relegated to the shelves as just another 'aromatic variety of rice' that you could buy in the supermarket. Indeed, it is not just in the US that basmati faces the risk of genericization.[16]

Attempts to Define and Protect the Uniqueness of Basmati Exports from India

In order to claim that basmati is a unique kind of rice, it is first necessary to identify the special characteristics of basmati by defining it, and then establish how this identity needed to be protected against infringers.

The first attempt to define and regulate the use of the term 'basmati rice' in India was through the Basmati Rice (Export) Grading and Marking Rules, 1979 ('Basmati Grading Rules, 1979'). These rules were notified by the ministry of agriculture under the pre-independence Agricultural Produce (Grading and Marking) Act, 1937. At around the same time, the Janata Party-led government in India decided to end the monopoly of the centrally-owned State Trading Corporation on basmati exports.[17] The consequent influx of private players in the basmati export business presumably required some form of regulation. These rules defined the 'general characteristics' of basmati rice as being dried matured kernels of *oryza sativa*, possessing in a marked degree the natural fragrance characteristic of basmati rice both in raw and cooked states, with each grain having a length of six millimetres and above, and a length-breadth ratio of three and above. Only 'authorised packers', that is, those issued a 'certificate of authorisation' by the agricultural marketing adviser to the Government of India, could grade and package such basmati rice for export. Before packaging, the authorized packers had to test basmati rice in the manner prescribed by the agricultural marketing adviser. The packaging would carry two sets of marks—'AGMARK' (with the figure of the rising sun and the words 'Produce of India'), a standard mark affixed on most Indian agricultural exports; and a 'grade designation mark,' indicating the grade of the basmati rice as per the criteria laid down in the schedule to the rules. This grading was based on amount of foreign matter, broken fragments, discoloured grains, and so on.

The grading criteria laid down in the Basmati Grading Rules, 1979, were soon adopted by a different ministry too. The ministry of commerce co-opted these rules into the Export of Basmati Rice (Inspection Rules), 1980 (notified under the Export (Quality Control and Inspection) Act, 1963). Although these export rules merely defined 'basmati rice' as 'basmati rice produced in India', a statutory order accompanying the rules expressly recognized the grade designations formulated under the Basmati Grading Rules, 1979.[18] With this, all export consignments could be graded and packed only by the authorized packer under instructions from agricultural marketing advisers. The consignments would then be inspected by an 'Inspecting Officer', authorized by the agricultural marketing adviser, who would issue the Agmark labels and a certificate of grading.

But these rules were not very effective in regulating the quality of basmati exports. An anecdote from the biography of television mogul Subhash Chandra, *The Z Factor*,[19] is revelatory here. Chandra narrates a tale of corruption and adulteration in basmati exports around when Indira Gandhi was voted back as the Prime Minister of India in 1980. At the time, Chandra's business associates suggested that he could make lucrative profits by exporting basmati rice to the Soviet Union, provided he could leverage high-level contacts within the Government of India to recommend him to the Soviets. Chandra tried to establish contact with Rajiv Gandhi, Indira Gandhi's son and political protégé. Chandra first met Swami Dhirendra Brahmachari, a yoga guru close to Indira Gandhi, apparently well-known for providing 'liaison services' for businessmen interested in contacting Gandhi's family.[20] Dhirendra Brahmachari agreed to introduce Chandra to Vijay Dhar, Rajiv Gandhi's close aide and son of D.P. Dhar, the then Indian ambassador to the Soviet Union. In exchange for setting up a meeting with Rajiv Gandhi, Dhirendra Brahmachari demanded a share of the profits, and was paid, as an advance, fifty lakh rupees. At the meeting where Dhar introduced Chandra to Rajiv Gandhi as a person sent by Swamiji, Rajiv assured Chandra of help, after having remembered Chandra from the time that he assisted the Gandhi family during the Shah Commission inquiry (which had been instituted to look into excesses committed during the Emergency proclaimed by Indira Gandhi in 1975). When the Soviets visited India, they gave Chandra a contract for supplying 30,000 tonnes of basmati rice, while also mentioning that the contract was being awarded because of the recommendation of 'our common friend'. Another contract for supplying 20,000 tonnes of basmati rice was given to Tulsi Tanna in Bombay, who, until then, had had a complete monopoly over basmati exports to the Soviet Union.

Meanwhile, the inexperienced Chandra was advised by multiple sources that basmati rice exports from India were never pure, but always mixed with lower-quality rice. Accordingly, Chandra ensured that his exports to the Soviets had 50 per cent basmati and 50 per cent parmal rice (an inferior grade of rice, lacking fragrance and other unique characteristics of basmati rice). Basmati rice was priced at Rs 3,000 per tonne, and parmal rice cost Rs 1,500 per tonne; the prospective profit margins were huge, especially since Chandra was exporting 30,000 tonnes. The first consignment reached the Soviet Union and was put through a quality inspection. Chandra recalls that the Russians were angry and agitated with the consignment quality, and told him that he was supplying B-grade rice while his competitor Tulsi Tanna was supplying A-grade rice. Chandra was shocked, because he had stuck to prevalent business practices of mixing basmati with non-basmati rice. When the Russians produced samples of Tanna's export consignment, Chandra discovered that the samples had only parmal rice. There was no basmati rice in Tanna's consignment at all! Since Tanna had had a monopoly on basmati rice exports until then, the Soviets had consumed only parmal rice, under the impression that it was basmati rice. Chandra quickly apologised to the Russians, and told his Indian office to return all existing consignments, and instead export only 100 per cent parmal rice, as basmati rice. In his biography Chandra speculates that the Europeans had not perhaps ever enjoyed the aroma of basmati rice, because they had never been made familiar with the notion of fragrant rice, at least until he came along.

Such large-scale adulteration in exports was clearly an indicator that India's basmati export inspection system was flawed and, perhaps, corrupt. As amusing as Chandra's story may be, practices like these cause irreparable injury to the basmati brand. There is, perhaps, now a large section of consumers in the former Soviet Union, who believe that basmati rice is the same as parmal rice, despite the world of difference between the two. The person at the losing end is, as with so many other such tales, the Indian farmer.

Elsewhere, from 1987, the European Communities (EC), after lengthy trade negotiations, allowed a tariff concession of 25 per cent on the import of up to 10,000 tonnes of long-grain aromatic basmati rice from India and Pakistan.[21] The tariff concession sought to operate as an equalizer in reducing the price of (the more expensive) basmati rice for European consumers, to the level of other long-grained rice. The Europeans were aware of the difficulty in defining basmati rice, noting in one regulation, that 'morphological characteristics alone do not enable Basmati rice to be distinguished from other long-grain rice'.[22] Consequently, the EC entrusted the task of authenticating basmati exports to the Indians and Pakistanis themselves. To qualify for concession, an export had to be accompanied by a certificate of authenticity, issued by an agency authorized to do so by the respective governments of India and Pakistan.

In 1990, with the worth of basmati rice exports increasing, the Indian ministry of commerce tried to tackle the quality control problem. It replaced the 1980 rules with the Basmati Rice (Quality Control and Inspection) Rules, 1990. Logically, with quality control being a known issue, and the EC being a high-value market, the new rules should have been more rigorous. Instead, the new rules allowed exporters to self-certify exports, after their quality control systems were vetted by the export inspection agency (EIA). In such cases, the EIA did not have to inspect each consignment. For exporters who lacked an in-house quality control mechanism, the EIA had to certify exports.

In 1996, after trade talks accompanying the creation of the World Trade Organization (WTO), the EC offered an even more generous concession for basmati rice. Under the Commission Regulation No. 1503/96, basmati rice from India was offered a concession of EUR 250 per tonne, with the intention to provide a more level playing field for basmati rice, which would have otherwise been even more expensive. Like previous regulations, this too required India to self-certify its basmati rice exports. Each consignment of basmati would have to be accompanied with a certificate of authenticity. Basmati rice exports to Europe spiked after being offered this tariff concession, increasing from 50,000 tonnes in 1994 to 160,000 tonnes in 2002.[23]

The increase in basmati rice exports also raised suspicion in some quarters. For instance, there were concerns of adulteration due to exporters mixing inferior quality non-basmati rice. The UK's Food Standards Agency (FSA) commissioned studies to examine the problem in greater detail. A 2003 study by the Natural Resources Institute (NRI) and University of Greenwich revealed troubling rates of adulteration in basmati rice imported from India and Pakistan.[24] Of 363 basmati samples drawn from the market by the FSA, 17 per cent of the samples had non-basmati content greater than 20 per cent, while 9 per cent of the samples had non-basmati content greater than 60 per cent.[25] Prevalent trade rules permitted mixing non-basmati rice up to a quantity of 20 per cent as some amount of co-mingling was inevitable during processing and shipping.[26] The FSA study became a key topic of discussion in the British media as the UK was the largest consumer of basmati rice within Europe, accounting for 70 per cent of basmati rice imported from India and Pakistan at the time.[27] Besides hurting consumers, large-scale adulteration also perhaps eroded the goodwill associated with the basmati product, because consumers now presumed that basmati was no different from normal rice. As a result, consumers would not wish to pay a premium for basmati in the future. Stronger quality control measures, enforced strictly by the Government of India, could surely have prevented further damage to the basmati brand.

Adulteration was not the only concern. A second study commissioned by the FSA, and conducted by the Plant Science Division of the University of Nottingham, pointed out that because traditional varieties of basmati were low-yielding and difficult to harvest, India and Pakistan had embarked on several cross-breeding programmes to increase yields. Traditional varieties are usually indigenous to a region, and have adapted to local soil and environmental conditions. Hybrid and evolved varieties are usually created by cross-breeding traditional varieties of basmati with another rice variety, the aim being to create varieties with beneficial properties of both types, combining taste and aroma, with higher yields and increased disease resistance. Whether hybrid and evolved or traditional varieties have the same taste and aroma, though, is disputed, with some arguing that traditional varieties have a better flavour than the other varieties.[28] The Nottingham study suggested that attempts to increase yields through cross-breeding resulted in the decreased expression of the characteristic basmati properties.[29] More recently, the Indian media has also commented on traditional varieties of basmati like 386, 370, 217, and Dehraduni having a much stronger scent or aroma when compared with other varieties like Pusa 1121, a high-yielding variety evolved by the Indian Agricultural Research Institute (IARI). Although Pusa 1121 had grains as long as traditional varieties, it reportedly lacked the scent or aroma characteristic of traditional basmati varieties.[30] Was it justified to classify hybrid and evolved varieties as basmati rice when they lacked some of the most essential features of the rice itself?

Besides the UK, India too was paying close attention to the distinction between traditional varieties, and hybrid and evolved varieties. In January 2003, the ministry of commerce replaced its 1990 rules with the Export of Basmati Rice (Quality Control and Inspection) Rules, 2003. For the first time, the rules linked the definition of basmati rice for export purposes to 11 varieties of basmati rice. Of these 11 varieties, six were traditional, and five were not. One report of the time suggests that the commerce ministry, backed by domestic lobbies, had been trying to convince the European and British authorities to recognize only traditional varieties as genuine basmati rice, and thus offer tariff concessions only to such traditional varieties.[31] Although reasons for the commerce ministry's efforts are not known, attempts can be made to deduce reasons from the context. First, Pakistan grew mostly non-traditional rice varieties, which would automatically be disqualified from the preferential tariffs if Europe limited such concessions to only traditional basmati, thus making Indian basmati exports more lucrative. Second, the commerce ministry and older exporters of basmati were, perhaps, genuinely concerned about the basmati brand being diluted by hybrid and evolved varieties. Third, basmati rice had always been regarded as a premium product, due to which market economics required that the supply of the product had to be controlled. This was because oversupply could reduce the price of basmati, which would then lead to the product losing premium status. Since traditional varieties were always low-yielding, the price would remain under control if basmati's definition was confined to traditional varieties. Including hybrid and evolved varieties within the definition would increase the global supply of the rice substantially, since these varieties were usually bred to increase yield tremendously.

In November 2003, the EU declared that from 1 January 2004, it would restrict the tariff concession of EUR 250 only to traditional basmati varieties.[32] There was some complex reasoning for this. After tariff concessions had been announced in 1996, basmati rice exports from India and Pakistan went up significantly.[33] The increase in exports led to a drop in prices, and especially lowered the value of hybrid and evolved varieties. Recall that tariff concessions had been granted to basmati in the first place because basmati prices had been excessively high. Basmati would not likely have found a market in Europe had its prices remained at those levels, and would not have threatened the domestic agricultural industry either. But with hybrid and evolved varieties now entering the market, and prices automatically falling, the tariff concessions no longer made any sense, because the subsidized prices of basmati would now become significantly lower than other varieties, thus giving basmati an unfair advantage in the market. Additionally, aromatic varieties from other parts of the world, such as Thai jasmine, were not recipients of such concessions, giving basmati a further advantage.[34] Thus, Europe decided that it should withdraw the concessions for these non-traditional basmati varieties selling at considerably lower prices, and limit the concessions to only traditional varieties.

The European regulation on withdrawing concessions led to panic in Pakistan because most of the country's basmati exports were of the non-traditional 'Super Basmati' variety.[35] In contrast, most Indian basmati exports were of the traditional variety.[36] The only Indian variety to be hit by Europe's decision was Pusa Basmati-I which was becoming increasingly popular with farmers because it was a high-yielding variety. But protests by both India and Pakistan led to the EU's decision being withdrawn. Instead, by August 2004, Europe agreed to expand the definition of basmati rice to include two non-traditional varieties, that is, Super Basmati and Pusa Basmati.[37] Hybrid varieties that lacked a traditional variety as a 'parent' were excluded from this list of basmati rice that could be imported into the EU. Following previous procedure, export consignments had to be accompanied by a certificate of authenticity from recognized agencies in India and Pakistan. The EU now also required both countries to create DNA analysis systems for basmati exports.

Back in India, the definition of basmati rice was yet to be entirely resolved. Starting from 2005, the Indian scientific establishment began pressurizing the government to widen the definition of basmati rice in the Export of Basmati Rice (Quality Control and Inspection) Rules, 2003 to include a new variety, Pusa 1121, which they claimed was superior to Pusa Basmati-I, in terms of both length of grain and aroma. Unlike Pusa Basmati-I, which had one traditional variety as a parent, Pusa 1121 had a traditional variety only as its grandparent.[38] One rice scientist at IARI, the organization that had developed Pusa 1121, reportedly said, '[i]n improved varieties, the rice grain may not have the same characteristics as the one notified. The exporters of the improved varieties will not get the same advantages like other Basmati exporters and the benefits cannot be given back to the farmers. That ends Basmati improvement programmes'.[39] Supporting the scientific community, the Director-General of the Indian Council of Agricultural Research (ICAR) wrote to the commerce secretary, '[c]onsidering the scientific viewpoint in national interest and benefit of Indian farmers, I would like to request the commerce ministry to ... modify the definition of evolved basmati and ... remove the embargo of one traditional parent clause in the proposed modification to facilitate improvement in basmati to effectively compete internationally'.[40] While the scientists tried to address the domestic definition of basmati, they did not appear to realize that lucrative export destinations like Europe would not extend duty waivers to Pusa 1121 because it did not meet the European definition for eligible non-traditional varieties (that is, with one parent as a traditional variety, which Pusa 1121 was not). They also failed to realize the economic impact of boosting basmati rice production on existing prices of basmati.

Eventually, in 2007, the ministry of commerce left the decision on expanding the definition of basmati to the ministry of agriculture.[41] By 2005, Pusa 1121 had already been identified as a notified rice variety under the Seeds Act (which meant that its seeds would now be regulated under that law).[42] It took until May 2008 for the ministry of agriculture to further notify Pusa 1121 as basmati rice.[43] In its notification of 29 October 2008, however, the ministry introduced a restrictive clause by requiring that the notified variety of Pusa 1121 in the Seeds Act, 1966, would be applicable only to 'Delhi, Punjab and Haryana'.[44] These geographic boundaries were possibly justified by the ministry because farmers in Karnataka and Andhra Pradesh, thousands of kilometres away from traditional basmati-growing areas, had also begun growing Pusa 1121.[45]

The inclusion of Pusa 1121 into the definition of basmati rice did not go down well with Pakistan due to fears that India's output would now increase.[46] The Pusa 1121 variety did well in the export markets,[47] earning significant revenue, but questions remain on whether including such high-yielding varieties will eventually destroy the basmati brand built on the basis of traditional varieties. Is it possible that consumers may eventually forget that basmati rice was known for its unique fragrance and taste, and not just the size of the grain?

These are difficult questions to answer, which the government got a second chance to address, when the process of registering basmati rice as a GI began.

The Origins of Geographical Indications

Efforts to define basmati rice in Indian trade regulations sought to ensure quality exports of basmati rice from India. But the many complaints of adulteration suggest that early attempts at quality control in India were less than effective. While trade regulations are useful in maintaining the distinctiveness of the basmati brand, they do not help stop the misuse of the brand either in India or abroad. Possible misuse could happen by non-basmati rice traders seeking to use a 'basmati-type' name to sell goods which are not basmati rice or equally problematically, by seeking to register the phrase 'basmati rice' under national laws.

After the 'Texmati' incident in the mid-1990s, the Government of India authorized the Agricultural and Processed Food Products Export Development Authority (APEDA) to defend the basmati rice brand across the world and in India. As per data provided by APEDA to the authors in response to an RTI application in 2012,[48] APEDA instituted 211 trademark actions in 55 countries across six continents, as well as 352 trademark actions in India, to protect against the wrongful registration of trademarks consisting of 'basmati'. Nearly all these cases were by way of oppositions filed before trademark registries across the world, at the time of filing of trademark applications. The information provided by APEDA reveals that several of these cases led to the blocking of trademark applications that incorporated the word 'basmati' or similar-sounding names. On many occasions, the trademark applicant simply surrendered the trademark application once APEDA filed an opposition, while in some other instances, APEDA obtained undertakings or clarifications from the applicants that the trademark would be used to sell only 'basmati rice from India/Pakistan'. But APEDA was not universally successful. Its oppositions, for instance, failed in Angola, the Benelux countries, Czech Republic, Denmark, Egypt, France, Greece, Jordan, New Zealand, Oman, and Yemen.

In Greece, it fought RiceTec over a trademark application for 'Texmati' all the way till its Supreme Court, and eventually lost.[49] In Egypt and Oman, APEDA lost oppositions against trademark applications for the phrase 'basma' because the word has a different meaning in Arabic. Most of the 352 trademark oppositions filed in India are still pending due to the slow pace of the Indian Trademark Registry, although in some cases, trademark applicants abandoned their applications after APEDA filed its opposition. One thing stands out in the list provided by APEDA, though, which is the absence of any *offensive* trademark action. In other words, there does not seem to be proof of APEDA having sued an Indian or foreign company for misusing the basmati brand to *sell* rice that was not 'basmati rice'. It is possible that APEDA was struggling to file such actions because it had not yet registered the 'basmati' mark under Indian or foreign IP laws. In this sense, APEDA was following only a defensive course of action. A defensive strategy includes not only trademark oppositions, but also exclusivity over the brand name by registering it under domestic IP laws.

In India, there are two IP laws which can offer exclusivity over the use of names. The first is trademark law and the second is a new law to protect GIs. India has had trademark laws since 1889 when the Merchandise Marks Act was enacted. This was then replaced by the Trade Marks Act, 1940 (which was the first law to allow for *registration* of trademarks) which was replaced by the Trademarks and Merchandise Marks Act, 1958, which was also repealed and replaced by the Trade Marks Act, 1999. Under the Trade Marks Act, 1999, once a trademark is registered, the owner of that mark can sue and seek an injunction and damages against any person using a similar or same mark for the same class of goods or services. The main objective of trademark law is to inform the consumer of the origin or source of particular goods or services. Normally, trademark law does not guarantee the *quality* of goods. However, Indian trademark law also has the concept of a 'certification trade mark'. This type of mark allows a proprietor to claim a trademark which certifies the *quality* of the goods or services in respect of origin or other characteristics. One example of an Indian certification trademark in relation to an agricultural product is that of 'Darjeeling Tea'. The Tea Board of India protected the name 'Darjeeling Tea' and logo (the silhouette of a lady smelling two leaves and a bud, embedded in a circular frame) as certification trademarks in India, the US, and the UK decades ago. There is an elaborate testing mechanism to ensure that tea certified as Darjeeling Tea meets the standards set by the Tea Board. Protection is also limited to teas grown, cultivated, or produced in one of the 87 tea gardens in Darjeeling district in the eastern Indian state of West Bengal. Like 'Darjeeling Tea', it could have been possible to protect 'basmati rice' as a certification trademark, but this was never done.

The second type of IP law in India to protect names of products that owe their unique properties to a specific geographical location is the Geographical Indications of Goods (Registration and Protection) Act, 1999, ('the GI Act'). In modern law, GIs are understood as indicators or designations that are appended to the names of goods. The specifics of the law vary from country to country, but it is generally accepted that GI is an umbrella term which refers to the fact that the goods are of a certain quality and possess characteristics that are a direct outcome of the geographical environment, including natural and human factors.[50]

The origin of GIs as a separate law can be traced to Europe. The chain of events leading to a GI law in Europe, started with an enthusiastic viniculturist in the town of Roquemaure in the region of Lirac, on the western side of the southern Rhône Valley in France, known for its rosés and reds, having cultivated and produced wines for several centuries. The viniculturist's friend from across the Atlantic sent some American grapevines by steamship in the mid-1800s.[51] Little did the French farmer know that the vines carried with them the deadly, fast-multiplying Phylloxera pest. Over the next few years, the pest completely destroyed most local vineyards and the local wine industry in what came to be known as the Great French Wine Blight. One version blames the epidemic on the invention of the steamship itself, suggesting that the pests survived because steamships were faster than the forms of transportation previously used.[52] With their livelihoods at risk, local farmers devised new botanical techniques of grafting pest-resistant American grapevines onto native vines. As a result, the farmers could 'reconstitute' their vineyards and develop the produce that is consumed to this day. But the original plants vanished with this reconstitution, and farmers could now pass off wines as belonging to a certain region, even if the plants from which they originated came from elsewhere.[53]

The wrongly-labelled wines led to a public outcry over consumer fraud (and even threats to public health), after which the French government passed a law in 1905. This law sought to identify wines belonging to a defined geographical area, and to prevent misuse of denominations or 'appellations of origin'. But the law indicated only the geographical region from which a wine emerged, and referred to nothing else, such as methods of production. To address this, another law came in 1919, under which the appellation of origin became a collective right of producers in the area, which could neither be trademarked nor become generic. The law made the courts responsible for determining the area and methods of production. The area would be defined by geographical boundaries, and the methods of production had to be 'local, fair and constant'.[54] But handing this over to courts proved to be another problem, as courts were ill-equipped to understand methods of production.[55]

Acknowledging that the institutional set-up had to change, in 1935, appellation d'origine contrôlée (AOCs) were created, where agricultural products, whether unprocessed or processed, would be formally identified in connection with their authenticity and geographical origins. The administrative and legal affairs of AOCs were handed to the *Institut national de l'origine et de la qualité* (or, the National Institute of Origin and Quality) in France. The institute, better known by its acronym INAO, exists even today, as a French public sector body under the ministry of agriculture, and is responsible for regulating domestic agricultural products. A definition for 'appellation of origin' came only in a 1966 law, which amended the 1919 law. 'Appellation of origin' was defined as 'the geographical name of a country, region, or locality, which serves to designate a · product originating therein, the quality and characteristics of which are due to the geographical environment, including natural and human factors'.[56] For many decades, AOCs could be used only in connection with wines and spirits. In 1990, the scope of the law was expanded to include other agricultural products.[57]

In 1992, AOCs were harmonized across Europe using the French system as its basis. This was done through the European regulation on the protection of GIs and designations of origin for agricultural products and foodstuff.[58] Eventually, this system was replicated globally through TRIPS, which was a part of the Marrakesh agreement of 1994 that created the WTO. The issue of GIs was specifically incorporated in TRIPS as a result of a demand from the Europeans, primarily because Europe has several wines, spirits, cheese, and other agricultural products that owe their quality to the geographical location of their production. Champagne is one of the most popular examples of a European GI, and its uniqueness is attributed to various factors such as the soil and climate at the Champagne vineyards. During the TRIPS negotiations, GIs were a hot topic for disagreement between the developed countries themselves. Jayashree Watal, who represented India in the TRIPS negotiations, describes the debate, in her book, as one between the 'old world' and 'new world'.[59] Europe was the 'old world', which had developed an enormous goodwill for a range of wines, spirits, cheese, and other agricultural products. The 'new world' comprised countries like the US, Canada, and Australia, which had developed a local industry that liberally used famous European GIs with the suffix of 'type' or 'style'.

Geographical indications remained a bone of contention between the US and EU even after signing the WTO Agreement. The US filed a complaint before the WTO Dispute Settlement Body (DSB) alleging that EEC No. 2081/92 (on protection of GIs) was in violation of TRIPS because it allegedly required foreign countries to adopt a system for GI protection that was equivalent to that in Europe. Such a system, the US argued, treated foreign GI applicants differently from domestic GI applicants within Europe and was, therefore, in violation of the national treatment principle embodied in TRIPS, which principle forbids members of the WTO from discriminating between domestic and foreign IP owners. The DSB constituted a panel to hear the dispute in 2004, and in its report made publicly available on 15 March 2005, the panel agreed with the US that several requirements of the European regulation were in violation of TRIPS.[60] This ruling forced Europe to change its law. The new EC regulations made it possible for GI applicants from non-European countries, to seek GI protection in Europe even if their home countries did not provide for a European-style GI legislation. As a result, countries like the US have not enacted a separate law to protect GIs, and instead, allow for such protection as trademarks, collective trademarks, or certification trademarks under its conventional trademark law. The USPTO justifies the advantage of protecting GIs under existing trademark law thus:

> Protecting GIs as trademarks, collective or certification marks employs the existing trademark regime, a regime that is already familiar to businesses, both foreign and domestic. Moreover, no additional commitment of resources by governments or taxpayers (for example, personnel or money) is required to create a new GI registration or protection system. A country's use of its existing trademark regime to protect geographical indications involves the use only of resources already committed to the trademark system for applications, registrations, oppositions, cancellations, adjudication, and enforcement.[61]

Policymaking in India was unfortunately not as nuanced as in the US. In 1999, when introducing the Geographical Indications of Goods (Registration and Protection) Bill in Parliament, the government justified the need for such a law on the ground that 'there is no codified law for [the] registration and protection of the geographical indication of goods'.[62] The minister introducing the Bill in the Rajya Sabha said: 'Some limited protection is available under the common law. There is also some protection under the Trade and Merchandise Marks Act of 1958, but there is no direct legal protection. The proposed legislation seeks to provide for registration and better protection of geographical indication of goods in India'.[63] However, this was not true, because, as explained earlier, GIs could have been protected under conventional trademark law. Neither the Indian government nor the Parliament seems to have assessed the need to introduce a new, separate legislation on GIs after thoroughly examining the alternatives that were already available. As a result, India has been saddled with a complex, technical, procedure-laden law, which, in over a decade of implementation has diverted resources into the creation of a new registry, with its attendant limitations and challenges.

The Basmati GI Applications

Although the GI Act was passed by Parliament and enacted in 1999, it was notified into law only in 2003. The first GI application was filed within weeks of the law coming into existence, on 15 September 2003.[64] This application was for Darjeeling Tea, filed by the Tea Board of India. For several months subsequently, the GI application process remained in the teething stage. Applicants for GI applications numbered 1 to 13 ranged from government agencies (the Tea Board of India, and the Karnataka Silk Industries Corporation Limited) to societies, associations, and foundations, representing different interest groups. According to the GI Act, any association, organization, or authority representing producers of the goods in question can apply for a GI. As a result, interest groups were built around goods that were potential GIs to qualify as applicants under law. Usually, a GI applicant would have first-mover advantage over other competing associations. Producers who did not join an association initially would thus have to combine resources with the first applicant to obtain the benefits that would follow from a registered GI.

By August 2004, in the agreement in the form of an exchange of letters between the EC and India accompanying the 2004 European regulations,[65] the EC effectively said that basmati was a GI and should be protected as such. Further to these developments, India obviously had to take action to protect basmati as a GI in its own jurisdiction. Thus, an application had to be made before the Indian registry. The question was: Who would file the application? This was a particularly tricky question because it involved hundreds, and potentially thousands, of basmati-growing farmers across north India.

The Heritage Application

The 14th application to be filed before the GI Registry on 19 August 2004 was to register 'basmati rice' as a GI, by an NGO called the Heritage Foundation. The application was doomed to failure from the beginning because of the applicant's tenuous link to the main stakeholders in the basmati rice industry. Like any other form of IP, a GI can be registered and owned only by a person or a group of persons who are producers of the goods in questions. The Heritage Foundation was not formed by any of the key stakeholders in the basmati rice industry such as the farmers, millers, or traders. Instead, the six-page-long statement of case, filed by the NGO before the GI

Registry, claimed that all basmati rice farmers would automatically become members of the NGO, and that once the GI was registered in the NGO's name, the benefits of the registration would automatically flow to these members. The application did not provide any details on its founding members or the list of its members at the time of filing the application before the GI Registry.

Given the vagueness of the GI application filed by the Heritage Foundation, the GI Registry should have rejected the application in a few months. Instead, it took the GI Registry six years and four meetings of a specially constituted consultative group before the Registrar of GIs to finally refuse the Heritage Foundation the GI application for basmati rice. The order of refusal acknowledged that the application had been delayed by more than five years 'for numerous reasons', but also expressed officious annoyance at the 'countless deficiencies and defects' in the application. The main ground of rejection listed in the Registrar's order of 16 July 2010, was the fact that the Heritage Foundation did not 'adequately represent the interest of all producers (farmers, millers, traders, and exporters spread across the entire Basmati Rice territory) which is the essential requirement for registration' under the GI Act.[66] The Heritage Foundation did not contest the Registrar's order before the Intellectual Property Appellate Board (IPAB).

The APEDA Application

The focus now shifted to another application for 'basmati rice' pending before the GI Registry, filed by APEDA in November 2008. As explained earlier, APEDA is a statutory authority functioning under the ministry of commerce and industry, which has been at the forefront of defending the misuse of the basmati name in India and other countries. Claiming that the aromatic rice was 'an iconic heritage of India which needs to be preserved in the national interest', the application sought to protect the interests of stakeholders, identified to include farmers, millers, traders, exporters, and importers; and to protect consumers against deception and acts of unfair trade competition.[67]

There are three important questions regarding APEDA's GI application that strike at the core of the GI debate. The first was whether APEDA actually represented the interests of the 'producers' of basmati rice; the second was the characteristics of the basmati grain and the varieties of basmati that would be included in APEDA's definition; and the third was the question of the geographical areas in which basmati was grown.

THE FIRST QUESTION: DID APEDA REPRESENT THE
INTERESTS OF ALL PRODUCERS OF 'BASMATI RICE'?

According to its application, APEDA's locus standi (or, the legal right) to file this application came from its statutory powers, as well as its proactive attempts to protect the basmati name in different parts of the world. In 1986, APEDA was established by law for the development and promotion of exports of specific agricultural and processed food products. Its statutory powers changed around the same time as its basmati GI application was filed. Until the APEDA (Amendment) Act, 2009, was passed, APEDA did not have an express mandate to protect IP in agricultural products. The amendment in 2009 introduced a clause that stated: '10A. Without prejudice to any law for the time being in force, it shall be the duty of the Authority to undertake, by such measures as may be prescribed by the central government for registration and protection of the Intellectual Property rights in respect of Special products in India or outside India'. These 'special products' were listed in a separate schedule. At the time of its enactment, the schedule contained only one item—'basmati rice'. Through this legislative change, APEDA claimed the legal authority and mandate to protect and enforce all rights in basmati.

But did the amendment in 2009 actually mean that APEDA could file a GI application in its own name, or was it supposed to take steps to assist producers of basmati rice to form an association for protecting basmati? This is relevant because although the APEDA Act was amended, Section 11 of the GI Act remained the same, allowing only 'any association of persons or producers or any organization or authority established by or under any law for the time being in force representing the interest of the producers of the concerned goods' to file GI applications. While APEDA's efforts to defend the basmati trademark over more than a decade were commendable, was it enough to qualify the organization as 'representing the interest of the producers' of basmati rice? Or did APEDA actually have to be under the 'effective control' of the producers of basmati rice? As per the APEDA Act, its membership consists of Members of Parliament (MPs), central government appointees representing various ministries, central government appointees representing states and union territories, central government appointees representing scientific research bodies, central government appointees representing various industries (such as fruits and vegetable products; meat, poultry and dairy products; other Scheduled or Special products, including basmati; and so on), and central government appointees representing specialists . in the field of agriculture, economics, and so on. This membership pattern clearly shows that the organization is under the control of the central government. There is no provision for representation of the farmers, millers, and traders of basmati rice, who could be classified as the producers of basmati rice. In such a case, could APEDA said to be actually representing the interests of the producers of basmati rice?

In contrast, GIs for Champagne and Scotch Whisky are protected by institutions that function under the democratic control of the main stakeholders. The Scotch Whisky Association (SWA), which owns the Scotch Whisky GI, is a company limited by guarantee comprising 55 members made up of Scotch Whisky distillers, blenders, bottlers, and brand owners.[68] The SWA is privately funded and under the effective control of the producers of Scotch Whisky. Another interesting model of GI ownership is the Comité Interprofessionnel du vin de Champagne (CIVC), which owns the Champagne GI in India. The CIVC is a public service body created by an Act of the French Parliament, to manage, promote, and protect the interests of persons involved in the production of wines sold under the Champagne GI. The law requires all the vine growers of the Champagne region (about 15,000), and all the Champagne houses (about 140), to mandatorily subscribe to the CIVC for a fee. The CIVC itself does not manufacture any product, but operates as an administrative authority that takes decisions relating to its members, and it relies on the financial contributions from its members to finance its activities. Its responsibilities include managing and defending the rights in the Champagne GI against abuse in France and overseas.[69] The decision-making bodies in the CIVC are made up of an equal number of representatives of vine growers and Champagne houses. Thus, although the CIVC was created through an Act of the French Parliament, it was designed in a manner which ensures that it is under the control of the Champagne industry. Both the SWA and CIVC are ideal examples of institutions that actually represent producers, because they are under the *effective control* of producers.

The standing of APEDA to file the GI application for basmati rice did come under challenge in a series of oppositions filed by rice producers from the state of Madhya Pradesh after they discovered that APEDA's application had excluded that state from the list of basmati-growing regions. The final order of the GI Registry is not very clear on the arguments raised by Madhya Pradesh, but the order does say that the opponents from the state argued that APEDA represented only exporters and not producers of basmati rice.[70] The Registrar dismissed this on the ground that since APEDA was established by law, it was in effect an 'authority established by the law' as defined in Section 11 of the GI Act. This reasoning ignores the fact that the language of Section 11 requires that the authority established by law represent the interests of the producers. In APEDA's case, the organization has no representation from the farmers, traders, or millers of basmati rice and cannot, therefore, be said to be representing the interests of the producers of basmati rice. One reason why the GI Registry held in favour of APEDA on this point could be that the GI Registry, since its inception, had been registering state-run institutions as proprietors of GIs, even though these institutions had absolutely no relation to the producers of the goods in question.

A brief study of the first 200 applications filed before the GI Registry by the authors revealed that public authorities were listed as applicants in over half of the cases. There is the peculiar case of the Central Leather Research Institute (located in Chennai, Tamil Nadu, that forms part of the pan-Indian Council of Scientific and Industrial Research (CSIR)) filing for handcrafted leather chappals from Kolhapur in Maharashtra, situated nearly a thousand kilometres away. The Anand Agricultural University has applied and been granted protection for a wheat variety (Bhalia wheat), and the Kerala Agricultural University was granted a GI for Central Travancore jaggery. A university applying for IP protection is not uncommon, but one would expect such protection to be restricted to patents, and associated rights, that are directly linked to research output. But claiming to step into the shoes of a producer, as an applicant for GI protection is expected to be, is anomalous behaviour for a research institute, unless mandates for such institutes extend to commercial production, marketing, and sale. The list goes on: Kancheepuram silks have been registered by the department of handlooms and textiles of the state government of Tamil Nadu; and Madhubani paintings have been registered by the director of industries, department of industries of the state government of Bihar. Over a dozen GIs have been registered by the development commissioner (handicrafts), under the ministry of textiles of the central government alone, including 'Coconut Shell Crafts of Kerala', 'Temple Jewellery of Nagercoil', 'Kathputlis of Rajasthan', 'Leather Toys of Indore', and 'Bagh Prints of Madhya Pradesh'. Effectively, the development commissioner, with its office located in Udyog Bhavan in the heart of Lutyens' Delhi, has registered GIs for handicrafts spanning the length and breadth of the country. Since the GI Act permits the producers of the underlying products to apply for protection, the only manner in which the development commissioner could have filed these applications was if it claimed to have been representing the interests of the producers of these handicrafts. Does the development commissioner for handicrafts, or indeed, do any of these public authorities, actually have the legal standing to represent such interests? Besides questions of legal standing, there are also ethical concerns—can an artificial body created by the state take over the rights of ownership that justly belong to communities of artisans or farmers? More importantly, GIs are community rights carefully nurtured over years, with a conscious effort to cultivate and maintain a certain standard and quality. But in these cases, the state has abruptly entered the picture, and taken control over private enterprise. By blessing such applications with registrations, the GI Registry has in effect nationalized GIs of several communities in traditional arts and agriculture. In doing so, it may have deprived these communities of the opportunity to build democratic forms of ownership over the goodwill constructed by their ancestors in relation to these GIs. When the GI Registry's decision in the opposition against APEDA's basmati application was appealed to the IPAB, the tribunal upheld the GI Registry's decision.[71] An appeal against the IPAB's order is pending before the Madras High Court.

THE SECOND QUESTION: THE CHARACTERISTICS OF BASMATI GRAIN AND VARIETIES OF BASMATI THAT WOULD BE RECOGNIZED WITHIN THE DEFINITION OF BASMATI IN THE GI APPLICATION

As mentioned earlier, the definition of basmati rice under the Basmati Grading Rules, 1979, and the now repealed Export of Basmati Rice (Inspection Rules), 1980 and the Basmati Rice (Quality Control and Inspection) Rules, 1990, was limited to two critical issues, that is, physical characteristics, such as the length of the grain (6 millimetre), a length/breadth ratio of 3, and a natural fragrance that was characteristic of basmati rice in both a raw and cooked state. The APEDA GI Application retained 'aroma' as one of the characteristics that would be required. The physical characteristics requirement was also retained, but the basmati rice would now have to be longer. Unlike the previous regulations which required the length of the grain to be 6 millimetre, APEDA's application now required the length of the grain to be 6.61 millimetre. It is odd that requirements with respect to physical characteristics of the grain were changed in this manner. If the length of 6 millimetre was enough to qualify as basmati in 1979, why did this requirement increase by 0.61 millimetre in 2008?

The second issue, closely related to the qualitative characteristics of basmati grain, is the type of basmati variety that is grown. As explained earlier, the issue of variety was central to several debates of classification of basmati in both Europe and India because the variety of basmati directly impacts the quality and quantity of basmati. Just as the Europeans did not want to classify non-traditional varieties as basmati for the purpose of tariff concessions, similarly there was resistance in India to include Pusa 1121 within the definition of basmati.

Given the past controversies on the issue of varieties, one would have expected APEDA to close the controversy by clearly mentioning, in the GI application, the varieties of basmati that would be recognized within the definition of basmati. Illustratively, the GI application for Champagne filed by the CIVC specifies only five varieties of grapes that can be used in the production of Champagne: Pinot Noir, Petit Meunier, Chardonnay, Arbanne, and Petit Meslier. There was precedent to this effect in India too, in the Basmati Rice (Quality Control and Inspection), Rules 2003, which recognized only 11 varieties of basmati. Surprisingly, APEDA did not take this approach. Instead of mentioning the specific varieties of basmati in the GI application, APEDA left the issue in the hands of agencies which are entirely outside its control. The GI application states it will abide by the standards prescribed in an office memorandum issued by the department of agriculture and cooperation on 29 May 2008.[72] This memorandum states that after a meeting with the department of commerce, a reference was made to the Central Sub-committee on Crop Standards Notification and Release of Varieties for Agricultural Crops constituted by the Central Seed Committee established under the Seeds Act, 1966, to define the standards and delineate the qualifications of the rice varieties to qualify as basmati. The standards and qualifications laid down by the Central Seed Committee for basmati are not static, for it leaves room for new varieties of basmati to be recognized. In order to be recognized as basmati, a variety would have to go through the National Basmati Trials (NBTs) conducted under the aegis of the National Agricultural Research System (NARS) administered by ICAR, state agricultural universities (SAUs), and various other government and higher education agencies. They will also have to meet set norms on length of grain, length-breadth ratio of grain, among others. Once released in the market, these new varieties could be grown in only the areas designated in the GI application in order to qualify for the basmati tag. This arrangement is problematic because APEDA as the proprietor of the GI should have control over the process of designating new basmati varieties since the issue of variety is crucial to both quality and price. If Indian scientists continue to develop new, higher-yielding varieties, at the cost of quality, then there is a real possibility of hurting the basmati brand.

In the opposition before the GI Registry, the opponents from Madhya Pradesh did not challenge these defining features of basmati, preferring instead to argue that the basmati grain produced by them met the physical and qualitative characteristics laid down in APEDA's GI application.

THE THIRD QUESTION: THE GEOGRAPHICAL AREA
WITHIN WHICH BASMATI CAN BE GROWN

The issue of geography is at the heart of the opposition filed by Madhya Pradesh against APEDA's GI application. As per APEDA's GI application, basmati can be grown only in an area limited to the foothills of the Himalayas in the Indo-Gangetic plains, described in strict cartographical terms, covering regions in the states of Delhi, Haryana, Himachal Pradesh, parts of Jammu and Kashmir, Punjab, Uttarakhand, and parts of Uttar Pradesh. The APEDA application argued that the unique characteristics of basmati rice were attributable to specific soil conditions, weather conditions, and quality of the snow-fed rivers from the Himalayas that flow through these specified regions.

Thus when APEDA's GI application was published in the GI Journal for general information to the public, several farmers and traders from the state of Madhya Pradesh, along with the state government, filed oppositions on grounds that basmati-growing areas of that state were excluded from the geographical areas mentioned in the application. In its defence, APEDA argued that Madhya Pradesh was not a traditional growing area for basmati rice, since it was not located at the foothills of the Himalayas, and also that it did not have the reputation of growing basmati. There was some truth to APEDA's argument since Madhya Pradesh is located more than a thousand kilometres from the Himalayas. But it is also pertinent to point out that the grading rules of 1979 and export rules from 1980 to 2003 that were discussed earlier in this chapter, never specified that basmati rice had to be grown in specific geographical regions. Only in 2003 did the export rules introduce the requirement of growing rice in the Indo-Gangetic plains. Although the opponents from Madhya Pradesh did not make this specific argument (linked to past rules) in the oppositions before the Registry, they did argue that certain regions of Madhya Pradesh were on the Indo-Gangetic plains, and that these regions had the soil and weather conditions specified in APEDA's application for protecting basmati as a GI. Combined with the argument that the rice produced in Madhya Pradesh met the physical characteristics of the grain laid down in the GI application, the opponents from Madhya Pradesh argued that their regions should be included in the list of basmati-growing areas.

In his final order dated 31 December 2013, the Registrar of GIs ordered APEDA to include not only the state of Madhya Pradesh, but also those of Rajasthan and Bihar in the list of basmati-growing areas, because all these states had been identified as basmati-growing areas in previous government reports.[73] However, the Registrar's order failed to explain the definition of basmati as adopted in the government reports which had included Rajasthan, Bihar, and Madhya Pradesh in the list of basmati-growing areas. The order also failed to analyse the vast volumes of evidence filed by either side to support their case. The Registrar's order regarding the inclusion of Madhya Pradesh was partially set aside by the IPAB, on appeal, in a judgment dated 5 February 2016. The IPAB's order was not a complete setback for the opponent because it remanded the case back to the Registrar, ordering him to reassess the evidence on record before passing a final order on whether Madhya Pradesh was to be included in the list of basmati-growing areas.[74] The IPAB's order was later appealed to the Madras High Court, where it is pending adjudication.

* * *

As things stand, basmati is at a very uncertain juncture. Within the territory of India itself, the appeals against the APEDA GI application are likely to eventually reach the Supreme Court. This will not be surprising, given the significant stakes involved in the business of basmati rice.

There is also the issue of dealing with Pakistan's concurrent claim over the basmati GI in international markets like Europe. The last decade has seen several joint attempts by India and Pakistan to coordinate their efforts to jointly protect the basmati brand. However, either due to terrorist attacks or other issues, all attempts at coordination have failed. Instead, basmati-growing associations have litigated against each other in their respective countries. Only time will tell how these countries jointly protect the basmati brand in foreign territories. There is also a possibility that the two countries fail to agree on a common strategy for basmati protection, which may lead to further chaos. A real risk, for instance, may lie in the form of competitors from entirely different jurisdictions. By filing trademark applications for similar sounding names, as a Thai company Siam Grain has done with the mark 'Basmali',[75] companies may be attempting to consciously dilute the basmati brand. This calls for a rethink on how the Indian establishment has tackled basmati, and the urgency in the matter cannot be made more obvious.

Notes

1. Case Details for Trade Mark UK00001081589, available at http://www. ipo.gov.uk/tmcase/Results/1/UK00001081589 (Last visited on 29 March 2015).
2. Historic Case Details for Trade Mark 1081589, available at http://www. ipo.gov.uk/trademark/history/GB50000000001081589.pdf (Last visited on 29 March 2015).
3. See US Patent 5,663,484 (filed 8 July 1994), available at http://patent images.storage.googleapis.com/pdfs/US5663484.pdf (Last visited on 29 March 2015).
4. See US Patent 5,663,484 (filed 8 July 1994), at lines 39–44, Column 40.
5. Bayer Co. v. United Drug Co., 272 F. 505 (S.D.N.Y. 1921).
6. DuPont Cellophane Co. v. Waxed Products Co., (US Court of Appeals for the Second Circuit) 85 F.2d 75 (2d Cir. 1936).
7. Kenneth L. Port, *Foreword: Symposium on Intellectual Property Law Theory*, 68(2) CHI.-KENT. L. REV. 585 (1993).
8. See, for example, Email interview by Amberish K. Diwanji with Robin Andrews, CEO, RiceTec Inc., Rediff, 7 July 1998, available at http://www. rediff.com/business/1998/jul/07rice.htm (Last visited on 20 August 2014), where the CEO of RiceTec argued, among other things, that 'basmati has long been a generic term used throughout the world to describe a class of rice'.
9. Federal Trade Commission, *About the FTC*, available at https://www.ftc. gov/about-ftc (Last visited on 17 August 2016).

10. *Announced Actions for 15 May 2001: Commission Denial of Petition for Rulemaking Proceeding, Federal Trade Commission*, 15 May 2001, available at http://www.ftc.gov/news-events/press-releases/2001/05/announced-actions-may-15-2001 (Last visited on 29 March 2015).

11. *Announced Actions for 15 May 2001*.

12. *Announced Actions for 15 May 2001*.

13. See various office actions of the USPTO, available at https://tsdrsec.uspto.gov/ts/cd/casedoc/sn77906591/OOA20100407062619/download.pdf (U.S. Trademark Application No. 77906591 for Caspian Basmati Rice Aged for), https://tsdrsec.uspto.gov/ts/cd/casedoc/sn77955451/OOA20100621130737/download.pdf (U.S. Trademark Application No. 77955451 for Heritage Basmati Rice), and https://tsdrsec.uspto.gov/ts/cd/casedoc/sn85562997/OOA20120615152930/download.pdf (U.S. Trademark Application No. 85562997 for Kamal Basmati Rice) (Last visited on 29 March 2015).

14. Office Action, Trademark Number: 85562997 (USPTO) (15 June 2012), available at https://tsdrsec.uspto.gov/ts/cd/casedoc/sn85562997/OOA20120615152930/download.pdf (Last visited on 29 March 2015).

15. Office Action, Trademark Number: 77906591 (USPTO) (7 April 2010), available at https://tsdrsec.uspto.gov/ts/cd/casedoc/sn77906591/OOA20100407062619/download.pdf (Last visited on 29 March 2015).

16. According to a UK report, countries such as Australia, Egypt, Thailand, and France also grow 'basmati-type' rice, and could possibly take the lead from the US to officially deem 'basmati' a generic term. See COMMISSION ON INTELLECTUAL PROPERTY RIGHTS, FINAL REPORT, *Chapter 4: Traditional Knowledge and Geographical Indications*, available at http://www.cipr.org.uk/papers/text/final_report/chapter4htmfinal.htm (Last visited on 29 March 2015).

17. Ajay Modi, *Long in Grained Wisdom*, BUSINESS TODAY, 22 December 2013, available at http://www.businesstoday.in/magazine/cover-story/anil-mittal-krbl-played-key-role-in-changing-basmati-trade/story/201070.html (Last visited on 22 April 2016).

18. S.O. No. 1025, THE GAZETTE OF INDIA – Part II sec. 3 (ii), 1086 (19 April 1980).

19. SUBHASH CHANDRA, THE Z FACTOR: MY JOURNEY AS THE WRONG MAN AT THE RIGHT TIME 75–96 (2016).

20. Chand Joshi and Suchitra Behal, *Sinning with Swami*, INDIA TODAY, 21 August 2014, available at http://indiatoday.intoday.in/story/exclusive-information-swami-dhirendra-brahmachari-past/1/435625.html (Last visited on 22 April 2016).

21. Commission Regulation (EEC) No 833/87 laying down detailed rules for the application of Council Regulation (EEC) No 3877/86 on imports of rice of the long-grain aromatic Basmati variety falling within subheading ex 10.06 B I or II of the Common Customs Tariff (23 March 1987), available at http://eur-lex.europa.eu/legal-content/EN/TXT/?uri=CELEX:31987R0833 (Last visited on 22 April 2016).

22. Commission Regulation (EEC) No 833/87.

23. World Trade Review, *India Should Negotiate with EU over Basmati Rice Exports*, 1–15 August 2003, available at http://www.worldtradereview.com/news.asp?pType=N&iType=A&iID=64&siD=8&nID=10246   (Last visited on 22 April 2016).

24. PTI, *EU Reports Basmati Adulteration*, REDIFF.COM, 30 October 2003, available   at   http://www.rediff.com/money/2003/oct/30basmati.htm (Last visited on 22 April 2016).

25. Food Standards Agency, *Survey on Basmati Rice*, Food Survey Information Sheet 47/04 (9 March 2004) (archived content), available at http://tna.europarchive.org/20080609145551/http:/www.food.gov.uk/science/surveillance/fsis2004branch/fsis4704basmati (Last visited on 22 April 2016).

26. Cahal Milmo, *The Heat is On: Investigators Discover that Half the Basmati Rice Sold in Britain is Adulterated*, THE INDEPENDENT, 27 June 2004, available   at   http://www.independent.co.uk/life-style/food-and-drink/news/the-heat-is-on-investigators-discover-that-half-the-basmati-rice-sold-in-britain-is-adulterated-44939.html (Last visited on 22 April 2016).

27. Milmo, *The Heat is On*.

28. Contrarily, according to one description of 'Pusa Basmati Rice', it 'is nearly same or better to traditional basmati rice in terms of its fragrance, alkali content and taste'. See Sunfood Overseas Rice Millers & Exporters, *Basmati Rice*, available at http://sunfood.co.in/?page_id=82 (Last visited on 15 January 2016).

29. PTI, *EU Reports Basmati Adulteration*.

30. Yudhvir Rana, *Traditional Basmati Loses Out to Evolved Strains*, THE TIMES OF INDIA, 30 October 2013, available at http://timesofindia.indiatimes.com/city/chandigarh/Traditional-basmati-loses-out-to-evolved-strains/articleshow/24898221.cms (Last visited on 22 April 2016).

31. Nidhi Nath Srinivas, *Now, India Wants Preferential Access for all Basmati Varieties*, THE ECONOMIC TIMES, 28 November 2003, available at http://articles.economictimes.indiatimes.com/2003-11-28/news/27542077_1_pusa-basmati-varieties-taraori (Last visited on 22 April 2016).

32. See Harish Damodaran, *'EU Policy Will Not Hit Basmati Exports':* *No Need for Immediate Worry, Say Officials*, BUSINESS LINE, 5 July 2003, available at http://www.thehindubusinessline.com/2003/07/06/ stories/2003070601550100.htm (Last visited on 22 April 2016); Harish Damodaran, *EU to Allow Duty-free Import of Brown Basmati*, BUSINESS LINE, 4 August 2004, available at http://www.thehindubusinessline. com/2004/08/07/stories/2004080701321200.htm (Last visited on 22 April 2016).

33. Damodaran, *EU to Allow Duty-free Import of Brown Basmati*.

34. Harish Damodaran, *Basmati Exports May be Hit on New EU Rule:* *Serious Impact on Shipments from Pakistan*, BUSINESS LINE, 30 November 2003, available at http://www.thehindubusinessline.com/2003/12/01/ stories/2003120100500700.htm (Last visited on 22 April 2016).

35. Amir Muhammed and Wajid H. Pirzada, *Pakistan: The Consequences of a Change in the EC Rice Regime*, Managing the Challenges of WTO Participation: Case Study 35 (2005), available at https://www.wto.org/ english/res_e/booksp_e/casestudies_e/casestudies_e.htm (Last visited on 14 May 2016).

36. Damodaran, *Basmati Exports May be Hit on New EU Rule*.

37. Commission Regulation (EC) No 1549/2004 of 30 August 2004 derogating from Council Regulation (EC) No 1785/2003 as regards the arrangements for importing rice and laying down separate transitional rules for imports of basmati rice, Official Journal L 280/13 (31 August 2004), available at http://eur-lex.europa.eu/legal-content/EN/ TXT/?uri=CELEX:32004R1549 (Last visited on 27 July 2014).

38. PTI, *Long Wait for Pusa 1121 before It Gets Basmati Tag*, THE ECONOMIC TIMES, 11 September 2008, available at http://articles.economictimes. indiatimes.com/2008-09-11/news/28486437_1_export-of-non-basmati-rice-traditional-basmati-varieties-seed-act (Last visited on 22 April 2016).

39. Kalyan Ray, *Govt, Experts in 'Define Basmati' Row*, DECCAN HERALD, 30 August 2005, available at http://archive.deccanherald.com/deccanherald/ aug302005/national1538332005829.asp (Last visited on 22 April 2016).

40. Nidhi Nath Srinivas, *IARI Not for Basmati Definition*, THE ECONOMIC TIMES, 25 July 2007, available at http://articles.economictimes. indiatimes.com/2007-07-25/news/27679350_1_basmati-iari-rice (Last visited on 22 April 2016).

41. G. Srinivasan, *Commerce Dept Leaves Basmati Rice Definition to Agri Ministry*, BUSINESS LINE, 14 December 2007, available at http://www. thehindubusinessline.com/todays-paper/commerce-dept-leaves-basmati-rice-definition-to-agri-ministry/article1677421.ece (Last visited on 22 April 2016).

42. Notification S.O. 1566 (E), THE GAZETTE OF INDIA, EXTRAORDINARY, Part II, Section 3, Sub-section (ii) (5 November 2005), available at http://egazette.nic.in/WriteReadData/2005/E_1162_2012_007.pdf (Last visited on 22 April 2016).

43. G. Srinivasan, *Problems Dog Basmati Rice Export Industry*, BUSINESS LINE, 18 August 2008, available at http://www.thehindubusinessline.com/todays-paper/tp-agri-biz-and-commodity/problems-dog-basmati-rice-export-industry/article1634433.ece (Last visited on 22 April 2016).

44. Notification S.O. 2547 (E), THE GAZETTE OF INDIA, EXTRAORDINARY, Part II, Section 3, Sub-section (ii) (29 October 2008), available at http://seednet.gov.in/seedgo/2008/2008-2547.pdf (Last visited on 22 April 2016).

45. G. Srinivasan, *Pusa 1121 Gets Notified as Basmati Rice*, BUSINESS LINE, 4 November 2008, available at http://www.thehindubusinessline.com/todays-paper/tp-agri-biz-and-commodity/pusa-1121-gets-notified-as-basmati-rice/article1640491.ece (Last visited on 22 April 2016).

46. PTI, *Entry of New Basmati Variety Angers Pakistan*, THE ECONOMIC TIMES, 25 November 2008, available at http://articles.economictimes.indiatimes.com/2008-11-25/news/27696360_1_pusa-basmati-aroma-and-elongation (Last visited on 22 April 2016).

47. Prabha Jagannathan, *Pusa Buffer Helps Indian Basmati Deflect Pak Punch*, THE ECONOMIC TIMES, 20 June 2009, available at http://epaper.timesofindia.com/Repository/getFiles.asp?Style=OliveXLib:LowLevelEntityToPrint_ET&Type=text/html&Locale=english-skin-custom&Path=ETD/2009/06/20&ID=Ar00701 (Last visited on 22 April 2016).

48. See Prashant Reddy, *Auditing the Worldwide Litigation Involving 'Basmati' and APEDA*, SPICYIP, 10 March 2013, available at http://spicyip.com/2013/03/auditing-worldwide-litigation-involving.html (Last visited on 22 April 2016), and the accompanying 'List of Cases in Foreign Jurisdictions', available at https://docs.google.com/file/d/0Bxi2TzVXul5ZQ3RPN3RQQ2RsUTg/edit (Last visited on 22 April 2016).

49. Application No. 119706 for the mark Texmati filed by RiceTec was first rejected, but on appeal to the First Instance Court, the mark was allowed to remain on grounds that it was different from Basmati. The subsequent appeal by APEDA to the Supreme Court in Greece was rejected. *See* Reddy, *Auditing the Worldwide Litigation Involving 'Basmati' and APEDA*.

50. World Intellectual Property Organization, *International Treaties and Conventions on Intellectual Property*, at 22, available at http://www.wipo.int/export/sites/www/about-ip/en/iprm/pdf/ch5.pdf (Last visited on 29 March 2015).

51. Beppi Crosariol, *Rhône Valley Wines: From Ruin to Raves for Superb Recent Vintages*, THE GLOBE AND MAIL, 29 November 2012, available at http://www.theglobeandmail.com/life/food-and-wine/wine/rhone-valley-wines-from-ruin-to-raves-for-superb-recent-vintages/article5731459/ (Last visited on 29 March 2015).

52. Wine Portfolio, *Great French Wine Blight*, available at http://www.wineportfolio.com/sectionLearn-Great-French-Wine-Blight.html (Last visited on 29 March 2015).

53. Wine Portfolio, *Great French Wine Blight*.

54. A reference to Article 1 of the 1919 law, as cited by Delphine Marie-Vivien, *The Role of the State in the Protection of Geographical Indications: From Disengagement in France/Europe to Significant Involvement in India*, 13(2) JOURNAL OF WORLD INTELLECTUAL PROPERTY 121(2010).

55. Marie-Vivien, *The Role of the State in the Protection of Geographical Indications*.

56. Article L115-1 of the 'Code de la Consommation', as cited by Marie-Vivien, *The Role of the State in the Protection of Geographical Indications*.

57. Marie-Vivien, *The Role of the State in the Protection of Geographical Indications*.

58. Marie-Vivien, *The Role of the State in the Protection of Geographical Indications*.

59. See JAYASHREE WATAL, INTELLECTUAL PROPERTY RIGHTS IN THE WTO AND DEVELOPING COUNTRIES 263 (2003).

60. REPORT OF THE PANEL, EUROPEAN COMMUNITIES, PROTECTION OF TRADEMARKS AND GEOGRAPHICAL INDICATIONS FOR AGRICULTURAL PRODUCTS AND FOODSTUFFS, WT/DS174/R, World Trade Organization (15 March 2005), available at https://www.wto.org/english/tratop_e/dispu_e/cases_e/ds174_e.htm (Last visited on 15 January 2016).

61. *Geographical Indication Protection in the United States*, United States Patent and Trademark Office, available at http://www.uspto.gov/sites/default/files/web/offices/dcom/olia/globalip/pdf/gi_system.pdf (Last visited on 15 January 2016).

62. *Rajya Sabha Debates* (16 December 1999), at 312.

63. *Rajya Sabha Debates* (16 December 1999), at 312.

64. Application No. 1 for 'Darjeeling Tea' (word) filed by Tea Board on 27 October 2003, available at http://ipindiaservices.gov.in/GirPublic/ViewApplicationDetails.aspx?AppNo=1&index=0&pIndex=0&status=0 (Last visited on 18 August 2016) and Application No. 2 for Darjeeling Tea (word) filed by Tea Board on 27 October 2003, available at http://

ipindiaservices.gov.in/GirPublic/ViewApplicationDetails.aspx?AppNo=
2&index=0&pIndex=0&status=0 (Last visited on 18 August 2016).

65. Agreement in the form of an Exchange of Letters between the European
Community and India pursuant to Article XXVIII of the GATT 1994
relating to the modification of concessions with respect to rice provided
for in EC Schedule CXL annexed to the GATT 1994, Official Journal
L 279/17, available at http://eur-lex.europa.eu/legal-content/EN/
TXT/?uri=CELEX:32004D0617 (Last visited on 27 July 2014).

66. Order of Grounds for refusal dated 16 July 2010 in respect of GI
Application No. 14.

67. Application No. 145, Statement of Case, filed by APEDA, GI Registry,
available at http://ipindiaservices.gov.in/GI_DOC/145/145%20-%20
Statement%20of%20Case%20-%2026-11-2008.pdf (Last visited on 23
February 2014).

68. GI Application No. 151, ¶ 8.2 (5 January 2009), available at
http://164.100.176.36/GI_DOC/151/151%20-%20Statement%
20of%20Case%20-%2005-01-2009.pdf (Last visited on 23 February 2016).

69. GI Application No. 140, filed by CIVC (29 September 2008), available at
http://164.100.176.36/GI_DOC/140/140%20-%20Statement%20of%20
Case%20-%2029-09-2008.pdf (Last visited on 23 February 2016).

70. Order of the GI Registry in Oppositions TOP 13, 14, 15, 16, 17 and 19,
dated 31 December 2013, GI Registry, available at http://ipindiaservices.
gov.in/GI_DOC/145/145%20-%20GI%20-%20Order%20in%20
TOP%2013,%2014,%2015,%2016,%2017,%2019%20-%2031-12-2013.
pdf (Last visited on 23 February 2014).

71. Order No. 6 of 2016, dated 5 February 2016, IPAB.

72. Office Memorandum, Department of Agriculture and Cooperation (29
May 2008), Annexure-12, GI Application No. 145.

73. Order of the GI Registry in Oppositions TOP 13, 14, 15, 16, 17 and 19.

74. Order 6 of 2016 (IPAB) (unreported, (order passed on 5 February 2016).

75. Tilda Riceland Pvt. Ltd. v. OHIM, Decision of the General Court (Sixth
Chamber), T-136/14 (30 September 2015).

11

OF GODS AND GURUS

Whenever the law has to confront traditional or personal beliefs, people are quick to take umbrage, depending on whose sensibilities are affected. Unsurprisingly, India has been either the arena or a key player in some unique intellectual property (IP) battles in this field in recent times, where interesting questions have been raised. For instance, who has the right to use the names of religious figures in trademarks? Or to whom does the intellectual estate of a spiritual leader belong? Or when does an authority decide that a combination of yoga postures or healing techniques can be legally protected? This chapter discusses some of these issues, representing the challenges that IP law faces in the new age.

The Gods

The prospect of dabbling in the business of religion is attractive to many. Over a century ago, the painter Raja Ravi Varma decided to venture into precisely this business, when he set up his lithography press at Ghatkopar, Bombay (now Mumbai). Varma was a portrait artist from the princely state of Travancore, where he had mastered the art of combining the Indian form with European painting techniques. Besides indulging his various royal patrons, notably in Baroda, he was best known for representations of mythological figures, and gods and goddesses. Anil Relia, an art collector, in his monograph on graphic prints, retells Varma's story.[1] Varma's paintings were wildly popular, and everyone who saw them wanted to own one. To cater to this demand, Varma set up his first printing press, from where, using German machines and technicians, he manufactured exquisite colour reproductions of his own works, for sale in different parts of India. But being an artist and not a businessman, he did not understand the vagaries of the trade, and soon found himself owning a floundering press. In search of profit, he shifted from Bombay to Lonavala, with little success. A year before he died in 1906, Varma sold the press, along with the copyright in 89 of his works to his (former) German business partner, Fritz Schleicher. The German was more astute, driving the press to unprecedented commercial success. At one point in time, every other Indian household was said to own a print of a Ravi Varma painting. Many would make these prints images of worship themselves, placing them in consecrated spaces in their homes, embellishing the pictures with vermillion and sandalwood paste. But, besides those coming from the official press, prints made by other presses were also available in the market. This influx of 'unoffocial' prints had reportedly prompted Varma to approach the Indian National Congress leader Gopal Krishna Gokhale to criminalize 'plagiarism'.[2] (Plagiarism and copyright are often used interchangeably, but are in fact very different concepts, and legal protection has traditionally been offered only to copyright holders under law.) Schleicher, too, complained to the government's legislative department, saying that the 'Ravi Varma Press is suffering a great deal of unfair competition and loss from the absence of a protecting Copyright Act'.[3] India already had a Copyright Act since 1847, and with limited information on Varma's and Schleicher's appeals, it is difficult to understand what their exact demands were. As it turned out, both the Indian artist and the German publisher were apparently unsuccessful in their demands being fulfilled.

Legal encounters with religious symbols have been more frequent in the domain of trademarks than copyrights. An early battleground was the Indo-British textile trade in the late nineteenth and early twentieth centuries.[4] Mills in Great Britain and India competed with each other for newer markets for cloth, and to help consumers identify the provenance of the cloth, they used product labels. Mill cloth would be labelled with trademarks consisting of an ornate rectangular frame with an image from Indian mythology, or British royalty, and so on (some were also adapted from Ravi Varma's paintings). Indian mills quickly caught on, and created their own labels. This competition prompted the Bombay Mill Owners' Association to petition the government in 1877 to introduce a trademark law for India, where marks would be registered within the country itself. When the government was not forthcoming, in 1886, the Bombay Mill Owners' Association defiantly decided to register the marks and labels of different mills in its own books, and resort to arbitration to resolve disputes.[5] Strangely, though the Association's private register of mill labels and trademarks came with the condition that names of gods and goddesses were not registrable.[6]

In the 1930s, deliberations began on creating a consolidated law on trademarks for India. Subbiah Venkateswaran, an examiner in the Patent Office, Calcutta, offered his views in his classic text, 'The Law of Trade and Merchandise Marks in India'.[7] Among others, he discussed the issue of restrictions on registering trademarks. Some conditions for restricting registrations already existed under English trademark law, such as refusing to register marks that were contrary to law or morality or that would otherwise not be entitled to protection in a court of law. Alongside these, he put forward a new ground, that is, the names of deities. But the restriction he proposed was not the outright non-registrability adopted by the Bombay Mill Owners' Association. Instead, Venkateswaran wrote:

> The names of Hindu deities are commonly used in India as trademarks and such marks have been protected by the courts in India. As these names are the common heritage of the country, the question may be raised whether such marks should be registrable under the Indian Act. It may be mentioned in this connection that trade names consisting of the names of gods and goddesses are regarded as non registrable by the Bombay Mill Owners' Association for purposes of registration in their private register. There does not, however, appear to be any need for introducing such a severe restriction on registration under the Indian Act. The names of Hindu gods and goddesses are legion and the adopting of one of these names as a trademark by one person will not unduly restrict the choice by others of this class of names. The same thing applies to the names of mythological persons.[8]

Venkateswaran also observed that associating deities with certain types of trade could 'offend the religious sentiment of the people', and said that no trademark could be granted in respect of beef where the trademark contains the name or pictorial representation of a Hindu deity.[9]

When the new Indian Trademark Act was passed in 1940, the provision dealing with non-registrability of trademarks was practically a reproduction of the 1938 United Kingdom (UK) law on trademarks, but contained an added clause in Section 8(b): 'No trade mark nor part of a trade mark shall be registered which consists of, or contains, any scandalous design, or any matter the use of which would ... (b) be likely to hurt the religious susceptibilities of any class of His Majesty's subjects'. This addition was 'introduced to deal with local conditions'.[10]

A legal provision with similar language can be found in the Indian Penal Code, 1860. Section 295A of the Code was introduced in 1927, criminalizing deliberate and malicious acts intended to outrage religious feelings of any class by insulting its religion or religious beliefs. The provision was introduced after a failed attempt to prosecute the publisher and seller of a controversial pamphlet titled *Rangila Rasula*, which criticized the personal life of Prophet Mohammed. The case had been brought under Section 153A of the Code that criminalized 'promoting enmity between different groups on grounds of religion, race, place of birth, residence, language etc'. At the time, the explanation to this provision (later dropped by amendment in 1961) had allowed for speech that did not have malicious intent.[11] The Lahore High Court decided in *Rajpal v. King Emperor* (1927)[12] that although the pamphlet was a 'scurrilous satire on the founder of the Muslim religion', it was not meant 'to attack the Mahomedan religion as such or to hold Mahomedans as objects worthy of enmity or hatred'. The court's decision did not mitigate the volatile communal situation that had followed the pamphlet's publication. Worried that things could worsen, the National Assembly agreed to accept an earlier version of Section 295A found in the Code today.[13] Were the 'local conditions'[14] referred to in the commentary to the 1940 Indian trademark law an acknowledgement of the 1927 amendment to the Indian Penal Code? The trademark law provision has remained in some form or other for decades, untouched by any government or expert committee. Courts, however, have ventured to understand its true import over the years.

A popular Hindu deity and a frequent subject of dispute in trademark law is the elephant-headed Ganesha. In 1987, one A.T. Raja contended that his religious sentiments were affected by the use of Ganesha's picture on the products sold by Mangalore Ganesh Beedi Works, and approached the court to have the company's trademarks cancelled. The company's main product offering was beedis, which are tendu leaves wrapped around betel nuts and tobacco, thinner than cigarettes, and smoked as substitutes, because they are locally manufactured and cheaper. The Madras High Court, in its 1996 decision,[15] observed that Raja was not an 'aggrieved person' under the law (certain types of legal actions may be instituted only by certain categories of persons), and thus, had no legitimate right to file the suit. In this case, Raja was not 'aggrieved' because he failed to demonstrate that his business would be affected if the company's trademarks remained valid.[16] Despite Raja's lack of rights, the court went on to examine the substantive question of whether the trademarks hurt religious susceptibilities. It noted that Mangalore Ganesh Beedi Works had been using the trademarks uninterruptedly since 1942, and even though 'the vast majority of the population in this country worship Lord Ganesh, none had objected to the use of the mark for over half a century'.[17] (This petition was filed in 1987, which was 45 years after the marks were registered). The court also said that the Hindu religion was 'generous and tolerant and does not easily take offence at the pictorial representation of the Gods or Goddesses who form part of the Hindu Pantheon'.[18] The court then referred to a list issued by the central government of terms and names of persons and mythological figures which could not be registered as trademarks, including Buddha, Sri Ramakrishna, Sri Sarada Devi, the Sikh Gurus, Venkateshwara, and Chhatrapathi Shivaji. Ganesha was not on the list, and therefore, the court concluded that the 'Central Government is apparently of the view that registration of a mark containing the name or pictorial representation of Lord Ganesh is not per se objectionable'.[19] The petition was eventually dismissed, but the court made some sweeping comments about the boundaries between legal and moral sanctity for co-opting certain names and symbols for commercial use:

The use of [the] name though in itself not objectionable, may become objectionable if it is used in relation to goods with which it would be objectionable to associate the name. Though smoking is now recognised as hazardous to health, smoking is not prohibited by the religious doctrines of the Hindus. The reason for that may be that the use of tobacco was discovered long after the founding of the Hindu religion. This is not to say that Hindu religion approves smoking.[20]

In 1993, another person in Uttar Pradesh objected to the same trademarks, claiming in a court[21] that smoking beedi was prohibited and considered a social evil in Hinduism. After beedi packets were used, he said, they were thrown on the roads and stepped upon, and the deity was brought to disrepute. The company said that it could not be responsible for individuals throwing wrappers on streets. If this issue of disposing wrappers was taken to its logical end, the company said, then the use of names or pictures of gods or goddesses on anything except in temples would be effectively disallowed. In its 2005 decision, the Allahabad High Court agreed with the company, observing that the complainant had failed to prove either religious feelings were hurt or beedi-smoking was prohibited in religious scriptures. And Ganesha remained steadfastly stuck on beedi packets.

This fashion of using deities or religious symbols as trademarks has not gone unnoticed by the Trademark Registry. In its manual of practice and procedure,[22] the Registry observes:

such use per se is not regarded by [the] public as offending religious sentiments of any class or section of [the] public. However, such use in relation to certain goods may offend the religious sentiments of the people. For Example, use of names/device of deities or religious heads on footwear will be considered distasteful and will be open to objection. Similarly, use of Hindu gods in respect of Beef or meat products or use of names of Muslim saints for pork products would offend the religious feeling of respective sections of the public to attract the objection under this Section [9(2)(b) of the Trade Marks Act, 1999, according to which a mark may be refused registration if it contains or comprises of any matter likely to hurt the religious susceptibilities of any class or section of the citizens of India].

Many trademark disputes revolve around popular names of deities of the Hindu pantheon, since entrepreneurs, looking to encash on the benevolence of their favourite gods, also prefer to name their businesses after them. One such case involved schools named after the Hindu deity Shri Ram.

A non-profit society was running schools in the national capital region under the name 'Shri Ram School' for several years. In 2014, a new 'ShreeRam World School' came up in the same city. The difference in spelling being inconsequential, the older school took the newer one to court[23] over its choice of name. The newer school tried the 'crowded market' argument. It said that Shri Ram, the Hindu deity, was 'known for learning and teaching and adopted and used by Hindus as their name, part of trading activities, business ventures',[24] and, being widely used, could not be monopolized by any one party.[25] According to the 'crowded market' principle, a mark that is one in a crowd of similar marks used for similar goods or services cannot be considered 'distinctive'. In such a crowd, customers would be wary and not be confused by any two marks, and would exercise discretion in their selection. Further, in a crowded market consisting of similar or 'look-alike' marks, each one is a 'weak' mark, because it cannot prevent any other mark from being used. But the court decided that the original school had managed to demonstrate, through its academic record and popular standing, that it was not merely part of the crowd, but rather, stood out in the crowd. ShreeRam World School lost its rights to use its name, and the issue of the use of religious names in Indian trademark law remained unsatisfactorily addressed.

In 2015, the Supreme Court of India was faced with the question of whether the word 'Ramayan' could be registered under trademark law for the sale of incense sticks and perfumes.[26] The Registrar of Trademarks had originally registered the trademark consisting of the word 'Ramayan' and the device of a 'crown' after dismissing an opposition filed by a competitor. The competitor appealed further, and the Intellectual Property Appellate Board (IPAB) set aside the trademark registration on various grounds without ruling conclusively on the issue of registering the name of a religious book as a trademark. The case was then further appealed to the Supreme Court. In its judgment of October 2015, the Supreme Court held that, '[t]he answer to the question as to whether any person can claim the name of a holy or religious book as a trade mark for his goods or services marketed by

him is clearly "NO"'.[27] Although there were factual grounds for the
court to deny registration to this particular trademark (for example,
other businesses were using similar marks to sell the same goods in
the same areas as the applicant), the judgment failed to provide any
principle of law to support the conclusion that names of religious
books are prohibited from being registered under trademark law,
even if the registration does not hurt any religious sensibilities. The
Supreme Court seems to have kept the door open for the registration
of these marks when it held that the addition of a suffix or prefix to
'Ramayan' may make the mark registrable as a trademark. However,
only time will tell as to how the Trademark Registry applies this
judgment to future trademark applications and whether it will become
more difficult to register religious names as trademarks.

It is a truism that religion today is a business in itself. What,
therefore, happens to the IP that accompanies such 'religious'
businesses? For instance, could a temple trust claim a trademark on
the image of the deity it guarded? This was precisely the question that
came before the Kerala High Court.[28]

The Attukal Bhagavathy temple in Kerala's capital,
Thiruvananthapuram, is dedicated to an avatar of Kannaki, the heroine
of the Tamil epic poem, *Silappadikaram*, who in turn is regarded as
an incarnation of the goddess Parvati. The temple is very popular
with women, with several rituals and ceremonies being observed
particularly by them. The temple's trust obtained a trademark on the
icon of the Attukal deity and an accompanying phrase, in connection
with temple services, social service, welfare services, and cultural
activities. A private citizen, R.S. Praveen Raj, filed a public interest
litigation in 2009 against the trust, arguing that a trademark on a
religious symbol was 'an affront on the faith of devotees, more so when
on such registration the place of worship is reduced to a "business
outfit" engaged in trade and commerce'.[29] By appropriating the
picture of the goddess through the trademark, Raj said the trust would
'seriously and prejudicially interfere with the rights of an individual
devotee', and the trademark would allow the trust to monopolize the
picture, and prevent persons from worshipping the deity themselves,
except with the trust's permission.

The court examined the status of the deity as a legal person, the status of the trust in relation to the deity, and the consequent rights that each—the deity and the trust—had. Temple trusts and the deities they are responsible for are not unfamiliar to Indian courts. Here, a 1925 decision[30] came useful:

A Hindu idol is, according to long established authority, founded upon the religious customs of the Hindus, and the recognition thereof by courts of law, a 'juristic entity'. It has a juridical status with the power of suing and being sued. Its interests are attended to by the person who has the deity in his charge and who is in law its manager with all the powers which would, in such circumstances, on analogy, be given to the manager of the estate of an infant heir. It is unnecessary to quote the authorities; for this doctrine, thus simply stated, is firmly established.

Using these established principles, the court decided that the Attukal idol was a perpetual minor, with the trust being the manager of the estate of the idol. The trust argued that its trademark was only to prevent the use of the picture of the deity for the specific services protected under the registration, and not to restrict devotees from worshipping the deity. In other words, the trust wanted to ensure that no person or body other than the trust itself would be able to offer, for instance, temple services associated with the Attukal temple. The court, too, agreed. Did this, however, mean that no one could open another temple dedicated to Attukal, or distribute prasadam (religious offerings) in the name of that deity? The court did not address this issue satisfactorily.

The petitioner's allegations that, by registering a trademark, the trust had reduced a place of religious worship to a business could not be substantiated. Instead, the court observed that the registration prohibited 'such activity in the name of the deity or the temple by any other and thus restrict[ed] the commercialization of the services offered in the name of the deity'.[31] It also threw out the argument of the trademark alienating devotees of the temple: 'However abstract be spiritual affairs, it would be sailing over the cusp of reason to hold that the registration would alienate the deity from the devotee. Worship is personal and the registration is inconsequential as far as the belief of a devotee is concerned and it has no effect, material or spiritual, on the deity'.[32]

Another dispute arose (and continues to subsist) in connection with a piece of jewellery associated with religious traditions. The Payyannur pavithra mothiram is a spectacularly crafted gold ring, with many gold strands coming together in the shape of a knot, worn when performing rituals for departed souls in the Hindu tradition. A pavithra ring is handed to its purchaser only after its presentation before the local temple. For many generations, this ring's manufacture has been associated with the municipality of Payyannur in northern Kerala. In February 2004, enthused by the (then) new law on geographical indications (GIs), the Payyannur Pavithra Ring Artisans and Development Society (PPRADS) applied to register the Payyannur pavithra ring. It was the sixth application to be made in India after the Geographical Indications of Goods (Registration and Protection) Act, 1999 (the GI Act), came into force. According to the applicants, the local Payyannur temple, after desecration during Tipu Sultan's reign (in the late eighteenth century), was renovated and consecrated again soon after by a priest. This priest apparently entrusted the task of making pavithra rings to a particular family, and the PPRADS was a group of artisans making these rings under the guidance of that family.

This application was challenged in just over a year by another Payyannur jeweller, who said that the pavithra ring had existed well before the temple's desecration, and that the priest in question had handed over the manufacture of the rings to another family, to which the opponent belonged. Claims and counter-claims flew back and forth. Each side tried to influence the decision of the GI Registry, bringing solicitations from the Kerala state government, the central ministry of commerce and industry, and so on. The GI registry issued an order in 2009,[33] but the opponent was unsatisfied. The matter even reached the high court, but was dismissed because another legal remedy was as yet unexplored, that is, the IPAB where appeals against the GI registry ordinarily lie.[34] In its 2012 decision,[35] the IPAB removed the original GI applicant from the register, and returned the file to the GI Registry for fresh consideration, saying that the Registry could, if suitable, register the applicant and the other party as joint proprietors of the GI. Towards this, a fresh GI application for the pavithra ring was filed in 2013.

The GI Registry decided to hand over the decision on both applications (filed in 2004 and 2013) to a consultative group specially constituted for this purpose. The group concluded[36] that Payyannur had different groups of artisans and stakeholders who were neither prepared to unite to form an association nor agreeable to accept a GI registration in favour of the other party. As a result, neither application could fulfil the legal definition of a 'registered proprietor'. Therefore, the consultative group asked the GI Registry to request the Kerala state government to intervene, and unite the producers of the pavithra ring, because until then, neither society nor the artisans' community would benefit. This raises the question, though, as to whether it is the government's task to establish the dubiety or genuineness of one artisan community over another before proceeding to registration, or whether attempts to arbiter a truce between disagreeing factions should take place through some other agency.

At the heart of the debates around the (unsuccessful) Attukal challenge, and the (unresolved) Payyannur pavithra ring GI, lies a fundamental unanswered question—why are people clamouring to obtain these registrations? The law on GI has not been a success in India by any means. While a few hundred products from different parts of the country are now registered as GIs, there is little or no documentation on whether these products have had commercial success after being registered as GIs. Products that have commercially succeeded as GIs are invariably those that were already profitable *before* being registered, such as Darjeeling Tea. The original mandate of GI law was to protect the interests of the communities of producers producing the goods, and to add to their economic prosperity. In the Payyannur pavithra ring case, correctly identifying the producers may help. But how will temples and trusts improve their fortunes through such registrations? Further, if consumers are to be protected from being deceived, and unauthorized use of GIs is to be prevented, other avenues could also have been explored for obtaining the same result. As a form of legal protection in India, GIs remain undeveloped and untested, more so because courts have rarely, if ever, been brought to deliberate on registrations on these grounds. But, besides the courts, surely stakeholders must themselves introspect on the GI system.

The Gurus

India has been home to hundreds of thousands of 'spiritual' teachers and philosophers over the centuries. In the modern era, many have found supporters across the world, while a handful have become extraordinarily popular, earning several new followers every year, regardless of whether they are living or dead. Where the works of such persons remain in copyright, controversy inevitably follows. This is usually because the person, while living, was careless or unclear about how their estate should be handled. Or sometimes, it is because the person handed over the management of their estate to certain individuals who have not managed it in a manner agreeable to other followers. This section discusses the IP issues surrounding the lives and works of some Indian gurus.

At least two cases prompt the theoretical question about the engagement of Indian copyright law with religious works. In these two cases, involving Sri Sri Thakur Anukulchandra Chakraborty (in 1972),[37] and Santhanantha Swamigal of Pudukottai (in 2000),[38] their respective disciples argued that their gurus' teachings and devotional works were not amenable to any exclusive copyright, and that they could use them without violating the law. Courts disagreed in both cases, pointing out that the works were in fact the gurus' original literary works, in which copyright subsisted;[39] in one observation, befittingly noting that '[m]erely because he is a Swamigal having renounced the world, he cannot be compelled to renounce his copyright too'.[40]

Shree Swami Satyanand Ji Maharaj was a spiritual teacher who lived up to the ripe old age of 100.[41] Under his instructions, Satyanand's disciples formed a trust in 1936 in Lahore, in present-day Pakistan, which later moved to New Delhi, with the stated objective of 'propagating his teachings and also printing and publishing of his holy works'.[42] Over the years, the trust printed and published at least 11 books for several decades, distributing them amongst devotees at no profit. In 1994, some devotees fell out, and broke away to form a new trust. The original trust, apprehensive about the intentions of the new trust, 'immediately rushed' to register copyrights for the 11 books. The breakaway trust, worried that the original trust would 'take out an infringement action' against it, if and when the new trust considered publishing any of the 11 books, filed a suit before the Delhi High Court.[43] The court found that the original trust had not, in fact, initiated or threatened to initiate any such infringement action. Instead, a statement issued by the original trust said that it did not object to the publication of the books so long as it was 'not done for profiteering and the works remain exact replica without any alteration, distortion etc'.[44] The court, therefore, found the new trust's apprehensions without merit. It also said that under law, they could not be considered rival 'traders', as they had a common goal, and merely wanted to spread their guru's message and teachings through the books, without any profit motive. This case was dismissed with the following observation: '[W]e would like to express our trust and hope that instead of trying to reach the Court with litigations on the subject, both the trusts should help each other in trying to reach the public including the devotees with the message and teachings of Swami Ji. That only will provide fulfilment of their objects and aims'.[45]

This case raises an interesting question of copyright in relation to religious works. A religious or spiritual leader usually writes books or treatises with the intention of spreading their word, and distributing or reproducing such works only furthers the aim of the guru. Unlike other literary works, where an author's livelihood or the idea of 'just reward' for creative contributions may be of importance, would such issues still remain for literary works by such gurus?

Questions of the true purpose of works of spiritual leaders have not in any measure prevented the Maharishi Foundation from trying to consolidate its title to the intellectual property rights (IPRs) relating to the signature transcendental meditation technique, and corresponding names and marks, associated with its founder, Mahesh Yogi. The Maharishi (as he is colloquially known), born Mahesh Prasad Verma in 1918 in Jabalpur, in present-day Madhya Pradesh, is especially known in Western popular culture for his association with performers and artists of the 1960s and 1970s (he even acquired notoriety through a song written by the Beatles—'Sexy Sadie'—which they wrote after visiting his ashram in Rishikesh). The Maharishi was internationally renowned, extremely well-travelled, and eventually settled (and died) in a small town in the Netherlands. It is no surprise that the disputes relating to his life and works are also located in non-Indian jurisdictions.

In the United States (US), the Maharishi Foundation, which owns the trademarks for 'Transcendental Meditation' and its short form 'TM', reportedly earns several million dollars each year (USD 7.2 million in 2010, although it claims to have spent more than that in advancing its mission). The meditation technique, of Vedic origin, involves the chanting of a mantra, and is to be practiced twice daily while sitting with eyes closed. The Foundation claims that the technique has been demonstrated to have health benefits such as reduced risk of heart disease, stress, and anxiety. But the transcendental meditation trademarks have been frequently challenged in the US, most recently in 2011, alleging that they are 'generic and invalid', and have been used to violate antitrust laws.[46]

In Europe too, the Foundation has struggled to convince the Office for Harmonisation in the Internal Market (Trade Marks and Designs) (OHIM) that its trademark in French, 'méditation transcendantale', is distinctive and not generic.[47]

In IP law, a trademark may be registered if it has distinctive character. Distinctiveness can be easily shown if a trademark is inherently distinctive, that is, it is based on a word that is invented, which had no meaning before its use as a trademark, such as Kodak. However, most trademarks are rarely made up of purely invented words. Thus, trademarks may also be registered if they exhibit distinctive characteristics *through use*. Registries and courts across the world determine distinctiveness through use differently, but usually, it is required that the trademark already be in wide use in the jurisdiction where it will be registered, and be recognized as a distinctive trademark by its consumers. This can be shown through data, such as the trademark's market share; its geographical extent, and length of use; and market surveys showing the proportion of people who associate the mark with the owner.

The Maharishi Foundation applied for the mark, 'méditation transcendantale', in 2009 in Europe for various goods and services. The trademark examiner rejected the application on grounds that the mark was generic, and the Foundation had no proof of having acquired distinctiveness through use in Belgium and France.[48] The Foundation appealed, but the Board of Appeal[49] also agreed that no registration could be granted. The mark, it said, was generic, because the words, in both French and English, 'directly informed the public' of the nature of the goods and services being provided. In other words, the mark was 'an obvious way' of referring to the mediation technique, and if registration were granted, it could confer a monopoly on the technique itself. The Board did not address distinctiveness by use, and returned that question to the examiner. Finally, the matter reached the General Court of the European Union,[50] which, in February 2013, held forth on various issues, including the descriptiveness of the trademark. The court said that there was sufficient direct and specific relationship between the sign 'méditation transcendantale' and the goods and services for which the trademark was applied. 'Transcendantale', according to the court, was something that goes beyond sensory perception, and 'méditation' meant to reflect or think deeply on a subject. Therefore, the court agreed with the Board of Appeal, that any average consumer would understand the meaning of the expression 'méditation transcendantale', that is, the act of thinking deeply on a subject that goes beyond the world of the senses.

A younger contemporary of the Maharishi, Osho, was equally embroiled in IP controversies, during and after his lifetime. Chandra Mohan Jain, better known as Bhagwan Shree Rajneesh or Osho, was also born in the (present-day) state of Madhya Pradesh in 1931. Osho was a professor of philosophy at the University of Jabalpur for nearly a decade, later becoming a spiritual teacher, courting controversy and garnering popularity in equal measure. His main ashram, or 'commune', as it is sometimes called, was in Pune, Maharashtra. He also briefly lived in a 'commune' on a 126-square mile former cattle ranch in Oregon in the US, until he was deported for immigration violations in 1985. A year before his death, Rajneesh officially adopted the name 'Osho'. He died in 1990, leaving behind a rich estate of speeches, books, sound and video recordings, and other works expounding his ideas.

During his lifetime, Osho encouraged his followers to disseminate his teachings as widely as possible, and centres dedicated to Osho's teachings and meditation techniques sprung up all around the world. At the height of his popularity, it is said that Osho centres were located in over 80 countries.[51] The centres were independent, unconnected, and without any form of control. When Rajneesh adopted 'Osho', he asked the centres to use Osho in their names, to help people recognize the connection, and most centres agreed.[52]

The Osho International Foundation (OIF), based in Zurich, Switzerland, wanted to register marks containing the word Osho, such as Osho Active Meditations, Osho Zen Tarot, and Osho Times. The OIF said that it had been controlling all work related to Osho's teachings since even before he 'left his body', and claimed to control Osho centres around the world.

After registering some trademarks with the United States Patent and Trademark Office (USPTO), the OIF set out to enforce them. An early target was Osho Dhyan Mandir, an Indian body, which, about a decade after Osho's death, was dragged to arbitration for registering the domain name oshoworld.com on the Internet.

Domain names form an important part of an enterprise's portfolio of intangible assets. The Internet Corporation for Assigned Names and Numbers (ICANN) is responsible for the internet's naming system, and keeping the roster of domain names dispute-free. Under ICANN's Uniform Domain Name Dispute Policy, a party complaining about another's domain name must prove three elements to cancel or transfer a domain name: first, that the domain name was identical or confusingly similar to a trademark or service mark in which the complainant had rights; second, that the other party had no rights or legitimate interests in the domain name; and third, that the domain name was registered and was being used in bad faith.

In the oshoworld.com case, the OIF could not prove any of these elements, and ICANN's domain name disputes' arbitration forum decided categorically in favour of the Indian body, and against the OIF. Of all the decisions in the many Osho IP disputes, the most apt observation of all came, perhaps, from this forum:[53]

> To grant Complainant's [OIF's] request for relief would be to permit virtual monopolization on the Internet by Complainant of any domain name which includes the name of a great spiritual teacher and leader. While making no judgment on the relative merits or validity of the world's religions or spiritual movements or any leader thereof, this Arbitrator finds that permitting this would be as improper as doing the same with Christianity, Judaism, Islam, Zoroastrianism, Hinduism, Buddhism, Taoism, Confucianism, Shintoism, or any of the several hundred other of the world's religions and/or spiritual movements.

The OIF's claims to the trademarks before the USPTO would not survive too long on the register either. Another organization called Osho Friends International was behind the next round of troubles for the OIF. Osho Friends International is an association of individuals and centres dedicated to prevent Osho's works being monopolized by any one body. The masthead on its website reads, 'Osho Everybody's Birthright Nobody's Copyright'.[54] The website contains exhaustive documentation (such as lawsuits, petitions, evidentiary documents, news reports, and court decisions) on the cases that were fought around Osho trademark claims, and the rights to publish and reproduce Osho's works.

Osho Friends International opposed the OIF's trademark registrations on grounds that the term 'Osho' was generic and descriptive in relation to the goods and services in question, and that, the OIF did not own any rights to file the marks. The dispute came before the US Trademark Trial and Appeal Board (TTAB), a body that functions like a court for trademark matters at the USPTO. In its 2008 decision,[55] the TTAB sought to understand how Osho used the term himself. It found that Osho neither owned nor used 'Osho' as a trademark, nor did he ever authorize or permit any one person or organization to use the term as a source for his teachings. The TTAB also decided that both parties to the dispute used the term 'Osho' in a generic sense, whose 'primary significance [was] a religious and meditative movement'.[56] Based on these factors, all the trademarks that the OIF wanted to register were cancelled. The TTAB also referred to an apposite statement by Osho himself, deriding Mahesh Yogi's attempts to protect his IP:

> Maharishi Mahesh Yogi has copyrighted transcendental meditation and just underneath in a small circle you will find written TM—that means trademark!
>
> For ten thousand years the East has been meditating and nobody has put trademarks upon meditations. And above all, that transcendental meditation is neither transcendental nor meditation ... just a trademark.
>
> I told [my secretary] to reply to these people, 'You don't understand what meditation is. It is nobody's belonging, possession. You cannot have any copyright. Perhaps if your country gives you trademarks and copyrights on things like meditation, then it will be good to have a copyright on stupidity. That will help the whole world to be relieved... Only you will be stupid and nobody else can be stupid; it will be illegal'.

However, Osho's long-time legal secretary, Ma Anando, suggested elsewhere that Osho was 'full of contradictions', and his views on copyright expressed on any one occasion could not be regarded as his final word on the subject.[57]

The trademark dispute was a small part of a much larger power struggle to control the multi-million-dollar Osho estate, which included 1,500 books published in 40 languages, selling several million copies annually; 400 tapes of music and sermons, selling a few hundred thousand each year; paintings and photographs; diamond robes; a fleet of Rolls Royce cars; and real estate in prime locations across the world.[58]

The origins of this fascinating and continuing dispute can be attributed to Osho himself. According to an *India Today* exposé[59] on the fight over Osho's estate, during his lifetime, Osho had established an 'Inner Circle' of 21 individuals handpicked from amongst his disciples. After Osho's death, the Inner Circle itself went through a power struggle. Fifteen members quit the group after disagreements with its chairperson, Prem Jayesh, a Canadian by birth, originally named Michael O'Bryne. The group's remaining members formed the OIF, headquartered in Zurich, Switzerland (even though most of its estate was in Pune, India). Jayesh built an elaborate and complex legal structure across jurisdictions, with the apparent mandate of 'charging royalty on all of Osho's works'.[60] This structure included Osho International (New York), allegedly run by Jayesh's brother D'Arcy O'Bryne. It further transpired that Osho International (New York) was merely a front, and in fact, was a trading name for Master Zones Limited, a UK-based company.

Meanwhile, Osho had made an 'absolute and unconditional transfer' of his copyrights between 1972 and 1993 to the Rajneesh Foundation, a Pune-based trust controlling Osho's ashram there. As a consequence of this assignment, OIF Zurich could arguably not have obtained ownership of the same, unless some further transfer of title took place. In proceedings in a European court, OIF Zurich apparently claimed that the rights in Osho's works were transferred to them in 1980. Elsewhere, they claimed that the rights were transferred through Osho's will. But even this claim has been challenged, including through a complaint filed with the Pune police, alleging that the OIF 'created a forged will to use the income from the spiritual leader's intellectual property'.[61]

Osho Friends International filed cases against the OIF for misappropriation of funds and other charges in India and Switzerland. In June 2014, the Swiss Federal Supervisory Board and Swiss Federal Department of Home Affairs provisionally suspended the OIF Zurich board, including Jayesh and his brother, revoking their signatory authority and freezing their bank accounts. The Indian matter is yet to conclude.[62]

The lack of clarity on Osho's views on the rights to his own works, and to IP in general, is only a minor concern in this story. More than anything else, the Osho property disputes demonstrate the consequences of poor estate planning. This is a concern that might well be true of many other 'spiritual' teachers and leaders in this country, whose followers may be left without clear instructions on what is to be done with their assets and works after their death.

The Traditions

A third thread of debates in the new age has been around the IP in various traditional systems. Who has the right to protect these traditions? In what form can they be protected? Should these traditions be protected at all? And so on.

Bikram Choudhury has gained worldwide fame (and notoriety) in this context. Choudhury's credentials are illustrious, having learnt hatha yoga from Bishnu Ghosh (the brother of Paramahansa Yogananda, whose book *Autobiography of a Yogi* remains a bestseller over 60 years after its first publication), and having won the National India Yoga Championship thrice consecutively as a teenager.[63] Choudhury is the founder of Bikram yoga, which he claims is a system of yoga containing a series of 26 asanas ('postures') and two breathing exercises performed in a heated (40°C/104°F) environment. Bikram yoga has become popular in the US (where Choudhury lives and works) and elsewhere, with celebrity students including Hollywood superstars, pop icons, and sporting heroes. Choudhury opened his first Bikram Yoga Studio in Beverly Hills, US, in 1973. Two decades later, he started the Bikram yoga teacher-training course to train people who wanted to teach others in the Bikram yoga style. Choudhury certifies roughly 500 to 600 teachers annually, of whom one-third open their own studios.[64]

Although the 26 asanas are taken from the ancient practice of hatha yoga, Choudhury claims he was the first to select and arrange them in a particular sequence. He said he made this selection and arrangement around 1965 or 1970, and taught the sequence in Southern California throughout the 1970s. In 1979, Choudhury published and copyrighted his book, *Bikram's Beginning Yoga Class*, and later filed five copyright registrations for books, audiotapes, and videotapes. Finally, in 2002, he filed for a copyright on the yoga sequence itself, as a supplemental registration to the copyright on the book he originally wrote. He also registered trademarks in connection with his work, including 'Bikram Yoga', 'Bikram's Beginning Yoga Class', and 'Bikram's Yoga College of India'. Soon after, Choudhury began to inform students that they needed a licence from him to teach Bikram yoga, and a licence to use the term 'Bikram Yoga'. Choudhury made it clear that he did not wish to impose these licence requirements, at least immediately, on individual yoga practitioners who did not teach but simply performed the Bikram yoga sequence, either at home with the books and tapes or in yoga classes.[65]

Towards enforcing his rights, Choudhury sent cease-and-desist letters to at least 25 yoga instructors who were teaching Bikram Yoga, for, among other things, violating his copyrights and trademarks and employing uncertified teachers. He asked them to stop using his trademarks and copyrighted works, and directed them to disclose specific information to help calculate damages. Many instructors agreed to most of his terms, mainly to avoid being sued. One couple, the Morrisons, who owned a yoga studio in Costa Mesa, California, chose to defy him. In 2002, Choudhury sued the Morrisons for infringement and related claims, and the matter was eventually settled by a confidential agreement, although Choudhury claimed he was 'victorious' in the settlement. After this settlement, he seems to have become more vocal about his claims of copyright protection over his set of 26 asanas.[66]

Soon, however, Choudhury was at the receiving end of a suit. This time, another party challenged the validity of his copyrights and trademarks in relation to Bikram yoga. The other party was an organization called Open Source Yoga Unity (OSYU), a collective of yoga studios seeking to keep the practice of yoga in the public domain.

The yoga studios collective wanted the court of the Northern District of California in the US to issue summary judgments on the issues it raised. Under US law, a summary judgment is granted only if there are no genuine issues of material fact, and the person requesting for such judgments is entitled to it as a matter of law. First, OSYU argued that individual yoga asanas in the Bikram yoga sequence were in the public domain, and that it constituted functional information, rather than expressive creative content. As a result, OSYU argued, Bikram yoga could not be copyrighted under law. A previous US court's decision in connection with the National Basketball Association (NBA) was cited, to show that physical exercise regimes could not be copyrighted. But copyright was not granted in the NBA case for another reason, that is, sport activities did not involve scripted routines and were a result of unanticipated movements. Thus, the NBA decision was not a useful precedent. Choudhury, in his defence, claimed that his yoga sequence was a copyrightable compilation of information in the public domain, because he had selected and arranged the asanas in a manner that was both aesthetically pleasing and designed to improve the practitioner's health. The court noted that two competing principles of copyright law were at play here. Ordinarily, copyright law does not protect either factual or functional information, or information that is already in the public domain. At the same time, copyright law *does* protect an arrangement of information that may be in the public domain but is assembled in a sufficiently creative fashion. In this case, there was not enough evidence to decide on whether the Bikram yoga sequence was sufficiently creative to be afforded copyright protection, and the court did not decide on this question.

Second, OSYU argued that the Bikram yoga routine had already entered the public domain in the 1970s, when Choudhury started his yoga classes. Under the US Copyright Act of 1909 (the law in force when Choudhury claimed to have created the Bikram yoga sequence), if a work that could be copyrighted was published without any notice that it was a copyrightable work, then, by default, the work would become irrevocably dedicated to the public, and would not be copyrightable in the future. Choudhury argued that he did not forfeit copyright protection merely by performing his yoga sequence. The court pondered over the word 'published', noting that it was undefined under the 1909 Act, and that courts had previously held that mere performance would not amount to publication. OSYU also could not prove that Choudhury had recorded the yoga sequence in some form ('memorialized the sequence') before his book was published, and this did not support their case.

Third, OSYU argued that Choudhury's legal notices to yoga instructors were a 'misuse of copyright', attempting to obtain a broad monopoly on teaching Bikram yoga, and, therefore, his copyrights were unenforceable. However, the court observed that Choudhury was well within his rights as the copyright owner to send out those notices, and that there was insufficient proof of copyright misuse.

Although the request for summary judgment on all three issues was dismissed, this lawsuit also ended in a confidential settlement agreement, in May 2005, when Choudhury and OSYU 'reached a mutually satisfactory resolution'.

Choudhury continued to sue others for copyright and trademark infringement over the next few years. One of these suits[67] was before the court of the Central District of California, against Evolation Yoga, a limited liability enterprise formed by Mark Drost and Zefea Samson, former students of Choudhury. According to the suit, Evolation Yoga opened several yoga studios to teach the Bikram yoga sequence without Choudhury's authorization. In his suit, he claimed that his copyrights covered not only his written or audiovisual works, but the yoga sequence as well. Specifically, he argued, his yoga sequence was like a pantomime or a choreographic work, and was entitled to protection under law. Contrary to the previous decision in the OSYU case, this court decided that the Bikram yoga sequence was not copyrightable for two reasons. First, it said that his copyrights covered his written and audiovisual works to the extent of only his expression of the facts and ideas contained in those works; the copyrights did not extend to the facts and ideas themselves. Second, it said that even though Choudhury's works described the sequence, and taught people how to do it, a compilation of exercises or yoga poses itself would not fall into any of the copyrightable categories under the law.

For the second part of this decision about 'copyrightable categories', the court relied on a recent 'Statement of Policy' issued by the US Copyright Office. The policy statement had appeared in June 2012 in the US Federal Register, which, like the Gazette of India, is the official journal of the federal US government containing government agency rules, proposed rules, and public notices.[68] The US Copyright Office periodically issues announcements, rules, and so on, in the Federal Register, but statements of policy by the Copyright Office are unusual and very rare. This was the first such policy to appear in several years.

This policy sought to clarify the registrability of compilations through 'a closer analysis of legislative intent'. The Copyright Office chose this issue because the copyrightability of the selection and arrangement of exercises that already existed, 'such as yoga poses', had 'occupied [its] attention ... for quite some time'. Under this policy, it clarified that 'a claim in a compilation of exercises or the selection and arrangement of yoga poses will be refused registration'.[69]

All of Choudhury's claims as to his yoga sequence having legitimate copyright were systematically analysed and rejected by the policy. First, exercise was not a category of authorship under law, and therefore, a compilation of exercises would not be copyrightable. Second, the yoga system was not a choreographic work, because mere compilations of physical movements would not 'rise to the level' of choreography, which required at least a 'minimum amount of original choreographic authorship'.[70] It explained that choreographic authorship, for the purpose of copyright, meant that the dance movements and patterns that were part of the work, had to be composed and arranged such that they came together as 'an integrated, coherent, and expressive whole'.[71] Therefore, a selection of functional physical movements such as sports exercises, and other motor activities alone would not qualify as choreographic works. Third, US copyright law prevented the registration of certain compilations that amount to an idea, process, system, or method of operation, regardless of the form in which it is described in the work. According to the US Copyright Office, a selection of yoga poses may be denied registration because they may be regarded as a functional system or process, particularly where the movements are said to result in improvements in one's health or physical or mental condition (as Choudhury had repeatedly claimed). As its dénouement, the Office admitted to having incorrectly, and 'in error', issued registration certificates that referred to the 'nature of authorship' as being 'compilations of exercises' or 'selection and arrangement of exercises'.[72] In its warning note for future transgressors, it said, when a compilation did 'not result in one or more congressionally-established categories of authorship', such applications' claims in compilation authorship would be refused.[73]

This policy statement effectively derecognized all copyright registrations that had been previously granted for compilations of exercises. Choudhury's sequence, of course, was the target. But what was the legal effect of a statement of policy in a court of law? This was precisely the question that Choudhury asked the US Court of Appeals for the Ninth Circuit in 2013. He argued that the Copyright Office's statement of policy was not entitled to any deference in a court, because the Copyright Office was not authorized to issue a policy that had the force of law. The Copyright Office's interpretation of the law could, at best, be regarded as persuasive, and certainly not decisive. Choudhury also suggested that the court ought to have independently examined the law on its own, and in relying on the Copyright Office's interpretation, it had made a mistake. He then went on to demonstrate how his yoga sequence was copyrightable, and contradicted every conclusion made in the statement of policy.[74]

In its opinion in 2015,[75] the appeals court upheld the district court's decision regarding the non-copyrightability of Choudhury's work, while noting that the 'Indian practice and philosophy of yoga date[d] back thousands of years [and was] derived from ancient Hindu scriptures, including the Bhagavad Gita'. Acknowledging that yoga had 'evolved into a diverse set of spiritual, physical and philosophical disciplines',[76] the appeals court went back to the basics of copyright to explain why the sequence could not be copyrighted. Copyright law makes a distinction between an idea and the expression of that idea, and allows protecting only the latter, and not the former. Following from this, 'courts have routinely held that copyright for a work describing how to perform a process does not extend to the process itself'.[77] In this case, the court observed that '[c]onsumers would have little reason to buy Choudhury's book if Choudhury held a monopoly on the practice of the very activity he sought to popularize'.[78] It finally dismissed, as the district court had, Choudhury's claims of copyright on the sequence of poses, for reasons that the sequence was an idea, process, or system, and not the expression of an idea. As the sequence itself was an unprotectable idea, it could also not obtain copyright protection as a compilation or a choreographed work.

The yoga case has garnered much attention in India, for obvious reasons. The very idea that a person should consider claiming exclusive rights to anything related to an ancient Indian tradition such as yoga is appalling to many. While Bikram yoga's efforts are often publicized in India, there has also been much misreporting (mainly about Choudhury having 'patented' yoga asanas, as against 'copyrighting' them).[79] No yoga-related case appears to have reached Indian courts, but that has not prevented Indian courts from discussing yoga-related developments elsewhere. Reference, for instance, was made to the US Copyright Office's statement of policy in a decision of the Delhi High Court relating to techniques of 'Pranic Healing'. The Philippines-based 'Institute for Inner Studies' (IIS), founded by Master Choa Kok Sui in 1987, claimed copyright protection over Pranic Healing techniques, as well as trademarks for the expression 'Pranic Healing'. This healing system is popular in India, with teachers and students spread across the country. The IIS contended that a person in India was conducting training programmes without valid licences, and was granting authorization to instructors who were not properly qualified and did not follow guidelines issued by the Master.

In its decision,[80] the Delhi High Court reiterated the rule that copyright subsists only in expressions and does not extend over facts or ideas, and referred to the Evolation Yoga case. Therefore, the court limited copyright protection to the manner in which the asanas were explained, the language and pictures used, and their arrangement and selection. However, copyright would not extend to the performance of the asanas. Even if this technique was an innovation of the Master, the court held that copyright protection does not extend to protect such an innovation, observing, 'giving the monopoly over the performance art or exercising techniques which are apparently pre-existing in the ancient history of India would be a serious intrusion in the Public domain'.[81] The IIS argued that Pranic Healing was a 'dramatic work', but the court rejected the contention, holding that Pranic Healing was not a dramatic work as it embodied 'daily routine exercises'. It referred extensively to the US Copyright Office policy statement of June 2012, where yoga and routine exercises were held not to qualify as 'dramatic works'. The IIS also lost the case on trademark protection, with the court observing that it had obtained trademark registrations through misrepresentations, and that 'Pranic Healing' was generic and lacked distinctiveness, and hence, could not be protected.

India responded to the yoga debate fuelled by Choudhury with great enthusiasm. While the approach paper for the Traditional Knowledge Digital Library (TKDL)[82] made no mention of yoga, when the TKDL Task Force proposed the traditional knowledge resource classification (TKRC) system as a new form of classifying traditional knowledge, yoga was introduced as a category of classification. Like any other library classification system, the TKRC is designed to help arrange and locate information on traditional knowledge resources. It follows the International Patent Classification system used by patent offices worldwide, and lists 'yoga' as one section, besides ayurveda, unani, and siddha (naturopathy and folklore medicine were part of the original TKRC proposal, but have since been abandoned).[83]

Task forces were set up for each of the sections, and the TKDL (Yoga) Task Force first met on 31 January 2003. Initial efforts were directed at traditional medicine and biopiracy, and the need to protect knowledge on yoga was 'not of great concern', but a database on yoga was found necessary to study the utility of yoga in 'combinatorial therapy' with ayurveda and unani.[84] Eight books containing yogic kriyas and asanas were selected in the first phase, and another eight would be taken up in the second phase of the project. These included classics like Patanjali's *Yogasutras*, and the *Vijnanabhairava*. Wherever available, (pre-existing or specially commissioned) videos on yoga techniques and postures would be included in the database. In its final report of 2006–7, the Task Force recommended the transcription of 1,500 asanas from original yoga texts,[85] but the actual documentation appears to have begun only in January 2008.[86] The estimated cost, in 2009, of the yoga database was about Rs 3 crore or Rs 30 million, nearly half of the total cost (Rs 7 crore or Rs 70 million) of the TKDL itself.[87]

Since then, nine 'well-known institutions' and 200 scientists and researchers from the Council of Scientific and Industrial Research (CSIR) and the department of AYUSH (Ayurveda, Yoga, and Naturopathy, Unani, Siddha, and Homeopathy), ministry of health, have collaborated to form the TKDL yoga database. Some 1,300 asanas (compiled from over a dozen yoga texts) have been documented, of which 200 also have video clips,[88] accompanied by textual commentary, Sanskrit slokas, and subtitles in English, Spanish, French, German, and Japanese, as well as reference to the benefits and contraindications of the asanas.[89] However, as has become TKDL policy, only 30 or 40 of the most popular yoga asanas would be available publicly; the rest would only be available to patent offices.[90] The objective for undertaking this yoga documentation project was that all forms of yoga had to be documented, and placed in the public domain, so that no one could claim exclusive rights to yoga through copyrights or any other form of IP. But, it is strange that the TKDL should, in practice, continue to make a distinction between the true public domain (that is, everyone), and signatories to the TKDL (that is, other patent offices); that discussion could be found in Chapter 9 in this volume. There is no clarity as to whether copyright offices, in India or abroad, would have access to this database. This is relevant because copyright offices are more likely to carry out yoga-related registrations than patent offices.

Initial activities surrounding the TKDL (Yoga) Task Force and TKRC can be traced to 2001–2, around when Bikram Choudhury began enforcing his copyrights in the US. The TKDL's chief architect, V.K. Gupta, had said that they would not 'legally challenge' Bikram yoga.[91] Nevertheless, the TKDL's intentions as advertised elsewhere indicate otherwise. After completing the TKDL yoga database, the organization is expected to move against yoga-related IPRs registered abroad.[92]

Why is the world so interested in yoga, though? What can be so fascinating about a combination of techniques involving breathing exercises, physical postures, and mantra chanting that has been known and practiced for centuries? As with any activity that holds out the promise of health benefits, the popularity of yoga has soared wildly, and a host of IP around it has also sprung up. More than 3,000 yoga-related patent applications are believed to have been granted or filed the world over,[93] and the USPTO alone has reportedly issued 150 yoga-related copyrights, 134 trademarks on yoga accessories, and 2,315 yoga trademarks.[94] According to the 'Yoga in America' study released by the Yoga Journal in 2012, 20.4 million Americans practice yoga, up by 29 per cent from the previous 15.8 million recorded in 2008.[95] Collectively, they spent an estimated USD 10.3 billion in 2012 on yoga classes and products, including equipment, clothing, vacations, and media, nearly twice the estimated USD 5.7 billion spent in 2008.[96] (To put this in perspective, foreign direct investment inflows into India in 2012–13 were USD 22.4 billion, just a little over double of the US yoga spend).[97] It is no wonder that the Indian political establishment has begun to get interested in this business too.

While the ministry of health has funded yoga-related research for some time,[98] active political interest in yoga really began with the 15th Prime Minister of India, Narendra Modi. On the floor of the United Nations (UN) General Assembly in September 2014, he called for an 'International Yoga Day' to be celebrated every year.[99] An overwhelming majority (over 170 sovereign nations acted as co-sponsors)[100] in the General Assembly adopted a resolution[101] in December 2014, proclaiming 21 June as the International Day of Yoga. In November 2014, Modi introduced a new minister for ayurveda, yoga, and other systems of medicine.[102] Upon appointment, the new minister promptly asked the central government to allocate more funds in future budgets (almost seven times its existing allocation), 'in view of its emerging importance'.[103] Commentators suggest that his remit may be to 'get a slice of' the multi-billion-dollar yoga industry in the US.[104]

Speculation is rife that India will attempt to protect yoga through the GI system.[105] But the outlook for such protection does not look too good.[106] The law at present does not allow for granting GI protection to anything other than goods. Thus, any such attempt would require a change in the law. Even if the law were different, who would be the persons authorized to benefit from such protection? Next, merely changing *Indian* law will not benefit anyone. The challenge is likely to be in jurisdictions other than India, for which international protocols would need to be addressed. The value of such protection has also not been considered. For example, what will obtaining a GI for yoga achieve? Nobody has any clear answers. Instead, it is best to leave yoga to evolve in whichever way it wants, for it will be the best gift that India can give to the world.

* * *

Religion and tradition are money-spinners like no other, and their recent entanglements with IP in India have thrown up some fascinating dilemmas. Can any one temple, community, or country claim to own any one religious or traditional practice or artefact? How is such ownership to be established? What are the consequences of such ownership? If an owner is successfully identified, does it mean that the owner has the singular right to use and interpret that practice to the exclusion of others? Does it mean that a person must necessarily seek and obtain the permission of its owner before using or interpreting it themselves? As the world cross-pollinates, contracts in size, and expands in perspective, the clamour for answers to such questions will only grow louder. These questions do not have easy or clear solutions, and certainly cannot be answered without lengthy debates, which will continue for many decades to come.

Notes

1. ANIL RELIA, THE INDIAN PORTRAIT III: A HISTORICAL JOURNEY OF GRAPHIC PRINTS UP TO INDEPENDENCE 122–30 (2014).

2. PARTHA MITTER, ART AND NATIONALISM IN COLONIAL INDIA, 1850–1922: OCCIDENTAL ORIENTATIONS 214 (1994).

3. RUPIKA CHAWLA, RAJA RAVI VARMA: PAINTER OF COLONIAL INDIA 285 (2010), as cited in Jyotindra Jain, *Bombay/Mumbai: Visual Histories of a City*, 1(3) IMAGENAAMA (2013), available at http://civicportale.org/manage/downloadminpdf.php?download_file=pdf_52f0cb5e8873a.pdf (Last visited on 1 February 2015).

4. Jain, *Bombay/Mumbai.*

5. Jain, *Bombay/Mumbai*.

6. S. Venkateswaran, *Some Guiding Principles for Trademark Legislation in India, in* THE LAW OF TRADE AND MERCHANDISE MARKS IN INDIA 563 (1937).

7. S. VENKATESWARAN, THE LAW OF TRADE AND MERCHANDISE MARKS IN INDIA (1937).

8. Venkateswaran, *Some Guiding Principles*, at 563.

9. Venkateswaran, *Some Guiding Principles*, at 563.

10. INDIA, MINISTRY OF COMMERCE AND INDUSTRY, REPORT ON TRADE MARKS LAW REVISION, ¶ 145 (1955).

11. Siddharth Narrain, *Hate Speech, Hurt Sentiment, and the (Im)Possibility of Free Speech*, 51(17) EPW, 119–26 (23 April 2016).

12. AIR 1927 Lah 590

13. For a discussion on the history of Section 295A of the Indian Penal Code, 1860, see Shivprasad Swaminathan, *Scribblers, Scholars in the Same Boat*, THE HINDU, 25 February 2014, available at http://www.thehindu.com/opinion/lead/scribblers-scholars-in-the-same-boat/article5723012.ece (Last visited on 20 April 2015); see also Neeti Nair, *Beyond the 'Communal' 1920s: The Problem of Intention, Legislative Pragmatism, and the Making of Section 295A of the Indian Penal Code*, 50(3) INDIAN ECONOMIC SOCIAL AND HISTORY REVIEW 317 (2013).

14. MINISTRY OF COMMERCE AND INDUSTRY, REPORT ON TRADE MARKS LAW REVISION, ¶ 145.

15. A.T. Raja, Madras v. Mangalore Ganesh Beedi Works, Mysore, MANU/TN/1419/1996; 1996 Indlaw MAD 555.

16. The facts of the case were more complex, suggesting that the case was prompted by insincere motives. Mr Raja had also been using 'Ganesha', in both word and pictorial representation, for similar products. But the company forced Mr Raja to withdraw his trademarked products from the market by filing a trademark injunction against him. Mr Raja came up with the petition only after he was injuncted. The court said that since he was no longer in the same business, he could no longer be regarded as an 'aggrieved person'.

17. A.T. Raja, Madras v. Mangalore Ganesh Beedi Works, Mysore, ¶ 2.

18. A.T. Raja, Madras v. Mangalore Ganesh Beedi Works, Mysore, ¶ 13.

19. A.T. Raja, Madras v. Mangalore Ganesh Beedi Works, Mysore, ¶ 14.

20. A.T. Raja, Madras v. Mangalore Ganesh Beedi Works, Mysore, ¶ 16.

21. Manglore Ganesh Beedi Works v. District Judge, Meerut and Others, 2005 Indlaw ALL 1606.

22. INDIA, OFFICE OF CONTROLLER GENERAL PATENTS, DESIGNS & TRADE MARKS, MINISTRY OF COMMERCE AND INDUSTRY, A DRAFT OF MANUAL OF

TRADE MARKS PRACTICE & PROCEDURE (2015), available at http://ipindia.
gov.in/tmr_new/TMR_Manual/TMR_DraftManual_11March2015.pdf
(Last visited on 20 April 2015).

23. Educare Limited v. S.K. Sachdev, CS(OS) No. 1151 of 2014 (Delhi High
Court) (unreported), (order passed on 14 November 2014).

24. Educare Limited v. S.K. Sachdev, CS(OS) No. 1151 of 2014, ¶ 46.

25. Educare Limited v. S.K. Sachdev, CS(OS) No. 1151 of 2014, ¶ 67.

26. Lal Babu Priyadarshi v. Amritpal Singh, CA No. 2138 of 2006 (Supreme
Court of India) (unreported), (order passed on 27 October 2015).

27. Lal Babu Priyadarshi v. Amritpal Singh, CA No. 2138 of 2006, ¶ 18.

28. *Suo Motu* Proceedings Initiated on a Petition Received from Sri R.S.
Praveen Raj, Thiruvananthapuram, Regarding Trademark Registration
on the Picture of the Deity of Attukal Temple, Thiruvananthapuram,
W.P.(C) No. 14153 of 2009 (Kerala High Court) (unreported), (order passed
on 12 September 2013).

29. *Suo Motu* Proceedings Initiated on a Petition Received from Sri R.S.
Praveen Raj, Thiruvananthapuram, ¶ 2.

30. Pramatha Nath Mullick v. Pradyumna Kumar Mullick, (1925) 52 IA 245,
cited in *Suo Motu* Proceedings Initiated on a Petition Received from Sri
R.S. Praveen Raj, Thiruvananthapuram.

31. Suo Motu Proceedings Initiated on a Petition Received from Sri R.S.
Praveen Raj, Thiruvananthapuram, ¶ 13.

32. Suo Motu Proceedings Initiated on a Petition Received from Sri R.S.
Praveen Raj, Thiruvananthapuram, ¶ 11.

33. Payyannur Pavithra Ring Artisans & Development Society v. K.
Balakrishnan, 2009 (41) PTC 719 GIG.

34. See Matthews P. George, *IPAB on Payyannur Ring*, SPICYIP, 18 November
2012, available at http://spicyip.com/2012/11/ipab-on-payyannur-ring.
html (Last visited on 30 March 2015).

35. See George, *IPAB on Payyannur Ring*. Order No 255 of 2012, issued on 14
November 2012, in OA/2/2010/GI/CH and M.P. Nos. 1/2010 & 269/2012
in OA/2/2010/GI/CH.

36. Minutes of the Consultative Group Meeting, GI Application No. 06 and
408, and order in the matter remanded by IPAB in appeal OA/2/2010/GI/
CH and MP Nos 1/2010 and 269/2012 in OA/2/2010/GI/CH (11 March
2014), available at http://164.100.176.36/GI_DOC/6/6%20-%20GI%20-%
20Order%20of%20Registrar%20-%2022-04-2014.pdf (Last visited on 30
March 2015).

37. Satsang and Anr. v. Kiron Chandra Mukhopadhyay, AIR 1972 Cal 533.

38. Sulamangalam R. Jayalakshmi v. Meta Musicals, AIR 2000 Mad 454.

39. Satsang and Anr. v. Kiron Chandra Mukhopadhyay.

40. Sulamangalam R. Jayalakshmi v. Meta Musicals.
41. See Param Pujya Shree Swami Satyanand Ji Maharaj, available at http://www.ibiblio.org/ram/swamiji.htm (Last visited on 4 February 2015).
42. See Swami Satyanand Dharmarth Trust, available at http://www.ibiblio.org/ram/trust.htm (Last visited on 4 February 2015).
43. Shri Ganga Vishnu Raheja v. Shri Swami Satyanand Dharmarth, 2005 (30) PTC 577 Del.
44. Shri Ganga Vishnu Raheja v. Shri Swami Satyanand Dharmarth, ¶ 26.
45. Shri Ganga Vishnu Raheja v. Shri Swami Satyanand Dharmarth, ¶ 33.
46. The suit between Maharishi Meditation and the Meditation House was filed before the district court of Iowa in 2011. See Associated Press, *Legal Feud Over Teaching of Transcendental Meditation Technique is Anything but Peaceful*, Fox News, 20 January 2013, available at http://www.foxnews.com/us/2013/01/20/legal-feud-over-teaching-transcendental-meditation-technique-is-anything-but/ (Last visited on 30 March 2015).
47. Maharishi Foundation Ltd. v. Office for Harmonisation in the Internal Market (Trade Marks and Designs) (OHIM), Case T-426/11 (The General Court of the European Union (Second Chamber)), (order passed on 6 February 2013), [2013] E.T.M.R. 22.
48. Community trade mark No. [2009] OJ L78/1 (Trademark Examiner), (order passed on 25 May 2010).
49. Community trade mark No. [2009] OJ L78/1 (Second Board of Appeal, OHIM), (order passed on 6 April 2011).
50. Maharishi Foundation Ltd. v. Office for Harmonisation in the Internal Market (Trade Marks and Designs) (OHIM), Case T-426/11.
51. Sheela Raval, *Royalty Ruckus*, India Today, 3 July 2000, available at http://archives.digitaltoday.in/indiatoday/20000703/religion.html (Last visited on 30 March 2015).
52. Osho Friends International v. Osho International Foundation, Trademark Trial and Appeal Board (United States Patent and Trademark Office), Opposition Nos. 91121040; 91150372; 91150379; 91152313; 91153103; 91155927; 91157465; 91157610; 91157698; and Cancellation No. 92031932 (order passed on 13 January 2009), available at http://www.oshofriendsinternational.com/documents/Osho_Trademark_Decision.pdf (Last visited on 30 March 2015).
53. Osho International Foundation v. Osho Dhyan Mandir and Atul Anand, Case No. FA0006000094990 (National Arbitration Forum, Minneapolis), (order passed on 28 July 2000), available at http://domains.adrforum.com/domains/decisions/94990.htm (Last visited on 30 March 2015).
54. See http://oshofriendsinternational.com/ (Last visited on 25 April 2016).

55. Osho Friends International v. Osho International Foundation, Trademark Trial and Appeal Board (United States Patent and Trademark Office).

56. Osho Friends International v. Osho International Foundation, Trademark Trial and Appeal Board (United States Patent and Trademark Office), at 33.

57. Raval, *Royalty Ruckus*.

58. Raval, *Royalty Ruckus*.

59. Raval, *Royalty Ruckus*.

60. Raval, *Royalty Ruckus*.

61. Aditi Pai, *Trouble Brewing as Followers Allege Osho's Will Was Forged, Pune Police Investigating*, INDIA TODAY, 16 December 2013, available at http://indiatoday.intoday.in/story/trouble-brewing-as-followers-allege-oshos-will-was-forged-pune-police-investigating/1/331548.html (Last visited on 30 March 2015).

62. Kaumudi Gurjar, *Osho's Swiss Copycat Shut Down*, PUNE MIRROR, 10 June 2014, available at http://www.punemirror.in/pune/others/Oshos-Swiss-copycat-shut-down/articleshow/36312920.cms (Last visited on 30 March 2015). A January 2016 order of the Bombay High Court, among other things, directed the Joint Charity Commissioner to expeditiously dispose of the proceedings involving the parties (Neo Sanyas Foundation and anr. v. Shri. Yogesh Thakkar alias Swami Prem Geet and ors., WP No. 522 and 523 of 2016, Bombay HC (unreported), judgment dated 19 January 2016). The decision of the High Court was appealed to the Supreme Court, but appears to have been dismissed (Neo Sanyas Foundation and anr. v. Shri. Yogesh Thakkar alias Swami Prem Geet and ors., SLP (C) 3639-3640 of 2016, disposed by the Supreme Court on 22 February 2016). Separately, in August 2016, the Bombay HC pulled up the Pune police for its 'tardy investigation' in the issue of Osho's will, but the matter has not as yet concluded (Vidya, *Osho's will: Bombay High Court fumes at tardy investigation by Pune Police*, INDIA TODAY, 3 August 2016, available at http://indiatoday.intoday.in/story/oshos-will-bombay-high-court-fumes-at-tardy-investigation-by-pune-police/1/731025.html (Last visited on 17 August 2016)).

63. See Bikram Choudhury's website: http://www.bikramyoga.com/Bikram/bikram.php (Last visited on 21 April 2015).

64. Katherine Machan, *Bending Over Backwards for Copyright Protection: Bikram Yoga and the Quest for Federal Copyright Protection of an Asana Sequence*, 12 UCLA ENT. L. REV. 29 (2004–2005).

65. Open Source Yoga Unity v. Bikram Choudhury, United States District Court, No. C 03-3182 PJH (1 April 2005), 2005 WL 756558 (N.D.Cal.).

66. Machan, *Bending Over Backwards for Copyright Protection*.

67. Bikram's Yoga College of India, L.P. and Bikram Choudhury v. Evolation Yoga, LLC, Mark Drost and Zefea Samson, 2012 WL 6548505 (C.D.Cal.).

68. FEDERAL REGISTER, *Registration of Claims to Copyright*, Vol. 77, No. 121 (22 June 2012), Rules and Regulations, available at http://www.copyright. gov/fedreg/2012/77fr37605.pdf (Last visited on 7 August 2014).

69. FEDERAL REGISTER, *Registration of Claims to Copyright.*

70. FEDERAL REGISTER, *Registration of Claims to Copyright.*

71. FEDERAL REGISTER, *Registration of Claims to Copyright.*

72. FEDERAL REGISTER, *Registration of Claims to Copyright.*

73. FEDERAL REGISTER, *Registration of Claims to Copyright.*

74. Appellant's Opening Brief, in Bikram's Yoga College of India, L.P. and Bikram Choudhury v Evolation Yoga, LLC, Mark Drost and Zefea Samson, United States Court of Appeals for the Ninth Circuit, Appeal No. 13-55763 (14 November 2013), available at https://www. yogaalliance.org/Portals/0/Articles/BikramBrief.pdf (Last visited on 30 March 2015).

75. Bikram's Yoga College of India v. Evolation Yoga, No. 13-55763, Opinion by Judge Wardlaw (US Court of Appeals for the Ninth Circuit), (order dated 8 October 2015), available at http://cdn.ca9.uscourts.gov/datastore/ opinions/2015/10/08/13-55763.pdf (Last visited on 10 October 2015).

76. Bikram's Yoga College of India v. Evolation Yoga, No. 13-55763, Opinion by Judge Wardlaw, at 3.

77. Bikram's Yoga College of India v. Evolation Yoga, No. 13-55763, Opinion by Judge Wardlaw, at 9.

78. Bikram's Yoga College of India v. Evolation Yoga, No. 13-55763, Opinion by Judge Wardlaw, at 16.

79. See, for example, *US Patent on Yoga? Indian Gurus Fume*, THE TIMES OF INDIA, 18 May 2007, available at http://timesofindia.indiatimes.com/ india/US-patent-on-yoga-Indian-gurus-fume/articleshow/2058285.cms (Last visited on 30 March 2015); Girish Shahane, *Yoga was Created 5,000 Years Ago, Right?*, SCROLL.IN, 7 January 2015, available at http://scroll.in/ article/699011/Yoga-was-created-5,000-years-ago,-right? (Last visited on 30 March 2015).

80. Institute for Inner Studies v. Charlotte Anderson, CS(OS) 2252 of 2011 (Delhi High Court) (unreported), (order passed on 10 January 2014), available at http://lobis.nic.in/dhc/MAN/judgement/13-01-2014/MAN 10012014S22522011.pdf (Last visited on 20 January 2015).

81. Institute for Inner Studies v. Charlotte Anderson, CS(OS) 2252 of 2011, ¶ 99.

82. V.K. Gupta, *An Approach for Establishing a Traditional Knowledge Digital Library*, 5 JIPR 307 (November 2000), available at http://nopr.

niscair.res.in/bitstream/123456789/26010/1/JIPR%205%286%29%20 307-319.pdf (Last visited on 20 January 2015).

83. V.K. Gupta, *Report of the Task Force on TKDL: A Gist*, 6 JIPR 121 (March 2001), available at http://nopr.niscair.res.in/bitstream/123456789/19463/ 1/JIPR%206%282%29%20121-133.pdf (Last visited on 20 January 2015). See also *Traditional Knowledge Resource Classification (TKRC)*, for present TKRC structure, available at http://www.tkdl.res.in/tkdl/ langdefault/common/TKRC.asp?GL=Eng (Last visited on 20 January 2015).

84. CSIR-NISCAIR, ANNUAL REPORT 2002–03, *Recent Initiatives*, 4–16, available at http://www.niscair.res.in/aboutus/AR2002/Recent%20Initi-atives.pdf (Last visited on 20 January 2015).

85. CSIR-NISCAIR, ANNUAL REPORT 2006–07, *Network Projects*, 29–31, available at http://www.niscair.res.in/aboutus/AnnRep06/networkpro-jects.pdf (Last visited on 20 January 2015).

86. See Item 33, *Major Milestones*, About TKDL, available at http://www. tkdl.res.in/tkdl/langdefault/common/Abouttkdl.asp?GL=Eng   (Last visited on 20 January 2015).

87. Kounteya Sinha, *Yoga Piracy: India Shows Who's the Guru*, THE TIMES OF INDIA, 22 February 2009, available at http://timesofindia.indiatimes.com/ india/yoga-piracy-india-shows-whos-the-guru/articleshow/4167939.cms (Last visited on 20 January 2015).

88. PTI, *India Videographs 200 Yoga Postures to Prevent Patent Piracy*, THE TIMES OF INDIA, 20 April 2011, available at http://timesofindia. indiatimes.com/india/India-videographs-200-yoga-postures-to-prevent-patent-piracy-/articleshow/8039122.cms?referral=PM (Last visited on 20 January 2015).

89. CSIR, Annual Report 2010–11, 13, available at http://www.csir.res.in/ External/heads/aboutcsir/Annual_report/AnnualReport_1011.pdf   (Last visited on 20 January 2015).

90. PTI, *India Videographs 200 Yoga Postures*

91. Kounteya Sinha, *India Pulls the Plug on Yoga as Business*, THE TIMES OF INDIA, 6 February 2011, available at http://timesofindia.indiatimes.com/ india/India-pulls-the-plug-on-yoga-as-business/articleshow/7432959. cms (Last visited on 20 January 2015).

92. Madan Jaira, *India to Patent Yoga Asanas*, HINDUSTAN TIMES, 7 June 2010, available   at   http://www.hindustantimes.com/india-news/newdelhi/ india-to-patent-yoga-asanas/article1-554149.aspx (Last visited on 20 January 2015).

93. Lhendup Gyatso Bhutia, *Saving Yoga from Copyright-mongers*, DNA, 18 July 2010, available at   http://www.dnaindia.com/lifestyle/

report-saving-yoga-from-copyright-mongers-1411206 (Last visited on 20 January 2015).

94. *US Patent on Yoga? Indian Gurus Fume.*

95. *Yoga Journal Releases 2012 Yoga in America Market Study*, YOGA JOURNAL, 6 December 2012, available at http://www.yogajournal.com/article/press-releases/yoga-journal-releases-2012-yoga-in-america-market-study/ (Last visited on 20 January 2015).

96. *Yoga Journal Releases 2012 Yoga in America Market Study.*

97. *FDI Inflows into India Contract 38% in 2012–13*, BUSINESS STANDARD, 28 May 2013, available at http://www.business-standard.com/article/economy-policy/fdi-inflows-into-india-contract-38-in-2012-13-11305 2701103_1.html (Last visited on 20 January 2015).

98. Kounteya Sinha, *Health Ministry Goes Big on Yoga, Funds Studies on Its Benefits*, THE TIMES OF INDIA, 13 August 2011, available at http://timesofindia.indiatimes.com/india/Health-ministry-goes-big-on-yoga-funds-studies-on-its-benefits/articleshow/9585188.cms (Last visited on 20 January 2015).

99. Chidanand Rajghatta, *Narendra Modi Calls for International Yoga Day*, THE TIMES OF INDIA, 28 September 2014, available at http://timesofindia.indiatimes.com/india/Narendra-Modi-calls-for-International-Yoga-Day/articleshow/43665102.cms (Last visited on 20 January 2015).

100. UN, *General Assembly Resolution, Adopted Without Vote, Recognizes Global Impact of Ebola, Need to Include Health Issues in Foreign Policy Formulation, Meetings Coverage and Press Releases*, GA/11601, 11 December 2014, available at http://www.un.org/press/en/2014/ga11601.doc.htm (Last visited on 19 January 2015).

101. UN General Assembly, *International Day of Yoga*, A/RES/69/131, Resolution adopted by the General Assembly on 11 December 2014 (9 January 2015), available at http://www.un.org/en/ga/search/view_doc.asp?symbol=A/RES/69/131 (Last visited on 17 August 2016).

102. *PM Modi Now Has a Minister for Yoga, Ayurveda*, NDTV, 10 November 2014, available at http://www.ndtv.com/article/india/pm-modi-now-has-a-minister-for-yoga-ayurveda-618896 (Last visited on 19 January 2015).

103. PTI, *AYUSH Ministry Asks for Enhanced Budgetary Allocation*, THE ECONOMIC TIMES, 16 January 2015, available at http://articles.economictimes.indiatimes.com/2015-01-16/news/58149766_1_drug-controller-budgetary-allocation-finance-ministry (Last visited on 19 January 2015).

104. Tanya Basu, *Who Owns Yoga?*, THE ATLANTIC, 12 January 2015, available at http://www.theatlantic.com/business/archive/2015/01/who-owns-yoga/384350/ (Last visited on 19 January 2015).

105. Annie Gowen, *India's New Prime Minister, Narendra Modi, Aims to Rebrand and Promote Yoga in India*, THE WASHINGTON POST, 2 December 2014, available at http://www.washingtonpost.com/world/asia_pacific/indias-new-prime-minister-narendra-modi-wants-to-rebrand-and-promote-yoga-in-india/2014/12/02/7c5291de-7006-11e4-a2c2-478179fd0489_story.html (Last visited on 20 January 2015).
106. Arundathi Venkataraman, *Guest Post: GI for Yoga? (De)Merits and Consequences*, SPICYIP, 11 January 2015, available at http://spicyip.com/2015/01/guest-post-gi-for-yoga-demerits-and-consequences.html (Last visited on 20 January 2015).

INDEX

African Symposium on Copyright
(1963), 129
Agricultural and Processed Food
Products Export Development
Authority (APEDA), 269,
299–300, 306–7
Agricultural Produce (Grading and
Marking) Act (1937), 291
Ahluwalia, Montek Singh, 66, 72–3
Akhtar, Javed, 185, 194, 202, 205,
207; lobbying for Copyright
(Amendment) Act (2012),
186–8; on reforming copyright
law, 206
American Association for the
Advancement of Science, 252
appellation d'origine contrôlée
(AOCs), 302
appellation of origin, 302
Attukal Bhagavathy temple, Kerala,
329–30
Avesthagen Limited, 276
AYUSH (Ayurveda, Yoga, and
Naturopathy, Unani, Siddha, and
Homeopathy), 348–9
Ayyangar Committee, 5, 8, 66, 73;
draft provision on Patents Bill,
8–9; report on reworking Indian

patent law, 10; on revisions to
Indian patent law, 15
Azad, Maulana (Abul Kalam
Muhiyuddin Ahmed Azad), 124,
128

baazee.com, 224–5
Basic Books v. Kinko's Graphic
(1991), 144
basmati: adulteration, 292–5, 299;
AGMARK, 291; APEDA's locus
standi on, 307–11; basmati 867,
288; basmati GI applications, xxiv,
304–7; certificate of authenticity,
293–4; characteristics of, 268,
289–93, 298, 300–2, 307, 311,
313–14; discovery of RiceTec
patent, 267–8; grading criteria,
291, 311, 313; export inspection
system, 291–4, 296–7, 311–12;
patents controversy, 266–9; Pusa
Basmati, xxiv, 295, 297–8, 311;
quality control, 291, 294–7, 299,
311–12; re-examination process
before the USPTO, 269; risk of
genericization in United States,
288–90; Super Basmati, 297;
tariff concession, 293; Texmati,

267, 287–9, 299–300; trademark, 266–7, 287–90, 299–300, 308, 315; and uniqueness of basmati exports from India, 290–9; *See also* Pakistan.

Basmati Rice (Export) Grading and Marking Rules (1979), 291, 311
Basmati Rice (Quality Control and Inspection) Rules (1990), 294, 296–7, 311–12
Baxi, Upendra, 155, 162, 164–5
Bently, Lionel, 129
Berne Convention (1886), xxii, 36, 116, 119, 121, 123, 131, 133, 139; Berne Safeguard Clause, 122; Berne Union, 122, 132–4, 138; Brussels Act and Conference (1948), 117, 119, 121, 157; copyright protection under, 139; founding principle of, 121; India's plot to walk out of, 120–2; Paris Act of, 139; revision of, 128–33; Rome Text of, 134; vote of allegiance to, 116–20
Bhandari, Dalveer (Justice), 103–4, 235–6
Bharatiya Janata Party (BJP), 46, 60, 77, 207
Bikram yoga, 340–3, 346; copyrights and trademarks in relation to, 341; TDKL and, 348
Billy Joel case, 234–5
Biological Diversity Act (2002), 258, 277
biopiracy, 252, 266, 277–8, 347
'Bolar' exception, 63
Bombay Mill Owners' Association, 324
book piracy, 139–40
book publishing industry, 3, 140, 198

British chemical industry, 4–5
British Copyright Act (1911), 155
British Joint Copyright Council, 123
Bureaux Internationaux Réunis pour la Protection de la Propriété Intellectuelle (BIRPI), 132

Cambridge University Press (CUP), 115, 129
Cancer Patients Aid Association (CPAA), 87, 108
Capital Film Works (India) Limited, 172
Cargill (American seed corporation), 254
Central Bureau of Investigation (CBI), 226–7, 229
Chagla, M.C. (Justice), 116, 128–9, 131
Chandra, Subhash, 169, 292–3; *Z Factor, The*, 292
Chidambaram, P., 46, 66
Chopra, Yash Raj, 171, 195
Choudhury, Bikram, 340–1, 343, 347; claims of copyright, 346
chronic myeloid leukemia (CML), *See* Glivec drug
Ciba-Geigy Corporation, 84–5
cinematograph films, in India. *See* Indian cinema
cinematograph work, definition of, 192
Committee on Revision of Patent Law, 2
Communist Party of India (Marxist) (CPI(M)), 46, 61, 67–9, 76
Communist Party of India (CPI), 16, 18
Company Law Board (CLB), 202, 204
compulsory licensing dispute, 1, 6, 10, 13, 15–17, 30, 48, 61, 64, 72–4,

77, 130, 131, 134, 136, 139, 145;
for translation of works, 131
Computer Emergency Response
Team, India (CERT-IN), 238–9
Confédération Internationale
des Sociétés d'Auteurs et
Compositeurs (CISAC). *See*
International Confederation
of Societies of Authors and
Composers
Constitution of India, Article 14 of,
96; arbitrariness test, 97; Article
51(c) of, 98; Article 253 of, 98;
challenge against Section 3(d),
Patents (Amendment) Ordinance
(1994), 96–8; interpretations of,
97; 'reasonable classification'
doctrine, 97; statutory
interpretation, principles of, 98
contributory infringement, liability
for, 219–22
Controller of Patents (India), 8, 15,
100–1
Convention on Biological Diversity
(1992), 258
Copyright (Amendment) Act
(2012), xxiv, 184–9, 193, 197;
Parliamentary debates, 206–8
Copyright Clearance Center (CCC),
144
copyright infringement, xxiv, 216,
218, 220, 228; claims of, 164–5;
criminal penalties and action
against, 140; defence to, 142;
'fair use' defence, 142, 144; in
film songs, 174; four-factor test
for, 143; in Indian cinema, 153,
157, 161; intermediary liability,
issue of, 243; legal action for,
121; liability of, 230, 232–3;
photocopying by libraries, 142;

requirement of court orders
in cases of, 240; 'safe harbour'
provision, 221, 243
copyright law, in Germany, 197
copyright law, in India, xxii, 115;
aims of, 128; Berne Convention
(1886) and, 116; Copyright Act
(1847), 129; Copyright Act (1914),
116, 120–1, 130, 153, 155, 159;
Copyright Act (1957), 115, 122–8,
130, 145, 154, 162, 184, 192, 197,
231, 278; Copyright (Amendment)
Act (2012), 184, 186–8, 197,
198, 209, 242; Copyright Bill
(1955), 124; Copyright Bill (1983),
145; Copyright (Amendment)
Bill (1984), 140; Copyright
(Amendment) Bill (2010), 206–8;
dilution of, 16; domestic, 121;
'educational use' exceptions,
115; fair dealing, doctrine of, 142;
'fair dealing' limitations, 115;
foreign copyrights, recognition of,
117–18; Imperial Copyright Act
(1911), 153; jurisdiction of, 155;
safe harbour provision, 239–43;
translation rights under, 129
copyright law, in US, 118, 122, 131
Copyright Office, 139
copyright owners, 'just
compensation' to, 137
copyright protection: benefits of,
118; under Berne Convention,
139; of cinematograph films, 154,
162; collective licensing agency
for, 144; of film songs, 173–7;
restoring the term of copyrights,
127; transactions in film music,
185–6; UCC's standards of, 122;
Washington Recommendations,
138

copyrights: ownership of, 186, 189; registration of, 121, 127
copyright transactions, in film music, 185–6; mandatory royalty sharing, 193–7
Council of Scientific and Industrial Research (CSIR), 256, 265, 267, 347; *See* also Gupta, V.K.; Mashelkar, R.A.; Subbaram, N.
cow-milk story, 275–6
crowbar diplomacy, 36–40
'crowded market' principle, for registration of trademark, 328

Dandekar, N., 28–9
Darjeeling Tea, 300–1, 305
Das, Suman K., 261, 266
Delux Films, 159
Department of Industrial Policy and Promotion (DIPP), 65, 69–70, 73, 76
Department of Information Technology (DIT), 226
Department of Telecommunications, 238
Dhirendra Brahmachari, Swami, 292
Digital Millennium Copyright Act (DMCA), US, 219–22; 'safe harbour' provisions, 221–2
Dinkar, Ramdhari Singh, 124–5, 130
Doha Declaration, 64
Dravida Munnetra Kazhagam (DMK), 18
droit d'auteur system, 196–7
Drug Price Control Order, 1955 (DPCO), 29
drug prices, control of, 10, 12, 20, 29, 63, 87
drug safety laws, requirements of, 90
due diligence, notion of, 223, 225–9, 233, 243

Dunkel Draft, 46, 73; Parliament hearings on, 47–9

East Asian Seminar on Copyright (1967), New Delhi, 132
East India Company, 129
e-commerce, 222, 226
economic crisis of 1990–1, 44
E.P. Royappa v. *State of Tamil Nadu* (1974), 97
Essential Commodities Act (1955), 29
European Communities Rental Rights Directive (ECRRD), 197
European Patent Office (EPO), 252, 261, 275
evergreening of patents, 68–9, 71; curbing of, 75, 90; threat of, 71
Evolation Yoga, 343, 346
exclusive marketing rights (EMRs), 56, 59, 61, 88
export inspection agency (EIA), 294
Export of Basmati Rice (Quality Control and Inspection) Rules (2003), 291, 296–7

fair dealing, in copyright law, 142, 144, 166; economic rationale for, 143; four-factor test, 143
Farbewerke Hoechst Aktiengesellschaft Vormals Meister Lucius & Bruning Corporation v. *Unichem Laboratories and Ors* (1968), 10
Federal Trade Commission (FTC), US, 289–90
Fernandes, George, 255
film certification, 158
film music, copyrights in, 185–6; assigning copyright in new technology, 197–8; idea of sharing

royalties, 189; problems faced, by lyricists and composers, 188–206; 'trading' of music, 199

film songs, copyrights in, 173–7

Food Standards Agency (FSA), UK, 294

foreign copyrights, recognition of, 117–19, 131

free market capitalism, 16

free market trade, 61

Gandhi, Indira, 26, 292

Gandhi, Rajiv, 292

Ganesan, A.V., 40, 47, 73

Garga, B.D., 163, 167

General Agreement on Tariffs and Trade (GATT): Dunkel Draft, 46; inclusion of IP at, 38; Indian government's stand against, 46; Uruguay Round negotiations, 36–7, 44, 73

General Court of the European Union, 336

geographical indications (GIs), xxiv, 266, 286; APEDA application, 306–7; 'appellation of origin', 302; basmati GI applications, 304–7; heritage application, 305–6; law on, 331; origins of, 299–304; protection of, 303

Geographical Indications of Goods (Registration and Protection) Act, 1999 (the GI Act), 301, 304–5, 331

GI Registry, 305–6, 309–12, 331–2

Glivec drug, 104; cancer-causing enzyme and, 84; for chronic myeloid leukaemia (CML), 84–5; clinical trials of, 85–6; exclusive marketing rights (EMRs) for, 88; generic version of, 87–8; Novartis patent application for, 86, 89–93; patenting of, 1, 71; Philadelphia

chromosome, 84; use of, 1, 71, 84; for war against cancer, 86; *See also* Novartis patent case

Glivec International Patient Access Program (GIPAP), 89

Google, 216–17, 240–1

Guha, Amitava, 41

Gujral, I.K., 47

Gupta, Anil, 257

Gupta, V.K., 348

Gupta, Kanwar Lal, 60

Gurudutt, Kambadur Nagaraja Rao, 269

Guruji.com, 216–17, 229–30, 243; Dod, Anurag, 216; Mishra, Gaurav, 216

Haffkine Institute, 1, 10, 13

Haffkine, Waldemar Mordecai, 1

Hamdard University, 264

Hamied, K.A., 9–10

Heritage Foundation, 305–6

Hills, Carla, 39, 42–3, 45

Hindi film industry. *See* Bollywood

Hindu deities, trademarks of, 324–8; religious sensibilities and, 329

Hollywood films, 167–8; *Independence Day* (1996), 170

human resource development (HRD) ministry of, 140–1, 205

Imperial Copyright Act (1911), British India, 121, 153

Indian Agricultural Research Institute (IARI), 269, 295

Indian cinema, xxiv; *Aaranya Kaandam* (2011), 172–3; *Aradhana* (1969), 176; Ardeshir Irani's *Alam Ara* (1931), 153; Bollywood, xxi, 184–5, 188–9, 196; borrowed songs, 173–7;

borrowed stories, 167–73;
censorship of, 154; *Chashme
Buddoor* (1981), 172–3;
Cinematograph Act (1952),
158; copyright in, 153, 157,
161; Dadasaheb Phalke's *Raja
Harishchandra* (1913), 153;
Dhoom 3 (2013), 171; exhibition
of, 155; film certification, 158;
film-production industry, 155;
future aspects of IP issues in,
177–8; 'golden era' of, 158,
163; *Indian Performing Right
Society* case, 168, 175; inspired
by Hollywood films, 167–8;
intellectual property (IP) issues
in, 153–8, 167; *Jyoti* (1981), 174;
lack of originality in, 166–77;
Ladies v. *Ricky Bahl* (2011), 171;
New Delhi (1956), 158; 'new
wave' of filmmakers, 163–6;
Phone Booth (2002), 168; piracy,
problem of, 153, 177; pirated
copies of, 155; plagiarism,
practices of, 157; Rangachariar
Committee (1951), 157, 166;
reciprocal protection, issue of,
167; registration of, 157–8; *R.G.
Anand* case, 168; *Sorry Bhai*
(2008), 176; Supreme Court
directives on, 158–63; *Waves of
Revolution* (1975), 165
Indian Cinematograph Committee
(1928), 154, 177
Indian Council of Agricultural
Research (ICAR), 267, 298
Indian Drug Manufacturers'
Association (IDMA), 10
Indian education system, reforms
in, 207
Indian Express, 163–4

Indian Motion Picture Producers
Association, 240
Indian Music Industry (IMI), 195,
199, 223–4, 240; global anti-piracy
campaign, 229; *versus* Internet,
229–34
Indian National Congress (INC), 16,
60, 323
Indian Patent Office, 88, 273–4,
276–7
Indian Penal Code (1860), 325
Indian Performing Right Society
Ltd. (IPRS), 187, 198–206, 208;
Ali, Naushad, 199; *Indian
Performing Right Society Ltd.* v.
*Eastern India Motion Pictures
Association* (1977), 162–3, 168,
175, 186, 190, 193; management
of, 206; music labels of, 205;
ringtone royalties, 203, 206
Indian Reprographic Rights
Organisation (IRRO), 141
Indian Science Congress, 272
Indo-British textile trade, 323
information technology (IT):
Computer Emergency Response
Team, India (CERT-IN), 238–9;
corporate criminal liability,
principles of, 225; information
location tools, 242; Information
Technology Bill (1999), 222–4;
Information Technology
Bill (2000), 225; Information
Technology (Amendment) Bill
(2006), 224–9; Information
Technology (Intermediaries
Guidelines) Rules (2011), 229;
Internet piracy, 236; liability law
under, 231; pornographic video
clipping, 224; transitory digital
network communications, 241

Institute for Inner Studies (IIS),
Philippines, 346–7
Intellectual Property Appellate
Board (IPAB), 94–5, 306, 328;
judgment on Novartis patent
case, 100–2
Intellectual Property Owners
Association (IPOA), 103
intermediary liability, in copyright
infringement, 243
International Confederation
of Societies of Authors and
Composers, 123, 194
International Copyright Act (1891),
US. *See* Chace Act, US
International Copyright Order (1999),
167, 181n50
International Federation of Organic
Agricultural Movements
(IFOAM), 254, 259
International Intellectual Property
Alliance (IIPA), 140
Internet Corporation for Assigned
Names and Numbers (ICANN),
337; Uniform Domain Name
Dispute Policy, 337
Internet service providers (ISPs),
217; as copyright cops, 234–9;
liability of, 223–4; uniform
resource locators (URLs), 237,
239
Iyer, V.R. Krishna (Justice), 74, 162

Jain, Chandra Mohan. *See* Osho,
Maharishi
John Doe injunctions, 234–5, 237
Joint Parliamentary Committees
(JPCs), 2, 16, 21, 60, 64, 122;
recommendation on restoring the
term of copyright, 127
judicial ethics, code of, 104

Karnataka Rajya Raitha Sangha
(KRRS), 259
Katju, Markandey (Justice), 102–3
Kefauver, Carey Estes, 10–14, 69,
90; on reformation of American
patent law, 75–6; report on
overcharging by pharmaceutical
companies, 13, 27
known substances: definition of, 109;
patentability of, 92–3, 106
Krishnamachari, T.T., 6
Krishnamurti, T.S., 116, 132, 133,
135, 137
Kumararaja, Thiagarajan, 172–3
Kya Khayein aur Kyun, 264, 272

Lahiri, Bappi, 174–6, 201
land reforms, 23, 117; legislation, 23
licenses of rights, 15, 19, 25, 37, 48,
55, 63
limited liability company, creation
of, 228
Literary Copyright Act (1842), UK,
129

Macmillan v. *Shamsul Ulama M.
Zaka* (1895), 129
Maharishi Foundation, 334–5;
'méditation transcendantale' sign,
335–6; transcendental meditation
trademarks, 334–5
Mahesh Yogi, Maharishi, 334, 338
Malik, Anu, 176
Margosan-O, 253
Marrakesh Agreement (1994), 49, 55,
57, 303
Masani, Minocher Rustom (Minoo
Masani), 16, 127
Mashelkar, R.A., 78, 265
Merchandise Marks Act (1958), 300,
304

mobile ringtone music, 197–8;
ringtone royalties, 203
Modi, Narendra, 349
Mody, Piloo, 26
monopoly, over patented drugs, 92
Mookerjee, Syama Prasad, 5
Mukherjee, H.N., 27–9
Mukherjee, I.P. (Justice), 238
Mukherjee, Pranab, 50, 66–7, 70
Mundhra, Jagmohan, 163–4
MySpace, 230–1, 233–4, 238, 240

Nambiar, Ananda, 21, 25, 27
Nanjundaswamy, M.D., 49, 254
Nath, Kamal, 67, 70, 77–8
National Association of
Manufacturers, US, 19
National Association of Software and
Services Companies (NASSCOM),
225
National Basketball Association
(NBA) case, US, 342
National Biological Authority, 258,
277
National Democratic Alliance
(NDA), 78
National Institute of Origin and
Quality, France, 302
National Working Group on Patent
Laws (NWGPL), 41
Navdanya movement, 254
Nayar, Sushila, 27, 29
neem: *azadirachtin*, use of, 251–3,
255–6; challenges to Grace's US
and EU patents, 258–60; neem-
based biopesticide, 253, 255;
protest petition against the US
neem patent, 254–5; response
from Grace, 255–8; shelf life and
effectiveness of, 255–6; traditional

knowledge in India, IP protection
of, 252
Nehru, Jawaharlal, 1, 26, 116
Nestlé, 276
Netcom, 219–22, 231, 233
Network Service Provider (NSP),
223–4
new chemical entity (NCE), 68,
70, 73, 87, 91; demand to limit
patents to, 77
Novartis patent case, 71, 76;
aftermath of the rejection,
94–5; appeal against the IPAB's
judgment, 104; appeals to
the Supreme Court of India,
102–4; conflict of interest, 102;
constitutional challenge, before
Madras High Court, 95–9;
disinclination to reduce the drug
price, 87; ex parte injunction,
88; first round of litigation,
87–9; Glivec drug, use of, 1, 71,
84; grant of EMR for Glivec,
88; impact of the Madras High
Court's ruling, 99–100; IPAB
judgment on, 100–2; judgment
and the media verdict on, 105;
patent application for Glivec,
89–93; pre-grant oppositions,
93–4; on pricing of Glivec drug,
87; Supreme Court's judgment on,
1, 105–10
NRI Film Production Associates, 170

Office for Harmonisation in the
Internal Market (OHIM), 335
Omnibus Trade and Competitiveness
Act (1988), US, 39
Online Copyright Infringement
Liability Limitation Act

(OCILLA), US, 221; 'safe harbour' provision, 221
online service provider (OSP), 217–18, 221
Open Source Yoga Unity (OSYU), 342–3
Organisation of Pharmaceutical Producers of India (OPPI), 14
Osho Active Meditations, 337
Osho Dhyan Mandir, 337
Osho Friends International, 337–8, 340
Osho International Foundation (OIF), 336–7; trademark claims, 337–8
Osho, 336–7; Anando, Ma, 338–9
Osho Times, 337
Osho Zen Tarot, 337
ownership of copyrights, 186, 189; first ownership, principle of, 189; and idea of sharing royalties, 189, 193–7; licence fees, 190; of 'music and lyrics' used in a movie, 189–93, 200
Oxford University Press (OUP), 115, 129–30

Pakistan: basmati case, 266–9, 286–99; basmati rice imported from, 294–5; claim over the basmati GI, 314; cross-breeding programmes for basmati rice, 295; cultivation of basmati rice in, 268; registered trademark for basmati rice in, 287; Stockholm Protocol negotiations, 138; super basmati variety, 297; WTO dispute against US, 58
Paranjape, Sai, 172–3
Paris Act (1971), 139
Paris Conference (1971), 138–9, 145

Parliamentary Standing Committee on Commerce, 59, 73, 78, 194–5, 206, 223, 226, 228; examination of IT (Amendment) Bill (2006), 233, 240; recommendation of, 229
Patel, Dahyabhai V., 30
Patent Co-operation Treaty, 36
patent law, in Germany, 3–4, 6–8, 21–2
patent law, in India, 1–2; amendment of, 55, 60–70; 'anti-national' legislation and, 63; Ayyangar's report on revisions to, 15; Committee on Revision of Patent Law, 2; enactment of, 22; failed amendments of, 56–8; first amendment, 60–3; Indian Patents and Designs (Amendment) Act (1950), 6; 'invention-protecting' patent law, 266; multiple process patents, problem of, 9; Patents Act (1970), 15, 46, 48, 55, 67, 277; Patents (Amendment) Act (1999), 63; Patents and Designs Act (1911), 2–3, 8, 23; Patents Bill (1953), 6–10; Patents Bill (1965), 14–15; Patents Bill (1967), 18–19, 23; Patents (Amendment) Bill (1995), 61; Patents (Amendment) Bill (1998), 59–60, 62; Patents (Second Amendment) Act (2002), 64, 70; Patents (Second Amendment) Bill (1999), 63–4, 70; Patents (Amendment) Bill (2005), 74, 76–8, 89; Patents (Third Amendment) Bill (2003), 64–70; Patents (Amendment) Ordinance (1994), 56, 58; Patents (Amendment) Ordinance (2004),

70; on 'second-use' patents, 72;
section 3(d), birth of, 73–8
patent law, in UK, 3; Act of 1907, 8;
on methods of manufacture, 3
Patents Enquiry Committee, 2, 6, 26,
66, 117
patents, for pharmaceutical products:
on compulsory licensing, 77;
and cost of paying a patent
lawyer, 92; disputes related with,
1–2; experts and their reports
on, 2–10; Glivec drug *See* Glivec
drug; imatinib mesylate, 91; for
incremental innovation, 91–2;
known substances, patentability
of, 92–3, 106; on life-saving drug,
86; lobbying against, 2; new
invention, 76; pharmaceutical
substances and, 76; pre-grant
opposition to, 77; royalties
for, 37; terms of, 2; Uruguay
Round negotiations, 37; *See also*
pharmaceutical patents, in India
patent *versus* prices debate, in the
US, 10–14
Patwardhan, Anand, 165
Payyannur Pavithra Ring Artisans
and Development Society
(PPRADS), 331
Pearce, David, 275–6
Permanent Mission of India (PMI),
71
pharmaceutical industry: allegations
of overcharging, 12; business
structure of, 11; compulsory
licensing, 1; effect of patents
on the growth of, 17; exclusive
marketing rights (EMRs), 88;
Haffkine Institute, 1; Novartis,
1; overcharging issues, 13; patent
dispute with, 1, 13; patenting of

'me-too' drugs, 69; profit margins
of, 11
Pharmaceutical Manufacturers
Association, US, 19, 39
pharmaceutical patents, in India:
abolition of, 13, 16, 19; exclusive
marketing rights (EMRs) and, 88;
licenses of rights, 19, 37; politics
over, 15–18; prohibitions against,
88
Pharmaceutical Research and
Manufacturers of America
(PhRMA), 37, 95
pharmaceutical substances,
definition of, 76
Phonographic Performance Limited
(PPL), 199
photocopying in libraries: as
copyright infringement, 142;
disrupting effect on book
publishing, 139–45; 'fair use'
exception under American law,
142; legal limits of, 143; licences
for, 143; for limited purposes, 144;
photocopy piracy, 140–1
photocopy piracy, 140–1; legislative
guidance on issue of, 143
pirate websites, war against, 234
plagiarism, practices of, 157, 323
Planning Commission Task Force
(1999), 273
Playboy Enterprises, Inc. v. *Frena*
(1993), 221
Pokhran nuclear tests, trade
sanctions after, 62
politics of patents, in Indian
Parliament, 15–18; Attorney
General's deposition over,
23–6; new patent law, 26–31;
testimonies of the foreign
witnesses and, 19–23

Pranic Healing, 346–7
Prevention of Money Laundering Act
(2002), 208
Prime Minister's Office (PMO), 72
Princeton Univ. v. *Michigan
Document Servs* (1996), 144
printing and publishing industries, of
developed countries, 138
Protection of Literary and Artistic
Works. *See* Berne Convention
(1886)
public interest litigation, 329
Puri, Hardeep, 71–3

Rahman, A.R., 185, 195
Raja, A.T., 326
Rajneesh, Bhagwan Shree. *See* Osho
Raj, R.S. Praveen, 329
Rajpal v. *King Emperor* (1927), 325
Rangachariar Committee (1951), 157,
166
Rangachariar, T., 154
Rangila Rasula, 325
Rao, Dasari Narayana, 196
reasonable classification, doctrine
of, 96–7
Reddy, Jaipal, 62
registered proprietor, 332
Register of Owners, 201–2, 204
Registrar of Copyrights, India, 134,
137, 200
Registrar of Trademarks, 328
religious figures, in trademarks, 322;
the Gods, 322–32; the Gurus,
332–40; the traditions, 340–50
Religious Technology Center v.
*Netcom On-line Communication
Services Inc.*, 219
Research Foundation for Science,
Technology and Ecology (RFSTE),
254

Research Services of Great Britain
(RSGB), 288
R.G. Anand v. *Delux Films* (1978),
158–65, 168
RiceTec Inc., 266–8, 287–8; Andrews,
Robin, 267–8; 'basmati 867,' 288;
claims of genericization, 289; rice
lines of the invention, 268; Tilda
Rice Limited, 287; *See also* basmati
Right to Information (RTI) Act
(2005), 139, 263
ringtone royalties, 203, 206
royalty sharing, idea of, 189, 193–7

'safe harbour' protection, 4, 221, 239,
243
Saregama India Limited, 174–6, 185,
202, 238, 240
Sargant Committee, 4
'second-use' patents, 72
section 3(d), of Patents (Amendment)
Ordinance (1994), 89; Article
14 challenge against, 96–8;
birth of, 73–8; burden of proof,
92; discretion to interpret, 98;
IPAB's interpretation of, 103;
known substance, definition
of, 109; on patentability of
known substances, 92–3, 106;
right to equality and, 96; and
risk of violating TRIPS, 91; to
safeguard against 'evergreening'
patents, 90; therapeutic
efficacy, 110; threshold for
patenting derivatives, 92; TRIPS
compatibility of, 90, 96, 98–9
section 301, of Trade Act (1974), US:
components of, 39; sanctions
under, 40, 42–5; Special 301, 39,
42; Super 301, 39, 43; for unfair
trade practices, 42

Seeds Act (1966), 298
Sehgal, Mohan, 159–61
Seid, Harry, 19–20
Senate Sub-Committee on Anti-trust
    and Monopoly, US, 11
Sen Gupta, Amit, 41
Sen, Ronen, 72
Shah Commission inquiry, 292
Shakti Films, 176
Sharma, Ravi Shankar (Bombay
    Ravi), 205
Shergill, Rabbi, 176–7
Shiva, Vandana, 49, 254
Shourie, Arun, 61–2
Shreya Singhal v. *Union of India,*
    243
Shrimali, K.L., 123–4, 127
Sibal, Kapil, 205, 207
Singh, Dinesh, 26, 43
Singh, Manmohan, 65
Sokhey, S.S., 1–2, 13
South Indian Film Chamber of
    Commerce, 196
South Indian Music Companies
    Association (SIMCA), 240
Star India Pvt. Ltd, 242
States Reorganisation Act (1956), 160
States Reorganisation Commission
    (SRC), 160
Statute of Anne (1710), 196
statutory interpretation, principles
    of, 98
Stockholm Act (1967), 135, 138
Stockholm Diplomatic Conference
    (1967), 131–2, 135; Protocol for
    Developing Countries at, 133
Stockholm Protocol, 135–9, 145
story bureau, idea of, 158
Subbaram, N., 261–3, 265
Super Cassettes Industries Ltd.
    (SCIL). *See* T-Series

Surjeet, Harkishan Singh, 70
Swamy, Subramanian, 44–5
Swatantra Party, xxii, 16, 26;
    See also Masani, Minocher
    Rustom (Minoo Masani);
    Patel, Dahyabhai; Mody, Piloo;
    Dandekar, N.
systematic instructional activities, 145

Tagore, Rabindranath, 130
Taj Television v. *Rajan Mandal*
    (2003), 235
Taylor and Francis (T&F), 115
Tea Board of India, 305
technology transfer, xxii, 17
Tek Chand, Bakshi, 2, 26, 66;
    Committee, 5, 7, 13, 66
Texmati, *See* trademarks
therapeutic efficacy, 69, 98, 100–1,
    107–10
Thorazine (drug), 12
Trade Act of 1974, US, 39; components
    of, 39; section 301 of, 39
trademark law: in England, 324–5
trademark law: in India 95, 324–5;
    Trade Marks Act (1940), 300;
    Trade Marks Act (1999), 300
Trademark Registry, of India, 327,
    329
trademarks, 42; 'basmati' tag,
    287, 299; 'crowded market'
    argument, 328; 'Ramayan',
    issue of, 328–9; registration of,
    324; in relation to Bikram yoga,
    341; religious figures in, 322;
    religious sensibilities and, 329;
    Trade Marks Act (1999), 95; for
    transcendental meditation, 335;
    UK Texmati trademark, 289
Trade-Related Intellectual Property
    Rights (TRIPS), Agreement

on, xxiii, 31, 36, 38, 251, 290,
303; anti-TRIPS alliance, 40;
Article 27 of, 90–1, 96, 109;
Article 70 of, 58, 88; dispute
resolution mechanism, 57;
Doha Declaration, 64; domestic
opposition to, 49; impact on
medicines, 44; India's obligation
under, 65, 74, 87; India's violation
of, 58–9; Marrakesh Agreement
(1994), 49, 55; Negotiating Group
on, 38; on patentability criteria,
91; protection of GIs as violation
of, 303; signing by India, 49–50; as
violation of fundamental rights of
Indian citizens, 49
Traditional Knowledge Digital
Library (TKDL), xxiv, 250, 269–
79, 347–8; chinks in, 276–9; costs
of creating and running, 273; cow-
milk patent application, 275–6;
mission to help patent offices,
271–5; origins of, 270–1; rerouting
of resources in, 274; targeting of
patent applications, 276; TKDL
(Yoga) Task Force, 347–8
traditional knowledge in India,
protection of: 'Ancient Science
through Sanskrit' symposium,
272; *azadirachtin,* use of, 251;
basmati patents controversy,
266–9; as common heritage of
mankind, 258; misappropriation
of, 250; neem as wonder plant,
252–4; neem-based biopesticide,
253, 255; *See also* basmati, neem,
turmeric
traditional knowledge resource
classification (TKRC) system, 347
traditional medicine, 250, 261, 263,
347

transcendental meditation
trademarks, 334–5
transitory digital network
communications, 241
T-Series, 208, 216, 230–1
turmeric patents controversy, 261–6;
prior art and opposition strategies,
263–4; re-examination process,
264–6; turmeric patent and
'national interest,' 261–3; on use
of turmeric in wound healing, 261
Twentieth Century Fox (film studio),
168–70

unfair competition, 323
unfair trade practices, 38–9, 42–3, 306
Unichem Laboratory, 10
uniform resource locators (URLs),
237, 239
United Nations Educational,
Scientific and Cultural
Organization (UNESCO), 118,
121; Intergovernmental Copyright
Committee of, 138
United Progressive Alliance (UPA),
65, 206
United States (US): Copyright Act
(1909), 142, 342; copyright law,
122; Copyright Office, 344, 347;
Federal Register, 344; patent law,
reformation of, 69, 75; Trademark
Trial and Appeal Board (TTAB),
338
United States Patent and Trademark
Office (USPTO), 252, 259, 264,
288, 304, 337, 348
United States Trade Representative
(USTR), xxiii, 45; watch-list, 39
Universal Copyright Convention
(UCC), 121, 131; standards of
copyright protection, 122

University of Delhi (DU) photocopy
case, xxii, 115; case filed by
academic publishers, 145–6;
disruption of book publishing,
139–45; photocopy piracy, 140–1
Uruguay Round negotiations, 36–7,
44, 73

Vajpayee, Atal Bihari, 60
Varma, Raja Ravi, 322–4
Venkateswaran, Subbiah, 324
Verma, Shrikant, 139
von Lewinski, Silke, 197

Washington Recommendations, 138
Watal, Jayashree, 303
Western music industry, 195
Whyte, Ronald M., 220–1, 231
Williams & Wilkins (publisher),
141–4
World Intellectual Property
Organization (WIPO), 132
World Trade Organization (WTO),
xxiii, 38, 55, 88, 251, 254,
294; Dispute Settlement Body
(DSB) of, 38, 55, 98–9, 303; EC
retaliation against India under,
59; trade disputes, 58–9
W.R. Grace (company), 251–2, 254–5;
azadirachtin, use of, 251–3,
255; neem patents controversy,
See neem patents controversy;
opposition of patent, 259–60;
scope of its patents and the
invention, 255

Yahoo!, 221, 230, 241
Yash Raj Films, 185
Yechury, Sitaram, 67
'Yoga in America' study, 349
Yogi, Mahesh, 338
YouTube, 217–18, 227, 230, 234,
241–2

zamindari system, abolition of, 117,
126
Zee Telefilms, 169
Zimmermann, Jurg, 85–6, 106

ABOUT THE AUTHORS

Prashant Reddy T. is currently a Yong Pung How Research Associate at the Applied Research Centre for Intellectual Assets and the Law in Asia (ARCIALA), School of Law, Singapore Management University. He holds a BA LLB (Honours) degree from the National Law School of India University, Bengaluru, India and an LLM degree in the field of Law, Science, and Technology from Stanford Law School, USA. He has previously practised as a lawyer with IP law firms in India. A long-time contributor to *SpicyIP*, he was named in Managing IP's list of 50 people shaping the future of IP in 2011.

Sumathi Chandrashekaran works at the intersection of law and policy, and has interests in regulatory and judicial reform. She graduated with honours in English literature from Lady Shri Ram College, and in law from the Faculty of Law, University of Delhi. She also has a dual master's degree in public policy and public affairs from the Lee Kuan Yew School of Public Policy, National University of Singapore, and Sciences PO Paris. She was editor-in-chief of *SpicyIP*, and was named in Managing IP's list of 50 people shaping the future of IP in 2011.